PROFESSIONAL
WINDOWS® PHONE 7 GAME DEVELOPMENT

INTRODUCTION	 xxiii
CHAPTER 1	Getting to Know the Windows Phone 7 Device 1
CHAPTER 2	Getting Started 11
CHAPTER 3	Orientation 25
CHAPTER 4	Touch Input 39
CHAPTER 5	Give Me Your Input 59
CHAPTER 6	The State of Things 93
CHAPTER 7	Let the Music Play 127
CHAPTER 8	Putting It All Together: Drive & Dodge 147
CHAPTER 9	Whoa! The World Isn't Flat After All 247
CHAPTER 10	It's Your Turn! 269
CHAPTER 11	The World Outside Your Window(s) 299
CHAPTER 12	Putting It All Together: Poker Dice with Friends 351
CHAPTER 13	Dude, Where's My Car? 425
CHAPTER 14	Take a Picture; It'll Last Longer! 441
CHAPTER 15	Putting It All Together: Picture Puzzle 455
CHAPTER 16	Where Do You Go from Here? 497
INDEX	 513

PROFESSIONAL

Windows® Phone 7 Game Development

PROFESSIONAL
Windows® Phone 7 Game Development
CREATING GAMES USING XNA GAME STUDIO 4

Chris G. Williams
George W. Clingerman

Wiley Publishing, Inc.

Professional Windows® Phone 7 Game Development

Published by
Wiley Publishing, Inc.
10475 Crosspoint Boulevard
Indianapolis, IN 46256
www.wiley.com

Copyright © 2011 by Wiley Publishing, Inc., Indianapolis, Indiana

Published simultaneously in Canada

ISBN: 978-0-470-92244-6
ISBN: 978-1-118-06798-7 (ebk)
ISBN: 978-1-118-06797-0 (ebk)
ISBN: 978-1-118-06796-3 (ebk)

Manufactured in the United States of America

10 9 8 7 6 5 4 3 2 1

No part of this publication may be reproduced, stored in a retrieval system or transmitted in any form or by any means, electronic, mechanical, photocopying, recording, scanning or otherwise, except as permitted under Sections 107 or 108 of the 1976 United States Copyright Act, without either the prior written permission of the Publisher, or authorization through payment of the appropriate per-copy fee to the Copyright Clearance Center, 222 Rosewood Drive, Danvers, MA 01923, (978) 750-8400, fax (978) 646-8600. Requests to the Publisher for permission should be addressed to the Permissions Department, John Wiley & Sons, Inc., 111 River Street, Hoboken, NJ 07030, (201) 748-6011, fax (201) 748-6008, or online at http://www.wiley.com/go/permissions.

Limit of Liability/Disclaimer of Warranty: The publisher and the author make no representations or warranties with respect to the accuracy or completeness of the contents of this work and specifically disclaim all warranties, including without limitation warranties of fitness for a particular purpose. No warranty may be created or extended by sales or promotional materials. The advice and strategies contained herein may not be suitable for every situation. This work is sold with the understanding that the publisher is not engaged in rendering legal, accounting, or other professional services. If professional assistance is required, the services of a competent professional person should be sought. Neither the publisher nor the author shall be liable for damages arising herefrom. The fact that an organization or Web site is referred to in this work as a citation and/or a potential source of further information does not mean that the author or the publisher endorses the information the organization or Web site may provide or recommendations it may make. Further, readers should be aware that Internet Web sites listed in this work may have changed or disappeared between when this work was written and when it is read.

For general information on our other products and services please contact our Customer Care Department within the United States at (877) 762-2974, outside the United States at (317) 572-3993 or fax (317) 572-4002.

Wiley also publishes its books in a variety of electronic formats. Some content that appears in print may not be available in electronic books.

Library of Congress Control Number: 2011920609

Trademarks: Wiley, the Wiley logo, Wrox, the Wrox logo, Programmer to Programmer, and related trade dress are trademarks or registered trademarks of John Wiley & Sons, Inc. and/or its affiliates, in the United States and other countries, and may not be used without written permission. All other trademarks are the property of their respective owners. Wiley Publishing, Inc., is not associated with any product or vendor mentioned in this book.

ABOUT THE AUTHORS

CHRIS G. WILLIAMS is a principal consultant for Magenic, delivering custom-built .NET solutions to clients. He founded Reality Check Games as a studio for his various XNA projects on Windows, Xbox 360, and Windows Phone 7. In addition to creating games, Williams is a Microsoft MVP in XNA/DirectX (for six years running). He is an active contributor to the XNA Indie Games community, and founded an XNA Developers Group in Minneapolis, MN. He speaks regularly at user groups, code camps, and professional conferences country-wide, lecturing on XNA game development, Windows Phone 7, and other topics. He has also authored articles for the magazines *CODE* and *Flagship*. You can follow him on Twitter (`@chrisgwilliams`).

GEORGE W. CLINGERMAN is a business developer who works with .NET and SQL to build WinForm and web software. He also develops games, has won a small game development contest using Managed Direct X, and has released an Xbox Live Indie Game designed for small children (sold worldwide). Clingerman runs an XNA community site, `http://XNADevelopment.com`, where he creates tutorials for beginning game development, and he helps out in the official Microsoft Creators Club forums. For this work, Clingerman was awarded a Microsoft MVP award for XNA four times. You can reach him at the Geekswithblogs blogging community, or follow him on Twitter (`@clingermanw`).

ABOUT THE TECHNICAL EDITOR

PIETER GERMISHUYS is a business applications developer by day and a game developer by night. He is the co-founder of www.mdxinfo.com and www.xnainfo.com. He enjoys dabbling in ASP.NET MVC and jQuery when not attempting to develop the next "big thing" in the game entertainment world. He has a blog at www.pieterg.com, and frequents on http://stackoverflow.com/.

CREDITS

ACQUISITIONS EDITOR
Paul Reese

PROJECT EDITOR
Kevin Shafer

TECHNICAL EDITOR
Pieter Germishuys

PRODUCTION EDITOR
Daniel Scribner

COPY EDITOR
Gayle Johnson

EDITORIAL DIRECTOR
Robyn B. Siesky

EDITORIAL MANAGER
Mary Beth Wakefield

FREELANCER EDITORIAL MANAGER
Rosemarie Graham

ASSOCIATE DIRECTOR OF MARKETING
David Mayhew

PRODUCTION MANAGER
Tim Tate

VICE PRESIDENT AND EXECUTIVE GROUP PUBLISHER
Richard Swadley

VICE PRESIDENT AND EXECUTIVE PUBLISHER
Barry Pruett

ASSOCIATE PUBLISHER
Jim Minatel

PROJECT COORDINATOR, COVER
Katherine Crocker

PROOFREADER
Candace English

INDEXER
Robert Swanson

COVER DESIGNER
Michael E. Trent

COVER IMAGE
© Daniel Stein/istockphoto.com

ACKNOWLEDGMENTS

THE SUCCESSFUL COMPLETION OF a project of this size and duration is never the sole effort of the author(s). I could not have succeeded without the influence and support of the following people:

- Melynda, who does the impossible every day and makes it look easy.
- Lisa, Nicki, Logan, Abigail, and Max; I hope this proves anything is possible if you try hard enough.
- Georgie, my co-author. Dude! We did it!
- Greg and Paul, co-founders of Magenic, who gave me room to grow for the last five years, without which this book might have never existed.
- My good friends Amanda and Rachel, who convinced me that life is too short to pass up experiencing everything you can.

I'd also like to thank Andy "The ZMan" Dunn for taunting me with the grisly remains of my past failed projects. Your personal "support" was truly motivating. Failure was not an option.

To the rest of my friends and family, who waited patiently for me to finish this book and rejoin society: It's party time!

— CHRIS G. WILLIAMS

FIRST AND FOREMOST, I would just like to give my love and thanks to my family. Shawna, Gareth, Owen, Reece, and Tennyson, thanks for not forgetting who I was, even though at times you probably wanted to! I love you!

Chris, thanks for giving me this opportunity to meet a life goal. Couldn't have done it without you! Thanks for taking years off your life staying up late and working through this book with me. Can't believe we did it!

To the XNA community on the forums, IRC, and Twitter, thanks for keeping my spirits up and keeping me motivated. You guys rock! I'd especially like to thank Michael McLaughlin for his extremely valuable technical support late at night, Björn Graf for always being there supporting me, and Andy Dunn for keeping me motivated. So many others, too — @Ubergeekgames, @Xalterax, @kriswd40… the list goes on, and I'm running out of room. But if you chatted me up while I was writing this book, thanks!

To friends, family, acquaintances, and everyone else I've been ignoring while writing this book, sorry, but I'm done now and I'm available again! Until I start my next project, of course….

— GEORGE W. CLINGERMAN

CONTENTS

INTRODUCTION   *xxiii*

CHAPTER 1: GETTING TO KNOW THE WINDOWS PHONE 7 DEVICE   **1**

Minimum Specifications   **1**
  Chassis Design   2
  Screen Resolution   3
Phone Features   **3**
  Capacitive Touch   3
  Sensors   4
    Accelerometer   4
    aGPS   4
    Compass   4
    Light Sensor   5
    Proximity Sensor   5
  Digital Camera   5
  DirectX 9 Acceleration   6
  Face Buttons   6
    Back Button   6
    Start Button   6
    Search Button   7
  QWERTY Keyboard   7
Software Features   **7**
  Start and Lock Screens   7
  Hubs   8
    People Hub   8
    Pictures Hub   8
    Music + Video Hub   8
    Games Hub   8
    Marketplace Hub   9
    Office Hub   9
  Other Applications   10
Summary   **10**

CHAPTER 2: GETTING STARTED   **11**

Getting the Tools You Need   **11**
  Meeting the System Requirements   12

Satisfying the Developer Requirements	12
What You Get	13
XNA Game Studio 4.0	**13**
Creating Your First Project	14
Spotting Differences Between the Windows Phone Game and Other XNA Game Projects	15
Setting Up a Windows Phone Device	**18**
Using the Windows Phone Emulator	**19**
Using Command-Line Options	**22**
Summary	**24**

CHAPTER 3: ORIENTATION — 25

Device Orientation	**25**
Setting Device Orientation	25
Hardware Scaling	26
Automatic Rotation	26
Detecting Device Orientation	29
Running in Full-Screen Mode	30
Phone Title-Safe Area	31
Accelerometer	**32**
AccelerometerSample	34
Summary	**37**

CHAPTER 4: TOUCH INPUT — 39

Responding to Touch Events	**39**
Overview of Touch Interfaces	40
Detecting Touch Input	40
Detecting Gestures	44
Tap	47
DoubleTap	47
Hold	48
HorizontalDrag	48
VerticalDrag	48
FreeDrag	48
DragComplete	49
Flick	49
Pinch	49
PinchComplete	50
Seeing Results	50
Custom Gestures	50
Designing for Touch Games	51

Remember Your Platform	51
Design for the Right Resolution	51
Be Consistent and Predictable	52
The Soft Input Panel (SIP)	**53**
Summary	**56**

CHAPTER 5: GIVE ME YOUR INPUT — 59

Building the Input Management System	**59**
Input.cs	59
GestureDefinition.cs	75
GameInput.cs	76
TouchIndicator.cs	81
TouchIndicatorCollection.cs	84
Using the Input Management System	**85**
Actions.cs	85
Game1.cs	86
Summary	**91**

CHAPTER 6: THE STATE OF THINGS — 93

Game State	**93**
Managing Game State	94
Option 1: Boolean Flags	94
Option 2: Enumerations	98
Option 3: Object-Oriented	107
Handling Multiple Layers of Screens	114
Phone Hardware Events	**115**
Detecting the Back Button	115
Overriding the Back Button	115
Game, Interrupted	**116**
Notifications and Temporary Interruptions	117
Game-Stopping Events	120
Somebody Save Me	**121**
Summary	**125**

CHAPTER 7: LET THE MUSIC PLAY — 127

Handling Audio	**127**
Playing Music with MediaPlayer	127
Do You Mind? I'm Playing Music Here	128
Background Music	129
Song Collections	131

Visualizations	132
SoundEffect	133
SoundEffectInstance	136
XACT 3.0	**137**
Recording Audio	**138**
The Microphone Class	138
Saving and Retrieving Captured Audio	143
Summary	**145**

CHAPTER 8: PUTTING IT ALL TOGETHER: DRIVE & DODGE — 147

Creating the Game	**148**
Screens	149
Screen.cs	149
ScreenStateSwitchboard.cs	153
Title.cs	155
Sprite.cs	157
Background.cs	159
Content	159
Game1.cs	160
Text.cs	162
screenFont.spritefont	168
Button.cs	170
The Input Wrapper	174
GameInput.cs	174
GestureDefinition.cs	179
Input.cs	181
TouchIndicator.cs	193
TouchIndicatorCollection.cs	195
Adding Sounds and Music	198
Music.cs	198
SoundEffects.cs	199
More Screens	202
MainGame.cs	203
InGameMenu.cs	203
GameOver.cs	204
Coding the Main Game Screen	207
Road.cs	207
Car.cs	210
Hazards.cs	212
Finishing the MainGame Screen: Hooking Up the Sprites and the Game Play	215

MainGame.cs	215
InGameMenu.cs	219
GameOver.cs	221
Keeping Score	**224**
Score.cs	224
ScoreList.cs	225
Scores.cs	226
SerializableDictionary.cs	228
Screen.cs	231
MainGame.cs	231
GameOver.cs	234
Proper Care and Feeding of the Back Button	**237**
Screen.cs	237
Title.cs	240
MainGame.cs	240
InGameMenu.cs	241
GameOver.cs	241
Creating a Base Game Template	**241**
Stripping Down to the Essentials	242
Title.cs	242
ScreenStateSwitchboard.cs	243
Creating the Templates	244
Using the Templates	244
Summary	**245**

CHAPTER 9: WHOA! THE WORLD ISN'T FLAT AFTER ALL — 247

3D Graphics	**247**
Creating 3D Models for Your Game	247
Getting the Bits	248
Getting Started with Blender	248
Creating Primitive Shapes	248
Changing Your Point of View	249
Combining Shapes	249
Bringing It All Together	250
Exporting Your Shapes	250
Using 3D Models in Your Game	251
Adding Models to Your Project	251
Displaying the Models Onscreen	251
Texturing a Basic 3D Model in Blender	254
Configuring Your Workspace	254
Texturing the Model	254

CONTENTS

Performing 3D Transformations	257
It's All Relative	257
Rotating Your 3D Object	257
Creating 3D Animations	258
Adding Bones to Your Model	258
Weight Painting	260
Animating in Blender	262
Adding the FBX for XNA Script	263
The Microsoft Skinning Sample	264
Working with Effects	**266**
Stock Effects	267
Using the Reach Graphics Demo	267
Summary	**268**
CHAPTER 10: IT'S YOUR TURN!	**269**
Understanding Push Notifications	**269**
Raw Notifications	270
PushItRawSample	271
PushItRawWindows	276
Pop-Up Toasts	279
PassTheToastSample	279
PassTheToastWindows	281
Consuming Toasts as Raw Notifications in Your Game	284
Tile Notifications	286
PushingTileSample	287
PushingTileWindows	290
Good Vibrations	**294**
The Microsoft.Devices Namespace	294
Environment	295
VibrateController	295
Summary	**297**
CHAPTER 11: THE WORLD OUTSIDE YOUR WINDOW(S)	**299**
Consuming Web Services	**300**
Live to Serve You	300
Serve Me	305
Adding a Service Reference	305
Game1.cs	308
I Get High Scores with a Little Help from My Friends	**310**
HighScoreService	310

ScoreMe	317
Anonymous Live ID	319
HighScoreClient	319
Push Notifications	321
HighScoreTester	325
Testing the High-Score Service	328
Got a Match?	**329**
MatchMaker	329
GameRequest.cs	330
Gamer.cs	330
IMatchMaker.cs	332
MatchMakerService.svc.cs	333
MatchMe	335
MatchMakerTester	340
Form1	340
Testing the MatchMaker Service	344
Working with HTTP Requests	**345**
WeatherWitch	345
Pulling an RSS Feed into Your Game	348
Time for a REST(ful Web Service)	349
Summary	**349**

CHAPTER 12: PUTTING IT ALL TOGETHER: POKER DICE WITH FRIENDS   351

Taking Care of the Preliminaries	**351**
Service Flow versus Screen Flow	352
Creating the Poker Dice Service	353
IPokerDice.cs	353
Game.cs	354
Gamer.cs	355
HandRank.cs	359
PokerDice.svc	363
Creating the Poker Dice Tester	365
PokerDiceTest	366
Using the PokerDiceTester	371
Creating "Poker Dice with Friends"	**372**
Setting Up the Game Project Template	372
Modifying the Templates	373
Title.cs	373
Enhancing the ScreenStateSwitchboard Class	374
ScreenStateSwitchboard.cs	375

Adding the PokerDiceService	382
Creating the GameInformation and DiceGame Supporting Classes	383
DiceGame.cs	383
GameInformation.cs	385
Button.cs	385
Creating the Game Lobby	386
GameLobby.cs	386
Message.cs	394
Creating the GameInfo Screen	397
GameInfo.cs	397
Adding the Dice Model	404
Die.cs	405
Creating the MainGame Screen	414
MainGame.cs	414
Creating the DiceSelect Screen	417
DiceSelect.cs	417
Enhancing Your Game	**423**
Summary	**424**
CHAPTER 13: DUDE, WHERE'S MY CAR?	**425**
Understanding and Accessing the Location API	**425**
Best Practices for Using Location Services	**425**
Asking Permission	426
Power Consumption	426
Level of Accuracy	426
Movement Threshold	426
Using Location Services in Your Games	**426**
CivicAddress	427
CivicAddressResolver	427
Did You Order Pizza?	427
Resolving an Address Synchronously	428
Resolving an Address Asynchronously	431
GeoCoordinate	433
GeoCoordinateWatcher	433
FindMe	435
GeoPosition	439
Summary	**439**
CHAPTER 14: TAKE A PICTURE; IT'LL LAST LONGER!	**441**
Launchers and Choosers	**441**
NowPictureThis	**443**

CameraCaptureTask	443
The Application Deployment Tool	445
Testing NowPictureThis	447
PhotoChooserTask	447
Classes for Messaging Tasks	**449**
SmsComposeTask	449
EmailComposeTask	450
EmailAddressChooserTask	451
MediaPlayerLauncher	**452**
The Controls Property	452
The Location Property	453
The Media Property	453
Summary	**454**

CHAPTER 15: PUTTING IT ALL TOGETHER: PICTURE PUZZLE — 455

Picture Puzzle	**455**
Designing the Screen Flow	**456**
Creating Picture Puzzle	**456**
Creating the Title Screen	457
Title.cs	457
Enhancing the ScreenStateSwitchboard	460
ScreenStateSwitchboard.cs	460
Creating the NewPuzzle Screen	463
NewPuzzle.cs	463
The Pieces of the Puzzle	468
PuzzlePiece.cs	468
StencilPiece.cs	470
Puzzle.cs	471
How It Works	478
Managing State Objects	479
StateObject.cs	479
Creating the SelectPuzzle Screen	480
SelectPuzzleScreen.cs	481
Creating the Playable Game Screen	485
MainGame.cs	485
Making the InGameMenu Screen	488
InGameMenu.cs	488
Creating the PuzzleComplete Screen	491
Message.cs	492
Enhancing Your Game	**494**
Summary	**495**

CHAPTER 16: WHERE DO YOU GO FROM HERE? — 497

Trial Mode — 497
- Understanding Trial Mode — 498
- Detecting Trial Mode — 498
  - ShowMarketplace() — 498
  - SimulateTrialMode() — 499
  - IsTrialMode() — 499
  - Sharing with a Friend — 504
  - Running the Sample — 504

Pinning Your Game Tile to the Start Area — 505

Publishing — 507
- Requirements — 507
- Submission — 508
- Code Signing — 511

Where to Get Help — 511
- Forums — 511
- Blogs — 512
- Search — 512

Summary — 512

INDEX — *513*

PREFACE

This is my second opportunity to get my XNA-related words published in real-life book form. The first time I did this, I was writing a book about how to make a game more or less exactly like the one I put on Xbox Live Arcade. It ended up being full of very long code snippets and phrases that read something like, "This next part is really cool, but before that we have to do something *very boring*."

I think my takeaway lesson from writing that book was that my tone is, in general, way too apologetic. Maybe I just assumed no one would have as much fun writing an animation editor as I did. Or maybe one too many times I'd watched the eyes of someone outside of the nerd-rock-star elite glaze over as I gushed electrically about how cool it is to get parallax scrolling working the first time. But I think I got distracted from a critical truth: Making games is *awesome*.

I used to be a bit spoiled. While going to school at SUNY Institute of Technology, I got by doing the bare minimum of studying to afford as much game-making time as possible. Then, when that end-of-semester time of reckoning approached, I'd redeem myself with a term project somehow powered by DirectX even though the course never called for it. "Exploding spacecraft, gushing blood, and not a PowerPoint slide in sight!? My only regret is there is no grade higher than A!" is what I liked to imagine my professors saying. But those were the risks I took to do my Favorite Thing on Earth.

Now I'm immensely spoiled. I get to stay up late, wake up late, and make games when I'm not sleeping. I can't imagine a more satisfying way to spend my time than to sit around creating little universes, breathing life into them, setting them in motion, and then creating little heroes, armed to the teeth, to obliterate the rest of my creation.

Making games is awesome. Making Xbox 360 games has always been awesome, because the console has a killer GPU and you can play Xbox 360 games on a couch with a controller. With XNA 4.0, we've just turned the corner on Mobile Awesome in the form of Windows Phone, where we can bring our existing frameworks, tools, and C#/XNA knowledge into the world of multitouch input and gyroscopes.

Over the past couple of years, hardware and software have propelled indie gaming into a uniquely great area. While AAA games now require massive development teams to produce immensely detailed graphics that don't impress anyone anymore, small-scale indie games that rely far more on creative presentation than on nanosecond-efficient algorithms end up leaving more of an impression on gamers.

Tools such as XNA Game Studio give developers an environment for rapid development, whereas hardware such as Xbox 360 gives coders a silly amount of performance-related breathing room. Not to encourage sloppy coding, but if it takes me 10 minutes to implement an algorithm that's 25 percent slower than a far more complex algorithm that could keep me up all night with funny bugs, where I'm getting 60 frames per second with cycles to spare either way, I won't lose any sleep (see what I did there?) over implementing the slower, yet readable, algorithm.

Of course, Windows Phone isn't quite the same hardware juggernaut as the Xbox 360. Sure, it demolishes the Pentium II I got started with, but compared to today's hardware, it presents some performance challenges. And even if you do get away with abusing the GPU while maintaining a smooth frame rate, you must then live with the guilt of abusing the battery of whoever is playing your game. (That's where it gets personal.) My initial experience with Windows Phone was a bit jarring, because it quickly became apparent that my game development "style" involved throwing lots and lots of sprites on the screen at 60 frames per second, and that wouldn't cut it anymore. I would have to start designing smarter, not harder.

Fortunately, this book was written by smart people. George and Chris are two of the XNA community's most talented members, and I'm so glad that they've been given this opportunity to share their combined knowledge and experience. They've put a ton of work into setting up this book as an excellent tool for introducing you to Windows Phone development, whether you're coming from an XNA background and are geared toward porting your tech to Windows Phone, or you're new to the XNA Framework and you need a crash course. (And it is quick — trust me!)

I haven't had the honor of meeting Chris yet, but I've known George for a couple years. He even almost bought me a beer once, but he was derailed by a last-minute check-splitting initiated by a third party. From what I've read, Chris and George don't rely nearly as much as I do on phrases like, "I think this should work, but I honestly have no idea why."

So, jump in and have some fun! You have some great tech to play with, tons of cool things to try out, and only so much time, so get going!

—JAMES SILVA, SKA STUDIOS
Xbox Live Arcade and Xbox Live Indie Games Developer
Creator of the games The Dishwasher: Dead Samurai *and*
I MAED A GAM3 W1TH Z0MBIES 1N IT!!!1

INTRODUCTION

THE PURPOSE OF THIS BOOK is to get you up to speed and excited about making games for Windows Phone 7 with XNA Game Studio 4.0.

Throughout the book, Windows and Xbox 360 game development are mentioned within the context of the material presented. But make no mistake — this is a book about Windows Phone 7, first and foremost.

This book covers the features of the Windows Phone 7 devices and how to use them in your games. In the course of 16 chapters, you'll make three games, learn a bunch of cool stuff, and hopefully have some fun along the way.

WHO THIS BOOK IS FOR

The target audience for this book is anyone who wants to learn about programming games for Windows Phone 7 using C# and XNA Game Studio 4.0.

It's also for people who think most tech books are dense and dull. We've tried to keep this book light and interesting, with a conversational tone, while still teaching you something useful.

Wherever relevant, we include anecdotes and comments that provide context or that lead to additional information that isn't critical to the main flow of the book.

Maybe you are one of the following:

➤ An iPhone or Android game developer who wants to port your games to Windows Phone 7

➤ An experienced Windows developer who is getting into game development for the first time

➤ A developer who is cranking out Xbox Live Indie Games titles and who wants to know what's new in XNA Game Studio 4.0 as it relates to Windows Phone 7

No matter what your story, you can find a way to connect with and learn from this book.

Because no book can be all things to all people, some assumptions had to be made. This book will be most useful to people who meet some or all of the following criteria:

➤ You have some experience coding in C# or VB.NET. Even though VB.NET is not used in the book, there's no reason why a .NET developer (of either flavor) can't keep up.

➤ You have at least some familiarity or experience working with XNA (which implies C# experience).

➤ You want to make games for Windows Phone 7.

INTRODUCTION

If you own a Windows phone, you can probably skim through the first chapter. But whether or not you own a phone, you'll want to read the section on the Emulator in Chapter 2.

If you are the impatient sort, and you only want to read the "build a game" chapters, you might go straight to Chapter 8 (Drive & Dodge), Chapter 12 (Poker Dice with Friends), and Chapter 15 (Picture Puzzle).

WHAT THIS BOOK COVERS

This book covers XNA Game Studio 4.0 as it relates to Windows Phone 7 game development. You can make games for Windows Phone 7 with Silverlight, but that topic is not covered in this book.

Furthermore, you may use XNA Game Studio 4.0 to make games for Windows and Xbox Live Indie Games. Those platforms are referenced in this book but are not covered in detail.

HOW THIS BOOK IS STRUCTURED

In this book, you will learn about the various phone features a chapter at a time. Where possible, the chapters are organized into related groups of information or functionality.

Starting with Chapters 1 and 2, you will learn about the hardware and software features of Windows Phone 7, download the tools, explore the Emulator, and finally create your first Windows Phone game project.

In Chapters 3 through 7, you will learn the basics of making a Windows Phone 7 game. This includes handling device orientation, touch input and transitions, and playing sound.

In Chapter 8, you build the Drive & Dodge game, which leverages all the features you learned about in previous chapters.

In Chapters 9 through 11, you learn about three-dimensional (3D) graphics, making your own model with Blender, the Microsoft Push Notification network, and how to create and use services external to your phone. As part of this, you will create a global high-scores service, a matchmaking service, and a simple weather app.

In Chapter 12, you take what you learned from the earlier chapters and build your second game, Poker Dice with Friends.

In Chapters 13 and 14, you explore hardware features such as Location Services and Camera, and the various other tasks and choosers.

In Chapter 15, you build your third game, Picture Puzzle, which leverages the Camera and Photo Chooser tasks you learned about in the previous chapters.

Finally, in Chapter 16, you learn about trial mode and what it takes to submit your game to the Windows Phone Marketplace.

INTRODUCTION

WHAT YOU NEED TO USE THIS BOOK

To get the most out of this book, you need access to a Windows Phone 7 device. The Emulator is great, but there is no substitute for running on actual hardware.

Additionally, you need to download the Windows Phone Developer Tools before you can begin to write any code. Complete instructions are provided in Chapter 2.

CONVENTIONS

To help you get the most from the text and keep track of what's happening, we've used a number of conventions throughout the book.

> *Boxes with a warning icon like this one hold important, not-to-be-forgotten information that is directly relevant to the surrounding text.*

> *The pencil icon indicates notes, tips, hints, tricks, or asides to the current discussion.*

As for styles in the text:

- We *italicize* new terms and important words when we introduce them.
- We show keyboard strokes like this: Ctrl+A.
- We show filenames, URLs, and code within the text like so: `persistence.properties`.
- We present code in two different ways:

```
We use a monofont type for most code examples.
We use bold to emphasize code that is particularly important in the present
context or to show changes from a previous code snippet.
```

SOURCE CODE

As you work through the examples in this book, you may type in all the code manually, or you may use the source code files that accompany the book. All the source code used in this book is available for download at www.wrox.com. When at the site, simply locate the book's title (using the Search box or one of the title lists) and click the Download Code link on the book's detail page to obtain all the source code for the book. Notes within the text direct you to code that is included on the website. After you download the code, decompress it with your favorite compression tool.

 Because many books have similar titles, you may find it easiest to search by ISBN; this book's ISBN is 978-0-470-92244-6.

Alternatively, you can go to the main Wrox code download page at `www.wrox.com/dynamic/books/download.aspx` to see the code available for this book and all other Wrox books.

ERRATA

We make every effort to ensure that there are no errors in the text or code. However, no one is perfect and mistakes do occur. If you find an error in one of our books, such as a spelling mistake or faulty piece of code, we would be grateful for your feedback. By sending in errata, you may save another reader hours of frustration, and at the same time you will help us provide even higher-quality information.

To find the errata page for this book, go to `www.wrox.com` and locate the title using the Search box or one of the title lists. Then, on the book details page click the Book Errata link. On this page, you can view all errata that have been submitted for this book and posted by Wrox editors. A complete book list, including links to each book's errata, is also available at `www.wrox.com/misc-pages/booklist.shtml`.

If you don't spot "your" error on the Book Errata page, go to `www.wrox.com/contact/techsupport.shtml` and complete the form there to send us the error you have found. We'll check the information and, if appropriate, post a message to the book's errata page and fix the problem in subsequent editions of the book.

P2P.WROX.COM

For author and peer discussion, join the P2P forums at `http://p2p.wrox.com`. The forums are a web-based system for you to post messages relating to Wrox books and related technologies, and to interact with other readers and technology users. The forums offer a subscription feature through which you are e-mailed topics of interest of your choosing when new posts are made to the forums. Wrox authors, editors, other industry experts, and your fellow readers are present on these forums.

At `http://p2p.wrox.com`, you will find a number of different forums that will help you not only as you read this book, but also as you develop your own applications. To join the forums, follow these steps:

1. Go to `http://p2p.wrox.com` and click the Register link.
2. Read the terms of use, and click Agree.

3. Complete the required information to join, as well as any optional information you want to provide, and click Submit.

4. You will receive an e-mail with information describing how to verify your account and complete the joining process.

> *You can read messages in the forums without joining P2P, but to post messages, you must join.*

Once you join, you can post new messages and respond to messages other users post. You can read messages at any time on the web. If you would like to have new messages from a particular forum e-mailed to you, click the "Subscribe to this Forum" icon next to the forum name in the forum listing.

For more information about how to use the Wrox P2P forums, be sure to read the P2P FAQs for answers to questions about how the forum software works, as well as many common questions specific to P2P and Wrox books. To read the FAQs, click the FAQ link on any P2P page.

Getting to Know the Windows Phone 7 Device

WHAT'S IN THIS CHAPTER?

➤ Getting to know the minimum specifications for Windows Phone 7 devices, including chassis design and screen resolution

➤ Understanding the phone hardware features

➤ Understanding the Start and Lock screens

➤ Understanding hubs and what goes in them

Microsoft has leveraged its considerable marketing muscle and published a very strict set of minimum guidelines on what hardware and features will be available on Windows Phone 7. These guidelines ensure that both users and developers will have a consistently high-quality experience, no matter who manufactures the device your games will be running on.

This chapter provides an overview of the minimum specifications every phone must have. It also discusses hardware features of the device and software features of the new Windows Phone 7 operating system, including the innovative hubs feature.

MINIMUM SPECIFICATIONS

When Windows Phone 7 was first announced, Microsoft created quite a stir with the initial feature set, as well as the promise that no hardware vendor would be allowed to sell a device branded as Windows Phone 7 unless it supported the following minimum specifications:

➤ *Two screen sizes* — 480 by 800 WVGA (available at launch, with 480 by 320 HVGA available at a later, unannounced date)

➤ *Capacitive touch* — Four or more contact points

- *Sensors* — Assisted Global Positioning System (aGPS), accelerometer, compass, ambient light sensor, proximity sensor
- *Camera* — 5 megapixel (MP) camera with a flash and dedicated camera button
- *GPU* — DirectX 9 acceleration
- *Hardware buttons* — Must be fixed on the face
- *Keyboard* — Optional
- *Multimedia* — Common detailed specifications, codec acceleration
- *Memory* — 256 MB, 8 GB Flash or more
- *Processor* — ARMv7 Cortex/Scorpion or better

In addition to establishing these minimum specifications, Microsoft has stated that certain features will not be allowed on devices branded as Windows Phone 7. Currently, that list of prohibited features includes removable memory (via microSD or any other format) and having any extraneous buttons on the face of the phone beyond the Back, Start, and Search buttons.

Chassis Design

One of the truly great things about Windows Phone 7 is the consistency of chassis design between manufacturers. This will likely change with future generations, but all the devices available at launch sport the same basic form factor. And, thanks to Microsoft's involvement, all devices also have a roughly identical feature set, as shown in Figure 1-1.

FIGURE 1-1: Two different Windows Phone 7 devices

Screen Resolution

All the Windows Phone 7 devices available at launch (sometimes called "Chassis 1" devices) are required to have a screen resolution of 480 by 800 pixels, also known as Wide Video Graphics Array (WVGA). Devices made available after launch (cleverly referred to as "Chassis 2" devices) may instead support a screen resolution of 480 by 320 pixels, also known as Half-size Video Graphics Array (HVGA).

PHONE FEATURES

In addition to a fixed resolution, all Windows Phone 7 devices are required to ship with support for multitouch, an accelerometer, GPS, a camera, and a number of other features. Let's take a closer look at some of these required features.

Capacitive Touch

All Windows Phone 7 devices are required to incorporate *capacitive-touch screens* that have support for at least four contact points. However, none of the default gestures shipping with XNA 4.0 (which are described in detail in Chapter 4) actually use more than two touches at once.

> Capacitive sensors *detect anything that is conductive or that has dielectric properties (meaning it can store and discharge magnetic or electric energy). This is why you can wipe the phone's screen on your shirt without worrying about launching every app you own at once. In contrast,* resistive-touch screens *detect all pressure as input.*

Capacitive-touch screens have advantages and disadvantages compared to resistive-touch screens, as shown in Table 1-1.

TABLE 1-1: Advantages and Disadvantages of Capacitive-Touch Screens

ADVANTAGES	DISADVANTAGES
Capacitive-touch screens respond only to materials that are conductive (such as your finger), so you can clean them with a cloth without accidentally triggering input.	A regular stylus cannot be used with a capacitive-touch screen unless it is tipped with some form of conductive material.
Capacitive-touch screens are faster and more responsive than their resistive counterparts.	Capacitive-touch screens are more expensive to manufacture.
	Capacitive-touch screens are less accurate than resistive-touch screens.

While resistive-touch screens definitely have appealing user interface implications for game development, capacitive-touch screens are currently (and are likely to remain) the only option for Windows Phone 7.

Sensors

All Windows Phone 7 devices come standard with a number of sensors, including the accelerometer, aGPS, compass, light sensor, and proximity sensor.

Accelerometer

The *accelerometer* in Windows Phone 7 is used primarily for user interface control to present landscape or portrait views based on the device's physical orientation. It is commonly called a *tilt sensor*. The accelerometer also provides data that can be captured and used by your games and applications.

> You'll learn how to access the accelerometer data in Chapter 3.

aGPS

Unlike a regular GPS, which can take up to a couple minutes to pinpoint your location, aGPS gets assistance from local cell towers to determine the satellites relevant to your location. The end result is a much faster start time and more accurate positioning.

With aGPS comes the proverbial good news and bad news:

- *The good news* — It's fast! Also, using aGPS typically requires less processing power, resulting in correspondingly longer battery life than with a regular GPS.
- *The bad news* — aGPS does not have a single unifying standard. Several different configurations are possible for aGPS, with actual implementation on the device largely left up to the device manufacturers and cellular providers.

Compass

All Windows Phone 7 phones are required to ship with a built-in *compass*. However, as of launch, there is no API support for the compass. The data may be accessed via device-specific APIs or open source libraries, both of which are beyond the scope of this book.

> Microsoft would like anyone using other means to access compass data to convert it once API support for the compass is available so as to provide a consistent user experience for everyone.

Light Sensor

The *ambient light sensor* built into the phone is responsible for adjusting the brightness of the display based on the amount of available light. This sensor cannot be accessed or controlled via API and is not covered in this book.

Proximity Sensor

The *proximity sensor* is built into the phone hardware. It deactivates the screen when you place the phone near your face or any other body part or inanimate object. This prevents accidental dialing or feature activation during a phone call.

> In the name of science, the authors of this book exhaustively tested hundreds (well, maybe not hundreds) of items to see what would trigger the proximity sensor. They are happy to report that putting the phone's screen next to nearly anything will suffice. The authors also determined during this testing that the phone's proximity sensor is active only during phone calls.
>
> Sadly, this means that you won't be using it in your games, unless your game happens to be called "Make Several Phone Calls and See if the Screen Goes Dark When You Put the Phone Next to Your Face"! Of course, stranger things have happened. Neither of the authors (or anyone else) ever expected "I MAED A GAM3 W1TH Z0MB1ES!!!1" to sell more than 300,000 copies on Xbox Live Indie Games. So, who knows? Go for it!

Digital Camera

No self-respecting, super-cool smart phone would consider itself complete without a built-in camera and flash. Fortunately, Windows Phone 7 is no exception. All phones, regardless of manufacturer, are required to have a digital camera that supports a minimum of 5 megapixels. They are also required to have a dedicated camera button (for that "OMG!" candid shot) and a flash.

> Megapixels *are calculated by multiplying the horizontal and vertical pixels of a camera's default image resolution — just like calculating the area of your backyard (assuming it's rectangular, like a picture from your new phone).*

Manufacturers aren't limited to 5 MP. Searching online reveals some upcoming phones that will start shipping with a 10 MP camera.

DirectX 9 Acceleration

If you've been paying attention to the media hype about Windows Phone 7, you've probably seen DirectX 9 acceleration mentioned a few times. It's an impressive bullet point, but what does it mean for your game?

When you're developing games (or any piece of software, for that matter), sometimes you push the edges of performance. Eventually, you will hit a limit on just how much more you can tweak your code to increase the performance. This is where hardware acceleration comes in and takes over.

Intensive tasks such as video playback and three-dimensional (3D) rendering can be moved from the CPU to the GPU, freeing the CPU for more of your game logic. Having a GPU that supports DirectX 9 acceleration means that you can write intense, high-performance games.

You might think that this acceleration is important only for 3D games. And you'd be right — sort of. Hardware acceleration is traditionally thought of as an important feature for developing 3D games, but it's important for two-dimensional (2D) games as well. This is especially true because there really isn't any such thing as a 2D game in XNA! You can make 2D games, but behind the scenes the XNA framework makes a 3D game with a fixed camera. Because of this, even your "basic" 2D games will benefit from DirectX 9 acceleration.

Face Buttons

Every device marketed as Windows Phone 7 is required to have the following three buttons on the face of the phone:

- Back button
- Start button
- Search button

Back Button

This works exactly as you would expect it to, just like the famous browser button of the same name. If you go to a new screen in your phone's user interface (UI) and click the Back button, you are magically transported — wait for it — back to the previous screen. Pure genius! Games and applications that you write can handle the Back button however you choose.

 You will learn how to write code that responds to pressing the Back button in Chapter 6.

Start Button

Pressing the Start button returns you to the main Start screen no matter where you are or what application or game you are running. Applications exited in this manner go into a suspended state, which can be detected and handled programmatically. This means that although you can't actually capture the Start button, you can still respond to the events it generates when it suspends your game.

 You'll read more about the Start button in Chapter 6.

Search Button

Pressing the Search button launches the Bing Search screen on your phone, allowing you to get answers to all your burning questions (including where to get the best sushi within walking distance of your downtown Seattle hotel because your loser friends decided to go to a party and took the rental car without telling you).

QWERTY Keyboard

Slide-out keyboards are not part of the minimum required specification for Windows Phone 7 devices, but hardware manufacturers are free to incorporate them in their designs. The Dell Lightning has a portrait sliding keyboard that extends from the bottom of the phone, and the LG phone has a keyboard that slides out to the left (or the bottom if you are in landscape mode).

If your phone has a slide-out keyboard, you can use this in addition to the Soft Input Panel (SIP, an onscreen keyboard) when you need to type something. You can also use XNA to detect and respond to any keys pressed during a game.

 You'll learn more about the SIP in Chapter 4.

Regardless of what model of phone or type of keyboard you have, it should work fine with XNA without any special configuration or code workarounds.

SOFTWARE FEATURES

In addition to an impressive array of hardware features and functionality, Windows Phone 7 devices sport some extremely cool software features. Let's look at a few.

Start and Lock Screens

The *Start screen* on Windows Phone 7 serves as your desktop and is the primary point of interaction with the device. This screen is designed to give you information at a glance about missed calls, text messages, unread e-mails, and more.

Hubs (discussed in the next section) are accessed via the Start screen. You can see previews of content along with notifications from their respective tiles.

You can also pin your games to their own tile on the Start screen. You will learn how to do this in Chapter 16.

The *Lock screen* secures your phone contents from prying eyes. It also keeps you from accidentally "butt dialing" your mom while at the office holiday party. Microsoft has also made the Lock screen useful by incorporating status updates similar to what you would find on the Start screen, just in a smaller fashion.

Hubs

Instead of simply offering screen after screen of unsorted icons for all your various applications and games, Windows Phone 7 organizes everything into *hubs*. These aren't just program groups or folders; they are actually highly interactive and quite revolutionary. You've never seen anything like hubs on a phone, so let's look at a few examples.

People Hub

The *People hub* pulls in contacts from a variety of social media sites (such as Twitter and Facebook), as well as any e-mail services you use (including Exchange and web-based mail such as Gmail and Windows Live). The People hub aggregates all your contacts, status updates, and images into a specially tailored set of views.

The main view dynamically sorts your contacts by their update timeline and allows you to quickly jump to their social network updates. In addition to letting you view the status updates of all your friends, this hub contains an area called "me," which allows you to view and update your own status.

Pictures Hub

The *Pictures hub* contains exactly what you would expect — pictures, and plenty of them. In addition to local storage, pictures are pulled from a variety of sources you define and control (including Facebook, Windows Live, and various online photo services, as well as the feeds of your contacts).

The Pictures hub also offers tight integration with the previously mentioned services, allowing you to upload and comment on photos directly from this hub.

Music + Video Hub

If you've seen one Zune HD, you've seen them all.

Seriously, this hub is virtually identical to the Zune HD, except that it's in your phone, which has the added bonus of making it way more useful than the Zune HD ever was. You also can use the super-cool Zune Pass to download unlimited music and video over WiFi and 3G. Video support includes the standard `.avi` and `.wmv` file formats, as well as DivX.

Games Hub

If you're not impressed by now, you will be shortly. The *Games hub* is made of 100 percent pure, undiluted "Awesomium." It integrates nicely with Xbox Live, featuring a 3D rendering of your Xbox Live avatar (not to be confused with the 7-meter-tall blue people who run around half-naked in the forest, or that little bald kid with the arrow tattooed on his head).

You also get Xbox Live games and achievements. Yes, you read that right. You're probably thinking, "Wow! Even the Xbox Live Indie Games developers don't get achievements." (Unfortunately, as of this writing, access to these features is restricted to developers who have a publishing relationship with Microsoft.)

Furthermore, you get Spotlight feeds and the ability to browse gamer profiles directly from your phone.

Make no mistake — multiplayer and Xbox Live integration is a really big deal to Microsoft. There has been a big push in Redmond for turn-based casual games, so expect to see a lot of your favorite iPhone games popping up on Windows Phone 7 in the months around launch time. Some rather impressive 3D XNA games also are in the pipeline, including some with shared Xbox achievements, but obviously those can take a bit longer to create.

Marketplace Hub

Unlike with the previous Windows Mobile offerings from Microsoft, you really don't have any alternatives when it comes to getting content on your phone. Much like with Apple and its App Store, everything you put on your phone has to come from the Windows Phone Marketplace.

The *Marketplace hub* isn't just Microsoft's version of the App Store. Think of it as more of a one-stop shop for content of all types, whether it's applications, games, music, videos, or whatever else they can dream up in Redmond. Expect to also see branding here from whatever carrier your phone is using, because carriers will be able to add their own highlighted content as well.

Currently, the Marketplace hub is actually a bit more restrictive than Apple's App Store, since there is no option for distribution that bypasses the Marketplace (such as for beta testing, internal company use, and so on). Microsoft has acknowledged that this is not an ideal situation, and it plans to introduce new options, along with support for "enterprise customers." However, Microsoft has not said when that will be, other than sometime post-launch.

On a happier note, if you've been brutalized in the past by Apple's secretive application-approval process, you will be pleased to learn that Microsoft has implemented a "predictable and transparent" process for approving games and applications for the Marketplace. You can read all about it in the Windows Phone 7 Application Certification Requirements document, which is available at http://create.msdn.com.

Even better, Microsoft also says that it will not reject anything based on "duplication of functionality." (iPhone developers know all about this little gem.) Clearly, this opens a lot of possibilities for alternatives on Windows Phone 7, such as creating your own music player or Voice over IP (VoIP) application — as long as you can do it in Silverlight or XNA.

 You will learn more about the Marketplace and how to get your own games on there in Chapter 16.

Office Hub

The authors would like to point out that if you skimmed past the sections on the Games hub and the Marketplace hub in your haste to get to this section, you are most likely reading the wrong book. We're just saying....

With the *Office hub*, you can view and comment on Word documents, Excel spreadsheets, and PowerPoint presentations, as well as use various aspects of OneNote and SharePoint to store and retrieve documents. In addition to documents, the Office hub lets you manage lists and tasks, as well as schedule appointments and meetings.

As long as you don't have any need for copy and paste, it's just like the real thing. Okay, not really, but it's as good as you're likely to get on a phone, and certainly better than on any other phone out there.

Other Applications

The following applications also ship with Windows Phone 7, but since they don't have any direct relationship to gaming or game development, there is little point in covering them in depth:

- E-mail
- Calendar
- SMS
- Internet Explorer
- Bing

In addition to this list, a number of third-party applications will ship with Windows Phone 7. Some of these will be on all devices, and others may be provider-specific or manufacturer-specific.

SUMMARY

The Windows Phone 7 device is a remarkably powerful and feature-laden phone that you can customize to fit your needs. Support is included for a broad set of hardware features, including aGPS, digital camera, light sensor, and more.

Hubs provide a means of collecting and interacting with content both locally and across the Internet. The Games hub brings the Xbox Live experience to your phone and everywhere you go. The Office hub provides document viewers, as well as support for OneNote and SharePoint. The Marketplace hub is how you get applications and games and music onto your phone.

In Chapter 2, you will learn how to download the tools and build your first XNA game using Visual Studio 2010 Express for Windows Phone.

2

Getting Started

WHAT'S IN THIS CHAPTER?

- ➤ Getting the tools you need to build Windows Phone 7 games
- ➤ Understanding the differences between Windows Phone Game projects and other XNA game projects
- ➤ Deploying your game to a Windows Phone device
- ➤ Getting acquainted with the Windows Phone Emulator
- ➤ Running the Windows Phone Emulator from the command line

Windows Phone 7 supports two development strategies: Silverlight, which is primarily used for application development, and XNA, which is used for game development. This book focuses on game development with XNA Game Studio 4.0.

The development tools for Windows Phone 7 are free downloads available from Microsoft: Visual Studio 2010 Express for Windows Phone and XNA Game Studio 4.0. This chapter covers what tools you need, where to get them, and how to get started using them.

As part of Visual Studio 2010 Express for Windows Phone, you also get the Windows Phone Emulator. It includes the actual Windows Phone 7 ROM running on your computer and takes advantage of any available hardware acceleration you may have. This chapter also provides an overview of Emulator features and explains how to do more with the Emulator than just what Visual Studio exposes you to.

GETTING THE TOOLS YOU NEED

Everything you need to start developing for Windows Phone 7, regardless of whether you choose XNA or Silverlight, can be found in one easy download. Point your browser to http://developer.windowsphone.com and look for a link to "Get the free tools." As of this writing, that link is in the top-left corner and should look similar to what is shown in Figure 2-1.

FIGURE 2-1: The website may change, but the link should be prominently featured.

Meeting the System Requirements

Before you begin your development efforts, you must ensure that your development machine meets the following minimum specifications:

➤ Your operating system must be Windows Vista (x86 or x64) ENU with Service Pack (SP) 2 (all editions except Starter Edition), or Windows 7 (x86 or x64) ENU (all editions except Starter Edition).

➤ You must have 3 GB of free disk space on the system drive to perform the installation.

➤ You must have 2 GB of RAM on your system.

➤ You must have a graphics card that supports DirectX 10 with a WDDM 1.1 driver.

If your development machine meets only some of these requirements, you may still be able to install the tools, but you will likely run into problems using the Windows Phone Emulator.

 If you meet all the hardware requirements and still run into problems with the Emulator, ensure that you have the latest hardware reference drivers from your video card manufacturer. It's not enough to just install DirectX, since that doesn't actually install all the drivers you need.

Satisfying the Developer Requirements

This book assumes that in addition to having a computer that meets the hardware requirements, you are at least familiar with the following programming languages and technologies:

- C# and object-oriented programming (OOP) techniques
- XNA Game Studio (any version)
- Visual Studio

What You Get

After you download and run the Windows Phone Developer Tools installer, you have the following tools on your machine:

- Visual Studio 2010 Express for Windows Phone
- Windows Phone Emulator
- Silverlight for Windows Phone
- XNA Game Studio 4.0

Interestingly, since the first release of the XNA framework, game developer hopefuls have been able to get started without investing any money. The XNA framework has worked with the Express versions of Visual Studio from day one. This has allowed game developers to create and sell PC versions of their games with the only cost being their time. Xbox 360 developers had to pay a small fee to deploy and test their games on Xbox hardware. But with the Windows Phone 7 Emulator, game development on the phone is free for developers to try.

After installing the tools, you have a choice of using Visual Studio 2010 Express or a more full-featured edition such as Visual Studio 2010 Professional (if you have it installed). In this book, all the examples and screenshots use Microsoft Visual Studio 2010 Express for Windows Phone, but you are free to use any edition of Visual Studio 2010.

The Windows Phone 7 SDK is not compatible with Visual Studio 2008 and earlier. This is true of XNA Game Studio 4.0 as well. You must use Visual Studio 2010 to develop for Windows Phone 7.

On Windows Phone 7, XNA is actually a part of the Silverlight runtime, and the XNA framework is available for Silverlight applications and games. In-depth coverage of Silverlight is beyond the scope of this book, so all the discussions throughout this book focus solely on XNA Game Studio 4.0.

XNA GAME STUDIO 4.0

After you fire up Visual Studio 2010 Express for Windows Phone for the first time, you'll notice that the Start page in Visual Studio 2010 Express has changed a bit from previous versions, as shown in Figure 2-2.

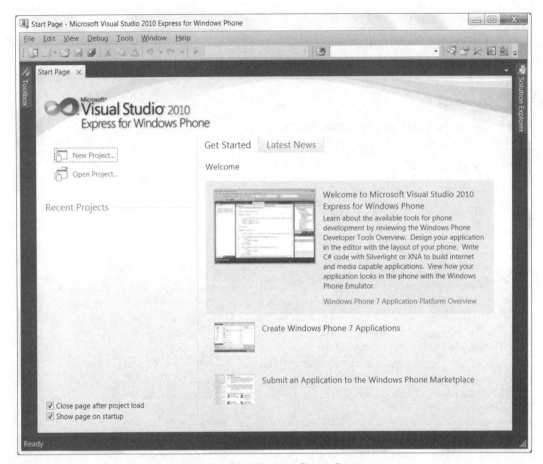

FIGURE 2-2: The Visual Studio 2010 Express for Windows Phone Start page

On the left are the familiar New Project and Open Project links, along with a Recent Projects section displaying links to the last ten projects you have opened. On the right, the Get Started tab contains links to additional information, including the Windows Phone 7 application platform overview, Windows Phone 7 class library reference, Windows Phone 7 UI Design and Interaction Guide, and the application submission requirements for Windows Phone 7.

If you were previously using Microsoft Visual Studio 2008, you'll be happy to know that the painfully slow Latest News page is now disabled by default and tucked away on a second tab. You can also add your own RSS news feeds to this page if you have a preferred source of information, such as the XNA Team blog or any of the resources discussed in Chapter 16.

Creating Your First Project

Now that you have XNA Game Studio 4.0 installed and running, it's time to create your first project by following these steps:

1. From the Start Page, click New Project.
2. Under Installed Templates in the New Project window, expand Visual C#. Select XNA Game Studio 4.0, as shown in Figure 2-3.
3. Select Windows Phone Game (4.0) Visual C#.
4. Click the OK button.

FIGURE 2-3: The New Project window

Throughout this book, you will be walked through an entire project for each sample. The complete code for each project is available for download at the book's companion website on www.wrox.com.

Don't worry about changing the name of the game project at this time. In this chapter, you're just taking a look around, so leave it as `WindowsPhoneGame1` if you like.

Spotting Differences Between the Windows Phone Game and Other XNA Game Projects

When you start a new Windows Phone Game project, there are a few key differences compared to projects from XNA Game Studio 3.1.

First, take a look in the Solution Explorer, where you see two projects. The first is your newly created `WindowsPhoneGame1`, and below that is the `WindowsPhoneGame1Content (Content)` project.

In XNA Game Studio 3.1, the `Content` folder was a part of each game project. Fortunately, in XNA Game Studio 4.0, this is no longer the case. `Content` projects now exist at the solution level, just like games. You can have as many or as few as you need.

> *An immediate benefit of having separate* Content *projects at the solution level is the sharing of sound effects, images, and other game assets between game projects. Much like including a reference to a physics library shared between game projects, game developers can now create separate* Content *projects and share those quite easily. This allows you to easily build a library of game assets to be reused for each game.*

Next, you see that your game project contains a file called `Game1.cs`. Open that file in the code editor and take a look. Listing 2-1 shows the complete `Game1.cs` file, with the differences highlighted in bold.

LISTING 2-1: Game1.cs

```
using System;
using System.Collections.Generic;
using System.Linq;
using Microsoft.Xna.Framework;
using Microsoft.Xna.Framework.Audio;
using Microsoft.Xna.Framework.Content;
using Microsoft.Xna.Framework.GamerServices;
using Microsoft.Xna.Framework.Graphics;
using Microsoft.Xna.Framework.Input;
using Microsoft.Xna.Framework.Input.Touch;
using Microsoft.Xna.Framework.Media;

namespace WindowsPhoneGame1
{
    /// <summary>
    /// This is the main type for your game
    /// </summary>
    public class Game1 : Microsoft.Xna.Framework.Game
    {
        GraphicsDeviceManager graphics;
        SpriteBatch spriteBatch;

        public Game1()
        {
            graphics = new GraphicsDeviceManager(this);
            Content.RootDirectory = "Content";

            // Frame rate is 30 fps by default for Windows Phone.
            TargetElapsedTime = TimeSpan.FromTicks(333333);

            // Pre-autoscale settings.
```

```csharp
        graphics.PreferredBackBufferWidth = 480;
        graphics.PreferredBackBufferHeight = 800;
    }

    /// <summary>
    /// Allows the game to perform any initialization it
    /// needs to before starting to run.
    /// This is where it can query for any required services
    /// and load any non-graphic related content.  Calling
    /// base.Initialize will enumerate through any components
    /// and initialize them as well.
    /// </summary>
    protected override void Initialize()
    {
        // TODO: Add your initialization logic here

        base.Initialize();
    }

    /// <summary>
    /// LoadContent will be called once per game and is the
    /// place to load all of your content.
    /// </summary>
    protected override void LoadContent()
    {
        // Create a new SpriteBatch, used to draw textures.
        spriteBatch = new SpriteBatch(GraphicsDevice);

        // TODO: use this.Content to load your game content here

    }

    /// <summary>
    /// UnloadContent will be called once per game and is
    /// the place to unload all content.
    /// </summary>
    protected override void UnloadContent()
    {
        // TODO: Unload any non ContentManager content here
    }

    /// <summary>
    /// Allows the game to run logic such as updating the world,
    /// collision checking, gathering input, and playing audio.
    /// </summary>
    /// <param name="gameTime">Provides a snapshot of timing
                values.</param>
    protected override void Update(GameTime gameTime)
    {
        // Allows the game to exit
        if (GamePad.GetState(PlayerIndex.One).Buttons.Back
                == ButtonState.Pressed)
            this.Exit();

        // TODO: Add your update logic here
```

continues

LISTING 2-1 *(continued)*

```
            base.Update(gameTime);
        }

        /// <summary>
        /// This is called when the game should draw itself.
        /// </summary>
        /// <param name="gameTime">Provides a snapshot of timing
                        values.</param>
        protected override void Draw(GameTime gameTime)
        {
            GraphicsDevice.Clear(Color.CornflowerBlue);

            // TODO: Add your drawing code here

            base.Draw(gameTime);
        }
    }
}
```

As you can see from the lines in bold, the only additions to the starter game template involve setting the default display resolution to 480 by 800 and setting the default frame rate to 30 frames per second (fps). The `TargetElapsedTime` property controls how often the `Update()` and `Draw()` methods are called, and 333333 ticks is approximately 0.033 seconds. From this, you can calculate that the line `TargetElapsedTime = TimeSpan.FromTicks(333333)` sets the target frame rate for your game at 30 fps.

 If you need to artificially reduce your game's frame rate below 30 fps, you can increase the `TimeSpan.FromTicks()` *that you pass into* `TargetElapsedTime`.

You might also be wondering why this line is included in the `Game1.cs` code, rather than being buried deeper in the `Game` base class, since the phone runs at 30 fps by default. It's there in case you need to artificially reduce your frame rate for testing or other purposes. Unfortunately, while you can tweak it to run slower, there's no way to make it faster than 30 fps.

Take a look in the `Update()` method, and you will see a call to `GamePad.GetState`, which checks to see if your player pressed the Back button on the phone.

You may think it looks odd to see code for checking the gamepad (also known as the Xbox 360 controller) in a Windows Phone Game project. However, this is actually the only way in XNA to check for the Back button on the phone. It also provides consistency between Windows, Xbox, and Windows Phone, since you use the exact same code on all three platforms.

SETTING UP A WINDOWS PHONE DEVICE

By default, your projects will deploy to the Windows Phone Emulator. If you have a Windows Phone 7 device, it's easy to change your deployment target to that instead.

On the XNA Game Studio Device Management Toolbar, find the XNA Game Studio Deployment Device drop-down, and select Windows Phone 7 Device, as shown in Figure 2-4.

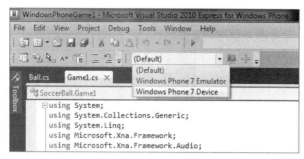

FIGURE 2-4: The XNA Game Studio Deployment Device drop-down

In addition to changing the deployment target, you must complete one more step. Before you can deploy any code to your Windows Phone 7 device, you must unlock it for development. Fortunately, it's quick and easy to do this. Just follow these steps:

1. Go to http://developer.windowsphone.com.
2. Follow the instructions to get your unlock code.
3. Enter that code into your phone.

Congratulations! Your Windows Phone 7 device is now unlocked for development.

USING THE WINDOWS PHONE EMULATOR

Visual Studio 2010 Express for Windows Phone includes a Windows Phone Emulator to make your development and testing process easier. The Emulator provides support for deploying, debugging, and running your game.

Press the F5 key to run your starting project. After a few seconds, you see the Emulator start (as shown in Figure 2-5), display the Windows Phone Start screen (as shown in Figure 2-6), and then launch your game (as shown in Figure 2-7).

> *CPU performance in the Windows Phone Emulator is not throttled to simulate the phone's processor, so be sure to test your game on an actual Windows Phone 7 device before publishing to the Marketplace.*

Another nice feature of the Emulator is that it persists until you shut it down, even after you terminate your game or shut down Visual Studio. This makes it very handy for demoing and testing multiple projects. The flip side of this is that every time you start the Emulator, it's like getting a brand-new phone. If your game persists anything to storage, it is wiped out when you close the Emulator.

If you click in the top of the screen area of the emulator, you will see a set of icons. That area of the screen is called the *system tray* and provides status information for your phone. The Emulator is set to autohide those icons after a few seconds (10 seconds, to be exact), but you can bring them back any time you want, just by touching (clicking in) the system tray.

20 | **CHAPTER 2** GETTING STARTED

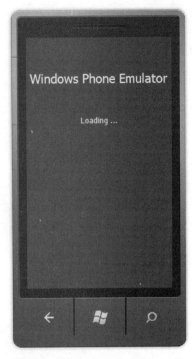

FIGURE 2-5: The Windows Phone Emulator boot screen

FIGURE 2-6: The Windows Phone Emulator Start screen

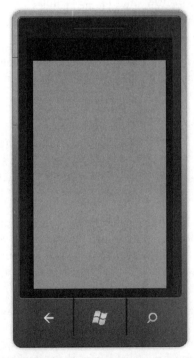

FIGURE 2-7: Your game, running on the Windows Phone Emulator

Figure 2-7 doesn't really capture the full majesty, but if you look at the Emulator, you'll see a lovely screen of cornflower blue. The default screen fill is set with the `Draw()` method, as shown earlier in Listing 2-1.

That's really all the starter game does. Although it is not very exciting, it does mean that everything is working correctly, and you're ready to move on to bigger challenges.

> *Clicking the Start button while your game is running immediately takes you to the Start screen of the Emulator (see Figure 2-6). Clicking the Back button from there returns you to your game, exactly where it left off. You will learn more about this, and how to handle the events that are triggered when this happens, in Chapter 5.*

Although it isn't quite identical to "the real thing," the Emulator is actually pretty impressive. It includes support for GPU emulation, GPS simulation, orientation, and phone skinning. You will learn more about these topics in later chapters of this book.

If your development machine has an active Internet connection, launch Internet Explorer from the Start menu, and click or tap in the address bar. You can type a destination address using the Soft Input Panel (SIP), as shown in Figures 2-8 and 2-9. The autocomplete feature kicks in after you type a few characters, providing you with a list of potential destinations.

FIGURE 2-8: The alpha keys of the SIP

FIGURE 2-9: The numeric and symbol keys of the SIP

If you have a touch-enabled development machine (such as a tablet or a desktop machine with a touch screen), you can also use those features in the Emulator without any additional configuration. You will learn about programming for multitouch and gestures in Chapter 4.

The Emulator also supports inputting text by typing on your keyboard. Some Windows Phone 7 devices also offer slide-out keyboards, so you can use either form of input.

If you want to visit Bing, you can type **www.bing.com**, or you can just press the Search button on the bottom right of the Emulator (or phone). This launches a mobile edition of the Bing start page, as shown in Figure 2-10.

USING COMMAND-LINE OPTIONS

There's no entry under All Programs for the Windows Phone Emulator, but you can run it outside of Visual Studio if you fire up an XNA Game Studio 4.0 command prompt and navigate to `C:\Program Files (x86)\Microsoft XDE\1.0`. You can run `XDE.exe` from the command line and see a list of all the additional parameters, as shown in Figure 2-11.

FIGURE 2-10: Windows Phone Emulator search screen

A number of command-line options are available. Some of the more interesting options include the following:

- *Mapping a directory to simulate a storage card* — The Windows Phone 7 specification doesn't allow for removable storage cards, but it does support local internal storage. Since the Emulator doesn't actually preserve anything between sessions, being able to simulate local storage with an actual directory on your development machine is very useful.

- *Loading a different skin file for the phone Emulator* — This doesn't affect the phone's UI, but rather how the phone looks in the Emulator. If you want to take screenshots of your game running on different simulated phones, you need to find or create skins for those phones.

- *Loading the Emulator rotated to a position other than the default* — This is a handy option, since XNA games default to landscape mode but the Emulator defaults to portrait mode.

- *Monitoring the serial port via a console window* — You can monitor the serial port by using the console window.

- *Simulating memory size (RAM) in megabytes* — This feature allows you to test your game's performance with varying amounts of memory.

While nothing can truly replace running your game on actual hardware, these command-line options really open up a lot of flexibility when you're developing and testing on the Emulator. To actually run the Emulator from a command prompt, you must pass in a path to the proper `bin` file. Unfortunately, this isn't kept in the same folder as the Emulator, so you must do a little digging.

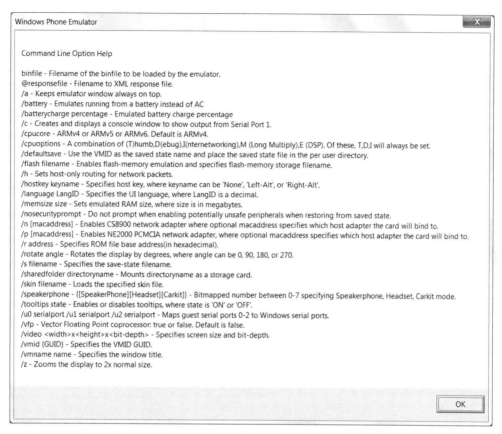

FIGURE 2-11: Windows Phone Emulator command-line parameters

The `bin` file is installed as part of the Windows Phone 7 SDK and can be found (on a 64-bit system) at `C:\Program Files (x86)\Microsoft SDKs\WindowsPhone\v7.0\Emulation\Images`. As of this writing, the `bin` file is named `WM70C1.bin`, but this is subject to change at any point as Microsoft updates the SDK and the Emulator. Knowing where to look is 99 percent of the battle, though, so with a little digging, you should have no trouble finding it.

Ensure that you are in the same folder as `XDE.exe`, and type the following at the command prompt:

```
xde "c:\program files (x86)\Microsoft SDKs\Windows Phone\v7.0\
    Emulation\Images\WM70C1.bin"
```

The Emulator should load right away, and, after about 15 seconds, you should see the familiar Windows Phone 7 Start Screen.

Now you don't have to launch Visual Studio every time you want to fire up the Emulator. But all that typing is still rather cumbersome, so there's an even easier way! Just follow these steps:

1. If you're in Windows 7, the next time you launch the Emulator, right-click it in the taskbar and select "Pin this program to taskbar."

2. Right-click it again. In the context-sensitive menu that pops up, right-click (a third time) Windows Phone Emulator and select Properties.

3. In the Properties window, find the Target textbox, and edit it to include the path to your `bin` file, like this:

   ```
   xde "c:\program files (x86)\Microsoft SDKs\Windows Phone\v7.0\
       Emulation\Images\WM70C1.bin"
   ```

4. Click OK.

You can launch the Emulator any time you like, straight from the desktop. If you want to add any command-line options, that's still easy. Just open the Properties window again, add them to the end of the Target textbox, and you're all set.

You may even want to set up multiple Emulator shortcuts with different command-line options enabled to help with testing your games. Just be sure to give them clear names so that you don't get them mixed up.

SUMMARY

Everything you need to download to get started creating Windows Phone 7 games with XNA can be found at `http://create.msdn.com/en-US/`. This includes the Windows Phone Emulator, which is a powerful and useful tool for creating, deploying, and testing your games.

In Chapter 3, you will learn about device orientation and how to make use of the accelerometer in your games.

3

Orientation

WHAT'S IN THIS CHAPTER?

- ➤ Understanding and using the accelerometer
- ➤ Determining what orientation strategies to use for your game
- ➤ Running your game in full-screen mode

All Windows Phone 7 devices contain an integrated accelerometer and compass that you can use to determine the device's direction and orientation.

The ability to play games on the phone without having to touch the screen creates numerous possibilities for interaction. Imagine how intuitive your game would be if you could steer a car or fly a jet by holding your phone like a steering wheel or yoke.

DEVICE ORIENTATION

When creating games, you must decide early in the process how you want to display your screens. The phone has two possible orientations: Portrait and Landscape. In the simplest possible terms, Portrait is the vertical orientation, and Landscape is horizontal.

A traditional arcade experience such as a building climber or a Space Invaders type of game would be best presented in Portrait mode. On the other hand, if your game requires a more tactical viewpoint, perhaps Landscape mode makes more sense.

Setting Device Orientation

By default, all games on Windows Phone 7 run in Landscape mode, meaning a backbuffer width of 800 pixels and a height of 480 pixels. To make your game run in Portrait mode, you must set the backbuffer width and height to 480 and 800 pixels, respectively.

Hardware Scaling

The phone includes a hardware image scaler, which means that your games can render to any size of backbuffer, and the image automatically stretches to fill the display.

If the backbuffer and display have different aspect ratios, you see black bars (also known as letterboxing) along the edges, just like on the Xbox 360.

Keep in mind that all phones available at launch will support 480 by 800 resolution (also known as Wide Video Graphics Array, or WVGA), but Microsoft plans to add a second supported resolution of 320 by 480 (also known as Half-size Video Graphics Array, or HVGA) sometime in the future.

The dedicated hardware scaling on Windows Phone 7 has a number of distinct advantages:

- ➤ You do not need to detect native resolution on future devices and code your game to adapt to them. Instead, you can just pick a resolution and stick with it, knowing that the scaler will handle it automatically.
- ➤ You have automatic scaling of touch inputs to match your game's resolution, regardless of the native resolution of the device you are running on.
- ➤ The automatic scaling is handled by dedicated hardware, so it has no impact on performance. No GPU resources are necessary.
- ➤ Dedicated hardware scaling allows for use of a higher-quality image filter than you could get by yourself with bilinear filtering on the GPU.

A deep dive into bilinear filtering is beyond the scope of this book. The short version is that bilinear filtering *is a software method used to smooth textures when displaying them at a size that doesn't match how they are stored.*

- ➤ Hardware scaling means that you can render your game at a lower resolution to conserve performance, and the scaler will still fill the display for you.

Be aware that if your game is using the scaler, the backbuffer resolution is scaled and is not the same as the screen resolution, which is not scaled.

Automatic Rotation

In addition to hardware scaling, the phone includes an automatic rotation feature. This is an improvement over the Zune way, which required you to draw everything to a `rendertarget`, and then rotate that when drawing it to the screen. Instead, you just use the `SupportedOrientations` property of the `GraphicsDeviceManager` class to specify which modes you want to support, and the rendering (and touch input) is adjusted accordingly.

To show off automatic rotation, even in the Emulator, create a new Windows Phone Game project, and call it RotationSample.

> *The complete code for this project is available for download at the book's companion website (www.wrox.com).*

Add a new SpriteFont to the RotationSampleContent project, and name it RotationFont .spritefont. Set the size to 20.

Next, add the following variable at the class level:

```
SpriteFont rotationFont;
```

Now you can load the SpriteFont into the rotationFont variable by adding the following line in the ContentLoad() method:

```
rotationFont = Content.Load<SpriteFont>("rotationFont");
```

Finally, add this block of code to the Draw() method, before the call to the base.Update() method:

```
spriteBatch.Begin();
spriteBatch.DrawString(rotationFont, "Check me out, I'm text.",
    new Vector2(50,50), Color.White);
spriteBatch.End();
```

At this point, if you build and run your game, it should look like Figure 3-1.

FIGURE 3-1: RotationSample in portrait orientation

If you have a phone, rotate it in your hand to see all the different orientations. If you are using the phone Emulator, click the rotation icons to the right of the Emulator. The phone (or the Emulator) should look like Figure 3-2 in Landscape orientation.

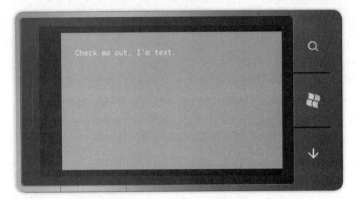

FIGURE 3-2: RotationSample in landscape orientation

This is not terribly impressive yet. Now, add the following code to your `Game` constructor:

```
graphics.SupportedOrientations = DisplayOrientation.Portrait
                               | DisplayOrientation.LandscapeLeft
                               | DisplayOrientation.LandscapeRight;
```

Build and run again. This time, when you rotate your phone (or the Emulator), you see that the text is displayed properly, as shown in Figure 3-3, regardless of the phone orientation.

FIGURE 3-3: RotationSample updated for automatic rotation

Listing 3-1 shows the `DisplayOrientation` enumeration (which you can find in the `Microsoft.XNA.Framework` namespace).

LISTING 3-1: DisplayOrientation enumeration

```
public enum DisplayOrientation
{
    Default = 0,

    // Display rotated counterclockwise 90 degrees in landscape orientation.
    LandscapeLeft = 1,

    // Display rotated clockwise 90 degrees in landscape orientation.
    LandscapeLeft = 2,

    // Orientation is a portrait, where height is greater than width.
    Portrait = 4,
}
```

Landscape games can automatically rotate between `LandscapeLeft` and `LandscapeRight`, so you don't actually have to set anything for them. But switching between Landscape and Portrait orientations is a bit more involved, because it alters the dimensions of the backbuffer, and you will almost certainly need to adjust your screen layout.

Not all games can gracefully handle both orientations. So, you must explicitly set the `SupportedOrientations` property to allow automatic switching between them.

If you find yourself needing to change orientation mid-game (from Landscape to Portrait, for example), use the following code snippet:

```
graphics.SupportedOrientations = DisplayOrientation.Portrait;
graphics.ApplyChanges();
```

If you want to allow automatic rotation of your game to different orientations, you need to know which orientation your game is currently in, so keep reading.

Detecting Device Orientation

Whenever your phone physically changes orientation, the `GameWindow.OrientationChanged` event gets raised. And, if you included the new orientation in the `SupportedOrientations` property, the graphics device is reset to support the new orientation.

Any time you need to check your current orientation, examining the `CurrentOrientation` property of the `GameWindow` class returns a value from the `DisplayOrientation` enumeration.

The `GameWindow` class is exposed as `Window` in your XNA game. So, the code to check the `CurrentOrientation` property in your game would look something like the following snippet:

```
if (Window.CurrentOrientation == DisplayOrientation.Portrait)
    {// code that does stuff}
```

To see it in action, go back into your `RotationSample` project and modify the `Draw()` method as shown in Listing 3-2.

LISTING 3-2: The Draw() Method of the Game1 Class

```
protected override void Draw(GameTime gameTime)
{
    GraphicsDevice.Clear(Color.CornflowerBlue);

    spriteBatch.Begin();
    spriteBatch.DrawString(rotationFont,
                        "Check me out, I'm "
                            + Window.CurrentOrientation.ToString()
                            + ".",
                        new Vector2(50,50),
                        Color.White);
    spriteBatch.End();

    base.Draw(gameTime);
}
```

Now, when you build and run, you see the text change when your orientation changes.

Here are a couple helpful tips when dealing with device orientation:

- Use the `DisplayOrientation` property of the `GraphicsDevice.PresentationParameters` class to check how your game is being displayed.
- If your phone is being held in a way that doesn't match one of your supported orientations, the `DisplayOrientation` and `CurrentOrientation` properties may not match.

Running in Full-Screen Mode

When designing an XNA game for Windows Phone 7, you must take into account the system tray. This is the 480-pixels-wide-by-32-pixels-high area at the top of your screen (in Portrait mode). It provides the status of things such as signal strength, battery, charging status, whether you are in airplane mode, and so on. It's up to you as the game developer to decide whether you want to keep this area visible while your game is active.

By default, your game will run in full-screen mode, meaning that the system tray is hidden. That's a perfectly valid option, and many games do this.

Maintaining a visible system tray while your game is running is really quite simple. Just add the following code in the constructor in your `Game` class:

```
graphics.IsFullScreen = false;
```

When you run your game, it draws as normal, but the system tray is drawn on top of it. So, you don't want to put any important information in that region, because your players won't be able to see it.

For some time now, Xbox Live Indie Games (XBLIG) developers have had a handy software tool known as the Safe Area Sample. It allows them to see the *title-safe area* (guaranteed visible area) of their monitor and TV screen.

Since all Windows Phone 7 devices are required to be one of two consistent resolutions (480 by 800 pixels or 320 by 480 pixels), you have it pretty easy. But if you plan to keep the system tray visible during game play, you may want to incorporate a similar Safe Area Sample into your bag of tricks.

Phone Title-Safe Area

This project displays a red bar in the area where the system tray would normally appear. This way, you can check your game to ensure that no important information is being obscured when you run your game as anything other than full screen.

Create a new Windows Phone Game project, and name it PhoneTitleSafe.

> *The complete code for this project is available for download at the book's companion website (www.wrox.com). If you have downloaded the sample code from this book's website (www.wrox.com), you already have everything you need, including the* PhoneTitleSafe.png *image.*

Next, fire up your browser and grab the PhoneTitleSafe.png image from this book's website (at www.wrox.com). Save it somewhere handy. Right-click the PhoneTitleSafeContent project, and add the image you just saved.

In your Game class, add the following code at the top:

```
Texture2D titleSafe;
```

In the constructor, add the following code to control whether the title-safe area is displayed in your game:

```
// True, red box displays
// False, red box disappears
graphics.IsFullScreen = true;
```

In the LoadContent() method, add the following line to load the PhoneTitleSafe image you added to your PhoneTitleSafeContent project earlier:

```
titleSafe = Content.Load<Texture2D>("PhoneTitleSafe");
```

Finally, add the following block of code to your Draw() routine:

```
spriteBatch.Begin();
spriteBatch.Draw(titleSafe, Vector2.Zero, Color.White);
spriteBatch.End();
```

That's it. Give it a run and take a look at the screen. You should see a red bar at the top indicating the area used by the system tray.

Now, stop the game and go back into the code. Switch the value of graphics.IsFullScreen to false. You see the system tray at the top of the screen.

At first glance, this may seem like a backwards approach, but it's not. Even if you are designing your game to run with the system tray visible, you should develop and test in full-screen mode with the title-safe area displayed. This will show you what might be getting obscured otherwise. Anything that shows up in the red area won't be visible when you run your game.

Just don't forget to take out this code before you submit your game to the Marketplace. Even though the red zone will be perfectly covered by the system tray, there's no point in wasting resources drawing something no one will ever see.

ACCELEROMETER

Your Windows Phone 7 includes at least one accelerometer sensor that measures and reports gravity and movement. The accelerometer API actually builds on a more generalized sensor framework. This means that if additional sensors are added later, you should be able to access them in mostly the same way.

> *Zune developers might be wondering what happened to the accelerometer. Don't worry; it's still around. However, to be accessible to both Silverlight and XNA developers, it no longer resides in the XNA Framework. You can now find it in the* `Microsoft.Devices.Sensors` *namespace.*

The `Accelerometer` class is the key to accessing the accelerometer sensor on your phone. As classes go, it's a rather simple one, as shown in Listing 3-3.

LISTING 3-3: Accelerometer Class Definition

```
public sealed class Accelerometer : IDisposable
{
    // Creates a new instance of the Accelerometer object.
    public Accelerometer();

    // Gets the current state of the accelerometer. The value is a member of
    // the Microsoft.Devices.Sensors.SensorState enumeration.
    public SensorState State { get; }

    // Occurs when new data arrives from the accelerometer.
    public event EventHandler<AccelerometerReadingEventArgs> ReadingChanged;

    // Releases the managed and unmanaged resources used by the Accelerometer
    public void Dispose();

    // Starts data acquisition from the accelerometer
    public void Start();
```

```
    // Stops data acquisition from the accelerometer
    public void Stop();
}
```

The `Dispose()`, `Start()`, and `Stop()` methods are pretty self-explanatory.

The read-only `State` property returns a `SensorState` enumeration containing one of the following six values:

- `NotSupported`
- `Ready`
- `Initializing`
- `NoData`
- `NoPermissions`
- `Disabled`

The `ReadingChanged()` event fires whenever new data comes in from the sensor. The `AccelerometerReadingEventArgs` object that gets passed into your handler provides the means for accessing the returned accelerometer data. Listing 3-4 lists the exposed methods and properties.

LISTING 3-4: AccelerometerReadingEventArgs Class Definition

```
public class AccelerometerReadingEventArgs : EventArgs
{
    // A timestamp indicating the time at which the accelerometer reading was
    // taken.
    public DateTimeOffset TimeStamp { get; }

    // The acceleration in the X direction.
    public double X { get; }

    // The acceleration in the Y direction.
    public double Y { get; }

    // The acceleration in the Z direction.
    public double Z { get; }
}
```

The X, Y, and Z properties each return a `double` with a range of -2 to 2 gravitational units, indicating the direction of acceleration for each axis.

The units typically used in describing gravitational acceleration are milliGals. A Gal is defined as a centimeter per second squared. Microsoft refers to these as gravitational units.

That's a good enough first glance at the key classes you will be working with. Now let's get started using them.

AccelerometerSample

Create a new Windows Phone Game (4.0) project, and name it `AccelerometerSample`.

The complete code for this project is available for download at the book's companion website (www.wrox.com).

Add a `SpriteFont` named `readings.spritefont` to your `AccelerometerSampleContent` project so that you can display your accelerometer readings on the screen. Set the size to 20.

As always, when adding external content, be sure you add a class-level variable to hold your `SpriteFont`, as shown here:

```
SpriteFont readingsFont;
```

Now, modify the `LoadContent()` method to load your font in memory:

```
readingsFont = Content.Load<SpriteFont>("readings");
```

Before you start writing any accelerometer code, you will expand the `References` section under your project in Solution Explorer and add a reference to the `Microsoft.Devices.Sensors` namespace.

With that out of the way, add the following `using` statement at the top of your `Game1` class file:

```
using Microsoft.Devices.Sensors;
```

This gives you access to the `Accelerometer` classes, so go ahead and add the following class-level variable:

```
Accelerometer accelerometer;
```

As you saw in Listing 3-2, the `Accelerometer` exposes X, Y, and Z properties that store acceleration for those directions. Add the following class-level variables to hold these values for use in the `AccelerometerSample` project:

```
double X;
double Y;
double Z;
```

You need to instantiate the `Accelerometer` class, so add this line to the `Initialize()` method of your `Game1` class:

```
accelerometer = new Accelerometer();
```

At this point, you have an `accelerometer` object in memory, but you can't do anything with it yet. You need to set up an event handler for the `ReadingChanged()` event discussed previously. You will do this in the `Initialize()` method as well, right after the code you just added to instantiate the `Accelerometer` class:

```
Accelerometer.ReadingChanged
    += new EventHandler<AccelerometerReadingEventArgs>
        (AccelerometerReadingChanged);
```

With the event handler defined, Visual Studio should be showing you an error saying that the `AccelerometerReadingChanged()` method doesn't exist yet. That's okay, because you will create it now. Add the method shown in Listing 3-5 to your `Game1` class.

LISTING 3-5: The AccelerometerReadingChanged() Method of the Game1 Class

```
void AccelerometerReadingChanged(object sender,
                                 AccelerometerReadingEventArgs e)
{
    Deployment.Current.Dispatcher.BeginInvoke(() => NewReading(e));
}
```

As mentioned earlier, the `AccelerometerReadingChanged()` method is called whenever the accelerometer sensor has new data. The event handler is called from a different thread than your main game thread. Therefore, you must use the `Dispatcher` class to invoke the `NewReading()` method in the game's main thread, passing in `AccelerometerReadingEventArgs` as a parameter.

Right now, Visual Studio doesn't know where to find the `Deployment` namespace, but that's an easy fix. In your Solution Explorer window, expand the `References` folder, and add a reference to the `System.Windows` namespace.

Now, add the following statement at the top of your `Game1` class:

```
using System.Windows;
```

You still have an error at this point, because Visual Studio doesn't know what or where the `NewReading()` method is. Take a look at Listing 3-6, and add it to your `Game1` class.

LISTING 3-6: The NewReading() Method of the Game1 Class

```
void NewReading(AccelerometerReadingEventArgs e)
{
    X = e.X;
    Y = e.Y;
    Z = e.Z;
}
```

In this method, you are taking the values returned and putting them in the variables you created earlier. You will write those values onscreen shortly.

Most of the plumbing is out of the way at this point. So, it's time to add some code to actually start and stop the accelerometer and display the returned values. Modify the `Initialize()` method to look like Listing 3-7.

LISTING 3-7: The Initialize() Method of the Game1 Class

```
protected override void Initialize()
{
    accelerometer = new Accelerometer();
    accelerometer.ReadingChanged
        += new EventHandler<AccelerometerReadingEventArgs>
            (AccelerometerReadingChanged);

    accelerometer.Start();

    base.Initialize();
}
```

For purposes of demonstrating the accelerometer and showing how to acquire readings from it, you are doing something here you wouldn't normally do in your games. To minimize battery usage and maximize performance, turn on the accelerometer only during the part of the game when you specifically need to get readings (such as during the main game screen). Leave it off otherwise.

Add the following line to your `UnloadContent()` method:

```
accelerometer.Stop();
```

The only thing left at this point is to display the coordinates onscreen. So, modify your `Draw()` method as shown in Listing 3-8.

LISTING 3-8: The Draw() Method of the Game1 Class

```
protected override void Draw(GameTime gameTime)
{
    GraphicsDevice.Clear(Color.CornflowerBlue);

    spriteBatch.Begin();
    spriteBatch.DrawString(readingsFont,
                    "X: " + X.ToString("0.00"),
                    new Vector2(50, 50),
                    Color.White);
    spriteBatch.DrawString(readingsFont,
                    "Y: " + Y.ToString("0.00"),
                    new Vector2(50, 75),
                    Color.White);
    spriteBatch.DrawString(readingsFont,
                    "Z: " + Z.ToString("0.00"),
                    new Vector2(50, 100),
                    Color.White);
    spriteBatch.End();

    base.Draw(gameTime);
}
```

That's all there is to capturing data from the built-in accelerometer. Fire it up, wave your phone around, and watch the values on the accelerometer change.

The authors would like to point out that if you are running in the Emulator instead of on actual hardware, waving around your laptop or desktop machine is not recommended and probably won't result in any changing values.

Before moving on to the next chapter, a few things about working with the accelerometer are worth pointing out:

- It is possible (if unlikely) for calls to the `Accelerometer Start()` and `Stop()` methods to throw an exception, so be sure to wrap them in a `try/catch` block.
- It may seem odd to include a reference to `System.Windows` in your XNA game. But in the case of the `Deployment` class, it's used with Silverlight and, on Windows Phone 7, XNA is a part of the Silverlight runtime.
- If you would like to see the `AccelerometerSample` do something a little more interesting than just display acceleration values on three axes, try this: Modify the `Draw()` routine to use `Vector2` variables instead of hard-coded `Vector2` positions, and then add some code to the `Update()` method to modify those variables based on accelerometer input.

SUMMARY

Device orientation is a critical part of game design, and Windows Phone 7 provides the option to hard-code orientation or to use the automatic rotation features.

The hardware scaler allows you to program to one resolution, knowing that it will "just work" on current and future devices. The scaler can also be used to improve performance by coding to a lower resolution and then scaling up.

The accelerometer provides a new and powerful means of control and input for your games, as well as providing feedback to your phone on how the device is oriented.

In Chapter 4, you will learn about touch input, including gestures and the Soft Input Panel (SIP), and polling hardware keyboards for input.

Touch Input

WHAT'S IN THIS CHAPTER?

- Understanding how to respond to touch events
- Understanding the different types of touch inputs and gestures
- Getting the proper layout of UI elements for touch-based interfaces
- Interacting with the Soft Input Panel (SIP)

Touch input is a vital part of the Windows Phone 7 user experience, and the capability to support up to four simultaneous touch points offers a tremendous number of options for game development.

In this chapter, you will learn how to detect and respond to touch input in the form of simple taps and more-complex gestures. You will also learn how to create your own gestures. Also included in this chapter is an examination of some best practices to consider when designing your own touch-based games.

RESPONDING TO TOUCH EVENTS

Previously, one of the biggest hurdles in developing games for mobile devices was the inability to predict what type of hardware your mobile game would be running on. Being compatible with Windows Mobile was no guarantee. Some phones had two buttons on the front, and others had six spread all over the device.

With the introduction of Windows Phone 7, this problem has been largely eliminated. While Microsoft has allowed phone manufacturers some limited flexibility in the form factor, the overall experience is consistent and predictable from one device to the next.

Having to develop games for a device with only three buttons sounds rather limited — until you consider the touch screen. The touch screen offers tremendous flexibility, and how you use it is entirely up to you. You can make your game control scheme as simple or robust as is appropriate for your game.

Overview of Touch Interfaces

Touch-based interfaces have actually been around almost three quarters of a century, with primitive implementations appearing in the mid-1940s. IBM created the first multitouch-capable screens in the late 1960s.

> *While Apple's claims in 2007 of having "invented multitouch" with the iPhone are primarily marketing fluff, it can certainly take credit for making multitouch mainstream. Without its innovation and the widespread adoption that followed, you almost certainly wouldn't be reading this chapter right now.*

Touch screens can be found in nearly every industry and in numerous devices, ranging from heavy-machinery assembly lines to automated teller machines (ATMs) to handheld gaming devices and, of course, phones. Additionally, touch screens are often used in places where more traditional input (mouse and keyboard) is either impossible or impractical for a variety of reasons, ranging from usability to security.

Touch capabilities have been available on phones for some time. For years, many smartphone or PDA devices could be used with your choice of stylus or fingertip, although the results of the latter were often unsatisfactory.

All that changed with the introduction of the iPhone and the devices that have followed. People who would never have considered purchasing a PDA or smartphone snapped up the iPhone and the devices that followed, without hesitation. Between the "Big 3" (Apple iPhone, Google Android, and Windows Phone 7), touch-based devices are rapidly becoming commonplace. Industry experts predict as many as 21 million touch-based devices will be in use by 2012.

Detecting Touch Input

Everything you need for using touch input in your Windows Phone 7 game can be found in the `Microsoft.Xna.Framework.Input` namespace.

To read touch input, you must call `TouchPanel.GetState` during the `Update` part of the game loop. This returns a `TouchCollection` that contains a `TouchLocation` object for every touch that was detected at the time. Once you have a `TouchCollection`, you can loop through and read the properties of each `TouchLocation` object to find out the location and state.

> *The fact that `TouchPanel.GetState()` returns a `TouchCollection` is one of the odd little inconsistencies in the XNA 4.0 framework. `Keyboard.GetState()` returns a `KeyboardState` object. `Gamepad.GetState()` returns a `GamepadState` object. There may be a perfectly logical reason why `TouchPanel.GetState()` returns a `TouchCollection`, but you would expect it to return a `TouchPanelState` object.*

In the following example, you will get the state of your touch panel and then loop through a collection of touch points. Next, you will check to see if the state of any touch points is equal to `Pressed` or `Moved`. Finally, you will update the location of a sprite onscreen, based on the location of your touch.

Start by creating a new Windows Phone Game project and adding an image to your `Content` project. It doesn't matter what image you use, as long as it is a `jpeg`, `png`, or `gif` file, fairly symmetrical, and small (less than 200 by 200 pixels).

The complete code for this project is available for download at the book's companion website (www.wrox.com).

On the Properties sheet for your image, change the asset name to `logo` if you plan on following along over the next few pages.

Add these two variables at the class level:

```
Texture2D logo;
Vector2 logoPosition;
```

Next, add this line to the `LoadContent()` method to load your sprite into memory:

```
logo = Content.Load<Texture2D>("logo");
```

The next line of code gets the current state of the touch screen. Put this in the `Update()` method, before the call to `base.Update()`:

```
TouchCollection touchCollection = TouchPanel.GetState();
```

After that, add the following block of code to read the touch data from each `TouchLocation` object in the collection, checking the state as you go:

```
foreach (TouchLocation touch in touchCollection)
{
    if ((touch.State == TouchLocationState.Pressed) ||
        (touch.State == TouchLocationState.Moved))
    {
        // update a sprite to be drawn at the touch location
        logoPosition.X = touch.Position.X;
        logoPosition.Y = touch.Position.Y;
    }
}
```

You are concerned with only two states in this sample, but the `TouchLocationState` enumeration actually has the following four possible values:

- `TouchLocationState.Invalid` — Usually, this occurs when a new touch location tries to access the previous state of itself.
- `TouchLocationState.Moved` — The position of this touch location was updated since the previous frame (or it continued to be pressed at the same position).

- ➤ `TouchLocationState.Pressed` — This touch location is new as of this frame. It did not exist in a prior frame. Lifting your finger and then touching in the exact same position still results in a new touch location.
- ➤ `TouchLocationState.Released` — This touch location was pressed in the previous frame but is no longer pressed in this frame.

Storing the previous state and comparing it to the current state can be the difference between a button that fires continuously if "held down" and a button that you must touch each time you want to fire.

The previous block of code set your sprite's x- and y-coordinates equal to your touch point. If you would rather center the sprite on your touch point, that's easy as well. Just find the following two lines:

```
logoPosition.X = touch.Position.X;
logoPosition.Y = touch.Position.Y;
```

Change them to look like this:

```
logoPosition.X = touch.Position.X - (logo.Width/2);
logoPosition.Y = touch.Position.Y - (logo.Height/2);
```

Add the following lines to the `Draw()` method, and you're in business:

```
spriteBatch.Begin();
spriteBatch.Draw(logo, logoPosition, Color.White);
spriteBatch.End();
```

Your sprite will be drawn *mostly* centered on your touch point. I say "mostly" because this is one of those cases where working with the Emulator is different from working with an actual device.

You probably do not have a touch-enabled developer workstation. This means that when you are working in the Emulator, you simulate a touch by using the cursor and clicking the screen where you would like to touch. Unless you have changed your cursor from the default arrow, it is likely a bit smaller than the average finger. To compensate for this, you can define and add an offset to the end of the position code, like so:

```
logoPosition.X = touch.Position.X - (logo.Width/2) + HorizontalOffset;
logoPosition.Y = touch.Position.Y - (logo.Height/2) + VerticalOffset;
```

The authors have found that a value of 20 for the vertical offset and 0 for the horizontal offset puts the cursor's point as close as possible to dead center. Feel free to experiment with your own values, but remember to disable these offsets when deploying to an actual device, or you may experience some unexpected behaviors.

If you would like the sprite to be visible only while you are touching the screen, you can do that, too. Just create a Boolean variable at the class level (name it something like `displayLogo`) and draw only if it's `true`. Take a look at the following code in bold:

```
spriteBatch.Begin();
if (displayLogo) spriteBatch.Draw(logo, logoPosition, Color.White);
spriteBatch.End();
```

Of course, for this to work, you must first add some more code to the `Update()` method. Your `foreach` loop will get a little bigger. Add the following bold code:

```
foreach (TouchLocation touch in touchCollection)
{
    if ((touch.State == TouchLocationState.Pressed) ||
        (touch.State == TouchLocationState.Moved))
    {
        // update a sprite to be drawn centered on the touch location
        logoPosition.X = touch.Position.X + HorizontalOffset;
        logoPosition.Y = touch.Position.Y + VerticalOffset;
        displayLogo = true;
    }

    if (touch.State == TouchLocationState.Released)
        displayLogo = false;
}
```

Up to this point, all of this has been built with the assumption that you have only one finger. (And, to be fair, as far as the Emulator is concerned, that's true, unless you have a multitouch-capable development machine.)

In the next example, you will detect multiple touch points and display a number corresponding to the Id property of each TouchLocation object at the current position.

Start by creating a new game project, and name it MultiTouchMe. Add a SpriteFont to the Content project. Leave the name SpriteFont1, but change the size to 20 to make your text more readable.

Add the following class-level variables:

```
SpriteFont spriteFont;
TouchCollection touchCollection;
```

Next, add the following line to the LoadContent() method to load your SpriteFont into memory:

```
spriteFont = Content.Load<SpriteFont>("SpriteFont1");
```

In the Update() method, add the following code before the call to base.Update():

```
touchCollection = TouchPanel.GetState();
```

 You've probably noticed a similar line at the bottom of both the Update() *and* Draw() *methods in your* Game *class. Each time you hit the* base.Update() *line in the* Update() *method of your game loop, it also calls the* Update() *method of any* GameComponent *or* DrawableGameComponent *objects you have registered. Additionally, if your game has any* DrawableGameComponent *objects,* base .Draw() *calls into their* Draw() *method as well.*

Finally, inside the Draw() method, add the following block of code just before base.Draw():

```
spriteBatch.Begin();

foreach (TouchLocation touch in touchCollection)
    spriteBatch.DrawString(spriteFont,
```

```
            "ID: " + touch.Id.ToString()
            + " (" + (int)touch.Position.X + "," + (int)touch.Position.Y + ")",
                        touch.Position,
                        Color.White);

spriteBatch.End();
```

That's it. Press F5 and run this code in the Emulator.

As you are running the code, touch/click the screen and hold it down. You should see a number at your touch point. Release it and touch/click elsewhere on the screen. The number you are seeing is the `Id` property of the `TouchLocation`.

Touch/click the screen again. This time, without releasing the touch, drag it across the screen. Notice how the `Id` number doesn't change, even though the `Location` coordinates obviously do.

This is an important concept, and it illustrates the key difference between the `TouchLocationState.Pressed` and `TouchLocationState.Moved` states. Even though the `Position` property of `TouchLocation` changed, it is still the same `TouchLocation` object — until you release it, and then it's gone forever.

Touch the screen a few more times. Notice how the `Id` number keeps going up by exactly 65536 each time. The reason has to do with the internal structure of how the `TouchLocation` objects are stored. But it's not important, because you should *never* rely on this number for anything — other than comparing it to another `TouchLocation` ID to ensure that they are different.

Running this in the Emulator gives you only one touch point. However, if you run the code on your phone, you can see multiple touch points on the screen at the same time, each with its own unique `Id`.

> One interesting thing to note about the Emulator is that if you have a multitouch screen, the Emulator responds to multitouch input from it! Having this as a resource when developing (especially when you don't have a phone handy) can be a very useful tool. This is an excellent example of how useful and well-designed the Windows Phone Emulator really is.

Detecting Gestures

In addition to providing support for single or multiple touch points on the same screen, XNA provides a set of common gestures that you can program against in your game. Whereas a simple touch often represents a selection or click event, *gestures* can represent more-complex actions and are modeled after natural human movements.

The various gestures included in XNA can be found in the `GestureType` enumeration. In the following discussion, you will learn about the available gestures and how they are implemented in XNA.

The best way to learn is by doing. So, create a new Windows Phone Game; you will add each of the gestures as you learn about them. Name your new project `Gestures`, and add a `SpriteFont` to the `Content` project. Accept the default `SpriteFont` name, and set the size to 20 to ensure readability.

The complete code for this project is available for download at the book's companion website (www.wrox.com).

Ensure that you have the following `using` statements at the top of your `Game` class file:

```
using System;
using Microsoft.Xna.Framework;
using Microsoft.Xna.Framework.Content;
using Microsoft.Xna.Framework.Graphics;
using Microsoft.Xna.Framework.Input;
using Microsoft.Xna.Framework.Input.Touch;
```

Next, add the code to load and instantiate your `SpriteFont`. At the class level, add these lines:

```
SpriteFont spriteFont;

String message = "Do Something";
Vector2 messagePos = Vector2.Zero;
Color color = Color.Black;
```

The last three lines will make more sense shortly, once you get into the gesture-handling code, so don't worry about them too much right now. You will use them to display messages based on the gesture you perform.

Inside the `LoadContent()` method, add this line:

```
spriteFont = Content.Load<SpriteFont>("SpriteFont1");
```

Now it's time to add the list of enabled gestures. You are required to tell the `TouchPanel` what gestures your game will be using, since none are enabled by default. Add the following block of code to the `Initialize()` method, just before the `base.Initialize()` line:

```
TouchPanel.EnabledGestures = GestureType.Tap
                           | GestureType.DoubleTap
                           | GestureType.Hold
                           | GestureType.HorizontalDrag
                           | GestureType.VerticalDrag
                           | GestureType.FreeDrag
                           | GestureType.DragComplete
                           | GestureType.Pinch
                           | GestureType.PinchComplete
                           | GestureType.Flick;
```

If you're curious about this syntax, take a look at the `GestureType` enumerator definition shown in Listing 4-1. The `[Flags]` attribute is used by enumerators to indicate that bitwise operations will be supported.

LISTING 4-1: GestureType Enumerator

```
[Flags]
public enum GestureType
```

continues

LISTING 4-1 *(continued)*

```
{
    None = 0,
    Tap = 1,
    DoubleTap = 2,
    Hold = 4,
    HorizontalDrag = 8,
    VerticalDrag = 16,
    FreeDrag = 32,
    Pinch = 64,
    Flick = 128,
    DragComplete = 256,
    PinchComplete = 512,
}
```

For these bitwise operations to work properly, the values in the enumerator must be powers of 2. By combining values with a bitwise OR (via the pipe symbol, |), you make it possible to retrieve one of those distinct values from the `EnabledGestures` property, although you won't be pulling anything out of this property. XNA handles that part for you.

Before executing code to respond to specific gestures, you must check to see if any touch gestures are actually available. Add the following block of code to the `Update()` method in your `Game` class. Make sure you put it before the `base.Update()` call.

```
if (TouchPanel.IsGestureAvailable)
{

}
```

This may seem like an odd thing to check, since you aren't actually passing in a gesture. However, `TouchPanel.IsGestureAvailable` lets you know if there are any gestures that you have enabled that are ready for reading. If none are available, you cannot call `TouchPanel.ReadGesture()`, because there are no gestures to read. Without this line, any attempt to read gestures will throw an `InvalidOperation` exception, and your game will fail to run.

Inside the `if` block that you just created, add the following line to the top:

```
GestureSample gesture = TouchPanel.ReadGesture();
```

This line reads the `TouchPanel` and returns a populated `GestureSample` struct that contains data from a multitouch gesture over a span of time. Listing 4-2 shows the properties exposed by `GestureSample`.

LISTING 4-2: GestureSample Properties

```
public struct GestureSample
{
    // Holds delta of first touchpoint in a multitouch gesture.
    public Vector2 Delta { get; }

    // Holds delta of second touchpoint in a multitouch gesture.
```

```
        public Vector2 Delta2 { get; }

        // The type of gesture in a multitouch gesture sample.
        public GestureType GestureType { get; }

        // Holds current position of first touchpoint in gesture sample.
        public Vector2 Position { get; }

        // Holds current position of second touchpoint in gesture sample.
        public Vector2 Position2 { get; }

        // Holds span of time represented by multitouch gesture sample.
        public TimeSpan Timestamp { get; }
    }
```

Even though Windows Phone 7 supports a minimum of four simultaneous touch points, the included gestures system currently doesn't use or support more than two touch points.

Immediately below the line that reads the `TouchPanel`, add the following `switch` statement to handle each of the returned gesture types:

```
switch (gesture.GestureType)
{

}
```

Inside the `switch` block, you will add code to handle each of the gestures you enabled previously.

Tap

The most basic of the touch gestures, a tap consists of a brief single touch on the screen. This is the equivalent of a click action in Windows.

To support the `Tap` gesture, add the following block of code:

```
case GestureType.Tap:
    message = "That was a Tap";
    color = Color.Red;
    break;
```

DoubleTap

To trigger this gesture, the user must tap the screen twice in quick succession. The `DoubleTap` gesture is always preceded by a `Tap` gesture at the same location. If the `TimeSpan` value between `Taps` is too long, the `DoubleTap` gesture is not detected, and a second `Tap` sample is returned instead.

```
case GestureType.DoubleTap:
    message = "That was a Double Tap";
    color = Color.Orange;
    break;
```

Hold

This works similar to the single Tap, except that you touch the screen for approximately 1 second before releasing or moving your finger.

In a game, this gesture might be used to provide a context menu on a specific unit, as opposed to the Tap gesture, which would be used to select the unit. To support the Hold gesture, add the following code block inside the switch block:

```
case GestureType.Hold:
    message = "That was a Hold";
    color = Color.Yellow;
    break;
```

HorizontalDrag

This gesture is a lot like the Tap gesture, except that you do not release your finger before moving it horizontally (left to right or right to left).

Add the following code to support the HorizontalDrag gesture:

```
case GestureType.HorizontalDrag:
    message = "That was a Horizontal Drag";
    color = Color.Blue;
    break;
```

VerticalDrag

The VerticalDrag gesture performs in much the same way as the HorizontalDrag gesture, except that it uses a vertical (top-to-bottom or bottom-to-top) motion.

Add the following block of code to support the VerticalDrag gesture:

```
case GestureType.VerticalDrag:
    message = "That was a Vertical Drag";
    color = Color.Indigo;
    break;
```

In touch-enabled games, Drag gestures are often used for moving units from one place to another, performing sliding adjustments, drawing lines, and more.

> When capturing a Drag gesture, keep in mind that only the initial motion is required to record the gesture. If you perform a VerticalDrag gesture and then a HorizontalDrag gesture without releasing your finger between them, only one GestureSample is returned, containing the data for the first gesture. This is also true of the FreeDrag gesture.

FreeDrag

You perform the FreeDrag gesture by touching the screen and moving your finger in a free-form manner (such as drawing a circle).

Add this block of code to support the `FreeDrag` gesture:

```
case GestureType.FreeDrag:
    message = "That was a Free Drag";
    color = Color.Green;
    break;
```

When coding support for the `FreeDrag` gesture in your game, carefully consider how you will use it, and whether to also support the `HorizontalDrag` and `VerticalDrag` gestures. If your primary purpose is to allow drawing in your game, you can likely get by with supporting only the `FreeDrag` gesture.

DragComplete

Working in complement to the three `Drag`-based gestures, the `DragComplete` gesture is returned when any of the `Drag` gestures are completed (by releasing the `TouchLocation`). This `GestureType` is included solely to indicate completion of the `Drag` gesture. No other `Position` or `Delta` data is provided for this sample type.

To receive notification when any of the `Drag`-based gestures have completed, add the following block of code to the `switch` statement:

```
case GestureType.DragComplete:
    message = "Drag gesture complete";
    color = Color.Gold;
    break;
```

Flick

You perform the `Flick` gesture by touching the screen and making a quick swipe in any direction. No positional data is returned from a `Flick` gesture, potentially making it of limited use for games. But you could use it to move the camera of your game, perhaps panning around on a large world map. Other uses include scrolling text.

You can retrieve the velocity by reading the `Delta` property of the returned `GestureSample` and then apply this as force to your calculations.

Add the following block of code to provide support for the `Flick` gesture:

```
case GestureType.Flick:
    message = "That was a Flick";
    color = Color.Violet;
    break;
```

Pinch

All the gestures covered so far are single-finger gestures. The `Pinch` gesture requires two fingers, with both touching the screen and then moving toward or away from each other. `Pinch` is treated like a two-finger drag internally and takes precedence over `Drag`-based gestures while two fingers are down.

The `Pinch` gesture is typically used to zoom in or out. This is accomplished by touching the screen with two fingers and sliding them apart to zoom in or bringing them together to zoom out.

First-person 3D games can use this gesture to alter the player's perspective by moving the camera forward or backward in relation to the character. Other uses might be to zoom in to specific parts of a game board, especially in a tile-placing game such as mahjong or Scrabble.

To add support for the `Pinch` gesture, add the following block of code inside your `switch` statement:

```
case GestureType.Pinch:
    message = "That was a Pinch";
    color = Color.Violet;
    break;
```

Unfortunately, if you don't have a Windows Phone 7 device or multitouch-capable development machine, you will be unable to test the `Pinch` gesture in this demo.

PinchComplete

Much like the `Drag`-based gestures and their complementary `DragComplete` gesture, `Pinch` has a similar gesture. The `PinchComplete` gesture does not return any `Position` or `delta` data. It is used only to signal completion of the `Pinch` gesture, regardless of the direction of the pinch.

```
case GestureType.PinchComplete:
    message = "Pinch gesture complete";
    color = Color.Silver;
    break;
```

Seeing Results

This marks the end of the XNA-provided gestures. Now that you have added them all to the sample, it's time to add the code that will enable you to see the results of your actions.

Add the following line of code inside the `if` statement, just after the closing bracket of the `switch` statement:

```
messagePos = gesture.Position;
```

The *messagePos* variable is used to store the current position of the gesture that will be used when drawing a message onscreen. To see this in action, go into the `Draw()` routine and add the following block of code just before the call to `base.Draw()`:

```
spriteBatch.Begin();
spriteBatch.DrawString(spriteFont, message, messagePos, color);
spriteBatch.End();
```

You're done! Press F5 to run the code and try performing the gestures you have defined. If you are using the Emulator instead of an actual device, some gestures may be a little more difficult to perform than others, especially `Flick` and `Pinch`.

Custom Gestures

In addition to the numerous gestures described here, it is possible (and highly encouraged) to create your own gestures. Just be sure to explain them to your players — how they work and what they are used for. Don't make them too complex, or you may end up with frustrated players. Also keep in mind that, although gestures are really cool, they can be difficult for children and for people with motor-control issues.

One of the gestures "missing" from XNA 4.0 is a Swipe *gesture that returns a location and has a configurable length. In Chapter 5, you will create a* Swipe *gesture as part of the input framework covered in that chapter.*

Designing for Touch Games

When designing the UI scheme for a touch-based game, it is especially important to make your controls easy to use. You don't have the luxury of a guaranteed keyboard on every device, or mapping controller buttons to all your various options and commands.

Part of the appeal of developing games using .NET, XNA, and Windows Phone 7 is that you can write your game once and run it on multiple platforms with minimal code changes. While that's certainly true in theory, it's a little different in practice.

The following sections discuss a few best practices to keep in mind when building your masterpiece. These will save you plenty of headaches later.

Remember Your Platform

The phone has no mouse support. This means there's no cursor, no hover events, and no right-click. There's no gamepad controller or guaranteed hardware keyboard either. Anything you can do with a hardware keyboard in your game must be possible via touch.

You may be able to recompile games designed for a PC and Xbox 360 and get them to run on Windows Phone 7. But if you want your players to have a good experience playing your game, you still have a fair amount of design work to do.

Let's take a look at some suggestions for ways to work around these limitations and ensure that your players are happy.

Design for the Right Resolution

At the very least, you should seriously consider that your screen resolution is fixed at 480 by 800 (or 480 by 320 for Chassis 2 devices).

Use an easy-to-read font, set to at least size 20. Small or fancy text looks fine on a HiDef platform such as the Xbox 360 or a Windows computer, but it can often become unreadable when displayed on a mobile device. If you are writing a game that targets multiple platforms, ensure that you check everywhere you display text to verify that it isn't running off the side of the screen or wrapping improperly.

Also make sure that your buttons or other touchable UI elements are sized appropriately. The average finger is roughly half an inch across, but the fingertip is actually capable of a much smaller impression. So, there's no need for huge buttons in your games (which is good, considering the rather limited screen real estate).

On the other hand, don't make UI elements too small either. If your game is fairly fast-paced, few things are more frustrating than being unable to hit the right button because it is too small.

Don't use buttons that look like the traditional Windows Forms buttons. Any text on these buttons would be extremely difficult to read unless the button were relatively large.

You have unlimited artistic freedom when creating a game. Make your onscreen buttons look like the action they are intended to perform. A buy/sell menu could be represented by a $ icon, or a pause button could be a toggle that alternates between stereo-style play and pause buttons. You are free to come up with whatever suits the style of your game; just make it intuitive.

If your game design supports it, keep the number of onscreen interactive (touchable) UI elements to a minimum. Instead of having one or more rows of icons always onscreen, consider displaying a pop-up menu when the player taps a noninteractive part of the screen. You can even make this menu context-sensitive and display only the options that are valid for a selected unit.

Try not to put small clickable regions too close together. If your players have any motor control (accessibility) issues, they will have difficulty playing your game if the controls are too small or too close together.

Be Consistent and Predictable

While there isn't a UI standard that every game should follow, there are basic expectations of what certain actions will do. Some of your players will never read the manual, no matter how good it is. Others will do so only as a last resort. If the interface for your game is difficult to figure out, most players will never make it past the demo.

Keep in mind the following action descriptions:

- ➤ *Tap* — A tap works just like a single click. When a unit in your game is tapped, a single tap should select that element (if possible), thus allowing the player to give it a command, mark it as a target, pick it up, or find out more about it. Mobile units could use a two-click system to define a movement destination. Immobile units could use the same system to define targets. When a button or action icon is tapped, that action should be performed one time, or toggled off/on. A single tap to the game's background should result in a pop-up menu.

> *Depending on the type of game you are creating, a unit could be a monster, item, door, container, playing card, puzzle piece, or anything the player can interact with, regardless of whether it is under the player's control.*

- ➤ *Double tap* — This should be used sparingly on units or buttons, because it is too easy to mistake it for two single taps. On a unit, a double tap should typically be used to perform a default action, such as shooting anything that comes too close, stacking a card in solitaire, flipping a puzzle piece, or moving a die to a keep zone. A double tap on the background or game board should zoom in and out if appropriate. This is common in puzzle games.

- ➤ *Hold* — This works just like a tap, but you leave your finger on the unit for roughly 1 second before something happens. Since phone games don't have any concept of a right click, the Hold gesture is a good replacement for anything you would do there. This is a good way to display an order menu for your army units, compared to a double tap, which could just execute the standing orders.

➤ *Drag* — This is the expected mechanism for moving nonintelligent units, such as a puzzle piece, letter tile, or die. Other uses would be to pan around on a map that is larger than the screen, or as a pencil in drawing games.

➤ *Flick* — The flick is used against any unit that can receive velocity or force. In XNA 4.0, flicks do not have a location, so there is no effective way to use them in a limited area or to have different effects on different units. Possible game uses would be if you need to start a unit moving (that is not under your control), such as kicking a soccer ball, hitting a baseball, or hurling a penguin at a polar bear.

➤ *Swipe* — Swipes are typically used to select items from a list. They could be used that way in an inventory or party-selection screen. Swipes are often used when marking things for deletion.

➤ *Pinch* — This is another gesture that might not be used all that often in some games. The pinch is an expected way to zoom a camera in and out with a finer degree of control than double-tapping offers.

The most important thing is that you be consistent. Once your players learn how to interact with your game, they expect most or all your games to work the same way, so don't change it without good reason, and let your players know if you do.

If you decide to create your own gestures, be sure to teach the player how to use them. A tutorial level or practice mode is the typical way of accomplishing this.

THE SOFT INPUT PANEL (SIP)

The *Soft Input Panel* (SIP) is automatically displayed by the Windows Phone 7 operating system whenever a text input control (such as a textbox) receives focus. Unfortunately, XNA doesn't ship with any text input controls, but that doesn't mean you can't use the SIP.

If you are working in the Emulator, you can also use the keyboard on your development machine, but only if the SIP is not onscreen. To toggle between the SIP and the hardware keyboard, press the Pause key on your computer keyboard. This works only in situations where you would normally display the SIP. It won't bring up the keyboard otherwise.

Let's take a look at how to access the SIP programmatically.

Create a new Windows Phone Game project, and call it `SIPSample`. Add a `SpriteFont` to the `Content` project. Leave the name as `SpriteFont1`, but change the size to at least `20`.

The complete code for this project is available for download at the book's companion website (www.wrox.com).

In the `Game` class file, at the very top, ensure that the following namespaces are included:

```
using System;
using System.Collections.Generic;
using Microsoft.Xna.Framework;
using Microsoft.Xna.Framework.GamerServices;
using Microsoft.Xna.Framework.Graphics;
using Microsoft.Xna.Framework.Input;
using Microsoft.Xna.Framework.Input.Touch;
```

Most of these should look familiar, but this is the first time you have included the `GamerServices` namespace. For Xbox Live Indie Games developers, `GamerServices` is how they access many of the cool features of Xbox Live. It's also how you will be accessing the SIP.

Add the `SpriteFont` declaration at the class level:

```
SpriteFont spriteFont;
```

Next, add the following familiar code to your `LoadContent()` method to load the `SpriteFont`:

```
spriteFont = Content.Load<SpriteFont>("SpriteFont1");
```

To display the SIP, you call the `BeginShowKeyboardInput()` method, and you call the `EndShowKeyboardInput()` method to close the SIP. Both of these are found in the `GamerServices.Guide` class.

The `Guide` class is static, so you don't need to instantiate it to use it. However, the methods you are calling do need a few extra things to work properly.

You'll need these for the SIP, so add the following `string` variables at the class level:

```
string sipTitle = "This is the title.";
string sipDescription = "This is the description that goes beneath the title.";
string sipResult = "You type stuff here.";
```

You are free to make them read however you like, and you can even pass in empty strings. For this example, however, it's good to know what will be displayed where.

To pass back a string from the SIP to your game, you must set up a callback delegate to be called by the `BeginShowKeyboardInput()` method after it has finished executing.

 A callback delegate is a pointer to a method that gets called when some type of predefined event fires. In this case, it gets called when you click the OK button on the SIP.

Next, add the following method to your `Game` class:

```
void keyboardCallback(IAsyncResult result)
{
    string retval = Guide.EndShowKeyboardInput(result);

    if (retval != null)
    {
```

```
            sipResult = retval;
        }
    }
```

The signature of the `keyboardCallback()` method defines an asynchronous result. Next, pass this result to the `EndShowKeyboardInput()` method, closing the SIP and getting back a string (or null) value that you assign back to the *sipResult* variable you defined a moment ago.

Now that you have the delegate in place, it's time to add the following block of code to your `Update()` method, between the check for the Back button and the call to `base.Update()` at the bottom:

```
// Display the SIP
TouchCollection touchCollection = TouchPanel.GetState();

foreach (TouchLocation touch in touchCollection)
{
    if (touch.State == TouchLocationState.Pressed)
        if (!Guide.IsVisible)
            Guide.BeginShowKeyboardInput(PlayerIndex.One,
                                         sipTitle,
                                         sipDescription,
                                         sipResult,
                                         keyboardCallback,
                                         new object());
}
```

The first thing you are doing here is setting up how to call the SIP — in this case, by touching the screen. After that, you ensure that the SIP isn't already onscreen by checking the `Guide.IsVisible` property. The call to `BeginShowKeyboardInput()` takes a `PlayerIndex` parameter, which is always `PlayerIndex.One` on the phone.

Next, you pass in your title and description, which are displayed at the top of the SIP. You also pass in the *sipResult* variable. It will contain any initial text to display in the SIP's textbox, as well as whatever you type into the SIP. After that, you pass in the name of the method to be called when the player touches the OK button on the SIP. Finally, an object is used to store state while the SIP is open.

Optionally, an overload supports passing in a Boolean flag that tells the SIP to use password mode, hiding the text as it is typed.

The last thing to add is the following code for your `Draw()` method, right after the call to the `GraphicsDevice.Clear()` method:

```
spriteBatch.Begin();
spriteBatch.DrawString(spriteFont, sipResult, new Vector2
    { X = 50, Y = 200 }, Color.Black);
spriteBatch.End();
```

This code initially displays the value of *sipResult* as you defined it at the class level. It will change to whatever you type into the SIP.

That's it for the SIP. Now, fire up the code and play with it for a bit. Try typing in your name or your dog's name or whatever you like. When you are finished, you can press the Back button (or the Escape key if you are in the Emulator).

As you probably have figured out, the SIP is great for naming your character or his or her pet, logging in to a website or service, or talking smack to your opponent.

Unfortunately, the SIP isn't much good for in-game commands, but all is not lost. On phones that have a hardware QWERTY keyboard, you can receive input from the keyboard the same way you do in Windows or Xbox games. The following code snippet shows how to acquire the keyboard state in your game's `Update()` method:

```
KeyboardState kbdState = Keyboard.GetState();
```

Once you have the keyboard state, it's just a matter of trapping for any keys you expect to be pressed and ignoring the rest, as shown here:

```
if (kbdState.IsKeyDown(Keys.Space))
{
    // Do Something
}
```

Interestingly, you can also detect whether specific keys are not pressed. This works just like the preceding example, except that it uses the `IsKeyUp()` method:

```
if (kbdState.IsKeyUp(Keys.Space))
{
    // Do Something
}
```

The `Keys` enumeration contains entries for all the keys available on a standard keyboard. It also contains additional special function buttons seen on various multimedia and OEM keyboards and the Xbox 360 chatpad (which is available as a snap-on extra for the Xbox 360 gamepad).

Unfortunately, much like with the Xbox, you cannot assume that everyone who downloads your game will possess a phone with a hardware keyboard. So, relying on that as your only means of input will cost you sales. Your best bet is to rely on the keyboard as an additional form of control, mapping keys to actions already covered in other ways.

Remember that, in addition to testing the SIP in the Emulator, you can use your development machine's hardware keyboard for input.

SUMMARY

As you have seen in this chapter, responding to touch events is handled by looping through the `TouchCollection` and processing each `TouchLocation`. Your XNA games can respond to a variety of inputs, including standard taps, as well as a number of gestures.

Part of designing your game for multitouch means being aware of the many differences in screen sizes from one platform to the next and defining your touch zones with this in mind. Handling touch input consistently throughout your game will keep your players from becoming frustrated with the control interface.

You also saw how to use the Soft Input Panel (SIP) to enter text into your game, and you wrote some code to handle hardware keyboard input when it's available.

In Chapter 5, you will use all the various input types you have learned about over the last few chapters and build an input management system. This system will allow you to map inputs to game actions and will greatly simplify your game development.

5
Give Me Your Input

WHAT'S IN THIS CHAPTER?

➤ Building your own input management system

➤ Mapping multiple sources of control input to the same actions

When developing games for multiple target platforms, you will quickly run into scenarios where your game requires several different ways to perform the same action based on the limitations of the individual platforms. The opposite can happen when you're developing a single-platform game. As your game gets progressively more screen states (and correspondingly more complex), you may find yourself needing to map different game actions to the same button, based on the active screen.

No matter which of these situations you find yourself in, there is a very simple answer. As described in this chapter, a properly designed *input management system* provides the freedom to map any number of actions to a single control and to map multiple controls to a single action.

BUILDING THE INPUT MANAGEMENT SYSTEM

The first step when creating an input management system is to disconnect individual actions from the control inputs that cause them. This allows you to map multiple input types to a single action and also makes it easier to change mappings (if necessary) from one screen to the next.

Input.cs

The purpose of the Input class is to store information about each input type that you will define in your game. This class will be used in the `Inputs` collection in the `GameInput` class defined later in this chapter.

CHAPTER 5 GIVE ME YOUR INPUT

The complete code for this project is available for download at the book's companion website (www.wrox.com).

Start by creating a new Windows Phone Game project and naming it `InputHandlerDemo`. Add a `SpriteFont` to the `Content` project, and accept the default name of `SpriteFont1.spritefont`. Set the `Size` property to 20 to ensure readability.

Before adding any new classes, you must do a little housekeeping. Start by right-clicking the project name in the Solution Explorer window and adding a new folder. Name this folder `Inputs`. When you do this, any classes you add to the `Inputs` folder are now contained in the `InputHandlerDemo.Inputs` namespace.

You also need to expand the References section and add a reference to the `Microsoft.Devices.Sensors` namespace. You can do this by right-clicking the References heading and selecting Add Reference.

Next, add a new class inside the `Inputs` folder and name it `Input.cs`.

Make sure the following `using` statements are at the top of the `Input` class file:

```
using System;
using System.Collections.Generic;
using Microsoft.Xna.Framework.Input;
using Microsoft.Xna.Framework.Input.Touch;
using Microsoft.Xna.Framework;
using Microsoft.Devices.Sensors;
```

Inside your `Input` class, create the following six `Dictionary` objects to store the keyboard, gamepad, touch (tap), touch (slide), gesture, and accelerometer inputs, respectively:

```
Dictionary<Keys, bool> keyboardInputs = new Dictionary<Keys, bool>();
Dictionary<Buttons, bool> gamepadInputs = new Dictionary<Buttons, bool>();
Dictionary<Rectangle, bool> touchTapInputs = new Dictionary<Rectangle, bool>();
Dictionary<Direction, float> touchSlideInputs = new Dictionary<Direction, float>();
Dictionary<int, GestureDefinition> gestureInputs =
    new Dictionary<int, GestureDefinition>();
Dictionary<Direction, float> accelerometerInputs =
    new Dictionary<Direction, float>();
```

`Buttons` is an enumeration containing a list of all buttons, sticks, and triggers found on the gamepad and is in the `Microsoft.Xna.Framework.Input` namespace. You can see the complete definition in Listing 5-1.

LISTING 5-1: The Buttons Enumeration

```
[Flags]
public enum Buttons
{
```

```
        DPadUp = 1,
        DPadDown = 2,
        DPadLeft = 4,
        DPadRight = 8,
        Start = 16,
        Back = 32,
        LeftStick = 64,
        RightStick = 128,
        LeftShoulder = 256,
        RightShoulder = 512,
        BigButton = 2048,
        A = 4096,
        B = 8192,
        X = 16384,
        Y = 32768,
        LeftThumbstickLeft = 2097152,
        RightTrigger = 4194304,
        LeftTrigger = 8388608,
        RightThumbstickUp = 16777216,
        RightThumbstickDown = 33554432,
        RightThumbstickRight = 67108864,
        RightThumbstickLeft = 134217728,
        LeftThumbstickUp = 268435456,
        LeftThumbstickDown = 536870912,
        LeftThumbstickRight = 1073741824,
    }
```

For a refresher on the significance of the `[Flags]` attribute, as well as the reason why the values all are powers of 2, take a look at Chapter 4.

The `Direction` enumeration contains a list of four directions (up, down, left, and right) and will be defined later.

You will create the `GestureDefinition` class after the `Input` class is complete. For now, you just need to know that it stores `GestureSample` information and provides a means to target a specific region with your gestures.

Next, add two more `Dictionary` objects, this time to store the current and previous `GamePadState` objects. You want to do this so that you can differentiate between pressing a button once and holding it down, and specify how your game responds to each action.

```
        static public Dictionary<PlayerIndex, GamePadState> CurrentGamePadState
            = new Dictionary<PlayerIndex, GamePadState>();
        static public Dictionary<PlayerIndex, GamePadState> PreviousGamePadState
            = new Dictionary<PlayerIndex, GamePadState>();
```

 Even though you can't connect any Xbox 360 gamepads to your phone, the `GamePadState` object is used to detect whether the Back button is being pressed. It also makes any code shared with Xbox and Windows games a little easier to maintain, since it's used the same way.

You want to do the same thing to store the current and previous `TouchLocation` and `Keyboard` states:

```
static public TouchCollection CurrentTouchLocationState;
static public TouchCollection PreviousTouchLocationState;
static public KeyboardState CurrentKeyboardState;
static public KeyboardState PreviousKeyboardState;
```

The next thing you must add to this section is the following line to track the `Gamepad` connection state:

```
static public Dictionary<PlayerIndex, bool> GamepadConnectionState
    = new Dictionary<PlayerIndex, bool>();
```

It's not necessary to check the `Gamepad` connection state on phone-only games. However, because this system supports all platforms, you will want it there for the Xbox 360 and Windows games. Phone games will simply always evaluate to a connected state.

Next, add the following line to store any gestures detected during a single pass. This variable will be cleared out at the beginning of the `Update` routine.

```
static private List<GestureDefinition> detectedGestures =
    new List<GestureDefinition>();
```

Now, add support for the `accelerometer` sensor and current `Accelerometer` readings:

```
static private Accelerometer accelerometerSensor;
static private Vector3 currentAccelerometerReading;
```

Finally, you will add an enumeration that stores possible directions for the custom `TouchSlide` gesture. This will be used by the *touchSlide* dictionary you defined earlier.

```
public enum Direction
{
    Up,
    Down,
    Left,
    Right
}
```

 A better name for this custom `TouchSlide` gesture might be `Swipe`, so why not call it that? Even though the `Swipe` gesture isn't currently offered by XNA 4.0, it might be added in a later version. So, to avoid confusion and potential conflicts, the authors have chosen to use the name `TouchSlide`.

Now that you have all the class-level variables out of the way, you can create the constructor for the `Input` class. This initializes the current and previous `GamePadState` dictionaries, the `GamepadConnectionState`, and the `Accelerometer` sensor.

```
public Input()
{
    if (CurrentGamePadState.Count == 0)
    {
```

```
        CurrentGamePadState.Add(PlayerIndex.One,
            GamePad.GetState(PlayerIndex.One));
        CurrentGamePadState.Add(PlayerIndex.Two,
            GamePad.GetState(PlayerIndex.Two));
        CurrentGamePadState.Add(PlayerIndex.Three,
            GamePad.GetState(PlayerIndex.Three));
        CurrentGamePadState.Add(PlayerIndex.Four,
            GamePad.GetState(PlayerIndex.Four));

        PreviousGamePadState.Add(PlayerIndex.One,
            GamePad.GetState(PlayerIndex.One));
        PreviousGamePadState.Add(PlayerIndex.Two,
            GamePad.GetState(PlayerIndex.Two));
        PreviousGamePadState.Add(PlayerIndex.Three,
            GamePad.GetState(PlayerIndex.Three));
        PreviousGamePadState.Add(PlayerIndex.Four,
            GamePad.GetState(PlayerIndex.Four));

        GamepadConnectionState.Add(PlayerIndex.One,
            CurrentGamePadState[PlayerIndex.One].IsConnected);
        GamepadConnectionState.Add(PlayerIndex.Two,
            CurrentGamePadState[PlayerIndex.Two].IsConnected);
        GamepadConnectionState.Add(PlayerIndex.Three,
            CurrentGamePadState[PlayerIndex.Three].IsConnected);
        GamepadConnectionState.Add(PlayerIndex.Four,
            CurrentGamePadState[PlayerIndex.Four].IsConnected);
    }

    if (accelerometerSensor == null)
    {
        accelerometerSensor = new Accelerometer();
        accelerometerSensor.ReadingChanged
            += new EventHandler<AccelerometerReadingEventArgs>
                (AccelerometerReadingChanged);
    }
}
```

You might be wondering why you are including code for four players when Windows Phone 7 supports only `PlayerIndex.One`. *The input management system you are building is designed to work with all supported platforms. This will make it significantly easier to share more of the same code base, regardless of which platforms you target.*

Now, add the following two methods. They set the current and previous states for the gamepad, touch panel, and keyboard and clear out any previously detected gestures before adding any newly detected gestures. A slightly abstracted version of these two methods will be called as part of your game's `Update()` method, wrapped around the code to detect player actions.

```
    static public void BeginUpdate()
    {
        CurrentGamePadState[PlayerIndex.One] = GamePad.GetState(PlayerIndex.One);
```

```csharp
        CurrentGamePadState[PlayerIndex.Two] = GamePad.GetState(PlayerIndex.Two);
        CurrentGamePadState[PlayerIndex.Three] = GamePad.GetState(PlayerIndex.Three);
        CurrentGamePadState[PlayerIndex.Four] = GamePad.GetState(PlayerIndex.Four);

        CurrentTouchLocationState = TouchPanel.GetState();
        CurrentKeyboardState = Keyboard.GetState(PlayerIndex.One);

        detectedGestures.Clear();
        while (TouchPanel.IsGestureAvailable)
        {
            GestureSample gesture = TouchPanel.ReadGesture();
            detectedGestures.Add(new GestureDefinition(gesture));
        }

    }

    static public void EndUpdate()
    {
        PreviousGamePadState[PlayerIndex.One] =
            CurrentGamePadState[PlayerIndex.One];
        PreviousGamePadState[PlayerIndex.Two] =
            CurrentGamePadState[PlayerIndex.Two];
        PreviousGamePadState[PlayerIndex.Three] =
            CurrentGamePadState[PlayerIndex.Three];
        PreviousGamePadState[PlayerIndex.Four] =
            CurrentGamePadState[PlayerIndex.Four];

        PreviousTouchLocationState = CurrentTouchLocationState;
        PreviousKeyboardState = CurrentKeyboardState;
    }
```

The next method to add is the target of the event you defined at the bottom of the `Input` class constructor. This method will be called to set the *currentAccelerometerReading* whenever the `Accelerometer` sensor reading changes.

```csharp
    private void AccelerometerReadingChanged(object sender,
        AccelerometerReadingEventArgs e)
    {
        currentAccelerometerReading.X = (float)e.X;
        currentAccelerometerReading.Y = (float)e.Y;
        currentAccelerometerReading.Z = (float)e.Z;
    }
```

The next methods you add are used to map a game action to a specific input. The great thing about this approach is the tremendous flexibility it offers. If you want to map multiple inputs to perform the same action, all you must do is define the action once in your game, and then you can map it to as many different inputs as necessary.

```csharp
    public void AddKeyboardInput(Keys theKey, bool isReleasedPreviously)
    {
        if (keyboardInputs.ContainsKey(theKey))
        {
            keyboardInputs[theKey] = isReleasedPreviously;
            return;
```

```
        }
        keyboardInputs.Add(theKey, isReleasedPreviously);
    }

    public void AddGamepadInput(Buttons theButton, bool isReleasedPreviously)
    {
        if (gamepadInputs.ContainsKey(theButton))
        {
            gamepadInputs[theButton] = isReleasedPreviously;
            return;
        }
        gamepadInputs.Add(theButton, isReleasedPreviously);
    }

    public void AddTouchTapInput(Rectangle theTouchArea, bool isReleasedPreviously)
    {
        if (touchTapInputs.ContainsKey(theTouchArea))
        {
            touchTapInputs[theTouchArea] = isReleasedPreviously;
            return;
        }
        touchTapInputs.Add(theTouchArea, isReleasedPreviously);
    }
```

It may seem like you're doing a lot of infrastructure work right now, but don't worry! It will all make sense once you start working on the Game *class and see the fruits of your labor.*

Did you notice that all three of these methods follow a similar pattern?

- ➤ In the AddKeyboardInput() method, you pass in two parameters. The first contains which key to map, and the second is a Boolean flag that indicates whether holding down that key counts as a single action (false) or repeats the same action until you release it (true).

- ➤ Much like the AddKeyboardInput() method, the AddGamepadInput() method accepts two parameters: which button to map, and a flag for whether holding down that button counts as a single action (false) or repeats the same action until you release it (true).

- ➤ In the AddTouchTapInput() method, you also pass in two parameters. The first parameter contains a rectangle of the screen area responsible for the action, and the second is the same auto-repeat flag just mentioned. In this case, keeping your finger on the screen after tapping it is effectively the same as holding down a button.

At their core, all three methods work basically the same:

1. Is the action you are adding already in the related dictionary?

2. If yes, update the flag to the passed-in value and get out.

3. If no, add the action to the proper dictionary, set the flag, and get out.

Now, add the following two methods to handle the custom `TouchSlide` gesture and the XNA-provided gestures:

```
public void AddTouchSlideInput(Direction theDirection, float slideDistance)
{
    if (touchSlideInputs.ContainsKey(theDirection))
    {
        touchSlideInputs[theDirection] = slideDistance;
        return;
    }
    touchSlideInputs.Add(theDirection, slideDistance);
}

public bool PinchGestureAvailable = false;
public void AddTouchGesture(GestureType theGesture, Rectangle theTouchArea)
{
    TouchPanel.EnabledGestures = theGesture | TouchPanel.EnabledGestures;
    gestureInputs.Add(gestureInputs.Count, new GestureDefinition(theGesture,
        theTouchArea));
    if (theGesture == GestureType.Pinch)
    {
        PinchGestureAvailable = true;
    }
}
```

The `AddTouchSlideInput()` method also accepts two parameters. This time, though, they are a bit different. The first contains the direction you are sliding your finger (from the `Direction` enumeration you defined earlier), and the second contains a floating-point number that says how far you must slide your finger to trigger the action.

The `AddTouchGesture()` method accepts a `GestureType` (which you first saw in Chapter 4) and a `Rectangle` object, which defines the possible touch area. You also expose the `PinchGestureAvailable` variable, which will be checked in the `GameInput` class.

The next two methods, combined with the `isAccelerometerStarted` flag, verify that the accelerometer is started. You are then allowed to add and remove accelerometer input from the `accelerometerInputs` dictionary.

In the first method, you supply a direction (from the `Direction` enumeration you created earlier) and a float that represents a tilt threshold for that input:

```
static private bool isAccelerometerStarted = false;
public void AddAccelerometerInput(Direction direction, float tiltThreshold)
{
    if (!isAccelerometerStarted)
    {
        try
        {
            accelerometerSensor.Start();
            isAccelerometerStarted = true;
        }
        catch (AccelerometerFailedException e)
        {
            isAccelerometerStarted = false;
```

```
            System.Diagnostics.Debug.WriteLine(e.Message);
        }
    }

    accelerometerInputs.Add(direction, tiltThreshold);
}

public void RemoveAccelerometerInputs()
{
    if (isAccelerometerStarted)
    {
        try
        {
            accelerometerSensor.Stop();
            isAccelerometerStarted = false;
        }
        catch (AccelerometerFailedException e)
        {
            // The sensor couldn't be stopped.
            System.Diagnostics.Debug.WriteLine(e.Message);
        }
    }

    accelerometerInputs.Clear();
}
```

Now, add the `IsConnected()` method, which returns a Boolean indicating whether the passed-in `PlayerIndex` is currently connected:

```
static public bool IsConnected(PlayerIndex thePlayerIndex)
{
    return CurrentGamePadState[thePlayerIndex].IsConnected;
}
```

Next, you add the overloaded `IsPressed()` method and the individual control input methods. These will make up the other half of this class, since they are responsible for determining if any of the defined inputs have actually occurred.

This next method contains six blocks of code that are responsible for detecting and handling any keyboard input, gamepad input (for a specific player index), touch (tap) input, touch (slide) input, gesture input (at a specific location), and accelerometer input, respectively. If none of these six input types are detected, the `IsPressed()` method simply returns false.

```
public bool IsPressed(PlayerIndex thePlayerIndex)
{
    return IsPressed(thePlayerIndex, null);
}

public bool IsPressed(PlayerIndex thePlayerIndex, Rectangle?
        theCurrentObjectLocation)
{
    if (IsKeyboardInputPressed())
    {
        return true;
    }
```

```
        if (IsGamepadInputPressed(thePlayerIndex))
        {
            return true;
        }

        if (IsTouchTapInputPressed())
        {
            return true;
        }

        if (IsTouchSlideInputPressed())
        {
            return true;
        }

        if (IsGestureInputPressed(theCurrentObjectLocation))
        {
            return true;
        }

        if (IsAccelerometerInputPressed())
        {
            return true;
        }

        return false;
    }
```

Now that the `IsPressed()` method is in place, Visual Studio should be lighting up and complaining about all the methods you haven't created yet. Fortunately, those are next on the list.

Start by adding the following method to detect if any of the keys you added to your `keyboardInputs` dictionary have been pressed. You will also check for a Boolean value (originally passed in to the `AddKeyboardInput()` method via the *isReleasedPreviously* parameter) to determine whether to only accept new presses, or to recognize when a key is being held down.

```
    private bool IsKeyboardInputPressed()
    {
        foreach (Keys aKey in keyboardInputs.Keys)
        {
            if (keyboardInputs[aKey]
            && CurrentKeyboardState.IsKeyDown(aKey)
            && !PreviousKeyboardState.IsKeyDown(aKey))
            {
                return true;
            }
            else if (!keyboardInputs[aKey]
            && CurrentKeyboardState.IsKeyDown(aKey))
            {
                return true;
            }
        }

        return false;
    }
```

The next method checks to see if your game has received any input from the gamepad associated with a specific player. In Windows Phone 7 games, this will always be `PlayerIndex.One`, but it could be any of the four controllers available on Xbox 360 or Windows games. This method also relies on the same technique as the previous method to differentiate between new or ongoing input.

```
private bool IsGamepadInputPressed(PlayerIndex thePlayerIndex)
{
    foreach (Buttons aButton in gamepadInputs.Keys)
    {
        if (gamepadInputs[aButton]
        && CurrentGamePadState[thePlayerIndex].IsButtonDown(aButton)
        && !PreviousGamePadState[thePlayerIndex].IsButtonDown(aButton))
        {
            return true;
        }
        else if (!gamepadInputs[aButton]
        && CurrentGamePadState[thePlayerIndex].IsButtonDown(aButton))
        {
            return true;
        }
    }

    return false;
}
```

This next method works much like the previous two. It determines if a touch input has occurred within the area of a rectangle you provided when defining the input (by adding it to the `touchTapInputs` dictionary).

```
private bool IsTouchTapInputPressed()
{
    foreach (Rectangle touchArea in touchTapInputs.Keys)
    {
        if (touchTapInputs[touchArea]
        && touchArea.Intersects(CurrentTouchRectangle)
        && PreviousTouchPosition() == null)
        {
            return true;
        }
        else if (!touchTapInputs[touchArea]
        && touchArea.Intersects(CurrentTouchRectangle))
        {
            return true;
        }
    }

    return false;
}
```

The possibilities for using this method are limitless. Maybe you have some onscreen buttons, or perhaps the rectangles represent targets or puzzle pieces. Being able to compare the location of a touch to the location of an item onscreen is extremely useful!

The next method detects whether the custom `TouchSlide` gesture was performed, along with the direction of the slide and whether the minimum slide length was met. You define the direction and length in the parameters passed into the `AddTouchSlideInput()` method.

```
private bool IsTouchSlideInputPressed()
{
    foreach (Direction slideDirection in touchSlideInputs.Keys)
    {
        if (CurrentTouchPosition() != null && PreviousTouchPosition() != null)
        {
            switch (slideDirection)
            {
                case Direction.Up:
                {
                    if (CurrentTouchPosition().Value.Y +
                            touchSlideInputs[slideDirection]
                        < PreviousTouchPosition().Value.Y)
                    {
                        return true;
                    }
                    break;
                }

                case Direction.Down:
                {
                    if (CurrentTouchPosition().Value.Y -
                            touchSlideInputs[slideDirection]
                        > PreviousTouchPosition().Value.Y)
                    {
                        return true;
                    }
                    break;
                }

                case Direction.Left:
                {
                    if (CurrentTouchPosition().Value.X +
                            touchSlideInputs[slideDirection]
                        < PreviousTouchPosition().Value.X)
                    {
                        return true;
                    }
                    break;
                }

                case Direction.Right:
                {
                    if (CurrentTouchPosition().Value.X -
                            touchSlideInputs[slideDirection]
                        > PreviousTouchPosition().Value.X)
                    {
                        return true;
                    }
                    break;
```

```
                    }
                }
            }
        }

        return false;
    }
```

Now, you add a method to detect gesture input. This method loops through your dictionary of gestures and compares it to the list of gestures detected in the current call to the Update() method. If a match is found, you then check to see if the gesture was performed in the right place onscreen.

```
    private bool IsGestureInputPressed(Rectangle? theNewDetectionLocation)
    {
        currentGestureDefinition = null;

        if (detectedGestures.Count == 0) return false;

        // Check to see if any of the Gestures defined in the gestureInputs
        // dictionary have been performed and detected.
        foreach (GestureDefinition userDefinedGesture in gestureInputs.Values)
        {
            foreach (GestureDefinition detectedGesture in detectedGestures)
            {
                if (detectedGesture.Type == userDefinedGesture.Type)
                {
                    // If a Rectangle area to check against has been passed in, then
                    // use that one; otherwise, use the one originally defined
                    Rectangle areaToCheck = userDefinedGesture.CollisionArea;
                    if (theNewDetectionLocation != null)
                        areaToCheck = (Rectangle)theNewDetectionLocation;

                    // If the gesture detected was made in the area where users were
                    // interested in Input (they intersect), then a gesture input is
                    // considered detected.
                    if (detectedGesture.CollisionArea.Intersects(areaToCheck))
                    {
                        if (currentGestureDefinition == null)
                        {
                            currentGestureDefinition
                                = new GestureDefinition(detectedGesture.Gesture);
                        }
                        else
                        {
                            // Some gestures like FreeDrag and Flick are registered
                            // many, many times in a single Update frame. Since
                            // there is only one variable to store the gesture
                            // info, you must add on any additional gesture values
                            // so there is a combination of all the gesture
                            // information in currentGesture.
                            currentGestureDefinition.Delta += detectedGesture.Delta;
                            currentGestureDefinition.Delta2 +=
                                detectedGesture.Delta2;
                            currentGestureDefinition.Position +=
```

```
                            detectedGesture.Position;
                    currentGestureDefinition.Position2 +=
                            detectedGesture.Position2;
                    }
                }
            }
        }
    }

    if (currentGestureDefinition != null) return true;

    return false;
}
```

This next method is the last one for the Input class. Once you add it and a few properties, you will be finished with this class. The purpose of this method is to compare the current accelerometer reading with the tilt threshold for a defined direction and to return true if the phone is tilted far enough in the appropriate direction.

```
private bool IsAccelerometerInputPressed()
{
    foreach (KeyValuePair<Direction, float> input in accelerometerInputs)
    {
        switch (input.Key)
        {
            case Direction.Up:
            {
                if (Math.Abs(currentAccelerometerReading.Y) > input.Value
                && currentAccelerometerReading.Y < 0)
                {
                    return true;
                }
                break;
            }

            case Direction.Down:
            {
                if (Math.Abs(currentAccelerometerReading.Y) > input.Value
                && currentAccelerometerReading.Y > 0)
                {
                    return true;
                }
                break;
            }

            case Direction.Left:
            {
                if (Math.Abs(currentAccelerometerReading.X) > input.Value
                && currentAccelerometerReading.X < 0)
                {
                    return true;
                }
                break;
            }

            case Direction.Right:
```

```
                    {
                        if (Math.Abs(currentAccelerometerReading.X) > input.Value
                        && currentAccelerometerReading.X > 0)
                        {
                            return true;
                        }
                        break;
                    }
                }
            }

            return false;
        }
```

At this point, you are finished with all the methods in this class. However, a few properties still must be added.

This first set of properties will be used to provide `Position` and `Delta` information back to the `GameInput` class, which you will create later in this chapter:

```
        GestureDefinition currentGestureDefinition;
        public Vector2 CurrentGesturePosition()
        {
            if (currentGestureDefinition == null)
                return Vector2.Zero;

            return currentGestureDefinition.Position;
        }

        public Vector2 CurrentGesturePosition2()
        {
            if (currentGestureDefinition == null)
                return Vector2.Zero;

            return currentGestureDefinition.Position2;
        }

        public Vector2 CurrentGestureDelta()
        {
            if (currentGestureDefinition == null)
                return Vector2.Zero;

            return currentGestureDefinition.Delta;
        }

        public Vector2 CurrentGestureDelta2()
        {
            if (currentGestureDefinition == null)
                return Vector2.Zero;

            return currentGestureDefinition.Delta2;
        }
```

The next two properties loop through the touch locations contained within the `State` object and return the positions of the current and previous screen touch points, respectively.

```csharp
public Vector2? CurrentTouchPosition()
{
    foreach (TouchLocation location in CurrentTouchLocationState)
    {
        switch (location.State)
        {
            case TouchLocationState.Pressed:
                return location.Position;

            case TouchLocationState.Moved:
                return location.Position;
        }
    }

    return null;
}

private Vector2? PreviousTouchPosition()
{
    foreach (TouchLocation location in PreviousTouchLocationState)
    {
        switch (location.State)
        {
            case TouchLocationState.Pressed:
                return location.Position;

            case TouchLocationState.Moved:
                return location.Position;
        }
    }

    return null;
}
```

The next property in this class is `CurrentTouchRectangle`, which returns a `Rectangle` object that defines where a touch was detected:

```csharp
private Rectangle CurrentTouchRectangle
{
    get
    {
        Vector2? touchPosition = CurrentTouchPosition();
        if (touchPosition == null)
            return Rectangle.Empty;

        return new Rectangle((int)touchPosition.Value.X - 5,
                             (int)touchPosition.Value.Y - 5,
                             10,
                             10);
    }
}
```

Finally, add the `CurrentAccelerometerReading` property, which returns (unsurprisingly) the current accelerometer reading:

```
public Vector3 CurrentAccelerometerReading
{
    get
    {
        return currentAccelerometerReading;
    }
}
```

You have finished the Input class. As you saw, in addition to the predefined inputs (such as keyboard, gamepad, accelerometer, and the gestures system), this class can be expanded further to include custom gestures of your own.

GestureDefinition.cs

The GestureDefinition class is used to contain information about the type of gesture being performed, the target rectangle where the gesture is expected to be performed, and information from the actual GestureSample object. The GestureDefinition class is used throughout the Input class.

To create this class, add a new class to your Inputs folder and name it GestureDefinition.cs. Ensure that the following using statements are present at the top of the newly created class file:

```
using System;
using Microsoft.Xna.Framework;
using Microsoft.Xna.Framework.Input.Touch;
```

Next, add the following public class-level variables to store all the information you need to expose:

```
public GestureType Type;
public Rectangle CollisionArea;
public GestureSample Gesture;
public Vector2 Delta;
public Vector2 Delta2;
public Vector2 Position;
public Vector2 Position2;
```

Finally, add the following overloaded constructors to your class:

```
public GestureDefinition(GestureType theGestureType, Rectangle theGestureArea)
{
    Gesture = new GestureSample(theGestureType, new TimeSpan(0),
                        Vector2.Zero, Vector2.Zero,
                        Vector2.Zero, Vector2.Zero);
    Type = theGestureType;
    CollisionArea = theGestureArea;
}

public GestureDefinition(GestureSample theGestureSample)
{
    Gesture = theGestureSample;
    Type = theGestureSample.GestureType;
    CollisionArea = new Rectangle((int)theGestureSample.Position.X,
                        (int)theGestureSample.Position.Y, 5, 5);

    Delta = theGestureSample.Delta;
```

```
        Delta2 = theGestureSample.Delta2;
        Position = theGestureSample.Position;
        Position2 = theGestureSample.Position2;
    }
```

The first overload accepts a `Gesture` type and a `Rectangle` that define the area where this `Gesture` is expected to be performed. From this, a new `GestureSample` object is created and initialized with default values for the `Position` and `Delta` properties.

The second overload accepts an existing `GestureSample` object and populates the `GestureDefinition` properties from the information contained within.

That's all there is to the `GestureDefinition` class. So, now it's time to put it and the `Input` class to use in the `GameInput` class.

GameInput.cs

The `GameInput` class wraps functionality from the `Input` and `GestureDefinition` classes and also provides a dictionary of the `Input` types you define for your game.

Add another new class to your project (also inside the `Inputs` folder) and name it `GameInput.cs`. Ensure that the following `using` statements are at the top of the class file:

```
using System;
using System.Collections.Generic;
using Microsoft.Xna.Framework;
using Microsoft.Xna.Framework.Input;
using Microsoft.Xna.Framework.Input.Touch;
```

Next, add the following class-level variable inside the `GameInput` class:

```
Dictionary<string, Input> Inputs = new Dictionary<string, Input>();
```

The *Inputs* dictionary will store all the input types you use in your game.

The following method returns the input type for whatever action you pass in. Additionally, if the action wasn't already in the dictionary, the method creates a new action entry automatically and then returns the input type.

```
public Input GetInput(string theAction)
{
    //Add the Action if it doesn't already exist
    if (Inputs.ContainsKey(theAction) == false)
    {
        Inputs.Add(theAction, new Input());
    }

    return Inputs[theAction];
}
```

The next two methods conveniently wrap the methods of the same name in the `Input` class, keeping things simple for your `Game` class. It has to deal with only the `GameInput` class, rather than both `Input` and `GameInput`.

```
    public void BeginUpdate()
    {
```

```
        Input.BeginUpdate();
    }

    public void EndUpdate()
    {
        Input.EndUpdate();
    }
```

The `IsConnected()` method returns the connection state of the `Gamepad` controller based on the `PlayerIndex` passed in:

```
    public bool IsConnected(PlayerIndex thePlayer)
    {
        // If there never WAS a gamepad connected, just say the
        // gamepad is STILL connected
        if (Input.GamepadConnectionState[thePlayer] == false)
            return true;

        return Input.IsConnected(thePlayer);
    }
```

Next, the overloaded `IsPressed()` method checks the local *Inputs* dictionary for an action. If the action does not exist in the dictionary, it returns `false`. Otherwise, it calls the `IsPressed()` method specific to the input object connected to that action. It returns `true` if the appropriate input was provided by the specified player; otherwise, it returns `false`.

```
    public bool IsPressed(string theAction)
    {
        if (!Inputs.ContainsKey(theAction))
        {
            return false;
        }

        return Inputs[theAction].IsPressed(PlayerIndex.One);
    }

    public bool IsPressed(string theAction, PlayerIndex thePlayer)
    {
        if (Inputs.ContainsKey(theAction) == false)
        {
            return false;
        }

        return Inputs[theAction].IsPressed(thePlayer);
    }

    public bool IsPressed(string theAction, PlayerIndex? thePlayer)
    {
        if (thePlayer == null)
        {
            PlayerIndex theReturnedControllingPlayer;
            return IsPressed(theAction, thePlayer, out theReturnedControllingPlayer);
        }

        return IsPressed(theAction, (PlayerIndex)thePlayer);
    }
```

This next overload is a real beast, so take a good look at what is going on inside. In this one, you are passing in an `Action` object and maybe a `PlayerIndex`. (Note the `?`, which implies a nullable type.)

1. If the `Action` object you pass in doesn't match anything in the *Inputs* dictionary, the method simply returns `false` and exits.
2. If you did pass in a valid `Action` object, but you didn't pass in a `PlayerIndex`, the method checks all four possible players (by recursively calling other overloads) to see if one of them generated the action.
3. If the responsible player is found, set the controlling player to the index of the player who generated the action and then return `true`.
4. If the responsible player can't be found, set the controlling player to `PlayerIndex.One` and return `false`.
5. If a `PlayerIndex` was actually passed in, set the controlling player to the appropriate index and then call one of the other `IsPressed` overloads with the `Action` and `PlayerIndex` parameters.

Following is the code to pull this off:

```
public bool IsPressed(string theAction, PlayerIndex? thePlayer,
    out PlayerIndex theControllingPlayer)
{
    if (!Inputs.ContainsKey(theAction))
    {
        theControllingPlayer = PlayerIndex.One;
        return false;
    }

    if (thePlayer == null)
    {
        if (IsPressed(theAction, PlayerIndex.One))
        {
            theControllingPlayer = PlayerIndex.One;
            return true;
        }

        if (IsPressed(theAction, PlayerIndex.Two))
        {
            theControllingPlayer = PlayerIndex.Two;
            return true;
        }

        if (IsPressed(theAction, PlayerIndex.Three))
        {
            theControllingPlayer = PlayerIndex.Three;
            return true;
        }

        if (IsPressed(theAction, PlayerIndex.Four))
        {
            theControllingPlayer = PlayerIndex.Four;
            return true;
```

```
            }

            theControllingPlayer = PlayerIndex.One;
            return false;
        }

        theControllingPlayer = (PlayerIndex)thePlayer;
        return IsPressed(theAction, (PlayerIndex)thePlayer);
    }
```

The next six methods are called directly by your `Game` class. They provide a means to map game actions and behavior with actual input.

```
    public void AddGamePadInput(string theAction, Buttons theButton,
                                bool isReleasedPreviously)
    {
        GetInput(theAction).AddGamepadInput(theButton, isReleasedPreviously);
    }

    public void AddTouchTapInput(string theAction, Rectangle theTouchArea,
                                 bool isReleasedPreviously)
    {
        GetInput(theAction).AddTouchTapInput(theTouchArea, isReleasedPreviously);
    }

    public void AddTouchSlideInput(string theAction, Input.Direction theDirection,
                                   float slideDistance)
    {
        GetInput(theAction).AddTouchSlideInput(theDirection, slideDistance);
    }

    public void AddKeyboardInput(string theAction, Keys theKey,
                                 bool isReleasedPreviously)
    {
        GetInput(theAction).AddKeyboardInput(theKey, isReleasedPreviously);
    }

    public void AddTouchGestureInput(string theAction, GestureType theGesture,
                                     Rectangle theRectangle)
    {
        GetInput(theAction).AddTouchGesture(theGesture, theRectangle);
    }

    public void AddAccelerometerInput(string theAction, Input.Direction theDirection,
                                      float tiltThreshold)
    {
        GetInput(theAction).AddAccelerometerInput(theDirection, tiltThreshold);
    }
```

The next four properties should look familiar. They grab the `Position` and `Delta` information from the `Input` object attached to the `Action` you pass in and return it to the `Game` class.

```
    public Vector2 CurrentGesturePosition(string theAction)
    {
        return GetInput(theAction).CurrentGesturePosition();
    }
```

```csharp
public Vector2 CurrentGestureDelta(string theAction)
{
    return GetInput(theAction).CurrentGestureDelta();
}

public Vector2 CurrentGesturePosition2(string theAction)
{
    return GetInput(theAction).CurrentGesturePosition2();
}

public Vector2 CurrentGestureDelta2(string theAction)
{
    return GetInput(theAction).CurrentGestureDelta2();
}
```

The next two properties return the current touch point or touch position data based on the `Action` you pass in:

```csharp
public Point CurrentTouchPoint(string theAction)
{
    Vector2? currentPosition = GetInput(theAction).CurrentTouchPosition();
    if (currentPosition == null)
    {
        return new Point(-1, -1);
    }

    return new Point((int)currentPosition.Value.X, (int)currentPosition.Value.Y);
}

public Vector2 CurrentTouchPosition(string theAction)
{
    Vector2? currentTouchPosition = GetInput(theAction).CurrentTouchPosition();
    if (currentTouchPosition == null)
    {
        return new Vector2(-1, -1);
    }

    return (Vector2)currentTouchPosition;
}
```

The next property is used specifically with the `Pinch` gesture type. It returns a positive or negative float value representing the scale change of the pinch (or 0 if no change occurred).

```csharp
public float CurrentGestureScaleChange(string theAction)
{
    // Scaling is dependent on the Pinch gesture. If no input has been set up for
    // Pinch then just return 0 indicating no scale change has occurred.
    if (!GetInput(theAction).PinchGestureAvailable) return 0;

    // Get the current and previous locations of the two fingers
    Vector2 currentPositionFingerOne = CurrentGesturePosition(theAction);
    Vector2 previousPositionFingerOne
        = CurrentGesturePosition(theAction) - CurrentGestureDelta(theAction);
    Vector2 currentPositionFingerTwo = CurrentGesturePosition2(theAction);
    Vector2 previousPositionFingerTwo
```

```
            = CurrentGesturePosition2(theAction) - CurrentGestureDelta2(theAction);

    // Figure out the distance between the current and previous locations
    float currentDistance = Vector2.Distance(currentPositionFingerOne,
        currentPositionFingerTwo);
    float previousDistance
        = Vector2.Distance(previousPositionFingerOne, previousPositionFingerTwo);

    // Calculate the difference between the two and use that to alter the scale
    float scaleChange = (currentDistance - previousDistance) * .01f;
    return scaleChange;
}
```

The last property you add returns the current accelerometer reading for the action you pass in:

```
public Vector3 CurrentAccelerometerReading(string theAction)
{
    return GetInput(theAction).CurrentAccelerometerReading;
}
```

You are now finished with the `GameInput` class.

TouchIndicator.cs

The `TouchIndicator` class is not a strict requirement of the input management system, but it is included here because it illustrates useful functionality. You use this class to provide a visual cue to your users (or players) of precisely where they are touching the screen. The `Game` class you will build later in this chapter takes advantage of the `TouchIndicator` and `TouchIndicatorCollection` classes.

Start by creating a new class inside the `Inputs` namespace and naming it `TouchIndicator.cs`. Verify that the following using statements are at the top of the class file:

```
using System;
using System.Collections.Generic;
using Microsoft.Xna.Framework;
using Microsoft.Xna.Framework.Graphics;
using Microsoft.Xna.Framework.Input.Touch;
using Microsoft.Xna.Framework.Content;
```

Next, add the following class-level variables:

```
int alphaValue = 255;
public int TouchID;
```

The *alphaValue* is modified in the `Update()` routine and also is used in the `Draw()` routine to control fading the indicator in or out. `TouchID` is set in the class constructor and is used to return a `TouchLocation` position to the `Game` class.

```
Texture2D touchCircleIndicatorTexture;
Texture2D touchCrossHairIndicatorTexture;
```

These two variables are used to store the images for the circle and crosshair indicators. They will be populated in the class constructor.

```
List<Vector2> touchPositions = new List<Vector2>();
```

The last of the class-level variables, *touchPositions*, contains a list of Vector2 values that correspond to the position of any active TouchLocation objects.

Before creating the constructor, add the files Circle.png and Crosshair.png to your Content project. These can be downloaded from this book's website, located at www.wrox.com. Next, create the constructor for this class. This constructor accepts an integer *touchID* and a ContentManager object, which you will use to load the indicator sprites into the two Texture2D variables you defined previously.

```
public TouchIndicator(int touchID, ContentManager content)
{
    TouchID = touchID;

    touchCircleIndicatorTexture = content.Load<Texture2D>("Circle");
    touchCrossHairIndicatorTexture = content.Load<Texture2D>("Crosshair");
}
```

In the next method, you accept a TouchCollection object and return position information for the TouchLocation that matches the *TouchID* variable. If nothing matches the ID, you return null.

```
private Vector2? TouchPosition(TouchCollection touchLocationState)
{
    TouchLocation touchLocation;
    if (touchLocationState.FindById(TouchID, out touchLocation))
    {
        return touchLocation.Position;
    }

    return null;
}
```

Next you add the Update() method. This method accepts a TouchCollection object as a parameter. The Update() method and the Draw() method that you will create shortly are both called from within the TouchIndicatorCollection class.

```
public void Update(TouchCollection touchLocationState)
{
    Vector2? currentPosition = TouchPosition(touchLocationState);
    if (currentPosition == null)
    {
        if (touchPositions.Count > 0)
        {
            alphaValue -= 20;
            if (alphaValue <= 0)
            {
                touchPositions.Clear();
                alphaValue = 255;
            }
        }
    }
    else
    {
        if (alphaValue != 255)
        {
            touchPositions.Clear();
```

```
            alphaValue = 255;
        }

        touchPositions.Add((Vector2)currentPosition);
    }
}
```

If position information is not available from `touchLocationState`, and touch positions are stored in the `touchPositions` list, you gradually decrement `alphaValue` and eventually clear the list as soon as the alpha value falls below 0. Otherwise, if the `TouchPosition()` method returns any positional data, you reset `alphaValue` to the starting value and add the current position to the list of touch positions.

The last two methods you must add to this class are `Draw()` and `DrawLine()`. Although these two methods could be combined, this approach makes the code cleaner and more maintainable.

First, add the `Draw()` method, passing in a `SpriteBatch` parameter. If any items are in the `touchPositions` list, set the previous position and loop through each item in the `touchPositions` list. Call out to the `DrawLine()` method at each position with the specified alpha channel value for transparency.

```
public void Draw(SpriteBatch batch)
{
    if (touchPositions.Count != 0)
    {
        Vector2 previousPosition = touchPositions[0];
        Vector2 offsetForCenteringTouchPosition = new Vector2(-25, 0);

        foreach (Vector2 aPosition in touchPositions)
        {
            DrawLine(batch,
                     touchCircleIndicatorTexture,
                     touchCrossHairIndicatorTexture,
                     previousPosition + offsetForCenteringTouchPosition,
                     aPosition + offsetForCenteringTouchPosition,
                     new Color(0, 0, 255, alphaValue));

            previousPosition = aPosition;
        }
    }
}
```

Finally, add the `DrawLine()` method. This method takes the parameters from the `Draw()` method and draws the crosshair image and a line as you drag your finger across the screen.

```
void DrawLine(SpriteBatch batch, Texture2D lineTexture, Texture2D touchTexture,
              Vector2 startingPoint, Vector2 endingPoint, Color lineColor)
{
    batch.Draw(touchTexture, startingPoint, lineColor);

    Vector2 difference = startingPoint - endingPoint;
    float lineLength = difference.Length() / 8;

    for (int i = 0; i < lineLength; i++)
```

```
        {
            batch.Draw(lineTexture, startingPoint, lineColor);
            startingPoint.X -= difference.X / lineLength;
            startingPoint.Y -= difference.Y / lineLength;
        }

        batch.Draw(touchTexture, endingPoint, lineColor);
    }
```

You might be wondering what happened to the calls to `batch.Begin()` and `batch.End()`, which would normally wrap the `batch.Draw()` calls. In this case, the `SpriteBatch` is actually being opened and closed lower in the call stack, back in the `Game` class, which you will create shortly.

Only one piece of the input management system is left — the `TouchIndicatorCollection` class, which you will add next.

TouchIndicatorCollection.cs

First, create a new class in the `Inputs` namespace and name it `TouchIndicatorCollection.cs`. Ensure that the following namespaces are present, adding any that may be missing and deleting any you don't need:

```
using System;
using System.Collections.Generic;
using Microsoft.Xna.Framework;
using Microsoft.Xna.Framework.Content;
using Microsoft.Xna.Framework.Input.Touch;
using Microsoft.Xna.Framework.Graphics;
```

Now, add the following class-level variable, which maintains a list of `TouchIndicator` objects:

```
List<TouchIndicator> touchPositions = new List<TouchIndicator>();
```

Much like the `TouchIndicator` class you created previously, this class also has `Update()` and `Draw()` methods. Both of these are called from their respective methods in your `Game` class.

In the `Update()` method, you get the current state of the touch panel and loop through the `TouchCollection`, comparing the `TouchLocation` ID to all the `TouchIndicator` IDs stored in the *touchPositions* list. If no match is found, you add a new `TouchIndicator` object to the *touchLocations* list. Finally, you call the `Update()` method of each `TouchIndicator` object stored in the list.

```
    public void Update(GameTime gameTime, ContentManager content)
    {
        TouchCollection currentTouchLocationState = TouchPanel.GetState();
        foreach (TouchLocation location in currentTouchLocationState)
        {
            bool isTouchIDAlreadyStored = false;
            foreach (TouchIndicator indicator in touchPositions)
            {
                if (location.Id == indicator.TouchID)
                {
```

```
                isTouchIDAlreadyStored = true;
                break;
            }
        }

        if (!isTouchIDAlreadyStored)
        {
            TouchIndicator indicator = new TouchIndicator(location.Id, content);
            touchPositions.Add(indicator);
        }
    }

    foreach (TouchIndicator indicator in touchPositions)
    {
        indicator.Update(currentTouchLocationState);
    }
}
```

The last method in this class is the `Draw()` method. It simply loops through the `touchPositions` list and calls the `Draw()` method of each `TouchIndicator` object in the list.

```
public void Draw(SpriteBatch batch)
{
    foreach (TouchIndicator indicator in touchPositions)
    {
        indicator.Draw(batch);
    }
}
```

Good work! You've built something that can serve as the foundation of many games, regardless of the platform (or platforms) you are targeting. Combining this input management system with the state management techniques you will learn in Chapter 6 will really give you a head start on your next game project.

Now, let's put this system to use in a sample game.

USING THE INPUT MANAGEMENT SYSTEM

This next part isn't essential, but in a large or complex game, it makes your life easier to have all your actions defined in one place and broken into a separate class. So, even though you don't need to do it here, it's a good habit to get into.

Actions.cs

Create a new class in your solution, and name it `Actions.cs`. You won't need any `using` statements in this file, so get rid of them. Since this will be a static class that contains only constants as definitions for your actions, add the `static` keyword to the class definition.

Next you add actions for this game. Your code should look like the `Actions` class shown in Listing 5-2.

LISTING 5-2: The Actions Class

```
static class Actions
{
    // Actions that will be defined for the "game" are declared as
    // constants so you don't have magic strings floating around
    // and more importantly so you can use IntelliSense to access
    // them in your code

    public const string Jump = "Jump";
    public const string Exit = "Exit";
    public const string Up = "Up";
    public const string Pause = "Pause";
}
```

This sample game contains only four actions, which can be triggered in many different ways. A larger or more complex game might have hundreds of possible actions. Having these defined in a separate class file keeps a lot of unnecessary clutter out of your main `Game` class.

Speaking of the `Game` class, that's next. You're almost done!

Game1.cs

You already have a `Game1` class in your project, so now it's time to work on that.

This class uses a `SpriteFont` to display text on the screen. So, right-click the `Content` project in your Solution Explorer and add a `SpriteFont`. Name it `Display.spritefont`. You will also add the image `Pixel.png`, which is available for download from this book's website at www.wrox.com.

Now, open your `Game1.cs` file and verify that you have the following `using` statements at the top of the file:

```
using System;
using Microsoft.Xna.Framework;
using Microsoft.Xna.Framework.Content;
using Microsoft.Xna.Framework.Graphics;
using Microsoft.Xna.Framework.Input;
using Microsoft.Xna.Framework.Input.Touch;

using InputHandlerDemo.Inputs;
```

One new thing is the inclusion of the `InputHandlerDemo.Inputs` namespace. This gives you access to all the classes you created previously, without having to fully qualify them in your code.

Next, add the following variables at the class level. These will be used to provide visual feedback that the input code is working properly.

```
SpriteFont font;
Texture2D square;
string action = "";
```

Add variables for the `GameInput` and `TouchIndicatorCollection` objects:

```
GameInput gameInput;
TouchIndicatorCollection touchIndicators;
```

Finally, add rectangle definitions for the four touch regions in your game. These will be used like onscreen buttons in the demo.

```
Rectangle JumpRectangle = new Rectangle(0, 0, 480, 100);
Rectangle UpRectangle = new Rectangle(0, 150, 480, 100);
Rectangle PauseRectangle = new Rectangle(0, 500, 200, 100);
Rectangle ExitRectangle = new Rectangle(220, 500, 200, 100);
```

Now that all the class-level variables are in place, add the following code inside the class constructor (also known as the `public Game1()` method):

```
graphics.PreferredBackBufferWidth = 480;
graphics.PreferredBackBufferHeight = 800;
```

These two lines of code are used to make your game use Portrait mode rather than the default Landscape mode.

In the `Initialize()` method of your `Game1` class, before the call to `base.Initialize()`, add the following lines to instantiate the `GameInput` and `TouchIndicatorCollection` classes and assign game inputs:

```
gameInput = new GameInput();
touchIndicators = new TouchIndicatorCollection();

AddInputs();
```

Visual Studio will complain a little because you haven't created the `AddInputs()` method yet. So, add the code shown in Listing 5-3. The purpose of this method is to map the various game actions to the inputs that trigger them.

LISTING 5-3: The AddInputs Method

```
private void AddInputs()
{
    // Add keyboard, gamepad and touch inputs for Jump
    gameInput.AddKeyboardInput(Actions.Jump, Keys.A, true);
    gameInput.AddKeyboardInput(Actions.Jump, Keys.Space, false);
    gameInput.AddTouchTapInput(Actions.Jump, JumpRectangle, false);
    gameInput.AddTouchSlideInput(Actions.Jump, Input.Direction.Right, 5.0f);

    // Add keyboard, gamepad and touch inputs for Pause
    gameInput.AddGamePadInput(Actions.Pause, Buttons.Start, true);
    gameInput.AddKeyboardInput(Actions.Pause, Keys.P, true);
    gameInput.AddTouchTapInput(Actions.Pause, PauseRectangle, true);
    gameInput.AddAccelerometerInput(Actions.Pause,
                                    Input.Direction.Down,
                                    0.10f);

    // Add keyboard, gamepad and touch inputs for Up
    gameInput.AddGamePadInput(Actions.Up, Buttons.RightThumbstickUp, false);
    gameInput.AddGamePadInput(Actions.Up, Buttons.LeftThumbstickUp, false);
    gameInput.AddGamePadInput(Actions.Up, Buttons.DPadUp, false);
    gameInput.AddKeyboardInput(Actions.Up, Keys.Up, false);
    gameInput.AddKeyboardInput(Actions.Up, Keys.W, true);
```

continues

LISTING 5-3 *(continued)*

```
        gameInput.AddTouchTapInput(Actions.Up, UpRectangle, true);
        gameInput.AddTouchSlideInput(Actions.Up, Input.Direction.Up, 5.0f);
        gameInput.AddAccelerometerInput(Actions.Up,
                                       Input.Direction.Up,
                                       0.10f);

        // Add keyboard, gamepad and touch inputs for Exit
        gameInput.AddGamePadInput(Actions.Exit, Buttons.Back, false);
        gameInput.AddKeyboardInput(Actions.Exit, Keys.Escape, false);
        gameInput.AddTouchTapInput(Actions.Exit, ExitRectangle, true);

        // Add some Gestures too, just to show them off...
        gameInput.AddTouchGestureInput(Actions.Jump,
                                      GestureType.VerticalDrag,
                                      JumpRectangle);
        gameInput.AddTouchGestureInput(Actions.Pause,
                                      GestureType.Hold,
                                      PauseRectangle);
}
```

You don't have to group your code by action if you don't want to, but doing so does keep it organized and makes it a lot easier to find the line you are looking for when you want to change something.

Take another look at Listing 5-3, and pay attention to the mappings for `Keyboard` and `GamePad` inputs.

> *While the intent of this example is to show off multiple platforms, keep in mind that some Windows Phone 7 devices will ship with slide-out hardware keyboards, and this code will work exactly the same way on those devices as it would with a regular keyboard attached to an Xbox 360 or a Windows PC.*

In the `LoadContent()` method of your `Game1` class, add the following two lines to load your game assets:

```
font = Content.Load<SpriteFont>("Display");
square = Content.Load<Texture2D>("Pixel");
```

Inside the `Update()` method of the `Game1` class, add the following block of code before the `base.Update()` line:

```
gameInput.BeginUpdate();

// Allows the game to exit
if (gameInput.IsPressed(Actions.Exit, PlayerIndex.One))
    this.Exit();

if (gameInput.IsPressed(Actions.Jump, PlayerIndex.One))
    action = Actions.Jump;
```

```
if (gameInput.IsPressed(Actions.Pause, PlayerIndex.One))
    action = Actions.Pause;

if (gameInput.IsPressed(Actions.Up, PlayerIndex.One))
    action = Actions.Up;

touchIndicators.Update(gameTime, Content);

gameInput.EndUpdate();
```

The calls to `BeginUpdate()` and `EndUpdate()` exist primarily to capture the current states of the various input types, and also to set the previous state to that current state right before the next pass through the game loop.

Notice that the usual code to detect the Back button has been replaced by code that simply checks to see if any of the inputs mapped to the `Exit` action have been triggered. This is much cleaner than having miles of code cluttering the `Update()` method.

The other three code blocks work the same way. Instead of explicitly checking for every possible input for the same action and then moving on to the next action, you now have to check only once for each action.

The last method you must update is the `Draw()` method. Add the following lines of code after `GraphicsDevice.Clear()` and before `base.Draw()`:

```
spriteBatch.Begin();

spriteBatch.Draw(square, UpRectangle, Color.Blue);
spriteBatch.DrawString(font,
                       "Up",
                       new Vector2(UpRectangle.Left + 20,
                           UpRectangle.Top + 20),
                       Color.Black);

spriteBatch.Draw(square, JumpRectangle, Color.Yellow);
spriteBatch.DrawString(font,
                       "Jump",
                       new Vector2(JumpRectangle.Left + 20,
                           JumpRectangle.Top + 20),
                       Color.Black);

spriteBatch.Draw(square, PauseRectangle, Color.Green);
spriteBatch.DrawString(font,
                       "Pause",
                       new Vector2(PauseRectangle.Left + 20,
                           PauseRectangle.Top + 20),
                       Color.Black);

spriteBatch.Draw(square, ExitRectangle, Color.Red);
spriteBatch.DrawString(font,
                       "Exit",
                       new Vector2(ExitRectangle.Left + 20,
                           ExitRectangle.Top + 20),
```

```
                    Color.Black);

spriteBatch.DrawString(font, action, new Vector2(100, 350), Color.White);

touchIndicators.Draw(spriteBatch);

spriteBatch.End();
```

The first four blocks of code you added after beginning your `SpriteBatch` set up the visual representation of the touch rectangles you defined earlier. The next line draws the name of the action that was detected. Finally, the touch indicators are drawn wherever a touch is registered.

That's it for the coding. Now it's time to fire it up and try it out. If you don't have a phone, you can still run and test this code, but you will be unable to trigger any of the `Accelerometer` actions.

When you have the demo running on your phone, it should look like Figure 5-1.

FIGURE 5-1: InputHandlerDemo running in the Emulator

This is a "kitchen sink" demo, meaning that it contains a bit of everything (but the kitchen sink). To test the demo, try the following actions:

1. Perform a simple tap anywhere in the blue area of the screen. You see a blue crosshair indicator appear for as long as you touch the screen.
2. Release the tap, and the blue crosshair indicator fades away.
3. Perform a `TouchSlide` gesture by touching the blue area of the screen and sliding your finger to the right. The word "Jump" appears on the screen.

4. Perform a `TouchSlide` gesture by sliding upward. The word "Up" appears on the screen.
5. If you are in the Emulator, press the A key on the keyboard. (If nothing happens, press the Pause/Break key to enable keyboard input.) The word "Jump" appears on the screen.
6. If you are using a phone with a keyboard, you can also perform Step 5 by sliding out the keyboard and pressing A.
7. If you are using a phone, tilt down the top end of the phone. The word "Down" appears on the screen. Tilt the phone up. The word "Up" appears on the screen.
8. Touch the yellow, blue, or green square. The label for that "button" appears on the screen.
9. Touch the red button. The game exits.

That's almost it for this demo, but you can take it a lot further. Look inside the `AddInputs()` method and try experimenting with adding other gestures and inputs.

If you have an Xbox 360 controller connected to your development machine, try performing some of the gamepad inputs listed in the `AddInputs()` method or adding some new ones mapped to other actions.

SUMMARY

In this chapter, you learned how to build a simple but powerful framework for managing the mapping of multiple sources of player input (including keyboard, controller, touch — that is, standard and gestures — and accelerometer sensor) to their respective in-game actions.

In Chapter 6, you will learn about properly managing game state and how to move between various states. You will build three progressively complex state management systems for use in your games.

The State of Things

WHAT'S IN THIS CHAPTER?

- Managing and tracking the state of your game
- Handling transitions between game states
- Detecting and handling phone hardware events
- Understanding what happens when your game is interrupted by a call
- Saving and restoring game state with local storage

A key part of game development is *state management.* This is how you handle the differences between the title screen and the middle of the game, as well as starting and ending your game, or even what goes on in the background while your game is paused.

When you receive an incoming phone call during your game, you don't just need to suspend game play and give control to the phone. You also must restore everything to the previous state when your player returns.

This chapter teaches you how to manage the state of your game and how to handle transitions between game states. You will also learn about detecting hardware events for the phone and how to use local storage to save and restore your game state.

GAME STATE

All video games go through various states as they run. Even the classic arcade machines used several states, such as running a demo in "attract" mode, the start screen displayed after you dropped in a quarter, an instructions screen, the actual game screen, and, of course, the high-score screen.

When designing a game, you must consider the various states and screens of your game before writing a single line of code. You need to know things like the following:

- What screens are displayed, and in what order?
- What screens can call other screens?
- What do those screens do?
- How will my players interact with those screens?
- What modes does my game support (for example, single-player, multiplayer, and so on)?

Having a system to manage these states and transitions is critically important, especially in a large or complex game.

Managing Game State

You can handle tracking the state of your game in a number of different ways. This section examines three different options that range from simple to complex. It's your call which one will work best for your game.

Option 1: Boolean Flags

This approach is the simplest; everything is contained in the main Game class. However, it doesn't provide any means of displaying layered or floating screens. So, use this option only if your game will never display more than one screen or window at a time.

The complete code for this project is available for download at the book's companion website (www.wrox.com).

To begin using this approach, start a new Windows Phone Game project and add the following flags to the Game class in your Game1.cs file:

```
bool IsSplashScreenShown;
bool IsTitleScreenShown;
```

This approach to state management makes it easy to add as many screens as you like. However, with everything in the main Game1.cs file, obviously it's not very practical for a large number of screens.

Next, in the Initialize() method, add the following lines of code to initialize the flags you just created:

```
IsTitleScreenShown = false;
IsSplashScreenShown = true;
```

Before you add anything to the Update() method, you must create a couple of additional methods — one for each screen to update.

The first method, `UpdateSplashScreen()`, checks to see if the game has been running for 4 seconds or longer and then flips the flags to show the title screen:

```
private void UpdateSplashScreen(GameTime gameTime)
{
    if (gameTime.TotalGameTime.Seconds > 4)
    {
        IsTitleScreenShown = true;
        IsSplashScreenShown = false;
        return;
    }
}
```

The next method, `UpdateTitleScreen()`, shows the title screen until you press the Back button, which closes the game.

```
private void UpdateTitleScreen()
{
    if (GamePad.GetState(PlayerIndex.One).Buttons.Back == ButtonState.Pressed)
        this.Exit();
}
```

Now, add the following code to the `Update()` method to call either of the previous methods, based on which of the screen state flags are set to `true`:

```
// Based on the screen state variables, call the proper update method
if (IsSplashScreenShown)
{
    UpdateSplashScreen(gameTime);
}
else if (IsTitleScreenShown)
{
    UpdateTitleScreen();
}
```

Everything is still pretty simple at this point, and you can see how easy it is to add more screens. As mentioned, this approach is good up to a point, but it can get out of hand from a code-management perspective if you have too many screens.

Next, add the following code to the `Draw()` method, just before the `base.Draw(gameTime);` line at the end of the method:

```
spriteBatch.Begin();

if (IsSplashScreenShown)
{
    GraphicsDevice.Clear(Color.White);
}
else if (IsTitleScreenShown)
{
    GraphicsDevice.Clear(Color.Green);
}

spriteBatch.End();
```

At this point, you've probably already figured out that this will be the most boring splash screen in the history of video games. But hopefully you agree that it's good enough for demo purposes.

If you run the game now, you should see a white "splash screen" for approximately 4 seconds, and then a green screen until you press the Back button and end your game.

If something isn't working, you can download the code from this book's companion website (www.wrox.com), or take a look at Listing 6-1 and compare the results. In the interest of brevity, most of the default comments have been trimmed from this listing.

LISTING 6-1: Flag-Based State Management

```
using System;
using Microsoft.Xna.Framework;
using Microsoft.Xna.Framework.Graphics;
using Microsoft.Xna.Framework.Input;

namespace SimpleStateManagementWithFlags
{
    public class Game1 : Microsoft.Xna.Framework.Game
    {
        GraphicsDeviceManager graphics;
        SpriteBatch spriteBatch;
        bool IsSplashScreenShown;
        bool IsTitleScreenShown;

        public Game1()
        {
            graphics = new GraphicsDeviceManager(this);
            Content.RootDirectory = "Content";

            // Frame rate is 30 fps by default for Windows Phone.
            TargetElapsedTime = TimeSpan.FromTicks(333333);

            // Pre-autoscale settings.
            graphics.PreferredBackBufferWidth = 480;
            graphics.PreferredBackBufferHeight = 800;
        }

        protected override void Initialize()
        {
            // TODO: Add your initialization logic here
            IsTitleScreenShown = false;
            IsSplashScreenShown = true;

            base.Initialize();
        }

        protected override void LoadContent()
        {
            // Create a new SpriteBatch, used to draw textures.
            spriteBatch = new SpriteBatch(GraphicsDevice);

            // TODO: use this.Content to load your game content here
        }
```

```csharp
protected override void UnloadContent()
{
    // TODO: Unload any non ContentManager content here
}

protected override void Update(GameTime gameTime)
{
    // Based on the screen flags, call the proper update method
    if (IsSplashScreenShown)
        UpdateSplashScreen(gameTime);
    else if (IsTitleScreenShown)
        UpdateTitleScreen();

    base.Update(gameTime);
}

protected override void Draw(GameTime gameTime)
{
    spriteBatch.Begin();

    if (IsSplashScreenShown)
        GraphicsDevice.Clear(Color.White);
    else if (IsTitleScreenShown)
        GraphicsDevice.Clear(Color.Green);

    spriteBatch.End();

    base.Draw(gameTime);
}

private void UpdateSplashScreen(GameTime gameTime)
{
    if (gameTime.TotalGameTime.Seconds > 4)
    {
        IsTitleScreenShown = true;
        IsSplashScreenShown = false;
        return;
    }
}

private void UpdateTitleScreen()
{
    if (GamePad.GetState(PlayerIndex.One).Buttons.Back
        == ButtonState.Pressed)

        this.Exit();
}
    }
}
```

That's it for Option 1. Now let's dive into something a little more complicated.

Option 2: Enumerations

Now that you've made it through the first example, you're probably wondering if there is a more sophisticated way of accomplishing things. Yes, there is!

In this example, instead of using Boolean flags to track state, you create an enumeration that lists all the possible screen states. You use a variable to keep track of the current screen to be drawn. This technique can be quite effective for small games. It is often used when you don't need multiple layers of screens displayed at the same time.

To begin, create a new Windows Phone Game for this example and call it `StateManagementWithEnum`.

The complete code for this project is available for download at the book's companion website (www.wrox.com).

Add a `SpriteFont` to your `Content` project as well. You can customize this for whatever font and size you like, or leave it at the default settings (although you should boost the font size to around `20` for better readability).

Leave the name as `SpriteFont1.spritefont` if you are typing in the rest of the code as you read along.

As with Option 1, all the code for this example will reside in `Game1.cs`. But when you are making your own games, you should consider placing the code in a separate file or namespace to keep your `Game` class as tidy as possible. You will see this approach in Chapter 8 when creating the Drive & Dodge game.

To start, you must add a couple of class-level variables to the `Game` class. First, create the enumeration that contains the screen states:

```
enum ScreenState
{
    Splash,
    Title,
    MainGame,
    Nag
}
```

Next, create the variables to contain the current screen state and the `SpriteFont`:

```
ScreenState currentScreen;
SpriteFont spriteFont;
```

As in the previous example, you need to add some initialization code. Set the current screen in the `Initialize()` method, just before the `base.Initialize();` line at the end:

```
currentScreen = ScreenState.Splash;
```

You must load your `SpriteFont`, so add the following code to your `LoadContent()` method:

```
spriteFont = Content.Load<SpriteFont>("SpriteFont1");
```

The `SpriteFont` isn't essential to the demo, but it makes the screens look a little nicer and doesn't take much time to add.

Each screen you create in your game needs an `Update()` method. So, include the following methods in your `Game` class:

```
private void UpdateSplashScreen(GameTime gameTime)
{
    if (gameTime.TotalGameTime.Seconds > 4)
        currentScreen = ScreenState.Title;
}

private void UpdateTitleScreen()
{
    //Checking to see if there's a touch anywhere on the screen
    TouchCollection currentTouchState = TouchPanel.GetState();

    if (currentTouchState.Count > 0)
    {
        //There was a touch registered somewhere on the screen
        currentScreen = ScreenState.MainGame;
    }
}

private void UpdateMainGameScreen()
{
    if (GamePad.GetState(PlayerIndex.One).Buttons.Back == ButtonState.Pressed)
        currentScreen = ScreenState.Nag;
}
```

The `UpdateSplashScreen()` method should look familiar, since it's the same as in the previous example, with the exception of how state change is handled.

You probably noticed a bit of touch code in the `UpdateTitleScreen()` method. For a simple demo like this, it really isn't worth your time to implement a whole input framework. The touch code in this method is sufficient for the job. If you need a refresher on handling touch input, glance through Chapter 4 again.

Take a look at the `UpdateMainGameScreen()` method. Notice that, instead of the usual behavior of instantly exiting the game when you press the Back button, the game displays a nag or "Buy Me!" screen. You will read more about overriding the Back button later in this chapter.

Add the following line at the top of the `Game` class, with the other variable declarations:

```
int nagStartTime = 0;
```

Finally, add this method to handle the nag screen:

```
private void UpdateNagScreen(GameTime gameTime)
{
    if (nagStartTime == 0)
        nagStartTime = gameTime.TotalGameTime.Seconds;

    if (gameTime.TotalGameTime.Seconds - nagStartTime > 4)
        this.Exit();
}
```

The `UpdateNagScreen()` method checks the current total game time when first called and then displays the nag screen for 4 seconds before ending the game.

Now you must modify the `Update()` method of your `Game` class. First, find the following block of code and comment it out or remove it:

```
// Allows the game to exit
if (GamePad.GetState(PlayerIndex.One).Buttons.Back == ButtonState.Pressed)
    this.Exit();
```

You don't want that in there, since you are handling the Back button behavior differently than the default of just dropping out of your game.

Next, still in the `Update()` method, add the following code:

```
// Update method associated with the current screen
switch (currentScreen)
{
    case ScreenState.Splash:
        UpdateSplashScreen(gameTime);
        break;

    case ScreenState.Title:
        UpdateTitleScreen();
        break;

    case ScreenState.MainGame:
        UpdateMainGameScreen();
        break;

    case ScreenState.Nag:
        UpdateNagScreen(gameTime);
        break;
}
```

Instead of an ugly pile of `if` and `else if` statements, as you saw in the first example, you can now use a single `switch()` statement. This will be much cleaner and easier to maintain!

With the individual update routines out of the way, it's time to add the `Draw()` methods for each screen. This is where the `SpriteFont` comes in handy. Since you now have several screens to deal with, it helps to know which one you are seeing and what to do to get to the next one.

First is the `DrawSplashScreen()` method:

```
private void DrawSplashScreen()
{
    GraphicsDevice.Clear(Color.White);
    spriteBatch.DrawString(spriteFont, "SPLASH", new Vector2(50f, 150f),
        Color.Tomato);
    spriteBatch.DrawString(spriteFont, "Wait 4 Seconds", new Vector2(50f,
        450f), Color.Tomato);
}
```

It's pretty straightforward. Like the first example, this method displays a white splash screen. This one also includes some red text telling your players what screen they are seeing.

Now, add the `DrawxxxScreen()` methods for the remaining three screens:

```
private void DrawTitleScreen()
{
    GraphicsDevice.Clear(Color.Green);
    spriteBatch.DrawString(spriteFont, "TITLE", new Vector2(50f, 150f),
        Color.White);
    spriteBatch.DrawString(spriteFont, "Touch Me", new Vector2(50f, 450f),
        Color.White);
}

private void DrawMainGameScreen()
{
    GraphicsDevice.Clear(Color.Black);
    spriteBatch.DrawString(spriteFont, "MAIN", new Vector2(50f, 150f),
        Color.Yellow);
    spriteBatch.DrawString(spriteFont, "Press the Back Button", new
        Vector2(50f, 450f), Color.Yellow);
}

private void DrawNagScreen()
{
    GraphicsDevice.Clear(Color.Pink);
    spriteBatch.DrawString(spriteFont, "NAG", new Vector2(50f, 150f), Color.Black);
    spriteBatch.DrawString(spriteFont, "BUY ME", new Vector2(150f, 250f),
        Color.Black);
    spriteBatch.DrawString(spriteFont, "NAG", new Vector2(50f, 350f),
        Color.Black);
    spriteBatch.DrawString(spriteFont, "BUY ME", new Vector2(150f, 450f),
        Color.Black);
    spriteBatch.DrawString(spriteFont, "NAG", new Vector2(50f, 550f),
        Color.Black);
    spriteBatch.DrawString(spriteFont, "BUY ME", new Vector2(150f, 650f),
        Color.Black);
}
```

There's a small chance that the code for that last method may go a bit overboard. However, if it's not at least a little annoying, it's not a very effective nag screen.

A good nag screen should be just annoying enough to make people want to register your game, but not so annoying that they stop playing it. It's a balancing act. Check out Chapter 16 for more about creating a compelling trial mode for your game and a nag screen to go with it.

You're almost done! Now you must modify the `Draw()` method of your `Game` class. Start by removing or commenting out the following line:

```
GraphicsDevice.Clear(Color.CornflowerBlue);
```

It doesn't hurt anything to leave this in, but this code is now unnecessary because you are handling screen color in the individual screen-draw routines.

Next, add the following code, also in the `Draw()` method, making sure you put it before the `base.Draw(gameTime)` call in the last line:

```
spriteBatch.Begin();
//Call the Draw method associated with the current screen
switch (currentScreen)
{
    case ScreenState.Splash:
        DrawSplashScreen();
        break;

    case ScreenState.Title:
        DrawTitleScreen();
        break;

    case ScreenState.MainGame:
        DrawMainGameScreen();
        break;

    case ScreenState.Nag:
        DrawNagScreen();
        break;
}
spriteBatch.End();
```

Using this approach makes it easy to add new screen states to your game. Just add any new screens to the enumeration, write your screen-specific draw and update routines, and add a new case in the `Update()` and `Draw()` methods. Then you're all set.

The only thing left at this point is to run the game. Assuming you followed along, you should see a splash screen for 4 seconds, followed by a title screen that waits for your touch. Next up is the main game screen and, finally, the nag screen. You can see the four screens in order in Figure 6-1.

If, at this point, your game isn't working as expected, you can download the code from this book's companion website (www.wrox.com), or compare it to the complete source in Listing 6-2. Extraneous comments have been removed to save space.

FIGURE 6-1: Splash screen, title screen, game screen, and nag screen

LISTING 6-2: Enum-Based State Management

```
using System;
using Microsoft.Xna.Framework;
using Microsoft.Xna.Framework.Content;
using Microsoft.Xna.Framework.Graphics;
using Microsoft.Xna.Framework.Input;
using Microsoft.Xna.Framework.Input.Touch;

namespace StateManagementWithEnum
{
    public class Game1 : Microsoft.Xna.Framework.Game
    {
        enum ScreenState
        {
            Splash,
            Title,
            MainGame,
            Nag
        }

        ScreenState currentScreen;
        GraphicsDeviceManager graphics;
        SpriteBatch spriteBatch;
        SpriteFont spriteFont;

        int nagStartTime = 0;
```

continues

LISTING 6-2 *(continued)*

```csharp
public Game1()
{
    graphics = new GraphicsDeviceManager(this);
    Content.RootDirectory = "Content";

    // Frame rate is 30 fps by default for Windows Phone.
    TargetElapsedTime = TimeSpan.FromTicks(333333);

    // Pre-autoscale settings.
    graphics.PreferredBackBufferWidth = 480;
    graphics.PreferredBackBufferHeight = 800;
}

protected override void Initialize()
{
    // TODO: Add your initialization logic here
    currentScreen = ScreenState.Splash;

    base.Initialize();
}

protected override void LoadContent()
{
    // Create a new SpriteBatch, used to draw textures.
    spriteBatch = new SpriteBatch(GraphicsDevice);

    spriteFont = Content.Load<SpriteFont>("SpriteFont1");
}

protected override void UnloadContent()
{
    // TODO: Unload any non ContentManager content here
}

protected override void Update(GameTime gameTime)
{
    // Update method associated with the current screen
    switch (currentScreen)
    {
        case ScreenState.Splash:
            UpdateSplashScreen(gameTime);
            break;

        case ScreenState.Title:
            UpdateTitleScreen();
            break;

        case ScreenState.MainGame:
            UpdateMainGameScreen();
            break;

        case ScreenState.Nag:
            UpdateNagScreen(gameTime);
```

```csharp
                break;
        }

        base.Update(gameTime);
    }

    protected override void Draw(GameTime gameTime)
    {
        spriteBatch.Begin();

        //Call the Draw method associated with the current screen
        switch (currentScreen)
        {
            case ScreenState.Splash:
                DrawSplashScreen();
                break;

            case ScreenState.Title:
                DrawTitleScreen();
                break;

            case ScreenState.MainGame:
                DrawMainGameScreen();
                break;

            case ScreenState.Nag:
                DrawNagScreen();
                break;
        }

        spriteBatch.End();

        base.Draw(gameTime);
    }

    private void UpdateSplashScreen(GameTime gameTime)
    {
        if (gameTime.TotalGameTime.Seconds > 4)
            currentScreen = ScreenState.Title;
    }

    private void UpdateTitleScreen()
    {
        //Checking to see if there's a touch anywhere on the screen
        TouchCollection currentTouchState = TouchPanel.GetState();

        if (currentTouchState.Count > 0)
        {
            //There was a touch registered somewhere on the screen
            currentScreen = ScreenState.MainGame;
        }
    }

    private void UpdateMainGameScreen()
    {
```

continues

LISTING 6-2 *(continued)*

```
        if (GamePad.GetState(PlayerIndex.One).Buttons.Back
            == ButtonState.Pressed)
            currentScreen = ScreenState.Nag;
    }

    private void UpdateNagScreen(GameTime gameTime)
    {
        if (nagStartTime == 0)
            nagStartTime = gameTime.TotalGameTime.Seconds;

        if (gameTime.TotalGameTime.Seconds - nagStartTime > 4)
            this.Exit();
    }

    private void DrawSplashScreen()
    {
        GraphicsDevice.Clear(Color.White);
        spriteBatch.DrawString(spriteFont, "SPLASH",
            new Vector2(50f, 150f), Color.Tomato);
        spriteBatch.DrawString(spriteFont, "Wait 4 Seconds",
            new Vector2(50f, 450f), Color.Tomato);
    }

    private void DrawTitleScreen()
    {
        GraphicsDevice.Clear(Color.Green);
        spriteBatch.DrawString(spriteFont, "TITLE",
            new Vector2(50f, 150f), Color.White);
        spriteBatch.DrawString(spriteFont, "Touch Me",
            new Vector2(50f, 450f), Color.White);
    }

    private void DrawMainGameScreen()
    {
        GraphicsDevice.Clear(Color.Black);
        spriteBatch.DrawString(spriteFont, "MAIN",
            new Vector2(50f, 150f), Color.Yellow);
        spriteBatch.DrawString(spriteFont, "Press the Back Button",
            new Vector2(50f, 450f), Color.Yellow);
    }

    private void DrawNagScreen()
    {
        GraphicsDevice.Clear(Color.Pink);
        spriteBatch.DrawString(spriteFont, "NAG",
            new Vector2(50f, 150f), Color.Black);
        spriteBatch.DrawString(spriteFont, "BUY ME",
            new Vector2(150f, 250f), Color.Black);
        spriteBatch.DrawString(spriteFont, "NAG",
            new Vector2(50f, 350f), Color.Black);
        spriteBatch.DrawString(spriteFont, "BUY ME",
            new Vector2(150f, 450f), Color.Black);
```

```
            spriteBatch.DrawString(spriteFont, "NAG",
                new Vector2(50f, 550f), Color.Black);
            spriteBatch.DrawString(spriteFont, "BUY ME",
                new Vector2(150f, 650f), Color.Black);
        }
    }
}
```

You should now be able to see how Option 2 would be not only more flexible, but also more maintainable than Option 1. With Option 3, you will take it even further by creating the same state management model that you will use when building the sample games in this book.

Option 3: Object-Oriented

This is where you really get into the good stuff. Flags and enumerations are fine for small or simple games, but as your games get more complex, so do your state management needs. For this option, you set up separate classes for each screen and use events to handle screen transitions.

> *The complete code for this project is available for download at the book's companion website (www.wrox.com).*

To begin, create a new Windows Phone Game and call it `OOStateManagement`. As with the previous project, add a `SpriteFont` to the `Content` project and set the size to 20.

Next, add a new class to your `OOStateManagement` project and name it `Screen.cs`. This will be the base class for all the screens you create in the demo game.

By default, new class files don't contain any of the appropriate `using` statements for XNA, so add these at the top:

```
using Microsoft.Xna.Framework;
using Microsoft.Xna.Framework.Graphics;
```

The constructor for your `Screen` class will accept three parameters, so add the following code inside the `Screen` class to store the `GraphicsDevice` and `SpriteFont` objects, along with an `EventHandler` object to raise events back to your `Game` class:

```
protected GraphicsDevice Graphics;
protected SpriteFont Font;
protected EventHandler ScreenEvent;
```

As you may remember from the previous examples, each screen has a unique background color, so add a line to handle that as well:

```
// The background color specific to the screen
public Color BackgroundColor;
```

The next thing to add is the constructor for the `Screen` class. This will accept an event handler you define in the main `Game` class, along with the `GraphicsDevice` and `SpriteFont` objects.

The `EventHandler` object is used to notify your game that it's time for a screen change, as a result of either user input or some other game condition:

```
public Screen(EventHandler screenEvent, GraphicsDevice graphicsDevice,
    SpriteFont spriteFont)
{
    ScreenEvent = screenEvent;
    Graphics = graphicsDevice;
    Font = spriteFont;
}
```

The last thing you must do in this class is add virtual methods for the Update() and Draw() routines:

```
// Update any information specific to the screen
public virtual void Update(GameTime gameTime){}

// Draw any objects specific to the screen
public virtual void Draw(SpriteBatch spriteBatch){}
```

You're finished with the base class for all your screens. Now it's time to create classes for each of the screens in your game. As with the previous example, you will have four screens, so go ahead and add four new classes to your project and name them as follows:

- SplashScreen.cs
- TitleScreen.cs
- GameScreen.cs
- NagScreen.cs

When creating your game, you should definitely move stuff like this into a separate namespace. Having all your related code under an appropriately titled namespace (such as Screens*) makes life much easier for you and your team.*

Now, it's time to do some prep work by going into each of the four screen classes you just created and adding the following using statements:

```
using Microsoft.Xna.Framework;
using Microsoft.Xna.Framework.Graphics;
```

You must also ensure that each of these screen classes inherits from the Screen base class you created. Using the SplashScreen class as an example, the first few lines should look like this:

```
using System;
using Microsoft.Xna.Framework;
using Microsoft.Xna.Framework.Graphics;

namespace OOStateManagement
{
    class SplashScreen : Screen
    {
```

Each class needs a constructor that will accept the EventHandler, GraphicsDevice, and SpriteFont objects and pass them to the base class. The constructor for the SplashScreen class has the following basic format. Add this to your SplashScreen class.

```
public SplashScreen(EventHandler screenEvent,
                GraphicsDevice graphicsDevice,
                SpriteFont spriteFont)
    : base(screenEvent, graphicsDevice, spriteFont)
{
    BackgroundColor = Color.White;
}
```

You want to add similar constructors to each of the remaining three screen classes. Be sure to name each one to match the class it is contained in. You will also want to set the `BackgroundColor` for each screen, based on Table 6-1.

TABLE 6-1: Screen Background Colors

SCREEN CLASS	BACKGROUND COLOR
SplashScreen	White
TitleScreen	Green
GameScreen	Black
NagScreen	Pink

Each screen class needs two more things: `Draw()` and `Update()` methods. Starting with the `SplashScreen` class, add the following code:

```
public override void Update(GameTime gameTime)
{
    // screen-specific update code goes here


    ScreenEvent.Invoke(this, new EventArgs());

    base.Update(gameTime);
}

public override void Draw(SpriteBatch spriteBatch)
{
    Graphics.Clear(BackgroundColor);

    // screen-specific draw code goes here


    base.Draw(spriteBatch);
}
```

See that `ScreenEvent.Invoke()` line in the `Update()` method? That's the key to the whole thing. Calling that line tells your `Game` class that it's time to pull the plug on this screen and queue up the next one.

As things stand, there are no conditional statements around that line, so it fires the event as soon as the `Update()` method is called. That would make for a pretty boring example, so it's time to add some more code.

In the `SplashScreen` class, add the following bold line just before the `ScreenEvent.Invoke` statement in your `Update()` method:

```
public override void Update(GameTime gameTime)
{
    if (gameTime.TotalGameTime.Seconds > 4)
        ScreenEvent.Invoke(this, new EventArgs());

    base.Update(gameTime);
}
```

Next, you add some familiar lines of code to the `Draw()` method, this time between setting the background color and calling the `base.Draw()` method:

```
public override void Draw(SpriteBatch spriteBatch)
{
    Graphics.Clear(BackgroundColor);
    spriteBatch.DrawString(Font, "SPLASH", new Vector2(50f, 150f),
        Color.Tomato);
    spriteBatch.DrawString(Font, "Wait 4 Seconds", new Vector2(50f, 450f),
        Color.Tomato);

    base.Draw(spriteBatch);
}
```

As with the previous example, your splash screen displays for 4 seconds and then triggers a transition to the next screen. The great thing about this approach is that none of the screen classes have to know or care what the next screen is. All they have to worry about is minding their own business and telling your `Game` class when they are finished.

The `SplashScreen` class is complete, so it's time to knock out the other three screens. Next up is the `TitleScreen` class.

In addition to the namespaces you added earlier, this screen requires the `Touch` namespace, so add the following line of code to the top of your class file:

```
using Microsoft.Xna.Framework.Input.Touch;
```

You should have already set the `BackgroundColor` for this screen, so the only remaining task is to modify the `Update()` and `Draw()` methods, as indicated by the following bold code:

```
public override void Update(GameTime gameTime)
{
    TouchCollection currentTouchState = TouchPanel.GetState();

    if (currentTouchState.Count > 0)
        ScreenEvent.Invoke(this, new EventArgs());

    base.Update(gameTime);
}

public override void Draw(SpriteBatch spriteBatch)
{
    Graphics.Clear(BackgroundColor);

    spriteBatch.DrawString(Font, "TITLE", new Vector2(50f, 150f), Color.White);
```

```
        spriteBatch.DrawString(Font, "Touch Me", new Vector2(50f, 450f), Color.White);

        base.Draw(spriteBatch);
    }
```

Again, this is mostly the same familiar screen-related code as in the previous examples; it's just being used in new and interesting ways.

Now it's time for the `GameScreen` class. This one uses controller input to detect the Back button, so you must add a `using` statement for the `Input` namespace to the top of your class file:

```
    using Microsoft.Xna.Framework.Input;
```

Next, add the following bold code to the `Update()` and `Draw()` methods of your `GameScreen` class:

```
    public override void Update(GameTime gameTime)
    {
        if (GamePad.GetState(PlayerIndex.One).Buttons.Back == ButtonState.Pressed)
            ScreenEvent.Invoke(this, new EventArgs());

        base.Update(gameTime);
    }

    public override void Draw(SpriteBatch spriteBatch)
    {
        Graphics.Clear(BackgroundColor);

        spriteBatch.DrawString(Font, "MAIN", new Vector2(50f, 150f), Color.Yellow);
        spriteBatch.DrawString(Font, "Press the Back Button", new Vector2(50f,
            450f), Color.Yellow);

        base.Draw(spriteBatch);
    }
```

This may seem like a fair amount of boilerplate code to put in place compared to the code that's actually different from one screen to the next, but keep in mind that this is a very simple example. The `Update()` and `Draw()` methods in a real game, like the one you will build in Chapter 8, will be a lot more complex.

That's three screens down and one to go. Switch over to the `NagScreen` class and add a class-level variable to keep track of when your nag screen starts displaying:

```
    int nagStartTime = 0;
```

Finally, add the following bold code to the `Update()` and `Draw()` methods:

```
    public override void Update(GameTime gameTime)
    {
        if (nagStartTime == 0)
            nagStartTime = gameTime.TotalGameTime.Seconds;

        if (gameTime.TotalGameTime.Seconds - nagStartTime > 4)
            ScreenEvent.Invoke(this, new EventArgs());

        base.Update(gameTime);
    }
```

```
public override void Draw(SpriteBatch spriteBatch)
{
    Graphics.Clear(BackgroundColor);

    spriteBatch.DrawString(Font, "NAG", new Vector2(50f, 150f), Color.Black);
    spriteBatch.DrawString(Font, "BUY ME", new Vector2(150f, 250f), Color.Black);
    spriteBatch.DrawString(Font, "NAG", new Vector2(50f, 350f), Color.Black);
    spriteBatch.DrawString(Font, "BUY ME", new Vector2(150f, 450f), Color.Black);
    spriteBatch.DrawString(Font, "NAG", new Vector2(50f, 550f), Color.Black);
    spriteBatch.DrawString(Font, "BUY ME", new Vector2(150f, 650f), Color.Black);

    base.Draw(spriteBatch);
}
```

You're done with screen classes (unless you decided to experiment and add a few extras). It's now time to crack open the `Game` class and tie everything together.

The `Game` class comes with all the namespaces you need. So, the first thing you must do is add the following class-level variables to handle the `SpriteFont` and various screens:

```
SpriteFont spriteFont;

Screen currentScreen;
SplashScreen splashScreen;
TitleScreen titleScreen;
GameScreen gameScreen;
NagScreen nagScreen;
```

You don't need to make any changes to the default constructor or the `Initialize()` method this time, so you can skip those and add the following bold code to the `LoadContent()` method:

```
protected override void LoadContent()
{
    spriteBatch = new SpriteBatch(GraphicsDevice);

    spriteFont = Content.Load<SpriteFont>("SpriteFont1");

    splashScreen = new SplashScreen(new EventHandler(SplashScreenEvent),
                                   GraphicsDevice,
                                   spriteFont);
    titleScreen = new TitleScreen(new EventHandler(TitleScreenEvent),
                                  GraphicsDevice,
                                  spriteFont);
    gameScreen = new GameScreen(new EventHandler(GameScreenEvent),
                                GraphicsDevice,
                                spriteFont);
    nagScreen = new NagScreen(new EventHandler(NagScreenEvent),
                              GraphicsDevice,
                              spriteFont);

    currentScreen = splashScreen;
}
```

You might be wondering why you are putting the screen initialization code in the `LoadContent()` method instead of in the `Initialize()` method. Try it if you like. If you know the answer, feel free to skip the next paragraph.

A couple of factors are at play here. The Initialize() method gets called before the LoadContent() method. So, if you pass the *spriteFont* variable into the screen constructors before loading the actual SpriteFont from disk, it gets passed in as null and blows up when called from within the screen.

Notice that you're setting the *currentScreen* variable here as well. The first screen loaded is the splash screen. In the Update() method of your Game class, add the following bold code:

```
protected override void Update(GameTime gameTime)
{
    currentScreen.Update(gameTime);

    base.Update(gameTime);
}
```

Pretty cool! Thanks to a little polymorphism, calling the Update() method of *currentScreen* actually calls the Update() method of the currently active screen.

The Draw() method works exactly the same way, for every screen. Add the following bold code to the Draw() method of your Game class:

```
protected override void Draw(GameTime gameTime)
{
    spriteBatch.Begin();
    currentScreen.Draw(spriteBatch);
    spriteBatch.End();

    base.Draw(gameTime);
}
```

See how nice and neat this is? It may not (okay, *will* not) improve game performance. However, keeping your Game class as clean as possible and breaking related functionality into namespaces sure makes your game easier to work on (especially in a team environment).

The last thing you need to do before running your game is to add the actual event handlers to your Game class. For the purposes of this example, let's keep them in the Game class (contradicting the excellent advice in the preceding paragraph).

In Chapter 8, you will implement a separate ScreenManager *class as part of the game so that you can break even more stuff out of the* Game *class.*

Add the following methods to the Game class:

```
public void SplashScreenEvent(object obj, EventArgs e)
{
    currentScreen = titleScreen;
    splashScreen = null;
}

public void TitleScreenEvent(object obj, EventArgs e)
{
    currentScreen = gameScreen;
```

```
        titleScreen = null;
    }

    public void GameScreenEvent(object obj, EventArgs e)
    {
        currentScreen = nagScreen;
        gameScreen = null;
    }

    public void NagScreenEvent(object obj, EventArgs e)
    {
        this.Exit();
        nagScreen = null;
    }
```

Remember how none of the screen classes know or care about any of the other screens? These screen event methods are the reason why. They take care of any transition from one screen to the next. They get called only from within the relevant screen, when that screen is ready to go away.

You're finished, so press F5 and give it a whirl. If you run into any problems or bizarre behavior, ensure that you have the correct namespaces listed at the top (in your using statements). You can also download the code from this book's companion website (www.wrox.com) and check against that.

Handling Multiple Layers of Screens

One thing you may have noticed about the state management techniques covered thus far is that they really don't specifically address layering one screen on top of another.

Imagine you had a "floating" options menu or a partially transparent inventory screen that you could call up during game play. Your game would keep running, visible in the background, while you interact with this screen. Given the phone's limited screen real estate, many games bring up a whole new screen for things like this, but it's good to know how to implement this anyway.

Fortunately, it's quite easy to handle layers. Create a new screen class for your layer, just like all the others. Include whatever functionality you need in it, but remove the call to `GraphicsDevice.Clear` in the `Draw()` method. That will prevent your secondary screen from erasing the parent screen beneath it.

Instantiate the secondary screen within the class of whatever parent screen you want to call it from (such as the `GameScreen` class). Then call the `Update()` and `Draw()` methods from those same methods in the parent screen.

Depending on the type of screen you are creating and the input you expect from your player, you may need to employ additional state management techniques (such as a Boolean flag) to indicate which screen (parent or floater) is accepting input. For example, touching the "floating" inventory screen may select a weapon, and touching the game screen may move a robot. Your players may not want to move their robots unpredictably while selecting their weapons.

PHONE HARDWARE EVENTS

It is important to ensure that your game interacts properly with the rest of the phone. This includes integrating with the Back button to ensure that users can cancel dialogs or dismiss the SIP.

Detecting the Back Button

The process of detecting the Back button is actually quite simple; it uses the same code you would use in an Xbox 360 or Windows game. This makes coding your game for multiple platforms that much easier.

This is the only GamePad *input supported by XNA in a Windows Phone Game project. If you are developing a game for Windows or Xbox, you will most likely have code for checking the thumbsticks or other button presses.*

Don't worry. You can leave all the multiplatform code intact, since it won't cause an error on the phone. It just never evaluates to true. To detect if someone has pressed the Back button while your game is running, use the GetState() method of the GamePad class:

```
GamePad.GetState(PlayerIndex.One).Buttons.Back
```

Overriding the Back Button

Without code to handle it, pressing the Back button has no effect on your game. You must evaluate against the ButtonState enumeration and provide your own code to handle shutdown, or any other event.

The simplest way to use the Back button to shut down your game is to just leave the code in place that comes in the Update() method of the starting Game1.cs file:

```
if (GamePad.GetState(PlayerIndex.One).Buttons.Back == ButtonState.Pressed)
    this.Exit();
```

This does exactly what you think. If your player presses the Back button, your game ends. No saves, no goodbyes, no "Buy Me!" screen. It just dumps you back out to the phone.

It's a safe bet that you (and your players) would prefer things to be handled a bit differently. As it turns out, so does Microsoft. Microsoft has published some very specific guidelines for how the Back button should behave in your game.

Section 5.2.4 of the "Windows Phone 7 Application Certification Requirements" document gives the following three rules for using the Back button in games:

➤ Pressing the Back button from the first screen of a game must exit the application.

➤ During game play, pressing the Back button in games must present an in-game menu. This menu must offer the option to resume the game. Pressing the Back button while this menu is up must exit the game. Microsoft recommends that you save the user game state or warn users of possible progress loss before exiting the game.

➤ While outside of game play (for example, when the user is viewing the Options or Help menu), pressing the Back button must return to the previous menu or page.

These guidelines are not mere suggestions. If your game does not behave exactly as outlined in this section, Microsoft will reject your game for inclusion in the Marketplace. So, disregard them at your own risk.

Using the input management system outlined in Chapter 5, along with the basic state management techniques from earlier in this chapter, it is easy to conform to these guidelines no matter what part of your game your players are in. The sample games you will build in Chapters 8, 12, and 15 all adhere to the Back button behavioral guidance described here.

Be consistent. Few things will frustrate your gamers more than unpredictable controls. You are free to define your control scheme however you like, of course, but ensure that when you define the controls for your game, they are consistent in similar situations.

Unfortunately, there's no way to remap the Start button in XNA. If your players press it, your game will exit. The good news is that you can still do some pre-shutdown processing to preserve the game state.

GAME, INTERRUPTED

No matter how compelling your game play is, your game eventually will be interrupted. Handling these interruptions gracefully will greatly improve the experience for your players and will make them more likely to recommend your game to their friends — as well as to buy your next release. In this section, you will learn how to address temporary interruptions such as notifications, and game-ending interruptions such as phone calls and pressing the Start button.

The complete code for this project is available for download at the book's companion website (www.wrox.com).

Start by creating a new Windows Phone Game project and calling it `InterruptionSample`. As usual, you will want to add a `SpriteFont` to the `Content` project and accept the default name.

Inside the `Game1.cs` file, ensure that the following `using` statements are present:

```
using System;
using Microsoft.Xna.Framework;
using Microsoft.Xna.Framework.Content;
using Microsoft.Xna.Framework.GamerServices;
using Microsoft.Xna.Framework.Graphics;
using Microsoft.Xna.Framework.Input;
```

Add a variable at the class level to store the `SpriteFont` you added to the `Content` project:

```
SpriteFont spriteFont;
```

In the `LoadContent()` method of your `Game` class, add the following line to load the `SpriteFont` into memory, and store it in the *spriteFont* variable:

```
spriteFont = Content.Load<SpriteFont>("SpriteFont1");
```

In the `Draw()` method, add the following code block to provide some status output onscreen:

```
spriteBatch.Begin();
spriteBatch.DrawString(spriteFont, "I'm running fine.", new Vector2(150f,
    150f), Color.Black);
spriteBatch.End();
```

At this point, you can press F5 and run the sample if you like, but it really doesn't do anything noteworthy. Next, you will add the code to handle game interruptions.

Notifications and Temporary Interruptions

When you receive a notification (such as a pop-up toast or reminder), your game receives an event indicating that it has been concealed. You can use this notification to autopause your game, or you can choose to ignore it.

How you handle these minor interruptions is up to you; it depends on the type of game you are creating. If you are making a fast-paced action arcade game, your players would most likely appreciate a break in the action until the notification is dismissed. In a turn-based game, it's probably not that big of a deal to let things continue to run (although good practice would dictate that any timers should be suspended).

Go back to your `InterruptionSample` project. Add an enumeration (again at the class level) containing the two relevant game states for this part of the demo, along with a variable to contain them:

```
enum State
{
    Running,
    Concealed
}

State state = State.Running;
```

You have a couple ways to tell if your game is in a concealed state. One way is to check the value of the `Guide.IsVisible` property. This property evaluates to `true` when the SIP is displayed or when a notification appears onscreen.

A better way to accomplish this is to override the `onDeactivated()` and `onActivated()` methods of the `Game` class.

> *The* `Guide.IsVisible` *property should look familiar to anyone who has been developing for Xbox Live Indie Games, since it is used there as well. This is just one more way XNA makes life easier by keeping code consistent between the various platforms. There is nothing wrong with using this approach, but the event-driven model offers more flexibility.*

Add the `OnDeactivated()` and `OnActivated()` overrides to your `Game` class:

```
protected override void OnDeactivated(object sender, EventArgs args)
{
    // This gets called when your game loses focus
    // (ex: game is concealed by SIP or notification)
    state = State.Concealed;

    base.OnDeactivated(sender, args);
}
```

The `OnDeactivated()` method is called any time your game loses focus, such as when the SIP is displayed or you receive a notification. This method is also called when your game is exiting, immediately after the call to the `OnExiting()` method (which is discussed later in this chapter).

In this method, you set the current state of the game to be used in the `Update()` method to control the game-play experience. You make a call to `base.OnDeactivated()`, which causes the same event to fire in any components you have registered in your game.

```
protected override void OnActivated(object sender, EventArgs args)
{
    // This gets called when your game regains focus
    state = State.Running;

    base.OnActivated(sender, args);
}
```

The `OnActivated()` method is called when your game receives focus, from either closing the SIP or dismissing a notification. This method is also called when your game first starts, although not before the game loop is entered and at least one call is made to the `Update()` method. In this method, much like the previous one, you update the state of your game and make a call to `base.OnActivated()`, which causes the same event to fire in any components you have registered in your game.

Next, modify the `Update()` method to control your game-play experience based on the game state. Add the following block of code, immediately after the code that checks the state of the gamepad:

```
// update the game based on the state
switch (state)
{
```

```
        case State.Running:
            // CheckPlayerInput();
            // UpdateHero();
            // PerformMonsterAction();
            // UpdateWorld();
            // UpdateAnimations();
            break;

        case State.Concealed:
            // UpdateIdleAnimations();
            break;
    }
```

At this point, your code knows something is going on. But how you handle it in your own game is up to you. For this example, let's use some pseudocode to illustrate how a game might behave in this situation. Take a look at the code for a moment, and consider what is going on and how you might change it for your own game.

In this example, if your game is running normally, you do the following:

1. Poll for player input (including the Back button).
2. Update the main character (or ship, and so on) based on player input.
3. Let all the enemies take their turn (to move, shoot, and so on).
4. Update the game world as necessary (time, weather, story, and so on).
5. Update any onscreen animation data.

Conversely, if your game has been temporarily interrupted by an onscreen notification or showing the SIP, you may want to do the following until the notification has been dismissed and control returns to your game:

1. Suspend player input and activity.
2. Suspend enemy activity.
3. Show "idle" animations.

Rather than resuming instantly after an interruption is dismissed, you may want to consider leaving the game in a paused state with an easy (and obvious) way to resume the game at the player's convenience. This gives your players a chance to get their heads back in the game (or not, in case they aren't quite ready).

To see this code in action, you must make one more change. Modify the call to `spriteBatch` `.DrawString()` to display the current state instead of a hard-coded string. (You only need to change the parameter shown here in bold.)

```
    spriteBatch.DrawString(spriteFont, state.ToString(), new Vector2(150f, 150f),
        Color.Black);
```

If you run the code, you see a screen that looks like Figure 6-2.

FIGURE 6-2: The DeactivationSample game in action

Unfortunately, there is no way to generate obscuring notifications in the Emulator, so you need a phone to test the `Concealed` state. While running this code on your phone, the easiest way to test this is to have someone send you a text message. Otherwise, you could be waiting a while for an obscuring event to happen.

After you receive a notification, the state displayed onscreen changes from Running to Concealed until the notification is dismissed. At that point it changes back to Running.

Game-Stopping Events

Sometimes you will also get events that you can't immediately resume from. Incoming phone calls and pressing the Start button are two examples of this. Both of these situations generate an `Exiting` event in your game.

The `Game` class provides a handler for this event, but it's not implemented by default. You must override the `OnExiting()` method if you want your game to do anything other than just dump everything from memory and return to the Start screen.

Implementing this functionality is entirely up to you. Of course, if your game requires a significant effort or time commitment from your players, you can bet they would appreciate it if they didn't have to start from the beginning every time they get an unexpected phone call.

Now you will modify your `InterruptionSample` project to recognize the `Exiting` event and handle it accordingly. Add the overridden `OnExiting()` method to your `Game` class:

```
protected override void OnExiting(object sender, EventArgs args)
{
    // There's no going back from here, so save everything and exit.
    // SaveGameState();
}
```

When your game has reached this point, shutdown is imminent, and all you can do is preserve state (if you choose) by saving the game to local storage. You will learn about saving and restoring game state shortly.

To test the code you just added, set a break point on the `OnExiting()` and `OnDeactivated()` methods and run the code. Once `InterruptionSample` is running on your phone (or Emulator), press the Start button and watch what happens. The `OnExiting()` method gets called, and the `OnDeactivated()` method is called as well, *after* the `OnExiting()` method, one last time before exiting.

If your game is ended because of a hardware event (such as a phone call), control is not returned to your game when the interrupting event ends. Instead, it is returned to your phone's Start screen.

SOMEBODY SAVE ME

So far in this chapter, you've learned how to manage screen state and also how to respond to changes in device state (such as when your game is temporarily hidden by notifications or is shut down by an incoming phone call). Now it's time to learn about saving the state of your game locally when one of these interruptions occurs, and how to retrieve this information when restarting your game later.

You will continue using the `InterruptionSample` project for this section, so start by adding the following `using` statements at the top of your `Game` class:

```
using System.IO;
using System.IO.IsolatedStorage;
```

Without these two namespaces, Visual Studio will refuse to work when you start adding code to talk to Isolated Storage.

Next, add the `GameState` class inside your `Game` class, outside of any method declarations.

```
public class GameState
{
    public int TimeState;
    public int Plays;
}
```

The `GameState` class stores some simple information about your game. The *GameState.TimeState* variable is incremented inside every call to the `Update()` method, and the `GameState.Plays` variable is incremented each time the game state is restored from storage. Both of these values are displayed onscreen while your game is running.

To save your game data, you must provide some information about what you are saving. Add the following class to your code, right after the `GameState` class:

```
public class SaveData
{
    public byte[] TimeState = new byte[4];
    public byte[] Plays = new byte[4];
}
```

This tells the code that saves and retrieves your data exactly how much space each piece of data will occupy.

Next, add the following block of code at the class level. The purpose of the first two lines should be fairly obvious. The last two are to store path information for your save file.

```
GameState gameState = new GameState();
SaveData saveData = new SaveData();
```

```
const string directoryName = "GameState";
const string fileName = "GameState.dat";
```

Now, you must modify the code you added to the `Update()` method. Inside the `State.Running` case, add the following line of code immediately before the `break;` statement:

```
gameState.TimeState++;
```

This increments the *TimeState* variable by 1 with every pass through the `Update()` method.

You must display the state data onscreen, so add the following code between the calls to `SpriteBatch.Begin()` and `SpriteBatch.End()` in your `Draw()` method:

```
spriteBatch.DrawString(spriteFont,
            "TimeState: " + gameState.TimeState.ToString(),
            new Vector2(150f, 300f),
            Color.Black);

spriteBatch.DrawString(spriteFont,
            "Plays: " + gameState.Plays.ToString(),
            new Vector2(150f, 350f),
            Color.Black);
```

Add a call to the `RetrieveGameState()` method at the bottom of `LoadContent()`, and then uncomment the call to `SaveGameState()` in your `OnExiting()` method. Visual Studio will complain a little, but you're adding both methods next, so it will be okay.

```
RetrieveGameState();
```

The `SaveGameState()` method begins by converting the game state data into bytes to be streamed to the save file and then placing them in the respective variables in the `saveData` object:

```
private void SaveGameState()
{
    saveData.TimeState = BitConverter.GetBytes(gameState.TimeState);
    saveData.Plays = BitConverter.GetBytes(gameState.Plays);
```

Next, you get the user storage area specific to your game and put together a file path (using the `directoryName` and `fileName` constants you added earlier). If the directory doesn't exist, it is created first.

```
    using (IsolatedStorageFile storage =
            IsolatedStorageFile.GetUserStoreForApplication())
    {
        if (!storage.DirectoryExists(directoryName))
            storage.CreateDirectory(directoryName);

        string filePath = Path.Combine(directoryName, fileName);
```

Once a file path has been assembled, call the `CreateFile()` method of the user store and create an `IsolatedStorageFileStream` object:

```
        using (IsolatedStorageFileStream stream = storage.CreateFile(filePath))
        {
            stream.Write(saveData.TimeState, 0, 4);
            stream.Write(saveData.Plays, 0, 4);
        }
    }
}
```

The `Write()` method of `IsolatedStorageFileStream` accepts the byte array you populated at the top of the `SaveGameState()` method, plus two additional values that represent an offset and total number of bytes to read from the array. This is useful if you need only a piece of data from a larger collection of information. However, for the purposes of this example, you just grab everything in each value.

> *If you are wondering about the `using` statements in these two methods, they are there to make memory management cleaner by automatically disposing of the object you are "using" once the block of code has completed executing. It's uncommon for C# to have the exact same keyword used in two different ways, but the context is totally different than the `using` statements at the top of your class file, which are used to add namespaces.*

> *For more information on the `using` statement, you may want to visit MSDN at http://msdn.microsoft.com/en-us/library/yh598w02.aspx.*

With that complete, you now save the game state information anytime this method is called. Now it's time to add the code that reads it all back into your game.

The `RetrieveGameState()` method starts by getting the user storage area specific to your game and checking to see if the directory you created earlier exists:

```
public bool RetrieveGameState()
{
    using (IsolatedStorageFile storage =
           IsolatedStorageFile.GetUserStoreForApplication())
    {
        if (storage.DirectoryExists(directoryName))
        {
```

Assuming it does, an `IsolatedStorageFileStream` object is created by calling the `OpenFile()` method of the user store and passing in the file path, file mode, and type of file access:

```
            try
            {
                string filePath = Path.Combine(directoryName, fileName);
                using (IsolatedStorageFileStream stream
                       = storage.OpenFile(filePath,
                                          FileMode.Open,
                                          FileAccess.Read))
                {
```

From this point, two reads are made in the same order the data was saved. This is important, because you are using only one file to store both pieces of information. You will read in the first 4 bytes, convert them to an integer, and store them in the appropriate property of `gameState`. You will do the same thing for each successive state value you want to read.

```
                    stream.Read(saveData.TimeState, 0, 4);
                    gameState.TimeState +=
```

```
                    BitConverter.ToInt32(saveData.TimeState, 0);

                stream.Read(saveData.Plays, 0, 4);
                gameState.Plays = BitConverter.ToInt32(saveData.Plays, 0) + 1;
            }
```

Once all the data has been read back into state, you return `true`, indicating that everything was read successfully:

```
            return true;
        }
```

If any errors are generated while the file is read, the following block of code catches them and returns `false`. This method also returns `false` if the requested directory was not found initially, skipping the read code.

```
        catch (Exception)
        {
            return false;
        }
    }

    return false;
}
```

That's it! All you have left to do is fire it up and take it for a spin. When you run the code, take a look at the screen on your phone (or the Emulator). It should look like Figure 6-3, although your numbers will be much lower initially.

FIGURE 6-3: The updated InterruptionSample screen

Now that you have it running, remember the values of *TimeState* and *Plays*, and press the Start button. Now, run the code again. (If you are using the Emulator, be sure to leave it running. Shutting down the Emulator wipes out internal storage.)

If you managed to remember where the previous run left off, when the new one restarts, you will notice that the *TimeState* picked up roughly where the previous one left off, and the *Plays* will have been incremented by 1.

You can use these techniques in your own games in many ways. If you want to experiment some more, try going back into the code and adding some additional state info to the `GameState` and `SaveData` classes. Just be sure to account for them in the `SaveGameState()` and `RetrieveGameState()` methods.

SUMMARY

As you have seen in this chapter, screen state can be managed in several ways of varying complexity, depending on the needs of your game. No matter how you manage state, your game should respond to hardware events, such as the Back button or incoming calls. Even with these interruptions, you can still save your game's state prior to exiting.

In this chapter, you learned how to persist your game data to local storage in the event of an interruption and how to restore your saved data when restarting the game later.

In Chapter 7, you will learn how to play audio and use the XACT tool to process audio. You will also capture an audio stream from the phone's microphone.

7

Let the Music Play

WHAT'S IN THIS CHAPTER?

- Playing audio in your game with MediaPlayer
- Working with the SoundEffect class
- Recording and playing back audio from the device microphone
- Saving and retrieving recorded audio to and from local storage

Every good game needs sound. XNA provides a robust Audio API that you can use to handle everything from sound effects to background music. Windows Phone 7 also includes a microphone for recording audio that you can leverage in your game.

HANDLING AUDIO

The Audio API in XNA Game Studio 4.0 provides a lot of functionality and makes using audio in your game very easy. To access the Audio API, you must include the `Microsoft.XNA.Framework.Audio` namespace in your code.

If you intend to load and play audio from disk, you also need to set references to the `Microsoft.XNA.Framework.Content` and `Microsoft.XNA.Framework.Media` namespaces.

Playing Music with MediaPlayer

To play music in your games, you must become acquainted with an object first. Say hello to `MediaPlayer`. Listing 7-1 shows an abbreviated version of the `MediaPlayer` class definition.

LISTING 7-1: The MediaPlayer Class

```
public static class MediaPlayer
{
    // Determines whether the game has control of the background music.
    public static bool GameHasControl { get; }

    // Gets or set the muted setting for the media player.
    public static bool IsMuted { get; set; }

    // Gets or sets the repeat setting for the media player.
    public static bool IsRepeating { get; set; }

    // Gets or sets the shuffle setting for the media player.
    public static bool IsShuffled { get; set; }

    // Gets the play position within the currently playing song.
    public static TimeSpan PlayPosition { get; }

    // Gets the media playback state, MediaState.
    public static MediaState State { get; }

    // Gets or sets the media player volume.
    public static float Volume { get; set; }

    // Moves to the next song in the queue of playing songs.
    public static void MoveNext();

    // Moves to the previous song in the queue of playing songs.
    public static void MovePrevious();

    // Pauses the currently playing song.
    public static void Pause();

    // Plays a Song.
    public static void Play(Song song);

    // Plays a SongCollection.
    public static void Play(SongCollection songs);

    // Plays a SongCollection, starting with the Song at the specified index.
    public static void Play(SongCollection songs, int index);

    // Resumes a paused song.
    public static void Resume();

    // Stops playing a song.
    public static void Stop();
}
```

Do You Mind? I'm Playing Music Here

One of the properties in the `MediaPlayer` class that you will want to pay attention to is `GameHasControl`. Checking this property lets you know whether you are allowed to play your game's music.

Read that last sentence again. "Allowed to play your game's music" refers to compliance with section 6.5.1 of the "Windows Phone 7 Application Certification Requirements" document:

> *"...when the user is already playing music on the phone when the application is launched, the application must not pause, resume, or stop the active music in the phone MediaQueue by calling the Microsoft.Xna.Framework.Media .MediaPlayer class.*
>
> *"If the application plays its own background music or adjusts background music volume, it must ask the user for consent to stop playing/adjust the background music (e.g. message dialog or settings menu)."*

In other words, on Windows Phone 7, your gamers can play their own music as the background to your game. If the game is currently playing this custom background music, calls to the `Play()`, `Stop()`, `Pause()`, `Resume()`, `MoveNext()`, and `MovePrevious()` methods have no effect.

Sound effects, as you will see later in this chapter, are fine, because they are mixed in with any music that is playing. But if you want to play your own music or adjust the volume, you must receive permission.

Background Music

Don't let all the properties and methods just listed scare you off. It's actually quite simple to start some background music playing in your game.

 The complete code for this project is available for download at the book's companion web site (www.wrox.com).

Create a new Windows Phone Game project, and call it `MusicSample`.

You need a piece of music to play, so grab the book files from www.wrox.com and add the `gameloop.wav` file to the `MusicSampleContent` project.

After you add the music file, click it in the Solution Explorer and look at the Properties window, shown in Figure 7-1. Change the Content Processor property from `Sound Effect - XNA Framework` to `Song - XNA Framework`.

If you don't change this, your game will build but will not run properly. This is because the Content Pipeline will process the file as a `Sound Effect` at build time, but the code will be looking for a `Song`, so a `CannotLoadException` will be thrown.

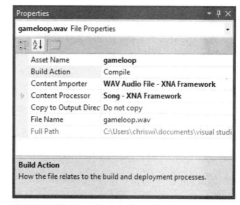

FIGURE 7-1: The Properties window

If you are wondering why XNA thought the music you added was a Sound Effect *and not a* Song, *take a look at the file extension. By default, XNA assumes that any* .mp3 *files you add are* Songs *and any* .wav *files are* Sound Effects. *Fortunately, you can override those assumptions by setting the Content Processor property individually for each item you add.*

Now you must add some code to your `Game1` class. Start by adding the following line at the class level:

```
Dictionary<string, Song> myMusic = new Dictionary<string, Song>();
```

Right about now, you're probably thinking that creating a `Dictionary` object solely for the purpose of storing a single song is overkill, and you're right. In this case, though, there's a method to the madness. Storing all your game music in a `Dictionary` object gives you an easy means of storing and referencing the music you need.

Now, add the `PlayMusic()` method shown in Listing 7-2.

LISTING 7-2: The PlayMusic() Method of the Game1 Class

```
public void PlayMusic(string song)
{
    if (!myMusic.ContainsKey(song))
        myMusic.Add(song, Content.Load<Song>(song));

    MediaPlayer.IsRepeating = true;
    MediaPlayer.Play(myMusic[song]);
}
```

Instead of loading every song for your entire game in `LoadContent()`, this method allows you to load songs as needed and store them in the `Dictionary` object. When songs are no longer needed (perhaps because of a level change or another reason), they can be easily deleted from memory as part of a cleanup routine.

When a song title is passed to the `PlayMusic()` method, it first checks the `Dictionary` object you created for the requested song. If it is not found, the method loads the song from disk into the `Dictionary`. Once the song is available, the `IsRepeating` property is set to `true`, and the song is played.

To call this method from your game, add the following code to your `Initialize()` method:

```
PlayMusic("gameloop");
```

At this point, you're done. Press F5 and fire up this example. There's nothing to look at other than a cornflower blue screen, but your music should start immediately.

Normally, you wouldn't put this kind of code in the `Initialize()` method, because the `LoadContent()` method is called after `Initialize()`, and your music files wouldn't be loaded yet. However, since you are actually loading the music into memory as part of the `PlayMusic()` method, it isn't a problem.

Of course, a more complex game would use a system of loading and managing screens (such as the one you learned about in Chapter 6). So you would put this code in the `Activate()` method of an individual screen or in the base `Screen` class. Be sure to take a good look at the Drive & Dodge game you will build in Chapter 8 for an example of how to handle an ongoing background music loop in a game with multiple screens.

Song Collections

The `MediaPlayer.Play()` method has two overloads, as shown in Listing 7-1. Both of these accept a `SongCollection` as a parameter, which represents one of the following collections of songs from a device's song library:

- All the songs in the media library
- Songs on a particular album
- Songs associated with a particular artist
- Songs associated with a particular genre

These collections are retrieved by using the various `MediaLibrary` properties, such as `Albums`, `Artists`, `Genres`, `Playlists`, and `Songs`. One important thing to keep in mind when working with these collections is that they do not immediately retrieve or instantiate all media objects. You must use the collections to individually fetch the appropriate media objects.

For an example of how to fetch a collection of `Songs` from the first `Album` of the first `Artist` in your collection, take a look at the following code:

```
MediaLibrary library = new MediaLibrary();
ArtistCollection artists = library.Artists;
AlbumCollection albums = artists[0].Albums;
Album album = albums[0];
MediaPlayer.Play(album.Songs);
```

You start by instantiating a `MediaLibrary` object. Next, you use the `Artists` property to return an `ArtistCollection`. Once you have that, you access the `Albums` property of the first `Artist` in the `ArtistCollection` to get an `AlbumCollection`. From there, you grab the first `Album` by that `Artist` and stick it into an `Album` object. Finally, you pass the `Songs` collection of that `Album` into the overloaded `MediaPlayer.Play()` method.

If you want to create an index of `Artists` by name, you use the following code, which iterates through the `ArtistCollection` returned from the call to `library.Artists`. Then it stuffs the `Artist` name and index into a `Dictionary` object for easy reference:

```
int i = 0;
var ArtistNames = new Dictionary<int, string>();
foreach (Artist artist in artists)
{
    ArtistNames.Add(i, artist.Name);
    i++;
}
```

You can see how it would be just as easy to create an indexed list of `Albums` by `Artist` or any other criteria.

Visualizations

Unfortunately, visualization data is not available on Windows Phone 7 with XNA 4.0. Any attempt to get visualization data on the phone will populate the `VisualizationData` class with zeros. If you would like to see how to do visualizations in a Windows XNA game, keep reading.

You will build a simple audio-spectrum display that updates onscreen as your music plays, as shown in Figure 7-2.

FIGURE 7-2: VisualizationSample

Create a Windows XNA Game and call it `VisualizationSample`.

You need a simple 1-pixel-by-1-pixel square image, which you can download from the book files (at www.wrox.com). Or you can quickly create your own in Microsoft Paint (or the program of your choice). If you make your own, call it `block.png` and add it to the `VisualizationSampleContent` project.

You also need the `gameloop.wav` file from earlier in this chapter. Add it to the `VisualizationSampleContent` project as well.

In your `Game1` class, add the following class-level variables:

```
VisualizationData visualizationData;
Texture2D block;
```

Next, in the `Game1` class constructor, add these lines at the bottom:

```
graphics.PreferredBackBufferWidth = 1280;
graphics.PreferredBackBufferHeight = 300;

visualizationData = new VisualizationData();
```

The first two lines set the screen size, giving you a nice skinny rectangle. The last line sets up your `VisualizationData` object, which stores the information returned from the `GetVisualizationData()` method of the `MediaPlayer` object (which you will add shortly).

In your `Initialize()` method, add these two lines just before the call to the `base.Initialize()` method:

```
MediaPlayer.IsRepeating = true;
MediaPlayer.Play(Content.Load<Song>("gameloop"));
```

This starts your music playing, and then the next line of code loads the graphic you will use to make the bars in your visualization appear. Add this line to the `LoadContent()` method:

```
block = Content.Load<Texture2D>("block");
```

You will want to grab the latest visualization data for each frame, so add the following line of code to the `Update()` method:

```
MediaPlayer.GetVisualizationData(visualizationData);
```

This grabs the visualization data from the current position of whatever song the `MediaPlayer` object is playing.

Finally, ensure that your `Draw()` routine looks like Listing 7-3.

LISTING 7-3: The Draw() Method of the Game1 Class

```
protected override void Draw(GameTime gameTime)
{
    GraphicsDevice.Clear(Color.Black);

    int screenWidth = graphics.PreferredBackBufferWidth;
    int screenHeight = graphics.PreferredBackBufferHeight;
    int freqCount = visualizationData.Frequencies.Count;

    spriteBatch.Begin();

    for (int freqCtr = 0; freqCtr < freqCount; freqCtr++)
    {
        int x1 = (screenWidth / freqCount) * freqCtr;
        int y1 = (int)(screenHeight
                    - (visualizationData.Frequencies[freqCtr]
                    * screenHeight));
        int y2 = (int)(visualizationData.Frequencies[freqCtr]
                    * screenHeight);

        spriteBatch.Draw(block,
                        new Rectangle(x1, y1, block.Width, y2),
                        Color.Orange);
    }

    spriteBatch.End();

    base.Draw(gameTime);
}
```

The meat of this method is in the `for` loop. You are building a rectangle to represent each of the 256 frequencies in the collection. Each frequency is returned as a `float`, so by multiplying the frequency by the height of the window, each bar is represented as a percentage of the window height.

That's all there is to it, so what are you waiting for? Press F5 and check out the frequencies while jamming to the `gameloop.wav` file.

SoundEffect

As mentioned previously, XNA assumes that game music will be in .MP3 format and that sound effects will be in .WAV format. To use .WAV files in your game, you can use the `SoundEffect` class or use the Microsoft Cross-Platform Audio Creation Tool (XACT) to create and play your sound effects. In this section, you will learn about the first option.

The complete code for this project is available for download at the book's companion web site (www.wrox.com).

First, create a new Windows Phone Game project and name it `SoundEffectSample`.

Next, you must add a file to your `SoundEffectSampleContent` project. Grab the `Crash.wav` file from the book files (at www.wrox.com) and add it. If you check the Properties window for this file, you see that the Content Processor is properly set to `Sound Effect - XNA Framework` by default.

Next, add a `SoundEffect` variable at the class level:

```
SoundEffect soundCrash;
```

The `SoundEffect` class exposes a variety of interesting properties and methods for working with audio. Listing 7-4 shows an abbreviated class definition.

LISTING 7-4: The SoundEffects Class

```
public sealed class SoundEffect : IDisposable
{
    // Initializes a new instance of SoundEffect based on an audio
    // buffer, sample rate, and number of audio channels.
    public SoundEffect(byte[] buffer,
                       int sampleRate,
                       AudioChannels channels);

    // Initializes a new instance of SoundEffect with specified
    // parameters such as audio sample rate, channels, looping
    // criteria, and a buffer to hold the audio.
    public SoundEffect(byte[] buffer,
                       int offset,
                       int count,
                       int sampleRate,
                       AudioChannels channels,
                       int loopStart,
                       int loopLength);

    // Gets or sets a value that adjusts the effect of distance
    // calculations on the sound (emitter).
    public static float DistanceScale { get; set; }

    // Gets or sets a value that adjusts the effect of doppler
    // calculations on the sound (emitter).
    public static float DopplerScale { get; set; }

    // Gets the duration of the SoundEffect.
```

```
        public TimeSpan Duration { get; }

        // Gets or sets the master volume that affects all
        // SoundEffectInstance sounds.
        public static float MasterVolume { get; set; }

        // Gets or sets the asset name of the SoundEffect.
        public string Name { get; set; }

        // Returns the speed of sound: 343.5 meters per second.
        public static float SpeedOfSound { get; set; }

        // Creates a new SoundEffectInstance for this SoundEffect.
        public SoundEffectInstance CreateInstance();

        // Creates a SoundEffect object based on the specified data stream.
        public static SoundEffect FromStream(Stream stream);

        // Returns the sample duration based on the specified sample size
        // and sample rate.
        public static TimeSpan GetSampleDuration(int sizeInBytes,
                                                 int sampleRate,
                                                 AudioChannels channels);

        // Returns the size of the audio sample based on duration,
        // sample rate, and audio channels.
        public static int GetSampleSizeInBytes(TimeSpan duration,
                                                int sampleRate,
                                                AudioChannels channels);

        // Plays a sound. Ref page contains links to code samples.
        public bool Play();

        // Plays a sound based on specified volume, pitch, and panning.
        public bool Play(float volume,
                        float pitch,
                        float pan);
}
```

The `DistanceScale`, `DopplerScale`, and `SpeedOfSound` properties are not included in the current demo, but they are important to understand when you're dealing with three-dimensional (3D) audio.

The `DistanceScale` property is used to manipulate a value that adjusts the effect of distance calculations on a sound. For example, in a 3D world, as you move closer to or farther away from a sound, it gets louder or quieter, respectively. If the sound is attenuating too fast (getting quiet too quickly), you need to increase the value of `DistanceScale`. If your sound isn't getting quiet fast enough, decrease `DistanceScale`.

The `DopplerScale` property is used to adjust the effect of Doppler calculations on your sound. If the pitch of your sound is shifting too much based on its velocity relative to your position, decrease the `DopplerScale` property.

You would think the speed of sound would be a constant, and on planet Earth, you would be right. But in a game world of your own making, things can change. The `SpeedOfSound` property is used to simulate these different environments. Increasing `SpeedOfSound` reduces the Doppler effect, and a decrease intensifies the effect.

You'll learn more about the `SoundEffects` class in a bit, but for now it's time to get back to the example project. Add the following line in the `LoadContent()` method to load your `Crash.wav` file into memory:

```
soundCrash = Content.Load<SoundEffect>("crash");
```

> *Did you notice the type you are passing into the generic* `Content.Load` *method? So far in this book, you have used this same method three different ways. You have loaded a sprite (*`Texture2D`*), a piece of music (*`Song`*), and a sound (*`SoundEffect`*) simply by specifying the proper data type and asset name. This is one of the numerous benefits of XNA.*

Now that the crash sound is in memory, you just need a way to trigger playing it. To keep things simple for this example, you will just map it to the Back button. Fortunately, you already have code in place for that, so just change the `if` statement in your `Update()` method to look like this:

```
if (GamePad.GetState(PlayerIndex.One).Buttons.Back == ButtonState.Pressed)
    soundCrash.Play();
```

At this point, the sound effect example is complete. Build and run your project. Once it is displaying on the phone (or in the Emulator), press the Back button to play the crash sound effect. Now, quickly press the Back button several times.

Notice how that sounds? Your game is not cutting off the sound and starting over with each press of the Back button. Actually, multiple crash sounds are playing at once. That is because each call to `soundCrash.Play()` produces a new `SoundEffectInstance` object with its own state separate from all the others.

SoundEffectInstance

In addition to `SoundEffectInstance` objects being automatically created by the `Play()` method of a `SoundEffect` object, you can create named `SoundEffectInstance` objects by calling the `CreateInstance()` method of a `SoundEffect` object.

The advantages of having named `SoundEffectInstance` objects become apparent when you realize that you can alter the `Pitch` and `Pan` properties individually per instance, as well as stopping and starting them. The class definition shown in Listing 7-5 gives a complete list.

LISTING 7-5: SoundEffectInstance Class Definition

```
public class SoundEffectInstance : IDisposable
{
    // Gets a value that indicates whether the object is disposed.
    public bool IsDisposed { get; }
```

```csharp
        // Gets a value that indicates whether looping is enabled for the
        // SoundEffectInstance.
        public virtual bool IsLooped { get; set; }

        // Gets or sets the panning for the SoundEffectInstance.
        public float Pan { get; set; }

        // Gets or sets the pitch adjustment for the SoundEffectInstance.
        public float Pitch { get; set; }

        // Gets the current state (playing, paused, or stopped) of the
        // SoundEffectInstance.
        public SoundState State { get; }

        // Gets or sets the volume of the SoundEffectInstance.
        public float Volume { get; set; }

        // Applies 3D positioning to the sound using a single listener.
        public void Apply3D(AudioListener listener, AudioEmitter emitter);

        // Applies 3D position to the sound using multiple listeners.
        public void Apply3D(AudioListener[] listeners, AudioEmitter emitter);

        // Pauses a SoundEffectInstance.
        public void Pause();

        // Plays or resumes a SoundEffectInstance.
        public virtual void Play();

        // Resumes playback for a SoundEffectInstance.
        public void Resume();

        // Immediately stops playing a SoundEffectInstance.
        public void Stop();

        // Stops playing a SoundEffectInstance, either immediately or
        // as authored.
        public void Stop(bool immediate);
    }
```

As you can imagine, having individual control over multiple instances of a sound effect gives you quite a bit of power over and flexibility for how to use them in your game. You may have up to 64 SoundEffectInstance objects in memory at one time.

Another thing to keep in mind is that, although the SoundEffect.Play() method creates multiple SoundEffectInstance objects, the same is not true of the SoundEffectInstance.Play() method. Executing the same SoundEffectInstance.Play() method repeatedly produces a noticeably different end result than executing SoundEffect.Play() repeatedly.

XACT 3.0

The Microsoft Cross-Platform Audio Creation Tool (XACT) is a graphical tool that enables you to author audio content, load .WAV files into groups, and play audio from in-game events via cues.

Unfortunately, XACT is not available for use with Windows Phone 7 and XNA 4.0. This is old news if you worked with XNA 3.1 on the Zune. Fortunately, the Audio API is quite good and can do anything you could have done with XACT.

RECORDING AUDIO

In addition to playing music and sound effects, the Audio API (found in the `Microsoft.XNA.Framework.Audio` namespace) lets you record audio in your games. Combined with local storage (which was covered in Chapter 6), you also can store and compare the captured audio.

The Microphone Class

The `Microphone` class provides a complete set of properties and methods for capturing audio data with the Windows Phone 7 microphone. For a complete list, see Listing 7-6.

LISTING 7-6: The Microphone Class

```
public sealed class Microphone
{
    // Returns the friendly name of the microphone.
    public readonly string Name;

    // Returns the collection of all currently available microphones.
    public static ReadOnlyCollection<Microphone> All { get; }

    // Gets or sets audio capture buffer duration of the microphone.
    public TimeSpan BufferDuration { get; set; }

    // Returns the default attached microphone.
    public static Microphone Default { get; }

    // Determines if the microphone is a wired or a Bluetooth device.
    public bool IsHeadset { get; }

    // Returns sample rate at which microphone is capturing audio data.
    public int SampleRate { get; }

    // Returns the recording state of the Microphone object.
    public MicrophoneState State { get; }

    // Event that occurs when the audio capture buffer is ready to be
    // processed.
    public event EventHandler<EventArgs> BufferReady;

    // Gets the latest recorded data from the microphone based on
    // the audio capture buffer.
    public int GetData(byte[] buffer);

    // Gets the latest captured audio data from microphone based on the
    // specified offset and byte count.
```

```
        public int GetData(byte[] buffer, int offset, int count);

        // Returns duration of audio playback based on buffer size.
        public TimeSpan GetSampleDuration(int sizeInBytes);

        // Returns the size of the byte array required to hold the
        // specified duration of audio for this microphone object.
        public int GetSampleSizeInBytes(TimeSpan duration);

        // Starts microphone audio capture.
        public void Start();

        // Stops microphone audio capture.
        public void Stop();
    }
```

The first two properties you will want to take a look at in the Microphone class are Default() and All(). These return the default attached microphone and a collection of all attached microphones, respectively. In the example for this section, you will focus on the Default() property.

The complete code for this project is available for download at the book's companion web site (www.wrox.com).

Speaking of examples, it's that time again, so create a new Windows Phone Game project and name it MicrophoneSample.

When Visual Studio finishes creating your solution, add a new SpriteFont to your MicrophoneSampleContent project and name it microphoneFont. While your newly created microphoneFont.spritefont file is open, take a moment and change the Size property to 20.

Inside the Game1 class, add the following spriteFont variable at the class level:

```
    SpriteFont spriteFont;
```

In your Content.Load() method, add the following line to load your microphoneFont into memory:

```
    spriteFont = Content.Load<SpriteFont>("microphoneFont");
```

Now, add a Microphone variable at the class level:

```
    Microphone mic;
```

In the Initialize() method, set it to the default attached microphone, as mentioned previously:

```
    mic = Microphone.Default;
```

Finally, add this block of code to your Draw() method, just before the call to base.Draw():

```
    spriteBatch.Begin();

    spriteBatch.DrawString(spriteFont,
                    "Mic Name: " + mic.Name,
                    new Vector2(50, 50),                            Color.Black);
```

```
spriteBatch.DrawString(spriteFont,
                    "Wired? " + mic.IsHeadset,
                    new Vector2(50, 100),
                    Color.Black);

spriteBatch.End();
```

At this point, if you build and run the project (by pressing F5), you see the "friendly name" of the microphone you have attached to, and whether it is wired (`true`) or Bluetooth (`false`). It's not much, but it's a start, so let's keep pressing forward.

Now you'll capture some audio from the microphone and play it back. To do this, you need a Record button and a Play button onscreen, as shown in Figure 7-3. So grab the `recorderbuttons.png` file from the book files (at www.wrox.com) and add it to your `MicrophoneSampleContent` project.

FIGURE 7-3: The Record and Play buttons

Add a `Texture2D` variable called `micButtons` at the class level:

```
Texture2D micButtons;
```

Now load the sprite into memory with this line in your `LoadContent()` method, right after loading `spriteFont`:

```
micButtons = Content.Load<Texture2D>("recorderbuttons");
```

For these buttons to be anything other than glorious works of art, you need to be able to interact with them like buttons rather than as just a sprite. To do this, you add two `Rectangle` variables at the class level, defining each button:

```
Rectangle recordButton = new Rectangle(50, 200, 100, 50);
Rectangle playButton = new Rectangle(150, 200, 100, 50);
```

You will be using a `Tap` gesture to interact with your buttons, which means you must set the `EnabledGestures` property of the `TouchPanel` class. Add this line to the end of the `LoadContent()` method:

```
TouchPanel.EnabledGestures = GestureType.Tap;
```

Now you must handle the `Tap` gesture, so add this block of code to your `Update()` method, just before the call to `base.Update()`:

```
while (TouchPanel.IsGestureAvailable)
{
    GestureSample gesture = TouchPanel.ReadGesture();

    switch (gesture.GestureType)
    {
        case GestureType.Tap:
        {
            Rectangle touchRect = new Rectangle((int)gesture.Position.X,
                                                (int)gesture.Position.Y,
                                                10,
```

```
                                    10);
            if (touchRect.Intersects(recordButton))
            {

            }

            if (touchRect.Intersects(playButton))
            {

            }

            break;
        }
    }
}
```

In this code, you're using the same gesture logic you learned in Chapter 4, combined with checking to see if the tap occurred within the area defined by your button rectangles (`recordButton` and `playButton`). Any `Tap` gestures or other touches outside those areas are discarded.

You'll come back to add some functionality to those buttons in a bit, but for now add these two variables at the class level:

```
String message = String.Empty;
byte[] audioBuffer;
```

The `message` variable indicates what's going on for the user of your application. `audioBuffer` is a byte array that stores the sound you will be recording for playback.

In your `Game1` class constructor, add these three lines to initialize your `Microphone` object and the audio buffer:

```
mic.BufferDuration = TimeSpan.FromSeconds(1);
audioBuffer = new byte[mic.GetSampleSizeInBytes(mic.BufferDuration)];
mic.BufferReady += BufferIsReady;
```

You're seeing some new properties of the `Microphone` class here, so let's stop and take a look. The `BufferDuration` property sets the maximum size of the audio buffer and allows a range between 100 and 1000 milliseconds (0.1 to 1 second). Anything outside that range, or not evenly divisible by 10, throws an `ArgumentOutOfRangeException`.

The `GetSampleSizeInBytes()` method is very handy. It saves you from having to manually calculate the size of your byte array (`audioBuffer`) based on the size of the buffer duration of your `Microphone` object (`mic`). Just pass in the `BufferDuration` property, and it returns a byte array size you can use to instantiate `audioBuffer`.

The last line sets a delegate to be called when your microphone's buffer is ready to start recording. Add the `BufferIsReady()` method shown in Listing 7-7.

LISTING 7-7: The BufferIsReady() Method of the Game1 Class

```
private void BufferIsReady(object sender, EventArgs e)
{
    mic.GetData(audioBuffer);
    message = "Start talking...";
}
```

This method doesn't get called until the input buffer on the microphone is ready. At that point it calls the `GetData()` method of the `Microphone` class and updates your status message.

Now you will add the Record and Play buttons and your status message onscreen. Modify the `spriteBatch` code block in your `Draw()` method to look like the following code (with changes in bold):

```
spriteBatch.Begin();

spriteBatch.DrawString(spriteFont,
                "Mic Name: " + mic.Name,
                new Vector2(50, 50),
                Color.Black);

spriteBatch.DrawString(spriteFont,
                "Wired? " + mic.IsHeadset,
                new Vector2(50, 100),
                Color.Black);

spriteBatch.Draw(micButtons, new Vector2(50, 200), Color.White);
spriteBatch.DrawString(spriteFont, message, new Vector2(50, 300), Color.Black);

spriteBatch.End();
```

At this point, the only thing you are missing is the code for the Record and Play buttons. Start by altering the `recordButton` block in your `Update()` method to look like this:

```
if (touchRect.Intersects(recordButton))
{
    mic.Start();
    message = "Preparing to record...";
}
```

If you were to tap the Record button at this point, you would briefly see a message that says, "Preparing to record...", followed by a message that says, "Start talking...". At this point, the phone microphone is on and recording.

You can talk as long as you want, but keep in mind that you have only 1 second of input buffer. This means that only the last second is saved in memory.

Normally, you would have a stream writing everything to local storage, and then you would fetch it later, at playback time. (You will, but that comes later in the demo.)

Change the `playButton` block in your `Update()` method to add the functionality necessary to stop the `Microphone` and play your sound buffer:

```
if (touchRect.Intersects(playButton))
{
```

```
            mic.Stop();
            message = "Playing...";

            if (audioBuffer == null || audioBuffer.Length == 0)
            {
                Message = "Buffer empty...";
                return;
            }

            SoundEffect recording = new SoundEffect(audioBuffer,
                                                   mic.SampleRate,
                                                   AudioChannels.Mono);
            recording.Play();
        }
```

In this method, the first thing you do is call the `Stop()` method of the `Microphone` object and set the status message to "Playing...".

Next, you check the byte array (`audioBuffer`) and ensure that it isn't null or empty. If it is, update the status message and exit the `Draw()` method.

The last task in this method is to convert the data in your byte array to a `SoundEffect` object. By passing in the audio buffer, the sample rate of the `Microphone` object, and whether the recording is in `Mono` or `Stereo` into your `SoundEffect()` constructor, you can return a `SoundEffect` object (called `recording`) that you can play via the `Play()` method of the `SoundEffect` class.

At this point, you can press F5 to build and run the `MicrophoneSample` project. Tap the Record button to record yourself speaking, and tap the Play button to hear what was recorded. Just remember: no matter how long you talk, only the last second will be in the memory buffer.

Saving and Retrieving Captured Audio

Continuing with the `MicrophoneSample` project from the previous section, you will add a memory stream object that will read the contents of the audio buffer and write to isolated storage on the phone. You will then add code to read the audio data back into memory and play the entire recorded audio.

You've already spent some time working with isolated storage, so if you need a refresher, jump back to Chapter 6. Start by adding the following `using` statements to the top of your `Game1` class:

```
using System.IO;
using System.IO.IsolatedStorage;
```

At the class level, add a `MemoryStream` variable:

```
MemoryStream memoryStream;
```

You don't need to make any additional changes to your class constructor, so you can skip that. But you need to add the following line to the `Initialize()` method to instantiate the memory stream object:

```
memoryStream = new MemoryStream();
```

In the `BufferIsReady()` method that gets called when the `Microphone` input buffer is ready, add this line immediately after the call to `mic.GetData(audioBuffer)`:

```
memoryStream.Write(audioBuffer, 0, audioBuffer.Length);
```

This line takes the entire `audioBuffer` variable with no offset and writes it out as a memory stream. Next, you add the `WriteBuffer()` method shown in Listing 7-8, which handles the task of writing your memory stream to isolated storage.

LISTING 7-8: The WriteBuffer() Method of the Game1 Class

```
private void WriteBuffer()
{
    using (var store =
        IsolatedStorageFile.GetUserStoreForApplication())
    {
        if (store.FileExists("audio.xna"))
            store.DeleteFile("audio.xna");

        using (var file = store.OpenFile("audio.xna",
                                        FileMode.CreateNew))
        {
            memoryStream.WriteTo(file);
        }
    }
}
```

This method creates a user store for the `MicrophoneSample` application and checks to see if the file you want to create already exists (and deletes it if so). Next, it takes the `memoryStream` variable and writes the contents to the `audio.xna` file.

With this in place, add the call to the `WriteBuffer()` method to your `playButton` code block in the `Update()` method, as shown in bold here:

```
mic.Stop();
WriteBuffer();
message = "Playing...";
```

Now add the `ReadBuffer()` method, which takes the file you persisted to local storage and reads it back into your `audioBuffer` object. Listing 7-9 contains the `ReadBuffer()` method.

LISTING 7-9: The ReadBuffer() Method of the Game1 Class

```
private void ReadBuffer()
{
    using (var store =
        IsolatedStorageFile.GetUserStoreForApplication())
    {
        if (store.FileExists("audio.xna"))
        {
            var file = store.OpenFile("audio.xna",
                                      FileMode.Open,
                                      FileAccess.Read);

            audioBuffer = new byte[file.Length];
            file.Read(audioBuffer, 0, audioBuffer.Length);
```

```
            }
        }
    }
```

The `ReadBuffer()` method opens the user store and checks for the existence of your `audio.xna` file. If the file is found, the method opens it and reads it into your byte array (`audioBuffer`).

The last thing you need to do is add one more line to the `Update()` method, inside the `playButton` code block, just like before. Add the following bold line immediately after the `message = "Playing...";` line, as shown here:

```
message = "Playing...";
ReadBuffer();
if (audioBuffer == null || audioBuffer.Length == 0)
```

That's it. Now you can build and run the application and record yourself singing the national anthem (or the song of your choice) and impress all your friends.

SUMMARY

In this chapter, you learned about the `MediaPlayer` class and how to play music in your games. You also learned about the `SoundEffect` class and how to play instanced sound effects with `SoundEffectInstance`.

You learned how to interact with the microphone on the phone, and how to record and play back audio.

Unfortunately, Windows Phone 7 does not support `VisualizationData`, but you learned how to work with the data in a Windows Game project. If Microsoft decides to add support for `VisualizationData` on the phone, you will be ready!

You also learned that even though Windows Phone 7 doesn't support XACT projects, you can do pretty much anything with the Audio API that you could do with XACT.

Chapter 8 helps you take everything you have learned thus far and build your first functioning game for Windows Phone 7.

Putting It All Together: Drive & Dodge

WHAT'S IN THIS CHAPTER?

➤ Using everything you've learned thus far and creating a game called Drive & Dodge

➤ Creating a basic game project template for reuse in other game projects

It's time to take everything you have learned in the previous chapters and create your first complete game for Windows Phone 7.

 The examples provided in the "Putting it All Together" chapters (Chapters 8, 12, and 15) assume knowledge of C#. Without that, the sample projects may be a bit overwhelming and confusing. These chapters are not for beginners, but for experienced developers who are familiar with C# and somewhat familiar with the XNA framework and game-development concepts.

When you begin developing games for a new system, it's always good to do a basic "Hello World!"–type game. It's important to pick a game with simple game play and mechanics so that you can spend time learning the ins and outs of the new API and hardware, instead of struggling with new game coding techniques. With that in mind, it's time to lay out the design of your "Hello World!" game, called Drive & Dodge.

If you were to buy Drive & Dodge at your favorite game store, the back of the box might read something like this: "You're in a car speeding down a perfectly straight road that seems to stretch on forever. The car keeps accelerating as you drive. Wait — what's this? Some kind of construction is going on, and hazard signs blocking portions of the road keep appearing in the lanes. No matter — the car has excellent steering. Why not make a game of it? Keep the pedal cranked, and see how many of these hazards you can avoid. Don't crash, though, or it's game over."

Game developers speak a slightly different language than marketers, so you might describe the game more like this to your boss: "Drive & Dodge is a single-player, top-down, vertical-scrolling driving game that uses touch-and-tilt functionality to control a car driving on the highway. As the game continues, the scrolling progressively speeds up until the player collides with an obstacle, ending the game."

This chapter introduces the concepts of collision detection and scoring. Collision will be signaled by vibrating the phone and playing a crash sound.

CREATING THE GAME

Before coding a single line, you should think about the various screens that will be in the game. Try to picture not just what's on the screen, but what inputs are important on each screen. For example, are there any menu items? What screens can you navigate to from this screen? Knowing this will help you get a good skeleton in place for your game and will also help remind you that there's far more to a game than game play.

It's easy to make a sample demonstrating game play (okay, relatively easy), but much more work is involved with adding all the screens and polish that really make the difference between a game demo and a complete game.

Figure 8-1 shows a diagram mapping out the screens that will be in Drive & Dodge. It also shows some of the buttons that will be on those screens, and the flow of the game between those screens from game start to game exit.

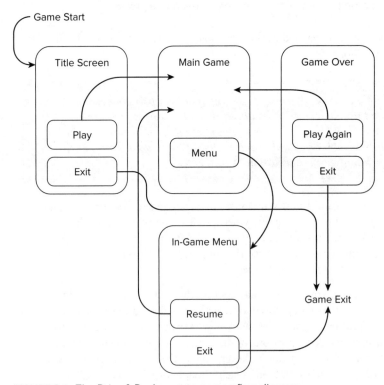

FIGURE 8-1: The Drive & Dodge game screen flow diagram

Now, you will create a new Windows Phone Game project and call it DriveAndDodge. In the next section, you will add the base functionality and supporting classes that will help shape this game and the other two games in this book.

 The complete code for this project is available for download at the book's companion website (www.wrox.com).

In Chapter 6, you learned about game and screen state, so that's where you will begin.

Screens

In your game project, create a new folder called Screens. This is where you will keep the various screens that make up the game and where you will store the base screen class. Not only does this folder keep the files organized, it also serves as a namespace definition to help keep your classes organized.

Screen.cs

Right-click the Screens folder and add a new class called Screen.cs. The code for the Screen class is shown in Listing 8-1.

LISTING 8-1: Screen.cs

```
using System;

using Microsoft.Xna.Framework;
using Microsoft.Xna.Framework.Content;
using Microsoft.Xna.Framework.Graphics;

namespace DriveAndDodge.Screens
{
    class Screen
    {
        protected static Game game;
        protected static ContentManager content;
        protected static SpriteBatch batch;
        protected static Random random = new Random();

        public ChangeScreen changeScreenDelegate;
        public delegate void ChangeScreen(ScreenState screen);

        public Screen(Game game, SpriteBatch batch,
                    ChangeScreen changeScreen)
        {
            Screen.game = game;
            Screen.content = game.Content;
            Screen.batch = batch;

            changeScreenDelegate = changeScreen;
```

continues

LISTING 8-1 *(continued)*

```
        }

        public virtual void Activate()
        {
        }

        public void LoadContent()
        {
            LoadScreenContent(content);
            SetupInputs();
        }

        protected virtual void SetupInputs()
        {
        }

        protected virtual void LoadScreenContent(ContentManager
                                                            content)
        {
        }

        public void Update(GameTime gameTime)
        {
            UpdateScreen(gameTime,
                game.GraphicsDevice
                    .PresentationParameters.DisplayOrientation);
        }

        protected virtual void UpdateScreen(GameTime gameTime,
                                        DisplayOrientation
                                            screenOrientation)
        {
        }

        public void Draw()
        {
            batch.Begin();
            DrawScreen(batch,
                    game.GraphicsDevice
                        .PresentationParameters.DisplayOrientation);
            batch.End();
        }

        protected virtual void DrawScreen(SpriteBatch batch,
                                        DisplayOrientation
                                            screenOrientation)
        {
        }

        public void SaveState()
        {
            SaveScreenState();
        }
```

```csharp
            protected virtual void SaveScreenState()
            {
            }

            static public int ScreenWidth
            {
                get { return
                        game.GraphicsDevice
                            .PresentationParameters.BackBufferWidth; }
            }

            static public int ScreenHeight
            {
                get { return
                        game.GraphicsDevice
                            .PresentationParameters.BackBufferHeight; }
            }

            static public Rectangle ScreenRectangle
            {
                get { return new Rectangle(0,
                                           0,
                                           ScreenWidth,
                                           ScreenHeight); }
            }

            static public Rectangle ScreenLeftHalf
            {
                get { return new Rectangle(0,
                                           0,
                                           (int)(ScreenWidth/2),
                                           ScreenHeight); }
            }

            static public Rectangle ScreenRightHalf
            {
                get { return new Rectangle((int)(ScreenWidth / 2),
                                           0,
                                           (int)(ScreenWidth / 2),
                                           ScreenHeight); }
            }
        }
    }
```

The `Screen` class defines the base functionality of all future screens. It's a little sparse right now, but you will add more as you develop the game.

The `Screen` class constructor takes in information about the `Game` class itself and then stores references to this information to be used later. The `Game` object and `SpriteBatch` objects are key components of every XNA game, so having these available to the `Screen` class will be advantageous. The `ChangeScreen` object will be used to raise change-screen events to other classes.

The `Activate()` method is provided for classes inheriting from `Screen` to override. The intent of the method is to provide a place for you to put any code that must be executed when a screen has been activated.

To use Drive & Dodge as an example, think about moving from the `GameOver` screen back to the `MainGame` screen. It's important that the game gets reset so that the player can start again with a score of 0, a slow speed, and, of course, not on top of any hazards. This code would be executed when the screen has been reactivated, and it would be placed in the `Activate()` method.

The `LoadContent()` method is called to load any particular content for the screens. The `LoadContent()` method in the base class is the public method, so it is the one that is called by external callers. This allows any other important calls to be wrapped, as well as a chance to place any specific content that all screens should be loading. The base class then calls the specific screen's `LoadScreenContent()` method if it has been overridden.

The previously mentioned `LoadScreenContent()` method is a way for an inheriting screen to load any specific content such as images, sound effects, or music. If that type of content is needed by the implementation of a screen, this would be the place to load it.

`SetupInputs()` is more of an organizational method to keep the code neat and tidy. If an implementation of a screen must set up some inputs (with the input wrapper classes you will add later), placing that type of setup code in this overridden method would be the way to go.

The public `Update()` method and the virtual `UpdateScreen()` method that immediately follow should be a familiar pattern. (The same type of pattern was used by the `LoadContent()` and `LoadScreenContent()` methods.)

The `Update()` method in the base class is the one that is called. It also manages the calling of any of the inheriting classes' `Update()` method if the `UpdateScreen()` method is overridden. Again, this allows you to set up common functionality that all screens should have when updating, as well as specific `Update` code for each inheriting screen class.

The `Draw()` and `DrawScreen()` methods also use the same pattern. The public-facing `Draw()` method in the base class calls the inheriting classes' specific implementation of `DrawScreen()`.

Notice that both the `UpdateScreen()` and `DrawScreen()` methods accept a `DisplayOrientation` object as a parameter. With Windows Phone games, the screen can be turned Landscape left, Landscape right, or Portrait. It is important for both the Update and Draw screens to make logic decisions (if the game requires it) based on that information.

For example, assume that, when the screen is changed from Portrait mode to Landscape, you want to rearrange the game's visual elements to make sense for that orientation. With the `DisplayOrientation` object you can find out the current orientation and adjust your game accordingly.

Next are the `SaveState()` and `SaveScreenState()` methods. These methods are provided in case of game interruption, such as an incoming phone call or other user interaction. They are used to persist important information about the game if necessary. There's not much to see in them right now, since they are just stubbed out until later.

Finally, the `Screen` class wraps up by providing a set of helper properties used to get the height and width of the screen, as well as determining the screen area and the left and right halves of the screen.

The base `Screen` class is done for now. Unfortunately, you can't compile yet because of the reference to the `ScreenState` enumeration in line 17. Don't worry, though; you will create this in the next section.

ScreenStateSwitchboard.cs

With the base screen created, it is time to start thinking about just how you will manage changing between all the various screens in your game.

Add a second new class to the `Screens` folder/namespace, and give it the name `ScreenStateSwitchboard.cs`. Listing 8-2 contains the complete code for this class.

LISTING 8-2: ScreenStateSwitchboard.cs

```csharp
using System.Collections.Generic;

using Microsoft.Xna.Framework;
using Microsoft.Xna.Framework.Graphics;


namespace DriveAndDodge.Screens
{
    public enum ScreenState
    {
        Title,
    }

    class ScreenStateSwitchboard
    {
        static Game game;
        static SpriteBatch batch;
        static Screen previousScreen;
        static Screen currentScreen;
        static Dictionary<ScreenState, Screen> screens
            = new Dictionary<ScreenState, Screen>();

        private delegate Screen CreateScreen();

        public ScreenStateSwitchboard(Game game, SpriteBatch batch)
        {
            ScreenStateSwitchboard.game = game;
            ScreenStateSwitchboard.batch = batch;
            ChangeScreen(ScreenState.Title);
        }

        private void ChangeScreen(ScreenState screenState)
        {
            switch (screenState)
            {
                case ScreenState.Title:
                {
                    ChangeScreen(screenState,
                            new CreateScreen(CreateTitleScreen));
                    break;
                }
            }
        }
```

continues

LISTING 8-2 *(continued)*

```
        private void ChangeScreen(ScreenState screenState,
                                  CreateScreen createScreen)
        {
            previousScreen = currentScreen;

            if (!screens.ContainsKey(screenState))
            {
                screens.Add(screenState, createScreen());
                screens[screenState].LoadContent();
            }
            currentScreen = screens[screenState];
            currentScreen.Activate();
        }

        private Screen CreateTitleScreen()
        {
            return new Title(game,
                             batch,
                             new Screen.ChangeScreen(ChangeScreen));
        }

        public void Update(GameTime gameTime)
        {
            currentScreen.Update(gameTime);
        }

        public void Draw()
        {
            currentScreen.Draw();
        }
    }
}
```

The `ScreenStateSwitchboard` class is the heart of controlling the game's screen state. It helps switch between the various screens and ensures that the `Update()` and `Draw()` methods are being called on the currently active screen.

You'll notice at the top of `ScreenStateSwitchboard.cs` file (outside of the class definition) that there's an enumeration called `ScreenState`. This is where you'll add more screen options as you develop them and want them to be available. The enumeration is placed outside of the class definition so that it's available throughout your game project. Currently, there's just a `Title` screen option, but there will be more as you add to the game.

Skipping over the class-level objects for now (you'll find out about them as you use them in the various class methods), take a look at the constructor. The `ScreenStateSwitchboard()` constructor gets references to the `Game` and `SpriteBatch` objects. You learned earlier how important these objects are in a game, and that's why you store references to them here.

The last line of the constructor calls a method called `ChangeScreen()` and passes in the `Title` enumeration value. This is what sets up the first screen of the game. If you don't want the first screen to be Title, you would change it here.

Next, take a look at the first of the two overloaded `ChangeScreen()` methods. The first one just takes in `ScreenState` as a parameter value. This method is the big switching station for screens. Based on the value of the `ScreenState` parameter passed in, the appropriate method is called to create the screen and make that one the current one. The meat of that work is done in the second `ChangeScreen()` method.

The second overload of the `ChangeScreen()` method takes in the `ScreenState` enumeration value again, as well as a delegate object for `CreateScreen()`. This allows the `CreateScreen()` method to call the appropriate class method to create a screen of that type.

`ChangeScreen()` starts by storing a reference to the current screen in a `Screen` object called `previousScreen`. The intent (you may have guessed by the clever name) is to keep track of what screen you just navigated from. This is useful for moving back through screens.

The `ChangeScreen()` method then looks to see if the screen has already been created. The various `Screen` objects are stored in a dictionary keyed by their `ScreenState` enumeration value. If this is the first time navigating to them, the new `Screen` object is created, the screen's `LoadContent()` method is called, and a reference to it is stored in the dictionary.

If the screen already exists, the `ChangeScreen()` method just makes that screen the current one and calls the `Activate()` method to run any screen-specific activation code. (Resetting levels and making the first menu item the selected one are some of the things that would commonly be found in a screen-specific implementation of the `Activate()` method.)

The next method in the `ScreenStateSwitchboard` creates the `Title` screen class. Eventually you'll add methods to create instances of each screen the game will need. When `ChangeScreen()` is called with the `ScreenState` enumeration value, the intent is that the specified screen is created, and it does this by calling the appropriate create-screen method. In this case, `CreateTitleScreen()` creates a new instance of a `Title` screen object.

Last, but certainly not least, are the `Update()` and `Draw()` methods. These public-facing methods draw and update the current screen.

So, now you can run the game and it's all done, right? Sadly, no. You still must fill in more of the pieces. At this point, Visual Studio should be complaining about the lack of a `Title` class. Don't worry; that's next.

Title.cs

With the basics of the `ScreenStateSwitchboard` class in place, it is time to make a screen for it to manage. The `Title` screen is a logical place to start.

Add the `Title` class shown in Listing 8-3 to your `DriveAndDodge` game project under the `Screens` folder.

LISTING 8-3: Title.cs

```
using Microsoft.Xna.Framework;
using Microsoft.Xna.Framework.Graphics;
using Microsoft.Xna.Framework.Content;
```

continues

LISTING 8-3 *(continued)*

```csharp
namespace DriveAndDodge.Screens
{
    class Title : Screen
    {
        public Title(Game game,
                     SpriteBatch batch,
                     ChangeScreen changeScreen)
            : base(game, batch, changeScreen)
        {
        }

        protected override void SetupInputs()
        {
        }

        public override void Activate()
        {
        }

        protected override void LoadScreenContent(ContentManager
                                                                content)
        {
        }

        protected override void UpdateScreen(GameTime gameTime,
                                             DisplayOrientation
                                                 displayOrientation)
        {
        }

        protected override void DrawScreen(SpriteBatch batch,
                                           DisplayOrientation
                                               displayOrientation)
        {
        }
    }
}
```

There are plenty of screen-specific implementation overrides of base class methods, but currently no code fills out those methods. The `Title` screen definitely needs more functionality, but before anything can be drawn to the screen, you must add some classes to help manage those drawn images (also known as *sprites*).

Sprites refer to just about anything drawn to the screen. A character is a sprite, a power-up is a sprite, a background image is a sprite, and even the text you write on the screen is a series of sprites.

Since you will be drawing many things on the screen, it makes sense to add a `Sprite` class to your game. So, put the `Title` screen aside for now, and focus on what the `Title` screen class will need.

Drawing a background image on the `Title` screen is a good place to start. Because, as you just learned, a background image is a sprite, it's time to create a new class.

Sprite.cs

Start by creating a new folder called `Sprites` under your `DriveAndDodge` game project, and then add the class shown in Listing 8-4 to the `Sprites` folder.

LISTING 8-4: Sprite.cs

```
using Microsoft.Xna.Framework;
using Microsoft.Xna.Framework.Content;
using Microsoft.Xna.Framework.Graphics;

namespace DriveAndDodge.Sprites
{
    class Sprite
    {
        public Vector2 Position;
        public delegate void CollisionDelegate();

        protected Texture2D texture;
        protected Color color = Color.White;

        public Sprite(ContentManager content, string assetName)
        {
            texture = content.Load<Texture2D>(assetName);
        }

        public void Update(GameTime gameTime)
        {
            UpdateSprite(gameTime);
        }

        protected virtual void UpdateSprite(GameTime gameTime)
        {
        }

        public void Draw(SpriteBatch batch)
        {
            batch.Draw(texture, Position, color);
            DrawSprite(batch);
        }

        protected virtual void DrawSprite(SpriteBatch batch)
        {
        }

        public bool IsCollidingWith(Sprite spriteToCheck)
        {
            return CollisionRectangle.Intersects
                    (spriteToCheck.CollisionRectangle);
        }

        public Rectangle CollisionRectangle
```

continues

LISTING 8-4 *(continued)*

```
        {
            get
            {
                return new Rectangle((int)Position.X,
                                     (int)Position.Y,
                                     Width,
                                     Height);
            }
        }

        public int Height
        {
            get { return texture.Height; }
        }

        public int Width
        {
            get { return texture.Width; }
        }
    }
}
```

The `Sprite` class will be the base class for every two-dimensional (2D) image drawn to the screen. Having a base class for all your in-game objects gives you tremendous power to change behaviors and can also be a useful debugging aid.

> *One common feature not implemented here that you might want to add to your base `Sprite` class is the ability to turn on and off a visible box around the collision area defined for your sprites. This lets you see just why a collision is (or is not) occurring.*

The `Sprite` class constructor takes a reference to a `ContentManager` object and then a string value for the name of the asset that will be loaded for this `Sprite`. The constructor then proceeds to load and store the texture for the `Sprite`. (A *texture* is an image loaded from disk.)

Next, you'll again see a familiar pattern with a public-facing `Update()` method that exists in the base class, and then a sprite-specific implementation that's called. This again gives you the freedom to add functionality in your base class. You know that every sprite in your game will automatically get the benefit of that change, since all calls to `Update()` are funneled through the base class. The `UpdateSprite()` method would then be overridden in an inherited class, and any sprite-specific update code would be placed there.

The `Draw()` and `DrawSprite()` methods use the same pattern, although the base public `Draw()` method draws the sprite to the screen.

Next, you have a helper method to handle collision detection. The `IsCollidingWith()` method takes in another `Sprite` object and then checks to see if the current sprite's collision rectangle intersects with the passed-in sprite's collision rectangle.

Last, a few helper properties are provided to help define the sprite's `Height` and `Width`, as well as defining the `CollisionRectangle`.

Now that you have your base `Sprite` class, you will implement a `Sprite`. As mentioned earlier, you will display a background on the `Title` screen, so that will be the class you make next.

Background.cs

Add the `Background` class in Listing 8-5 to the `Sprites` folder in your `DriveAndDodge` project.

LISTING 8-5: Background.cs

```csharp
using Microsoft.Xna.Framework.Content;

namespace DriveAndDodge.Sprites
{
    class Background : Sprite
    {
        public Background(ContentManager content)
            : base(content, "Images/Background")
        {
        }
    }
}
```

Backgrounds don't do much other than sit there and look pretty. (Well, they *could* do more, if you wanted triple parallax scrolling or animated backgrounds, for example, but this particular background doesn't do much.)

You can see there's really not much to this class. You may also notice that it passes in the string `"Images/Background"` to the base `Sprite` class constructor. That's the name (and path) of the asset, and the base class will use the Content Pipeline to load the asset with that name. That's a bit of a problem right now, since you don't actually have a folder called `Images` in the `Content` project, or an image asset called `Background`. Let's add those now.

Content

The `Content` project in your `DriveAndDodge` solution is where you will add all the assets (things like music, sound effects, and images) for your game. One of the improvements in XNA 4.0 is that the `Content` project has become an actual project in your solution, rather than just a "special folder." This allows you to share projects between game titles and target platforms, as well as gives you greater flexibility.

Keeping your assets organized is definitely a good thing, so start by adding a folder called `Images` to the `DriveAndDodge Content` project. Next, add the `Background.png` image to that folder. You can download it from this book's downloadable code files at www.wrox.com.

Now that you have your image placed in the `Content` folder, it is time to add the rest of the code so that you can finally start seeing something on the screen.

Game1.cs

To start seeing things, you must tie everything together. Start by adding some code to the `Game1.cs` class. (That class was created automatically when you created a new Windows Phone Game project.)

First, you must add some code to the `Game1` constructor to set the game to run in full-screen mode and to start the game in Portrait mode by default.

Change the `Game1()` constructor in the `Game1.cs` class to look like Listing 8-6, paying special attention to the code in bold.

LISTING 8-6: The Game1 Class Constructor

```
public Game1()
{
    graphics = new GraphicsDeviceManager(this);
    Content.RootDirectory = "Content";

    // Frame rate is 30 fps by default for Windows Phone.
    TargetElapsedTime = TimeSpan.FromTicks(333333);

    // Set the game up to be in portrait mode
    graphics.PreferredBackBufferWidth = 480;
    graphics.PreferredBackBufferHeight = 800;

    // Use the full phone screen real estate by setting this to true
    graphics.IsFullScreen = true;
}
```

Next, add a `using` statement to the top of the `Game1.cs` class file:

```
using DriveAndDodge.Screens;
```

Then add a class-level variable called `screen` for the `ScreenStateSwitchboard` class:

```
ScreenStateSwitchboard screen;
```

You will create the `ScreenStateSwitchboard` object in the `LoadContent()` method. Change the `LoadContent()` method in the `Game1.cs` file to look like Listing 8-7. The new line is in bold.

LISTING 8-7: The LoadContent() Method of the Game1 Class

```
protected override void LoadContent()
{
    // Create a new SpriteBatch, which can be used to draw textures.
```

```
        spriteBatch = new SpriteBatch(GraphicsDevice);

        screen = new ScreenStateSwitchboard(this, spriteBatch);
    }
```

With the `screen` object created, you will use it in the `Update()` and `Draw()` methods. Change both methods in the `Game1.cs` class to look like the methods shown in Listing 8-8. The changed lines are in bold.

LISTING 8-8: The Update() and Draw() Methods of the Game1 Class

```
    protected override void Update(GameTime gameTime)
    {
        screen.Update(gameTime);
        base.Update(gameTime);
    }

    protected override void Draw(GameTime gameTime)
    {
        GraphicsDevice.Clear(Color.CornflowerBlue);
        screen.Draw();
        base.Draw(gameTime);
    }
```

With those changes, the `ScreenStateSwitchboard` object now ensures that the appropriate screens are being drawn and updated.

At this point, the `ScreenStateSwitchboard` has been integrated into the game loop.

Jump back into the `Title` screen class briefly to add the drawing of the background. Inside the `Title.cs` file, add the following `using` statement at the top:

```
using DriveAndDodge.Sprites;
```

Next, you will take advantage of the new `Background` class you created. Add a class-level variable of type `Background` and name it `background`, as shown here:

```
Background background;
```

The `background` variable needs to be instantiated and loaded before it can be used. Earlier, you defined a `Screen` base class and some methods. The `LoadScreenContent()` method is where you would instantiate the `background` variable.

Add the following line of code inside the `LoadScreenContent()` method of the `Title` class:

```
background = new Background(content);
```

Finally, the background must be drawn to the screen. Add the following line of code to the `DrawScreen()` method of your `Title` class:

```
background.Draw(batch);
```

And that's it (for now).

Save the solution, and press F5 to build and run.

If you skipped all the chapters before this one so that you could jump right into building a game, you have to be patient while the Emulator starts for the first time, since it can take a while. The great thing is that you can keep the Emulator open even when your game isn't running so that repeated deployments don't take as long.

If you've followed along correctly, you should be seeing a background other than Cornflower Blue being displayed by your currently active `Title` screen, much like what is shown in Figure 8-2.

FIGURE 8-2: The Drive & Dodge background screen, running in the Windows Phone 7 Emulator

It may seem like you did a lot of work for such simple results, but there is plenty more work to do before you have a proper game. All that groundwork you put in will help you do so.

Now that the `Title` screen is drawing and the background is displaying, it's time to start adding even more functionality to that screen and the game. A `Title` screen is pretty pointless without a title, so you will fix that next.

To display a title, you could create a new image and draw another sprite on the screen, or you could just write some text and display that. Next you will create some helper classes to make drawing text even easier.

Text.cs

First, create a new folder called `Texts` in the `DriveAndDodge` project. Then add the class shown in Listing 8-9 to that folder.

LISTING 8-9: Text.cs

```csharp
using Microsoft.Xna.Framework;
using Microsoft.Xna.Framework.Graphics;

namespace DriveAndDodge.Texts
{
    class Text
    {
        public Vector2 Position;
        public Color DisplayColor = Color.White;

        public enum Alignment
        {
            None,
            Horizontal,
            Vertical,
            Both
        }

        SpriteFont font;
        string text;
        Vector2 textSize;
        Color outlineColor = Color.White;
        bool isTextOutlined = false;

        public Text(SpriteFont displayFont,
                    string displayText,
                    Vector2 displayPosition)
            : this(displayFont,
                   displayText,
                   displayPosition,
                   Color.White,
                   Color.White,
                   false,
                   Alignment.None,
                   Rectangle.Empty)
        {
        }

        public Text(SpriteFont displayFont,
                    string displayText,
                    Vector2 displayPosition,
                    Color displayColor)
            : this(displayFont,
                   displayText,
                   displayPosition,
                   displayColor,
                   Color.White,
                   false,
                   Alignment.None,
                   Rectangle.Empty)
        {
        }
```

continues

LISTING 8-9 *(continued)*

```
        public Text(SpriteFont displayFont,
                    string displayText,
                    Vector2 displayPosition,
                    Color displayColor,
                    Alignment alignment,
                    Rectangle displayArea)
            : this(displayFont,
                   displayText,
                   displayPosition,
                   displayColor,
                   Color.White,
                   false,
                   alignment,
                   displayArea)
        {
        }

        public Text(SpriteFont displayFont,
                    string displayText,
                    Vector2 displayPosition,
                    Color displayColor,
                    Color outlineColor)
            : this(displayFont,
                   displayText,
                   displayPosition,
                   displayColor,
                   outlineColor,
                   true,
                   Alignment.None,
                   Rectangle.Empty)
        {
        }

        public Text(SpriteFont displayFont,
                    string displayText,
                    Vector2 displayPosition,
                    Color displayColor,
                    Color outlineColor,
                    Alignment alignment,
                    Rectangle displayArea)
            : this(displayFont,
                   displayText,
                   displayPosition,
                   displayColor,
                   outlineColor,
                   true,
                   alignment,
                   displayArea)
        {
        }

        private Text(SpriteFont displayFont,
                     string displayText,
```

```csharp
                Vector2 displayPosition,
                Color displayColor,
                Color outlineColor,
                bool isTextOutlined,
                Alignment alignment,
                Rectangle displayArea)
{
    font = displayFont;
    text = displayText;
    Position = displayPosition;
    DisplayColor = displayColor;

    this.isTextOutlined = isTextOutlined;
    this.outlineColor = outlineColor;

    CenterText(alignment, displayArea);
}

private void CenterText(Alignment alignment,
                        Rectangle displayArea)
{
    textSize = font.MeasureString(text);

    int positionX = (int)Position.X;
    int positionY = (int)Position.Y;

    switch (alignment)
    {
        case Alignment.Horizontal:
            {
                positionX = (int)((displayArea.Width / 2)
                            - (textSize.X / 2))
                            + displayArea.X;
                break;
            }

        case Alignment.Vertical:
            {
                positionY = (int)((displayArea.Height / 2)
                            - (textSize.Y / 2))
                            + displayArea.Y;
                break;
            }

        case Alignment.Both:
            {
                positionX = (int)((displayArea.Width / 2)
                            - (textSize.X / 2))
                            + displayArea.X;
                positionY = (int)((displayArea.Height / 2)
                            - (textSize.Y / 2))
                            + displayArea.Y;
                break;
            }
```

continues

LISTING 8-9 *(continued)*

```
            case Alignment.None:
                {
                    //Nothing to do
                    break;
                }
        }

        Position = new Vector2(positionX, positionY);
    }

    public void Draw(SpriteBatch batch)
    {
        if (isTextOutlined)
        {
            int outlineWidth = 3;
            batch.DrawString(font,
                            text,
                            Position - new Vector2(0,
                                                    outlineWidth),
                            outlineColor);

            batch.DrawString(font,
                            text,
                            Position + new Vector2(0,
                                                    outlineWidth),
                            outlineColor);

            batch.DrawString(font,
                            text,
                            Position - new Vector2(outlineWidth,
                                                    0),
                            outlineColor);

            batch.DrawString(font,
                            text,
                            Position + new Vector2(outlineWidth,
                                                    0),
                            outlineColor);

            batch.DrawString(font,
                            text,
                            Position + new Vector2(outlineWidth,
                                                    outlineWidth),
                            outlineColor);

            batch.DrawString(font,
                            text,
                            Position + new Vector2(outlineWidth,
                                                    -outlineWidth),
                            outlineColor);

            batch.DrawString(font,
```

```
                        text,
                        Position + new Vector2(-outlineWidth,
                                                outlineWidth),
                        outlineColor);

            batch.DrawString(font,
                        text,
                        Position + new Vector2(-outlineWidth,
                                                -outlineWidth),
                        outlineColor);
        }

        batch.DrawString(font, text, Position, DisplayColor);
    }

    public void ChangeText(string displayText)
    {
        text = displayText;
        CenterText(Alignment.None, Rectangle.Empty);
    }

    public Rectangle CollisionRectangle
    {
        get { return new Rectangle((int)Position.X,
                                    (int)Position.Y,
                                    (int)textSize.X,
                                    (int)textSize.Y); }
    }
  }
}
```

The Text class provides the ability to quickly color, center, and outline text. In examining the class, you'll see that it has many overloaded constructors. This gives you the option of simply displaying some text in a particular position on the screen, along with coloring, outlining, and centering the text.

The CenterText() method is used by the Text class to position the given text with the supplied SpriteFont in the appropriate position. It starts by measuring the size of the text based on the size of the font. (This is a fairly imprecise sizing, so don't expect to be able to do much with that information.) Then CenterText() properly positions the text in the rectangular display area that's been defined.

As expected, the Draw() method handles the actual drawing of the text to the screen. First, it checks to see if the text should be outlined. If so, it draws the text repeatedly at various offsets to create an outline shape around the text. Then it draws the actual text over those "outlines" to create the effect. It's a simple technique, but very effective.

Next, the ChangeText() method is provided so that external callers can change the text if necessary. Static text is great, but sometimes you may need to continually update the Text object to display a different value, such as when you are displaying a countdown timer. This method is provided to give that type of functionality to your text objects.

After the new text has been set, a call to the CenterText() method is made to remeasure the string, with Alignment.None passed in to indicate that the text should not be repositioned.

Last, the `CollisionRectangle` property is part of the `Text` class for those occasions when you need to know if something is colliding with your text. Remember, for all practical purposes, onscreen text can be treated as a sprite.

screenFont.spritefont

Now that the `Text` class has been created, let's enhance the `Title` screen to actually display a title. You will do this by adding a `SpriteFont` object to your `Content` project.

First, add a new folder to the `Content` project, and name it `Fonts`. Then add a new `SpriteFont` object to that folder, and name it `screenFont.spritefont`.

`screenFont` will become the generic `SpriteFont` object that every screen in the game can use and has available. The default font size is a little on the small side, especially on the phone, so you will adjust the `screenFont.spriteFont` XML file to have the following `Size` information:

```
<!--
Size is a float value, measured in points. Modify this value to change the size
    of the font.
-->
<Size>40</Size>
```

Now that the `SpriteFont` has been added to the `Content` project, you need to actually create an object in the code to store it once you have loaded it. You want this font to be available to all screens, so you will modify the base `Screen` class.

In the `Screen.cs` class file, add the following class-level variable:

```
protected SpriteFont font;
```

Next, modify the `LoadContent()` method to look like Listing 8-10, paying special attention to the line in bold.

LISTING 8-10: The LoadContent() Method of the Screen Class

```
public void LoadContent()
{
    font = content.Load<SpriteFont>("Fonts/screenFont");
    LoadScreenContent(content);
    SetupInputs();
}
```

With the `SpriteFont` now available in the base `Screen` class, you can finally modify the `Title` screen to display that title you've been hearing so much about.

In the `Title.cs` class file, add the following `using` statement at the top of the file:

```
using DriveAndDodge.Texts;
```

Next, add the following class-level variable:

```
Text titleText;
```

Next, in the `LoadScreenContent()` method, add the bold code shown in Listing 8-11.

LISTING 8-11: The LoadScreenContent() Method of the Title Class

```
protected override void LoadScreenContent(ContentManager content)
{
    background = new Background(content);
    titleText = new Text(font,
                    "Drive & Dodge!",
                    new Vector2(0, (int)(ScreenHeight / 3)),
                    Color.Brown,
                    Color.Beige,
                    Text.Alignment.Horizontal,
                    new Rectangle(0, 0, ScreenWidth, 0));
}
```

As you can see, you are creating a new `Text` object, passing in the font from the `Screen` base class, giving it the text, and doing some positioning.

To display the title (as stored in the `Text` object) on the screen, modify the `DrawScreen()` method to look like Listing 8-12.

LISTING 8-12: The DrawScreen() Method of the Title Class

```
protected override void DrawScreen(SpriteBatch batch,
                                    DisplayOrientation
                                        displayOrientation)
{
    background.Draw(batch);
    titleText.Draw(batch);
}
```

Take a look at this code. The background is drawn, and then the title is drawn.

Remember, order is important, and drawing is always done in layers. If you drew the title before the background, you'd never see the text, because the background would be drawn over it in every frame!

And now you have a title! Run the game and see the progress you've made. If everything went well, it should look like Figure 8-3.

Continuing with the `Title` screen, it would be nice to have a way to tell the user that he or she should press something to play the game, or press something else to exit. Buttons might be a good choice. It's time to add a button class to the game.

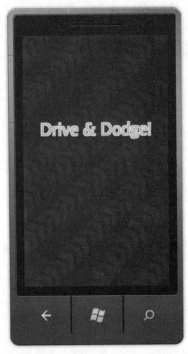

FIGURE 8-3: The title screen with a title

Button.cs

Before adding the class, you will add a button image and button font to the Content project so that they're available and ready for your soon-to-be-made button class.

If you have downloaded the book project files from the website, grab the Button.png image and add it to the Images folder in the DriveAndDodge Content project. If you haven't grabbed them yet, get them at www.wrox.com.

Next, create a new SpriteFont and add it to the Fonts folder in the DriveAndDodge Content project. Name it buttonFont.spritefont so that it's clear what the font is intended to be used for. Change the size of the font to 40, just like before. While you're in there, change the style of the font to Bold.

Next, add the Button class shown in Listing 8-13 to the Sprites folder of your DriveAndDodge project.

LISTING 8-13: Button.cs

```
using Microsoft.Xna.Framework;
using Microsoft.Xna.Framework.Content;
using Microsoft.Xna.Framework.Graphics;
```

```csharp
using DriveAndDodge.Texts;

namespace DriveAndDodge.Sprites
{
    class Button : Sprite
    {
        Text buttonText;
        SpriteFont buttonFont;

        private Rectangle touchArea;
        public Rectangle TouchArea
        {
            get { return touchArea; }
        }

        string displayText;
        public string DisplayText
        {
            get { return displayText; }
        }

        public Button(ContentManager content,
                    string displayText,
                    Vector2 displayPosition,
                    Color color)
              : base(content, "Images/Button")
        {
            Position = displayPosition;
            this.displayText = displayText;
            this.color = color;

            touchArea = new Rectangle((int)displayPosition.X,
                                    (int)displayPosition.Y,
                                    texture.Width,
                                    texture.Height);

            buttonFont = content.Load<SpriteFont>("Fonts/buttonFont");
            buttonText = new Text(buttonFont,
                                displayText,
                                Vector2.Zero,
                                Color.White,
                                Text.Alignment.Both,
                                TouchArea);
        }

        public void ChangePosition(Vector2 adjustment)
        {
            Position += adjustment;
            touchArea = new Rectangle((int)Position.X,
                                    (int)Position.Y,
                                    texture.Width,
                                    texture.Height);
```

continues

LISTING 8-13 *(continued)*

```
            buttonText.Position += adjustment;
        }

        protected override void DrawSprite(SpriteBatch batch)
        {
            buttonText.Draw(batch);
        }
    }
}
```

The `Button` class inherits from `Sprite`, so it gets a lot of the benefits of that class already. The `TouchArea` and `DisplayText` properties give external classes a way of getting the text currently being displayed on the button, and the collision area that's been defined.

The `Button` class constructor passes the `Button` asset name to the base sprite constructor and then defines and creates the `Text` object to be positioned over the top of the button image. The `touchArea` is also defined, matching the size and shape of the button sprite.

The `ChangePosition()` method is used to move the button around on the screen. When the button position is adjusted, the collision area must be recalculated, and the text must be repositioned as well. This feature is useful if you need to create a scrollable list of buttons, or if you want to change your user interface (UI) layout because of a phone orientation change.

Finally, `DrawSprite()` draws the `Text` object to the screen. The drawing of the button image is handled in the base `Sprite` class.

With the creation of the `Button` class, you can now add some buttons to the `Title` screen. It would be nice to be able to play or exit the game, so you will add both of those buttons to the screen.

In the `Title` class, add the following class-level variables:

```
Button startButton;
Button exitButton;
```

Change the `LoadScreenContent()` method to look like Listing 8-14. As usual, the changed lines are in bold.

LISTING 8-14: The LoadScreenContent() Method of the Title Class

```
protected override void LoadScreenContent(ContentManager content)
{
    background = new Background(content);
    titleText = new Text(font,
                        "Drive & Dodge!",
                        new Vector2(0, (int)(ScreenHeight / 3)),
                        Color.BurlyWood,
                        Color.Beige,
                        Text.Alignment.Horizontal,
                        new Rectangle(0, 0, ScreenWidth, 0));

    startButton = new Button(content,
                            "Start Game",
```

```
                            new Vector2(30, 500),
                            Color.BurlyWood);

    exitButton = new Button(content,
                            "Exit",
                            new Vector2(30, 650),
                            Color.BurlyWood);
}
```

Finally, change the `DrawScreen()` method to look like Listing 8-15.

LISTING 8-15: The DrawScreen() Method of the Title Class

```
protected override void DrawScreen(SpriteBatch batch,
                                    DisplayOrientation displayOrientation)
{
    background.Draw(batch);
    titleText.Draw(batch);
    startButton.Draw(batch);
    exitButton.Draw(batch);
}
```

Press F5 to build and run your game and experience the miracle of Start Game and Exit buttons being drawn on the Title screen, as shown in Figure 8-4. This is pretty amazing stuff. You can imagine how much more impressive it will be once your buttons actually do something.

FIGURE 8-4: The title screen for your game, with buttons that don't do anything — yet

The Input Wrapper

The input wrapper classes were covered in Chapter 5, so if you need a refresher (or if you skipped that chapter), you can find more information on the implementation and theory there.

Before you add the classes, you need to add a reference in your Solution Explorer to the `Microsoft.Devices.Sensors` namespace so that the accelerometer code will work.

After you have done that, create a folder called `Inputs` in your `DriveAndDodge` project, and add the following five classes to that folder. These classes will enable you to add all kinds of inputs to your game quickly and easily.

GameInput.cs

The `GameInput` class in Listing 8-16 is the object that other classes will instantiate for adding and checking on inputs. With it, you can quickly define the types of inputs you're watching for, map them to a particular action, and then query whether any of the inputs you've defined have been triggered for that action.

LISTING 8-16: GameInput.cs

```csharp
using System.Collections.Generic;

using Microsoft.Xna.Framework;
using Microsoft.Xna.Framework.Input;
using Microsoft.Xna.Framework.Input.Touch;

namespace DriveAndDodge.Inputs
{
    class GameInput
    {
        Dictionary<string, Input> inputs
            = new Dictionary<string, Input>();

        public GameInput()
        {
        }

        public Input MyInput(string theAction)
        {
            // Add the Action if it doesn't already exist
            if (inputs.ContainsKey(theAction) == false)
            {
                inputs.Add(theAction, new Input());
            }

            return inputs[theAction];
        }

        public void BeginUpdate()
        {
            Input.BeginUpdate();
```

```csharp
    }

    public void EndUpdate()
    {
        Input.EndUpdate();
    }

    public bool IsConnected(PlayerIndex thePlayer)
    {
        // If there never WAS a gamepad connected, then just
        // say that the gamepad is still connected...
        if (Input.GamepadConnectionState[thePlayer] == false)
        {
            return true;
        }

        return Input.IsConnected(thePlayer);
    }

    public bool IsPressed(string theAction,
                          Rectangle theCurrentObjectLocation)
    {
        if (!inputs.ContainsKey(theAction))
        {
            return false;
        }

        return inputs[theAction].IsPressed(PlayerIndex.One,
                                           theCurrentObjectLocation);
    }

    public bool IsPressed(string theAction)
    {
        if (!inputs.ContainsKey(theAction))
        {
            return false;
        }
        return inputs[theAction].IsPressed(PlayerIndex.One);
    }

    public bool IsPressed(string theAction, PlayerIndex thePlayer)
    {
        if (inputs.ContainsKey(theAction) == false)
        {
            return false;
        }

        return inputs[theAction].IsPressed(thePlayer);
    }

    public bool IsPressed(string theAction, PlayerIndex? thePlayer)
    {
        if (thePlayer == null)
        {
```

continues

LISTING 8-16 *(continued)*

```
            PlayerIndex theReturnedControllingPlayer;
            return IsPressed(theAction,
                            thePlayer,
                            out theReturnedControllingPlayer);
        }

        return IsPressed(theAction, (PlayerIndex)thePlayer);
    }

    public bool IsPressed(string theAction,
                          PlayerIndex? thePlayer,
                          out PlayerIndex theControllingPlayer)
    {
        if (!inputs.ContainsKey(theAction))
        {
            theControllingPlayer = PlayerIndex.One;
            return false;
        }

        if (thePlayer == null)
        {
            if (IsPressed(theAction, PlayerIndex.One))
            {
                theControllingPlayer = PlayerIndex.One;
                return true;
            }

            if (IsPressed(theAction, PlayerIndex.Two))
            {
                theControllingPlayer = PlayerIndex.Two;
                return true;
            }

            if (IsPressed(theAction, PlayerIndex.Three))
            {
                theControllingPlayer = PlayerIndex.Three;
                return true;
            }

            if (IsPressed(theAction, PlayerIndex.Four))
            {
                theControllingPlayer = PlayerIndex.Four;
                return true;
            }

            theControllingPlayer = PlayerIndex.One;
            return false;
        }

        theControllingPlayer = (PlayerIndex)thePlayer;
        return IsPressed(theAction, (PlayerIndex)thePlayer);
    }
```

```csharp
        public void AddGamePadInput(string theAction,
                                    Buttons theButton,
                                    bool isReleasedPreviously)
        {
            MyInput(theAction).AddGamepadInput(theButton,
                                                isReleasedPreviously);
        }

        public void AddKeyboardInput(string theAction,
                                     Keys theKey,
                                     bool isReleasedPreviously)
        {
            MyInput(theAction).AddKeyboardInput(theKey,
                                                 isReleasedPreviously);
        }

        public void AddTouchTapInput(string theAction,
                                     Rectangle theTouchArea,
                                     bool isReleasedPreviously)
        {
            MyInput(theAction).AddTouchTapInput(theTouchArea,
                                                 isReleasedPreviously);
        }

        public void AddTouchSlideInput(string theAction,
                                       Input.Direction theDirection,
                                       float slideDistance)
        {
            MyInput(theAction).AddTouchSlideInput(theDirection,
                                                   slideDistance);
        }

        public void AddTouchGestureInput(string theAction,
                                         GestureType theGesture,
                                         Rectangle theRectangle)
        {
            MyInput(theAction).AddTouchGesture(theGesture,
                                                theRectangle);
        }

        public void AddAccelerometerInput(string theAction,
                                          Input.Direction theDirection,
                                          float tiltThreshold)
        {
            MyInput(theAction).AddAccelerometerInput(theDirection,
                                                      tiltThreshold);
        }

        public Vector2 CurrentGesturePosition(string theAction)
        {
            return MyInput(theAction).CurrentGesturePosition();
        }

        public Vector2 CurrentGestureDelta(string theAction)
```

continues

LISTING 8-16 *(continued)*

```
    {
        return MyInput(theAction).CurrentGestureDelta();
    }

    public Vector2 CurrentGesturePosition2(string theAction)
    {
        return MyInput(theAction).CurrentGesturePosition2();
    }

    public Vector2 CurrentGestureDelta2(string theAction)
    {
        return MyInput(theAction).CurrentGestureDelta2();
    }

    public Point CurrentTouchPoint(string theAction)
    {
        Vector2? currentPosition =
                MyInput(theAction).CurrentTouchPosition();
        if (currentPosition == null)
        {
            return new Point(-1, -1);
        }

        return new Point((int)currentPosition.Value.X,
                    (int)currentPosition.Value.Y);
    }

    public Vector2 CurrentTouchPosition(string theAction)
    {
        Vector2? currentTouchPosition =
                MyInput(theAction).CurrentTouchPosition();
        if (currentTouchPosition == null)
        {
            return new Vector2(-1, -1);
        }

        return (Vector2)currentTouchPosition;
    }

    public float CurrentGestureScaleChange(string theAction)
    {
        // Scaling is dependent on the Pinch gesture.
        // If no input has been set up for Pinch then just
        // return 0 indicating no scale change has occurred.
        if (!MyInput(theAction).PinchGestureAvailable)
        {
            return 0;
        }
```

```csharp
            // Get the current and previous locations of
            // the two fingers
            Vector2 currentPositionFingerOne =
                    CurrentGesturePosition(theAction);

            Vector2 previousPositionFingerOne =
                    CurrentGesturePosition(theAction)
                    - CurrentGestureDelta(theAction);

            Vector2 currentPositionFingerTwo =
                    CurrentGesturePosition2(theAction);

            Vector2 previousPositionFingerTwo =
                    CurrentGesturePosition2(theAction)
                    - CurrentGestureDelta2(theAction);

            // Figure out the distance between current &
            // previous locations
            float currentDistance =
                    Vector2.Distance(currentPositionFingerOne,
                                    currentPositionFingerTwo);

            float previousDistance =
                    Vector2.Distance(previousPositionFingerOne,
                                    previousPositionFingerTwo);

            // Calculate the diff between the two & use it to
            // alter the scale
            float scaleChange = (currentDistance - previousDistance)
                                    * .01f;
            return scaleChange;
        }

        public Vector3 CurrentAccelerometerReading(string theAction)
        {
            return MyInput(theAction).CurrentAccelerometerReading;
        }
    }
}
```

You need a few more classes before you can build again, so just keep at it. Next up is the `GestureDefinition` class.

GestureDefinition.cs

The `GestureDefinition` class is a helper class for the `Input` class. It allows you to store information about gestures that have been detected so that they can be retrieved later. It's not quite a wrapper for the `GestureSample` object that is built into XNA 4.0, but it is close. For a refresher on gestures, be sure to check out Chapter 4.

Add the `GestureDefinition` class shown in Listing 8-17 to the `Inputs` folder in your project.

LISTING 8-17: GestureDefinition.cs

```csharp
using System;
using Microsoft.Xna.Framework;
using Microsoft.Xna.Framework.Input.Touch;

namespace DriveAndDodge.Inputs
{
    class GestureDefinition
    {
        public GestureType Type;
        public Rectangle CollisionArea;
        public GestureSample Gesture;
        public Vector2 Delta;
        public Vector2 Delta2;
        public Vector2 Position;
        public Vector2 Position2;

        public GestureDefinition(GestureType theGestureType,
                                 Rectangle theGestureArea)
        {
            Gesture = new GestureSample(theGestureType,
                                        new TimeSpan(0),
                                        Vector2.Zero,
                                        Vector2.Zero,
                                        Vector2.Zero,
                                        Vector2.Zero);
            Type = theGestureType;
            CollisionArea = theGestureArea;
        }

        public GestureDefinition(GestureSample theGestureSample)
        {
            Gesture = theGestureSample;
            Type = theGestureSample.GestureType;
            CollisionArea = new Rectangle((int)theGestureSample.Position.X,
                                          (int)theGestureSample.Position.Y,
                                          5,
                                          5);

            Delta = theGestureSample.Delta;
            Delta2 = theGestureSample.Delta2;
            Position = theGestureSample.Position;
            Position2 = theGestureSample.Position2;
        }
    }
}
```

You should have a fistful of errors in Visual Studio at this point. (For future reference, a fistful is 10.) This next class will clear those up and get everything back on track.

Input.cs

The `Input` class is the meat of the input wrapper classes. It does all the heavy lifting. The `Input` class is what queries each type of input and then checks to see if inputs that have been triggered match any that the game cares about. Add the class shown in Listing 8-18 to your `Inputs` folder.

LISTING 8-18: Input.cs

```csharp
using System;
using System.Collections.Generic;

using Microsoft.Xna.Framework.Input;
using Microsoft.Xna.Framework.Input.Touch;
using Microsoft.Xna.Framework;
using Microsoft.Devices.Sensors;

namespace DriveAndDodge.Inputs
{
    class Input
    {
        Dictionary<Keys, bool> keyboardDefinedInputs
            = new Dictionary<Keys, bool>();
        Dictionary<Buttons, bool> gamepadDefinedInputs
            = new Dictionary<Buttons, bool>();
        Dictionary<Rectangle, bool> touchTapDefinedInputs
            = new Dictionary<Rectangle, bool>();
        Dictionary<Direction, float> touchSlideDefinedInputs
            = new Dictionary<Direction, float>();
        Dictionary<int, GestureDefinition> gestureDefinedInputs
            = new Dictionary<int, GestureDefinition>();
        Dictionary<Direction, float> accelerometerDefinedInputs
            = new Dictionary<Direction, float>();

        static public Dictionary<PlayerIndex, GamePadState>
            CurrentGamePadState = new
            Dictionary<PlayerIndex, GamePadState>();
        static public Dictionary<PlayerIndex, GamePadState>
            PreviousGamePadState = new Dictionary<PlayerIndex,
            GamePadState>();
        static public KeyboardState CurrentKeyboardState;
        static public KeyboardState PreviousKeyboardState;
        static public TouchCollection CurrentTouchLocationState;
        static public TouchCollection PreviousTouchLocationState;
        static public Dictionary<PlayerIndex, bool>
            GamepadConnectionState = new Dictionary<PlayerIndex,
                                                        bool>();

        static private List<GestureDefinition>
                    detectedGestures = new List<GestureDefinition>();
        static private Accelerometer accelerometerSensor;
        static private Vector3 currentAccelerometerReading;
```

continues

LISTING 8-18 *(continued)*

```csharp
    public enum Direction
    {
        Up,
        Down,
        Left,
        Right
    }

    public Input()
    {
        if (CurrentGamePadState.Count == 0)
        {
            CurrentGamePadState.Add(PlayerIndex.One,
                              GamePad.GetState(PlayerIndex.One));
            CurrentGamePadState.Add(PlayerIndex.Two,
                              GamePad.GetState(PlayerIndex.Two));
            CurrentGamePadState.Add(PlayerIndex.Three,
                              GamePad.GetState(PlayerIndex.Three));
            CurrentGamePadState.Add(PlayerIndex.Four,
                              GamePad.GetState(PlayerIndex.Four));

            PreviousGamePadState.Add(PlayerIndex.One,
                                GamePad.GetState(PlayerIndex.One));
            PreviousGamePadState.Add(PlayerIndex.Two,
                                GamePad.GetState(PlayerIndex.Two));
            PreviousGamePadState.Add(PlayerIndex.Three,
                                GamePad.GetState(PlayerIndex.Three));
            PreviousGamePadState.Add(PlayerIndex.Four,
                                GamePad.GetState(PlayerIndex.Four));

            GamepadConnectionState.Add(PlayerIndex.One,
                    CurrentGamePadState[PlayerIndex.One].IsConnected);
            GamepadConnectionState.Add(PlayerIndex.Two,
                    CurrentGamePadState[PlayerIndex.Two].IsConnected);
            GamepadConnectionState.Add(PlayerIndex.Three,
                    CurrentGamePadState[PlayerIndex.Three].IsConnected);
            GamepadConnectionState.Add(PlayerIndex.Four,
                    CurrentGamePadState[PlayerIndex.Four].IsConnected);
        }

        if (accelerometerSensor == null)
        {
            accelerometerSensor = new Accelerometer();
            accelerometerSensor.ReadingChanged += new
                    EventHandler<AccelerometerReadingEventArgs>
                        (AccelerometerReadingChanged);
        }
    }

    static public void BeginUpdate()
    {
        CurrentGamePadState[PlayerIndex.One] =
```

```csharp
                        GamePad.GetState(PlayerIndex.One);
        CurrentGamePadState[PlayerIndex.Two] =
                        GamePad.GetState(PlayerIndex.Two);
        CurrentGamePadState[PlayerIndex.Three] =
                        GamePad.GetState(PlayerIndex.Three);
        CurrentGamePadState[PlayerIndex.Four] =
                        GamePad.GetState(PlayerIndex.Four);

        CurrentKeyboardState = Keyboard.GetState(PlayerIndex.One);
        CurrentTouchLocationState = TouchPanel.GetState();

        detectedGestures.Clear();
        if (TouchPanel.EnabledGestures != GestureType.None)
        {
            while (TouchPanel.IsGestureAvailable)
            {
                GestureSample gesture = TouchPanel.ReadGesture();
                detectedGestures.Add(new GestureDefinition(gesture));
            }
        }
    }

    static public void EndUpdate()
    {
        PreviousGamePadState[PlayerIndex.One] =
                        CurrentGamePadState[PlayerIndex.One];
        PreviousGamePadState[PlayerIndex.Two] =
                        CurrentGamePadState[PlayerIndex.Two];
        PreviousGamePadState[PlayerIndex.Three] =
                        CurrentGamePadState[PlayerIndex.Three];
        PreviousGamePadState[PlayerIndex.Four] =
                        CurrentGamePadState[PlayerIndex.Four];

        PreviousKeyboardState = CurrentKeyboardState;
        PreviousTouchLocationState = CurrentTouchLocationState;
    }

    private void AccelerometerReadingChanged(object sender,
                                AccelerometerReadingEventArgs e)
    {
        currentAccelerometerReading.X = (float)e.X;
        currentAccelerometerReading.Y = (float)e.Y;
        currentAccelerometerReading.Z = (float)e.Z;
    }

    public void AddKeyboardInput(Keys theKey, bool isReleasedPreviously)
    {
        if (keyboardDefinedInputs.ContainsKey(theKey))
        {
            keyboardDefinedInputs[theKey] = isReleasedPreviously;
            return;
        }
        keyboardDefinedInputs.Add(theKey, isReleasedPreviously);
    }
```

continues

LISTING 8-18 *(continued)*

```
        public void AddGamepadInput(Buttons theButton,
                                    bool isReleasedPreviously)
        {
            if (gamepadDefinedInputs.ContainsKey(theButton))
            {
                gamepadDefinedInputs[theButton] = isReleasedPreviously;
                return;
            }
            gamepadDefinedInputs.Add(theButton, isReleasedPreviously);
        }

        public void AddTouchTapInput(Rectangle theTouchArea,
                                     bool isReleasedPreviously)
        {
            if (touchTapDefinedInputs.ContainsKey(theTouchArea))
            {
                touchTapDefinedInputs[theTouchArea] = isReleasedPreviously;
                return;
            }
            touchTapDefinedInputs.Add(theTouchArea, isReleasedPreviously);
        }

        public void AddTouchSlideInput(Direction theDirection,
                                       float slideDistance)
        {
            if (touchSlideDefinedInputs.ContainsKey(theDirection))
            {
                touchSlideDefinedInputs[theDirection] = slideDistance;
                return;
            }
            touchSlideDefinedInputs.Add(theDirection, slideDistance);
        }

        public bool PinchGestureAvailable = false;
        public void AddTouchGesture(GestureType theGesture,
                                    Rectangle theTouchArea)
        {
            TouchPanel.EnabledGestures = theGesture |
                                        TouchPanel.EnabledGestures;
            gestureDefinedInputs.Add(gestureDefinedInputs.Count,
                                     new GestureDefinition(theGesture,
                                                           theTouchArea));
            if (theGesture == GestureType.Pinch)
            {
                PinchGestureAvailable = true;
            }
        }

        static private bool isAccelerometerStarted = false;
        public void AddAccelerometerInput(Direction direction,
                                          float tiltThreshold)
        {
```

```csharp
        if (!isAccelerometerStarted)
        {
            try
            {
                accelerometerSensor.Start();
                isAccelerometerStarted = true;
            }
            catch (AccelerometerFailedException e)
            {
                isAccelerometerStarted = false;
            }
        }

        accelerometerDefinedInputs.Add(direction, tiltThreshold);
    }

    public void RemoveAccelerometerInputs()
    {
        if (isAccelerometerStarted)
        {
            try
            {
                accelerometerSensor.Stop();
                isAccelerometerStarted = false;
            }
            catch (AccelerometerFailedException e)
            {
                // The sensor couldn't be stopped...
            }
        }

        accelerometerDefinedInputs.Clear();
    }

    static public bool IsConnected(PlayerIndex thePlayerIndex)
    {
        return CurrentGamePadState[thePlayerIndex].IsConnected;
    }

    public bool IsPressed(PlayerIndex thePlayerIndex)
    {
        return IsPressed(thePlayerIndex, null);
    }

    public bool IsPressed(PlayerIndex thePlayerIndex,
                          Rectangle? theCurrentObjectLocation)
    {
        if (IsKeyboardInputPressed())
        {
            return true;
        }

        if (IsGamepadInputPressed(thePlayerIndex))
        {
```

continues

LISTING 8-18 *(continued)*

```
            return true;
        }

        if (IsTouchTapInputPressed())
        {
            return true;
        }

        if (IsTouchSlideInputPressed())
        {
            return true;
        }

        if (IsGestureInputPressed(theCurrentObjectLocation))
        {
            return true;
        }

        if (IsAccelerometerInputPressed())
        {
            return true;
        }

        return false;
    }

    private bool IsKeyboardInputPressed()
    {
        foreach (Keys aKey in keyboardDefinedInputs.Keys)
        {
            if (keyboardDefinedInputs[aKey]
                && CurrentKeyboardState.IsKeyDown(aKey)
                && !PreviousKeyboardState.IsKeyDown(aKey))
            {
                return true;
            }
            else if (!keyboardDefinedInputs[aKey]
                && CurrentKeyboardState.IsKeyDown(aKey))
            {
                return true;
            }
        }

        return false;
    }

    private bool IsGamepadInputPressed(PlayerIndex thePlayerIndex)
    {
        foreach (Buttons aButton in gamepadDefinedInputs.Keys)
        {
            if (gamepadDefinedInputs[aButton]
                && CurrentGamePadState[thePlayerIndex].IsButtonDown(aButton)
```

```
                && !PreviousGamePadState[thePlayerIndex]
                                    .IsButtonDown(aButton))
            {
                return true;
            }
            else if (!gamepadDefinedInputs[aButton]
                && CurrentGamePadState[thePlayerIndex].IsButtonDown(aButton))
            {
                return true;
            }
        }

        return false;
    }

    private bool IsTouchTapInputPressed()
    {
        foreach (Rectangle touchArea in touchTapDefinedInputs.Keys)
        {
            if (touchTapDefinedInputs[touchArea]
            && touchArea.Intersects(CurrentTouchRectangle)
            && PreviousTouchPosition() == null)
            {
                return true;
            }
            else if (!touchTapDefinedInputs[touchArea]
            && touchArea.Intersects(CurrentTouchRectangle))
            {
                return true;
            }
        }

        return false;
    }

    private bool IsTouchSlideInputPressed()
    {
        foreach (Direction slideDirection in
                            touchSlideDefinedInputs.Keys)
        {
            if (CurrentTouchPosition() != null
            && PreviousTouchPosition() != null)
            {
                switch (slideDirection)
                {
                    case Direction.Up:
                        {
                            if (CurrentTouchPosition().Value.Y
                              + touchSlideDefinedInputs[slideDirection]
                              < PreviousTouchPosition().Value.Y)
                            {
                                return true;
                            }
                            break;
```

continues

LISTING 8-18 *(continued)*

```
                        }
                    case Direction.Down:
                        {
                            if (CurrentTouchPosition().Value.Y
                              - touchSlideDefinedInputs[slideDirection]
                              > PreviousTouchPosition().Value.Y)
                            {
                                return true;
                            }
                            break;
                        }
                    case Direction.Left:
                        {
                            if (CurrentTouchPosition().Value.X
                              + touchSlideDefinedInputs[slideDirection]
                              < PreviousTouchPosition().Value.X)
                            {
                                return true;
                            }
                            break;
                        }
                    case Direction.Right:
                        {
                            if (CurrentTouchPosition().Value.X
                              - touchSlideDefinedInputs[slideDirection]
                              > PreviousTouchPosition().Value.X)
                            {
                                return true;
                            }
                            break;
                        }
                }
            }
        }

        return false;
    }

    private bool IsGestureInputPressed(Rectangle?
                                      theNewDetectionLocation)
    {
        // Clear out the current gesture definition each time through so
        // the information stored there is always the most recent
        currentGestureDefinition = null;

        // If no gestures have been detected immediately just exit
        if (detectedGestures.Count == 0)
        {
            return false;
        }
```

```csharp
// Check to see if any of the Gestures have been fired
foreach (GestureDefinition userDefinedGesture
                    in gestureDefinedInputs.Values)
{
    foreach (GestureDefinition detectedGesture
                        in detectedGestures)
    {
        if (detectedGesture.Type == userDefinedGesture.Type)
        {
            // If a Rectangle area to check against has been
            // passed in, use that one. Otherwise use
            // the one the Input was originally set up with
            Rectangle areaToCheck =
                        userDefinedGesture.CollisionArea;
            if (theNewDetectionLocation != null)
            {
                areaToCheck = (Rectangle)theNewDetectionLocation;
            }

            // If the gesture detected was made in the area where
            // users were interested in Input (they intersect),
            // then a gesture input is considered detected.
            if (detectedGesture.CollisionArea
                            .Intersects(areaToCheck))
            {
                if (currentGestureDefinition == null)
                {
                    currentGestureDefinition = new
                            GestureDefinition(detectedGesture
                                            .Gesture);
                }
                else
                {
                    // Many gestures like FreeDrag and Flick are
                    // registered many, many times in a single
                    // Update frame. Since you only store one
                    // variable for the currentGestureInformation
                    // you add on any additional gesture values
                    // so you have a composite of all the gesture
                    // information in currentGesture
                    currentGestureDefinition.Delta
                                += detectedGesture.Delta;
                    currentGestureDefinition.Delta2
                                += detectedGesture.Delta2;
                    currentGestureDefinition.Position
                                += detectedGesture.Position;
                    currentGestureDefinition.Position2
                                += detectedGesture.Position2;
                }
            }
        }
    }
}
```

continues

LISTING 8-18 *(continued)*

```
        if (currentGestureDefinition != null)
        {
            return true;
        }

        return false;
    }

    private bool IsAccelerometerInputPressed()
    {
        foreach (KeyValuePair<Direction, float>
                            input in accelerometerDefinedInputs)
        {
            switch (input.Key)
            {
                case Direction.Up:
                    {
                        if (Math.Abs(currentAccelerometerReading.Y)
                         > input.Value && currentAccelerometerReading.Y
                         < 0)
                        {
                            return true;
                        }
                        break;
                    }

                case Direction.Down:
                    {
                        if (Math.Abs(currentAccelerometerReading.Y)
                         > input.Value && currentAccelerometerReading.Y
                         > 0)
                        {
                            return true;
                        }
                        break;
                    }

                case Direction.Left:
                    {
                        if (Math.Abs(currentAccelerometerReading.X)
                         > input.Value && currentAccelerometerReading.X
                         < 0)
                        {
                            return true;
                        }
                        break;
                    }

                case Direction.Right:
                    {
                        if (Math.Abs(currentAccelerometerReading.X)
                         > input.Value && currentAccelerometerReading.X
```

```
                        > 0)
                    {
                        return true;
                    }
                    break;
            }
        }
    }

    return false;
}

// These properties return the Position and Delta information about
// the current gesture that was detected. If no gesture was detected,
// then the values returned are set to safe default values.
GestureDefinition currentGestureDefinition;
public Vector2 CurrentGesturePosition()
{
    if (currentGestureDefinition == null)
    {
        return Vector2.Zero;
    }
    return currentGestureDefinition.Position;
}

public Vector2 CurrentGesturePosition2()
{
    if (currentGestureDefinition == null)
    {
        return Vector2.Zero;
    }
    return currentGestureDefinition.Position2;
}

public Vector2 CurrentGestureDelta()
{
    if (currentGestureDefinition == null)
    {
        return Vector2.Zero;
    }
    return currentGestureDefinition.Delta;
}

public Vector2 CurrentGestureDelta2()
{
    if (currentGestureDefinition == null)
    {
        return Vector2.Zero;
    }
    return currentGestureDefinition.Delta2;
}

// Get the touch point for the current location. This doesn't use
// any of the Gesture information, but the actual touch point on
```

continues

LISTING 8-18 *(continued)*

```
        // the screen
        public Vector2? CurrentTouchPosition()
        {
            foreach (TouchLocation location in CurrentTouchLocationState)
            {
                switch (location.State)
                {
                    case TouchLocationState.Pressed:
                        return location.Position;

                    case TouchLocationState.Moved:
                        return location.Position;
                }
            }

            return null;
        }

        private Vector2? PreviousTouchPosition()
        {
            foreach (TouchLocation location in PreviousTouchLocationState)
            {
                switch (location.State)
                {
                    case TouchLocationState.Pressed:
                        return location.Position;

                    case TouchLocationState.Moved:
                        return location.Position;
                }
            }

            return null;
        }

        private Rectangle CurrentTouchRectangle
        {
            get
            {
                Vector2? touchPosition = CurrentTouchPosition();
                if (touchPosition == null)
                {
                    return Rectangle.Empty;
                }
                return new Rectangle((int)touchPosition.Value.X - 5,
                                     (int)touchPosition.Value.Y - 5,
                                     10,
                                     10);
            }
        }

        public Vector3 CurrentAccelerometerReading
```

```
            {
                get
                {
                    return currentAccelerometerReading;
                }
            }
        }
    }
```

Next up is the `TouchIndicator` class. Before you can start creating the `TouchIndicator` class, you must add a couple more image files. Download the `Circle` and `Crosshair` images from this book's website (www.wrox.com), and add them to the `Images` folder in the `DriveAndDodge Content` project.

TouchIndicator.cs

The `TouchIndicator` class is used to give visual feedback to the user for where he or she has touched. With a touch screen, this becomes quite important, because it's easy to lose your place or wonder if the screen has actually registered your touch.

Add the `TouchIndicator` class shown in Listing 8-19 to the `Inputs` folder of your `DriveAndDodge` project.

LISTING 8-19: TouchIndicator.cs

```
using System.Collections.Generic;

using Microsoft.Xna.Framework;
using Microsoft.Xna.Framework.Graphics;
using Microsoft.Xna.Framework.Input.Touch;
using Microsoft.Xna.Framework.Content;

namespace DriveAndDodge.Inputs
{
    class TouchIndicator
    {
        int alphaValue = 255;
        public int TouchID;

        Texture2D touchCircleIndicatorTexture;
        Texture2D touchCrossHairIndicatorTexture;
        List<Vector2> touchPositions = new List<Vector2>();

        public TouchIndicator(int touchID, ContentManager content)
        {
            TouchID = touchID;

            touchCircleIndicatorTexture =
                        content.Load<Texture2D>("Images/Circle");
            touchCrossHairIndicatorTexture =
                        content.Load<Texture2D>("Images/Crosshair");
        }
```

continues

LISTING 8-19 *(continued)*

```
        public void Update(GameTime gameTime,
                           TouchCollection touchLocationState)
        {
            Vector2? currentPosition = TouchPosition(touchLocationState);
            if (currentPosition == null)
            {
                if (touchPositions.Count > 0)
                {
                    alphaValue -= 20;
                    if (alphaValue <= 0)
                    {
                        touchPositions.Clear();
                        alphaValue = 255;
                    }
                }
            }
            else
            {
                if (alphaValue != 255)
                {
                    touchPositions.Clear();
                    alphaValue = 255;
                }

                touchPositions.Add((Vector2)currentPosition);
            }
        }

        private Vector2? TouchPosition(TouchCollection touchLocationState)
        {
            TouchLocation touchLocation;
            if (touchLocationState.FindById(TouchID, out touchLocation))
            {
                return touchLocation.Position;
            }

            return null;
        }

        public void Draw(SpriteBatch batch)
        {
            if (touchPositions.Count != 0)
            {
                Vector2 previousPosition = touchPositions[0];
                Vector2 offsetForCenteringTouchPosition
                                              = new Vector2(-25, 0);
                foreach (Vector2 aPosition in touchPositions)
                {
                    DrawLine(batch,
                             touchCircleIndicatorTexture,
                             touchCrossHairIndicatorTexture,
                             previousPosition
```

```
                                + offsetForCenteringTouchPosition,
                                aPosition + offsetForCenteringTouchPosition,
                                new Color(0, 0, 255, alphaValue));
                    previousPosition = aPosition;
                }
            }
        }

        void DrawLine(SpriteBatch batch,
                      Texture2D lineTexture,
                      Texture2D touchTexture,
                      Vector2 startingPoint,
                      Vector2 endingPoint,
                      Color lineColor)
        {
            batch.Draw(touchTexture, startingPoint, lineColor);

            Vector2 difference = startingPoint - endingPoint;
            float lineLength = difference.Length() / 8;
            for (int i = 0; i < lineLength; i++)
            {
                batch.Draw(lineTexture, startingPoint, lineColor);
                startingPoint.X -= difference.X / lineLength;
                startingPoint.Y -= difference.Y / lineLength;
            }

            batch.Draw(touchTexture, endingPoint, lineColor);
        }
    }
}
```

TouchIndicatorCollection.cs

The `TouchIndicatorCollection` is a helper class for `TouchIndicator`. `TouchIndicatorCollection` allows `TouchIndicator` to store all the places that a touch has occurred so that lines can be shown for where inputs have been dragged on the touch surface.

In the `Inputs` folder, add the `TouchIndicatorCollection` class, as shown in Listing 8-20.

LISTING 8-20: TouchIndicatorCollection.cs

```
using System.Collections.Generic;

using Microsoft.Xna.Framework;
using Microsoft.Xna.Framework.Content;
using Microsoft.Xna.Framework.Input.Touch;
using Microsoft.Xna.Framework.Graphics;

namespace DriveAndDodge.Inputs
{
    class TouchIndicatorCollection
    {
```

continues

LISTING 8-20 *(continued)*

```
            List<TouchIndicator> touchPositions = new List<TouchIndicator>();

            public void Update(GameTime gameTime, ContentManager content)
            {
                TouchCollection currentTouchLocationState
                                    = TouchPanel.GetState();
                foreach (TouchLocation location in currentTouchLocationState)
                {
                    bool isTouchIDAlreadyStored = false;
                    foreach (TouchIndicator indicator in touchPositions)
                    {
                        if (location.Id == indicator.TouchID)
                        {
                            isTouchIDAlreadyStored = true;
                            break;
                        }
                    }

                    if (!isTouchIDAlreadyStored)
                    {
                        TouchIndicator indicator
                                = new TouchIndicator(location.Id, content);
                        touchPositions.Add(indicator);
                    }
                }

                foreach (TouchIndicator indicator in touchPositions)
                {
                    indicator.Update(gameTime, currentTouchLocationState);
                }
            }
            public void Draw(SpriteBatch spriteBatch)
            {
                foreach (TouchIndicator indicator in touchPositions)
                {
                    indicator.Draw(spriteBatch);
                }
            }
        }
    }
```

With the `Input` classes added to the `DriveAndDodge` project, you need to tie them into your screens so that they can be utilized. To begin, add the following `using` statement to the top of the `Screen.cs` file:

```
using DriveAndDodge.Inputs;
```

Add the following class-level variables to the `Screen.cs` class:

```
protected GameInput input = new GameInput();
public bool IsTouchIndicatorEnabled = false;
private TouchIndicatorCollection touchIndicator;
```

Next, you must initialize your `touchIndicator` object, so add the following line to the end of your `Screen` constructor:

```
touchIndicator = new TouchIndicatorCollection();
```

You must manage the `Input` class by telling it when an `Update` began and ended. This allows it to collect the current state of inputs, as well as store the previous states of those inputs.

Modify the `Update()` method in the `Screen` class to look like Listing 8-21. Pay special attention to the code in bold, both before and after the call to the `UpdateScreen()` method.

LISTING 8-21: The Updated Update() Method of the Screen Class

```
public void Update(GameTime gameTime)
{
    input.BeginUpdate();

    if (IsTouchIndicatorEnabled)
    {
        touchIndicator.Update(gameTime, content);
    }

    UpdateScreen(gameTime,
                 game.GraphicsDevice
                     .PresentationParameters.DisplayOrientation);

    input.EndUpdate();
}
```

Finally, you must draw any touches to the screen when appropriate. Modify the `Draw()` method in the `Screen` class to look like Listing 8-22. Be sure to focus on the lines in bold.

LISTING 8-22: The Updated Draw() Method of the Screen Class

```
public void Draw()
{
    batch.Begin();
    DrawScreen(batch,
               game.GraphicsDevice
                   .PresentationParameters.DisplayOrientation);

    if (IsTouchIndicatorEnabled)
    {
        touchIndicator.Draw(batch);
    }

    batch.End();
}
```

The input wrapper classes are now tied into the base `Screen` class. You may need to tie them into other classes later, but that's good for now.

It's time to continue building this game!

Adding Sounds and Music

At this point you're probably getting a little tired of adding all this basic game functionality and very little game. Have no fear. You're almost done laying the foundation of your game.

Sounds and music will be the last of the base functionality you will add for this game. After these last classes have been added, you will finally start piecing together the actual game.

Having some background music in a game is a fairly common thing. To do that, you must add some songs to your `Content` project. Add a new folder called `Music` to the `DriveAndDodge Content` project. Then either download `racesong.wav` from this book's website (www.wrox.com) or copy it from the project files, and add it to the `Music` folder.

Ensure that the Content Processor property for the song you add is set to "Song" and not "Sound Effect" after it's been added.

Music.cs

Create a folder called `Sounds` in the `DriveAndDodge` project, and add the class shown in Listing 8-23 to that folder.

LISTING 8-23: Music.cs

```csharp
using System.Collections.Generic;

using Microsoft.Xna.Framework;
using Microsoft.Xna.Framework.Audio;
using Microsoft.Xna.Framework.Content;
using Microsoft.Xna.Framework.Media;

namespace DriveAndDodge.Sounds
{
    class Music
    {
        ContentManager content;
        Dictionary<string, Song> backgroundMusic
                            = new Dictionary<string, Song>();

        public Music(ContentManager contentManager)
        {
            content = contentManager;
        }

        public void PlayBackgroundMusic(string song)
        {
            MediaPlayer.Stop();
            if (!backgroundMusic.ContainsKey(song))
            {
                backgroundMusic.Add(song, content.Load<Song>(song));
            }

            MediaPlayer.IsRepeating = true;
```

```
                MediaPlayer.Play(backgroundMusic[song]);
            }
        }
    }
```

The `Music` class is pretty simple. The constructor stores a reference to a `ContentManager` object that it will use to load any `Song`s you need to play.

The `PlayBackgroundMusic()` method takes in a song's asset name and then stops any currently playing music. It either loads and adds a new song to an internal dictionary of songs or just replays a song it previously had loaded.

SoundEffects.cs

Create a new folder called `SoundEffects` in the `DriveAndDodge Content` project. Then grab the sample sound effect `Select.wav` from the files on this book's website (www.wrox.com) and add it to the `SoundEffects` folder.

Now, add the `SoundEffects` class shown in Listing 8-24 to the `Sounds` folder in the `DriveAndDodge` project.

LISTING 8-24: SoundEffects.cs

```csharp
using System.Collections.Generic;

using Microsoft.Xna.Framework;
using Microsoft.Xna.Framework.Content;
using Microsoft.Xna.Framework.Audio;

namespace DriveAndDodge.Sounds
{
    class SoundEffects
    {
        ContentManager content;
        Dictionary<string, SoundEffect> sounds
            = new Dictionary<string, SoundEffect>();

        public SoundEffects(ContentManager contentManager)
        {
            content = contentManager;
        }

        public void PlaySound(string sound)
        {
            if (!sounds.ContainsKey(sound))
            {
                sounds.Add(sound, content.Load<SoundEffect>(sound));
            }
            sounds[sound].Play();
        }
    }
}
```

`SoundEffects` helps make it easy to play sounds in your game. The constructor takes a reference to a `ContentManager` object. Then the `PlaySound()` method loads (if the sound hasn't been loaded already) and plays the sounds.

With the `Music` and `SoundEffects` classes created, you must now tie them into the base `Screen` class in the same way as the `Input` class.

Start by adding the following `using` statement to the top of the `Screen.cs` class file:

```
using DriveAndDodge.Sounds;
```

Next, add the following class-level variables for the `Music` and `SoundEffects` objects that the `Screen` class will use:

```
protected static Music music;
protected static SoundEffects soundEffects;
```

Now, you must actually load and create these objects. Since they're static and need to be created only once for every instance of the `Screen` class, you should ensure that you create them only once.

Modify the `Screen()` class constructor to include the bold lines shown in Listing 8-25.

LISTING 8-25: The Screen() Constructor of the Screen Class

```
public Screen(Game game, SpriteBatch batch, ChangeScreen changeScreen)
{
    Screen.game = game;
    Screen.content = game.Content;
    Screen.batch = batch;

    changeScreenDelegate = changeScreen;

    touchIndicator = new TouchIndicatorCollection();

    if (music == null)
    {
        music = new Music(content);
    }

    if (soundEffects == null)
    {
        soundEffects = new SoundEffects(content);
    }
}
```

With this code, every screen that inherits from your base `Screen` class will have easy access to playing music and sound effects.

By now, your `Title` screen is looking pretty good. It needs only a few more things for you to finish it. You are displaying the background, title, and buttons but are not responding to input or playing any music or sound effects.

To finish the `Title` screen, start by adding the following `using` statement to the top of the `Title.cs` class file:

```
using Microsoft.Xna.Framework.Input.Touch;
```

Next, add the following string constants at the class level. These will be used to query the inputs.

```
const string ActionStart = "Start";
const string ActionExit = "Exit";
```

Using the handy `Input` wrapper classes you added earlier, you can now set up the inputs in the `SetupInputs()` method. Modify it to look like Listing 8-26.

LISTING 8-26: The SetupInputs() Method of the Title Class

```
protected override void SetupInputs()
{
    input.AddTouchGestureInput(ActionStart,
                               GestureType.Tap,
                               startButton.CollisionRectangle);
    input.AddTouchGestureInput(ActionExit,
                               GestureType.Tap,
                               exitButton.CollisionRectangle);
}
```

A little music would be nice, so you need to set it up to start playing every time the `Title` screen is activated. To make that happen, add the following line to the `Activate()` method:

```
music.PlayBackgroundMusic("Music/RaceSong");
```

Now that you have inputs hooked up for the game, you can check to see if they were detected in the `UpdateScreen()` method and react accordingly. So, modify the `UpdateScreen()` method to look like what is shown in Listing 8-27.

LISTING 8-27: The UpdateScreen() Method of the Title Class

```
protected override void UpdateScreen(GameTime gameTime,
                                    DisplayOrientation displayOrientation)
{
    if (input.IsPressed(ActionStart))
    {
        soundEffects.PlaySound("SoundEffects/Select");
        changeScreenDelegate(ScreenState.MainGame);
    }
    else if (input.IsPressed(ActionExit))
    {
        soundEffects.PlaySound("SoundEffects/Select");
        changeScreenDelegate(ScreenState.Exit);
    }
}
```

At this point, you should have two compile errors, because you haven't defined any enumeration value for `MainGame` and `Exit` in the `ScreenState` enumeration. So, do that now.

Switch over to your `ScreenStateSwitchboard` class and modify your `ScreenState` enumeration to look like Listing 8-28.

LISTING 8-28: The ScreenState Enumeration of the ScreenStateSwitchboard Class

```
public enum ScreenState
{
    Title,
    MainGame,
    GameOver,
    InGameMenu,
    PreviousScreen,
    Exit
}
```

You only needed to add `MainGame` and `Exit` to fix the compile errors, but since you were in there, the authors figured it was a good idea to get you ready for the other screens and functionality soon to follow.

The authors would like to thank Mike Hodnick for donating the cool background music used in Drive & Dodge. You can contact Mike about music for your game at www.hodnick.com.

With the compile errors fixed and your `Title` screen coded, take your game for a spin (by pressing F5 to build and run) and see how it behaves. Some awesome background music should be playing and the buttons should now respond to your touch input. When you tap the Start button, you should hear a brief sound effect as well.

Now you have a working `Title` screen and a metric crapload of base classes coded and ready for use. You're finally ready to start really digging into making this game happen.

A "metric crapload" is a term used by highly professional programmers to indicate a very large quantity. All the great programmers use this terminology. Give it a try in your next conversation with your boss.

More Screens

The next step is to add more screens. The game needs a `Title` screen (which you've already added), a main game screen, an in-game menu screen, and a game-over screen. Let's add them in one blast to the `Screens` folder in the `DriveAndDodge` game project.

MainGame.cs

Don't worry too much about implementation details at this point. You're just stubbing out this screen and the others right now. You'll come back to this one later to add the fun stuff. Remember to put the code shown in Listing 8-29 in the `Screens` folder.

LISTING 8-29: MainGame.cs

```csharp
using Microsoft.Xna.Framework;
using Microsoft.Xna.Framework.Content;
using Microsoft.Xna.Framework.Graphics;

namespace DriveAndDodge.Screens
{
    class MainGame : Screen
    {
        public MainGame(Game game,
                        SpriteBatch batch,
                        ChangeScreen changeScreen)
            : base(game, batch, changeScreen)
        {
        }

        protected override void SetupInputs()
        {
        }

        protected override void LoadScreenContent(ContentManager content)
        {
        }

        public override void Activate()
        {
        }

        protected override void UpdateScreen(GameTime gameTime,
                                              DisplayOrientation
                                                  displayOrientation)
        {
        }

        protected override void DrawScreen(SpriteBatch batch,
                                            DisplayOrientation
                                                displayOrientation)
        {
        }
    }
}
```

InGameMenu.cs

The in-game menu can be displayed to give players of your game some choices. Sounds pretty generic, right? You'll get back to it in more detail later, but for now, you are just stubbing out the class. Add the class shown in Listing 8-30 to your `Screens` folder.

LISTING 8-30: InGameMenu.cs

```csharp
using Microsoft.Xna.Framework.Content;
using Microsoft.Xna.Framework.Graphics;
using Microsoft.Xna.Framework;

namespace DriveAndDodge.Screens
{
    class InGameMenu : Screen
    {
        public InGameMenu(Game game,
                         SpriteBatch batch,
                         ChangeScreen changeScreen)
            : base(game, batch, changeScreen)
        {
        }

        protected override void SetupInputs()
        {
        }

        protected override void LoadScreenContent(ContentManager content)
        {
        }

        public override void Activate()
        {
        }

        protected override void UpdateScreen(GameTime gameTime,
                                            DisplayOrientation
                                                displayOrientation)
        {
        }

        protected override void DrawScreen(SpriteBatch batch,
                                           DisplayOrientation
                                               displayOrientation)
        {
        }
    }
}
```

GameOver.cs

The `GameOver` screen is displayed when — well, you can probably figure it out. Listing 8-31 shows the code for this screen. Stub it out, like the two before it, and then you'll be ready to get to the good stuff.

LISTING 8-31: GameOver.cs

```csharp
using Microsoft.Xna.Framework.Content;
using Microsoft.Xna.Framework.Graphics;
```

```csharp
using Microsoft.Xna.Framework;

namespace DriveAndDodge.Screens
{
    class GameOver : Screen
    {
        public GameOver(Game game,
                        SpriteBatch batch,
                        ChangeScreen changeScreen)
            : base(game, batch, changeScreen)
        {
        }

        protected override void SetupInputs()
        {
        }

        protected override void LoadScreenContent(ContentManager content)
        {
        }

        public override void Activate()
        {
        }

        protected override void UpdateScreen(GameTime gameTime,
                                             DisplayOrientation
                                                 displayOrientation)
        {
        }

        protected override void DrawScreen(SpriteBatch batch,
                                           DisplayOrientation
                                               displayOrientation)
        {
        }
    }
}
```

With all the game screens stubbed out, you can now complete the work in the `ScreenStateSwitchboard` class to handle moving between and creating all of them.

In the `ScreenStateSwitchboard` class, make the changes shown in Listing 8-32 to the `ChangeScreen()` method.

LISTING 8-32: The ChangeScreen() Method of the ScreenStateSwitchboard Class

```csharp
private void ChangeScreen(ScreenState screenState)
{
    switch (screenState)
    {
        case ScreenState.Title:
        {
```

continues

LISTING 8-32 *(continued)*

```
                ChangeScreen(screenState,
                        new CreateScreen(CreateTitleScreen));
                break;
        }

        case ScreenState.MainGame:
        {
            ChangeScreen(screenState,
                    new CreateScreen(CreateMainGameScreen));
            break;
        }

        case ScreenState.GameOver:
        {
            ChangeScreen(screenState,
                    new CreateScreen(CreateGameOverScreen));
            break;
        }

        case ScreenState.InGameMenu:
        {
            ChangeScreen(screenState,
                    new CreateScreen(CreateInGameMenuScreen));
            break;
        }

        case ScreenState.PreviousScreen:
        {
            currentScreen = previousScreen;
            currentScreen.Activate();
            break;
        }

        case ScreenState.Exit:
        {
            game.Exit();
            break;
        }
    }
}
```

At this point you will have a few errors, since the additional create-screen methods don't exist yet. So, next you must add code to support them all. Add the `CreateMainGameScreen()`, `CreateGameOverScreen()`, and `CreateInGameMenuScreen()` methods shown in Listing 8-33 to the `ScreenStateSwitchboard` class.

LISTING 8-33: Additional Create-Screen Methods for the ScreenStateSwitchboard Class

```
private Screen CreateMainGameScreen()
{
    return new MainGame(game,
```

```
                    batch,
                    new Screen.ChangeScreen(ChangeScreen));
}

private Screen CreateInGameMenuScreen()
{
    return new InGameMenu(game,
                    batch,
                    new Screen.ChangeScreen(ChangeScreen));
}

private Screen CreateGameOverScreen()
{
    return new GameOver(game,
                    batch,
                    new Screen.ChangeScreen(ChangeScreen));
}
```

This is a good time to compile your solution and run the game again. If everything builds correctly, you should now be able to tap the buttons on the `Title` screen and watch the screen change (although the screen it changes to will just be Cornflower Blue for now), as well as exit the game.

Coding the Main Game Screen

It's finally time to start coding the actual game play. You'll begin by coding the sprites that the game uses. In Drive & Dodge you drive a car on a road filled with hazards that you must dodge, so you need some classes to define those three game elements.

Begin by adding the images to the `Content` project. Add the `Road`, `Car`, and `Hazard` images (available in the book-files download at www.wrox.com) to the `Images` folder in the `DriveAndDodge Content` project.

Road.cs

First, create the `Road` class. Add the class shown in Listing 8-34 to the `Sprite` folder in your `DriveAndDodge` project.

LISTING 8-34: Road.cs

```
using System.Collections.Generic;

using Microsoft.Xna.Framework.Content;
using Microsoft.Xna.Framework.Graphics;
using Microsoft.Xna.Framework;

namespace DriveAndDodge.Sprites
{
    class Road : Sprite
    {
        int velocity;
```

continues

LISTING 8-34 *(continued)*

```csharp
        public Road(ContentManager content) : base(content, "Images/Road")
        {
            Reset();
        }

        public void Reset()
        {
            velocity = 5;
            Position.Y = 0;
        }

        protected override void UpdateSprite(GameTime gameTime)
        {
            Position.Y -= velocity;
        }

        protected override void DrawSprite(SpriteBatch batch)
        {
            batch.End();

            batch.Begin(SpriteSortMode.Immediate,
                    null,
                    SamplerState.LinearWrap,
                    null,
                    null);

            batch.Draw(texture,
                    Vector2.Zero,
                    new Rectangle(0,
                                (int)Position.Y,
                                Width,
                                Height),
                    Color.White);
            batch.End();

            batch.Begin();
        }
    }
}
```

The `Road` class draws the road your car will be driving on. This will be an endlessly scrolling straight road, and all that logic will be handled in this class.

The `velocity` variable tracks how fast the road should scroll. This game uses a classic technique in which the background images move while the main character remains stationary.

The `Reset()` method puts the road sprite back into its original state. This will be useful to call when the car has crashed and the game needs to be restarted.

In the `UpdateSprite()` method, you can see that the road's position changes each time the method is called. This moves your road position down through the screen, making it look like the car is driving along at a merry little clip.

The `DrawSprite()` method is one of the more interesting methods in this class. Some odd stuff is going on here, so let's take a closer look and break down what's happening.

```
protected override void DrawSprite(SpriteBatch batch)
{
    batch.End();

    batch.Begin(SpriteSortMode.Immediate,
            null,
            SamplerState.LinearWrap,
            null,
            null);
    batch.Draw(texture,
            Vector2.Zero,
            new Rectangle(0, (int)Position.Y, Width, Height),
            Color.White);
    batch.End();

    batch.Begin();
}
```

First, notice that `batch.End()` is called right away. This finishes any previous drawing the batch was doing. This is necessary because the scrolling effect for the road requires changing some of the values the `SpriteBatch` object uses when drawing. Calling `batch.End()` sets you up to pass in those new values.

Immediately after calling `End()`, you call `Begin()` on the `batch` object and pass in some new values. The first is `SpriteSortMode.Immediate`. This tells the batch object that you're not sorting the sprites by any sort of depth, so don't spend any processing time on this — just draw the sprite on the screen immediately.

With the XNA 4.0 framework, changing various "states" that the `Batch` can draw with can do all sorts of neat tricks. The way the states are handled is new for XNA 4.0. This topic is worth reading about more in the MSDN help files, but it's a little too much to cover in this chapter.

The second value passed in is one of those precreated states you can choose from. (In this case, however, since all you want is the batch's default state, you just pass in a null value.) The only state you want to change the behavior for is the `SamplerState`, and for that, you want to choose `LinearWrap`. This allows you to use the framework to do a neat little trick to scroll the image.

Next, you draw the `Road` texture to the screen. It's a mostly standard draw call, except that you are defining the source rectangle for the `Sprite` a little differently. In this case, you are telling it to draw from the original image starting from your current Y position. Because of the `LinearWrap` sampler state, it gives your game the effect of scrolling.

> *The source rectangle parameter of the* `SpriteBatch.Draw()` *method tells the batch just where in the original image files to draw from. Typically, the source rectangle is really useful when you have a spritesheet and are "cutting out" sprites from it to draw on the screen. So, you might say the sword sprite is at this rectangular position in the sheet, and the hero-character sprite is at this other position. With one spritesheet image, you would then be able to draw either one by just specifying a different source rectangle. Pretty handy, right?*

In this case, you are specifying the position but are telling the `SpriteBatch.Draw()` call to start "cutting out" the road image you want to draw at a different Y starting point. Because the `SamplerState` is set to `LinearWrap`, it then wraps the image to fill in the rest of the `Height` and `Width` specified.

If you tell `SpriteBatch` to start cutting out the `Road` texture at an offset of 20 pixels down in the image (the Y position), it will do so. Then it will fill in the first 20 pixels above that with the bottom 20 pixels of the image, wrapping around so that it's seamless.

Now the reason it's called `LinearWrap` starts to make a little more sense. This is how you can easily and effectively use the XNA framework to create a simple scrolling image for your game.

> *The authors would love to take credit for discovering that technique, but we can't. This handy little trick was discovered by searching the XNA forums (`http://forums.xna.com`) and MSDN. Both of those free sites are incredibly valuable resources when you're working on your games.*

Car.cs

With the `Road` class added, now it's time to add the car. Before adding the `Car` class, you need to grab the `ChangeLane.wav` file from the book files (at `www.wrox.com`) and add it to your `DriveAndDodge Content` project, in the `SoundEffects` folder.

Now you can add the `Car` class shown in Listing 8-35 to the `Sprites` folder in the `DriveAndDodge` project.

LISTING 8-35: Car.cs

```
using Microsoft.Xna.Framework;
using Microsoft.Xna.Framework.Content;
```

```csharp
using DriveAndDodge.Inputs;
using DriveAndDodge.Sounds;

namespace DriveAndDodge.Sprites
{
    class Car : Sprite
    {
        SoundEffects soundEffects;
        string moveLeftAction;
        string moveRightAction;
        int leftLanePosition;
        int rightLanePosition;
        Vector2 startPosition;
        GameInput input;

        public Car(Vector2 startPosition,
                   ContentManager content,
                   SoundEffects soundEffects,
                   GameInput input,
                   string moveLeftInputAction,
                   string moveRightInputAction,
                   int leftLanePosition,
                   int rightLanePosition)
            : base(content, "Images/Car")
        {
            this.soundEffects = soundEffects;
            this.input = input;
            this.startPosition = startPosition;
            this.moveLeftAction = moveLeftInputAction;
            this.moveRightAction = moveRightInputAction;
            this.leftLanePosition = leftLanePosition;
            this.rightLanePosition = rightLanePosition;
        }


        public void Reset()
        {
            Position = startPosition;
        }

        protected override void UpdateSprite(GameTime gameTime)
        {
            if (input.IsPressed(moveLeftAction))
            {
                ChangeLanes(leftLanePosition);
            }
            else if (input.IsPressed(moveRightAction))
            {
                ChangeLanes(rightLanePosition);
            }
        }

        private void ChangeLanes(int lanePosition)
```

continues

LISTING 8-35 *(continued)*

```
            {
                soundEffects.PlaySound("SoundEffects/ChangeLane");
                Position.X = lanePosition;
            }
        }
    }
```

The `Car` class handles the position and movement of the only playable character in the game — the car. It queries the update class, moves the car into one of two positions (basically changing lanes), and then plays any appropriate sound effects.

The constructor of the `Car` class sets all the base information the class needs, including what input keys are mapped to moving the car left and right, and just how far the car should move if those inputs are detected.

The `Reset()` method allows the car to reset all its important information to the default starting values. This will be used after the car has crashed and the player has restarted the game.

`UpdateSprite()` and `ChangeLanes()` handle the movement of the `Car` between the left and right lanes. The input object is queried and, if the correct inputs are detected, the car's position is changed and a movement sound effect is played.

Hazards.cs

Finally, you want to add some obstacles to dodge in the game. You will manage those with the `Hazards` class. Add the class shown in Listing 8-36 to the `Sprites` folder in your `DriveAndDodge` project.

LISTING 8-36: Hazards.cs

```
using System;
using System.Collections.Generic;

using Microsoft.Xna.Framework;
using Microsoft.Xna.Framework.Content;
using Microsoft.Xna.Framework.Graphics;

using DriveAndDodge.Screens;

namespace DriveAndDodge.Sprites
{
    class Hazards
    {
        Random random = new Random();
        List<Sprite> roadHazards = new List<Sprite>();
        int velocity;
        int lastYPositionOfHazardInChain;
        int leftLanePosition;
        int rightLanePosition;
        ContentManager content;
```

```csharp
public int HazardCount;

public Hazards(ContentManager content,
               int velocity,
               int leftLanePosition,
               int rightLanePosition)
{
    this.content = content;
    this.velocity = velocity;
    this.leftLanePosition = leftLanePosition;
    this.rightLanePosition = rightLanePosition;
    Reset();
}

public void Reset()
{
    HazardCount = 0;
    PlaceHazards();
}

public void PlaceHazards()
{
    roadHazards.Clear();
    for (int aNumberOfHazards = 0;
             aNumberOfHazards < 10;
             aNumberOfHazards++)
    {
        Sprite hazard = new Sprite(content, "Images/Hazard");

        int yPosition = aNumberOfHazards * -300;
        hazard.Position = new Vector2(GetLanePosition(), yPosition);
        roadHazards.Add(hazard);

        if (yPosition < lastYPositionOfHazardInChain)
        {
            lastYPositionOfHazardInChain = yPosition;
        }
    }
}

public void Update(GameTime gameTime,
                   Sprite collisionSprite,
                   Sprite.CollisionDelegate collisionDelegate)
{
    foreach (Sprite hazard in roadHazards)
    {
        if (collisionSprite.IsCollidingWith(hazard))
        {
            collisionDelegate();
            return;
        }

        if (hazard.Position.Y >= Screen.ScreenHeight)
        {
            HazardCount += 1;
```

continues

LISTING 8-36 *(continued)*

```
                hazard.Position.Y = GetLanePosition();
                hazard.Position.Y = lastYPositionOfHazardInChain
                                    - 300;
                lastYPositionOfHazardInChain = (int)hazard.Position.Y;
            }

            hazard.Position.Y += velocity;
        }
        lastYPositionOfHazardInChain += velocity;
    }

    private int GetLanePosition()
    {
        int xPosition = leftLanePosition;
        if (random.Next(0, 2) == 0)
        {
            xPosition = rightLanePosition;
        }

        return xPosition;
    }

    public void Draw(SpriteBatch batch)
    {
        foreach (Sprite hazard in roadHazards)
        {
            hazard.Draw(batch);
        }
    }
}
}
```

One of the first things to notice about the `Hazards` class is that, although you stuck it in the `Sprites` namespace, it doesn't actually inherit from the base `Sprite` class. The `Hazards` class instead manages a collection of `Sprite` objects (specifically, the hazards) that it will move and display on the screen.

The `Hazards` class constructor gathers the information necessary to manage the hazard sprites it will display on the screen. The `ContentManager` object loads the sprite images. The `velocity` variable handles how fast to move the hazards down the screen. The `leftLanePosition` and `rightLanePosition` variables help the `Hazards` class decide where to place the sprites on the screen.

The `Reset()` method clears the hazards and re-places them on the screen. It calls the `PlaceHazards()` method, which is used to randomly place the hazard sprites spaced out in the left and right lanes (that is, the left and right positions that were passed into the `Hazards` class constructor).

The `Update()` method of the `Hazards` class not only moves the `Hazards` sprites down the screen, but also checks for collisions with other `Sprite` objects. For this game, you are passing in the `Car` sprite object. If a collision is detected with one of the hazard sprites, the `collisionDelegate` is called so that the caller knows a collision has occurred.

`GetLanePosition()` is used by the `PlaceHazards()` method and the `Update()` method to place the sprites randomly in the left and right positions. In the `Update()` method, this is important, because as hazards move down the screen and out of the viewable area, you want to recycle them and place them back at the top of the screen in a new random position. Recycling is good for the planet and saves on garbage collection in your games, as well!

Finally, the `Draw()` method draws all the sprites to the screen. That's all you need to handle the "enemies" in your game. Now it's time to start making this game playable.

Finishing the MainGame Screen: Hooking Up the Sprites and the Game Play

With the various sprite classes added to your project, it's time to hook them up and add the game-play logic to the `MainGame` screen. When you initially stubbed it out, not much was going on. That's all about to change.

Before jumping back into the code for the `MainGame` screen, you need to grab the `HazardPass.wav` and `Crash.wav` files from the book's downloadable files and add them to the `SoundEffects` folder of your `DriveAndDodge Content` project.

MainGame.cs

Modify the `MainGame` class to look like Listing 8-37. As usual, the relevant changes are in bold.

LISTING 8-37: MainGame.cs

```csharp
using System;
using Microsoft.Xna.Framework;
using Microsoft.Xna.Framework.Content;
using Microsoft.Xna.Framework.Graphics;
using Microsoft.Xna.Framework.Input.Touch;
using Microsoft.Devices;
using Microsoft.Phone.Tasks;

using DriveAndDodge.Sprites;
using DriveAndDodge.Texts;
using DriveAndDodge.Inputs;

namespace DriveAndDodge.Screens
{
    class MainGame : Screen
    {
        Background background;
        Road road;
        Car car;
        Hazards hazards;
```

continues

LISTING 8-37 *(continued)*

```
    int previousHazardCount;

    const string ActionMoveLeft = "Left";
    const string ActionMoveRight = "Right";

    public MainGame(Game game,
                SpriteBatch batch,
                ChangeScreen changeScreen)
        : base(game, batch, changeScreen)
    {
        IsTouchIndicatorEnabled = true;
    }

    protected override void SetupInputs()
    {
        input.AddTouchSlideInput(ActionMoveLeft,
                                Input.Direction.Left,
                                5.0f);

        input.AddAccelerometerInput(ActionMoveLeft,
                                    Input.Direction.Left,
                                    0.10f);

        input.AddTouchGestureInput(ActionMoveRight,
                                   GestureType.Tap,
                                   ScreenRightHalf);

        input.AddTouchSlideInput(ActionMoveRight,
                                 Input.Direction.Right,
                                 5.0f);

        input.AddAccelerometerInput(ActionMoveRight,
                                    Input.Direction.Right,
                                    0.10f);

        input.AddTouchGestureInput(ActionMoveRight,
                                   GestureType.Tap,
                                   ScreenLeftHalf);
    }

    protected override void LoadScreenContent(ContentManager content)
    {
        background = new Background(content);
        road = new Road(content);
        car = new Car(new Vector2(120, 599),
                      content,
                      soundEffects,
                      input,
                      ActionMoveLeft,
                      ActionMoveRight,
                      120,
                      280);
```

```csharp
            hazards = new Hazards(content, 5, 120, 280);
        }

        public override void Activate()
        {
            car.Reset();
            hazards.Reset();
            road.Reset();
        }

        protected override void UpdateScreen(GameTime gameTime,
                                             DisplayOrientation
                                                 displayOrientation)
        {
            road.Update(gameTime);
            car.Update(gameTime);
            hazards.Update(gameTime,
                    car,
                    new Sprite.CollisionDelegate(HandleCarCollision));

            if (previousHazardCount != hazards.HazardCount)
            {
                soundEffects.PlaySound("SoundEffects/HazardPass");
                previousHazardCount = hazards.HazardCount;
            }
        }

        private void HandleCarCollision()
        {
            soundEffects.PlaySound("SoundEffects/Crash");

            VibrateController vibrate = VibrateController.Default;
            vibrate.Start(TimeSpan.FromSeconds(1));

            changeScreenDelegate(ScreenState.GameOver);
        }

        protected override void DrawScreen(SpriteBatch batch,
                                           DisplayOrientation
                                               displayOrientation)
        {
            background.Draw(batch);
            road.Draw(batch);
            car.Draw(batch);
            hazards.Draw(batch);
        }
    }
}
```

Notice that the new `Sprite` classes have been added as objects to the top of the `MainGame` class. These will be used to display and update the `Sprite` objects for your game.

The `MainGame()` constructor doesn't do much other than turn on the `TouchIndicator`. Setting this value to `true` indicates that you want to indicate visually where the player is touching the screen.

In `SetupInputs()`, you define what inputs you want to accept for your game, and what key they are mapped to. For Drive & Dodge, you have only two types of inputs — moving left and moving right. For both of those, you will accept a tap, a slide, or tilting the phone in that direction as your input. Using your new homemade input wrapper makes adding those easy and makes checking them even easier!

`LoadScreenContent()` is where you actually create all your `Sprite` objects. This calls `LoadContent()` for each of them and gets the images loaded from disk and into the `Road`, `Car`, and `Hazard` sprite classes you wrote.

`Activate()` is where you will put any screen-specific code that needs to be called when a screen is activated. This would typically be called when navigating to one screen from another. This will be useful when navigating from the `GameOver` screen back to the `MainGame` screen. In this case, the `Activate()` method calls the `Reset()` method on the sprite objects to restore them to their default positions and state.

`UpdateScreen()` calls the `Update()` method for all sprite objects being managed by the `MainGame` screen. It also tracks when a new hazard has been passed and plays a sound to give some audio feedback to the player.

Notice that the `Update()` method to the `Hazard` object passes a delegate pointing to the `HandleCarCollision()` method. This method will be called in the `MainGame` class when the `Hazard` class detects a collision between a hazard sprite and the car sprite passed in to the `Update()` method.

`HandleCarCollision()` is called when a collision is detected between the `Car` sprite and one of the `Hazard` sprites. When a collision is detected, the crash sound effect is played, and the phone vibrates briefly. The `MainGame` screen then notifies the `ScreenStateSwitchboard` to change the screen to the `GameOver` screen.

The `DrawScreen()` method handles drawing everything, including the background image, the road, the car, and the hazards.

Remember, you are not using the `SpriteBatch` sprite-sorting functionality. It is in Immediate mode by default, and it draws your sprites on a first-come, first-served basis. So the order you draw in is very important! If you draw the background last, it will cover everything, and that is all you will see onscreen.

After you code all that, some compiler errors will still exist. This is because you are using some new Windows Phone 7 functionality for vibrating. To use the Vibration feature, you must add a new DLL reference to your project. Add the `Microsoft.Phone.dll` reference and rebuild. All your compiler errors should be gone.

At this point, the game should be mostly playable. Start it and check out your new `MainGame` screen, which should look like Figure 8-5.

It feels fairly complete — until you crash into a hazard. Then you are greeted with that wonderful Cornflower Blue screen that is currently your `GameOver` screen.

Creating the Game | 219

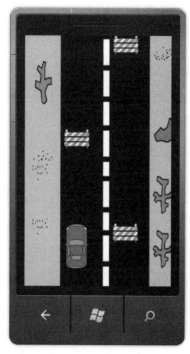

FIGURE 8-5: The MainGame screen, doing something interesting

Now that you've had a chance to play a bit, it's time to get back to coding so that you can finish the `InGameMenu` and `GameOver` screens.

InGameMenu.cs

The in-game menu is what players will see when the game is paused. You haven't actually added the ability to pause the game yet, but when you *do* add it, this is the screen players will see.

You stubbed out the `InGameMenu` screen earlier, so now just modify the `InGameMenu` class to look like Listing 8-38.

LISTING 8-38: InGameMenu.cs

```
using Microsoft.Xna.Framework;
using Microsoft.Xna.Framework.Content;
using Microsoft.Xna.Framework.Graphics;
using Microsoft.Xna.Framework.Input.Touch;

using DriveAndDodge.Sprites;

namespace DriveAndDodge.Screens
{
    class InGameMenu : Screen
```

continues

LISTING 8-38 *(continued)*

```csharp
{
    Background backgroundSprite;
    Button resumeButton;
    Button exitButton;

    const string ActionResume = "Resume";
    const string ActionExit = "Exit";

    public InGameMenu(Game game,
                     SpriteBatch batch,
                     ChangeScreen changeScreen)
        : base(game, batch, changeScreen)
    {
    }

    protected override void SetupInputs()
    {
        input.AddTouchGestureInput(ActionResume,
                                   GestureType.Tap,
                                   resumeButton.TouchArea);
        input.AddTouchGestureInput(ActionExit,
                                   GestureType.Tap,
                                   exitButton.TouchArea);
    }

    protected override void LoadScreenContent(ContentManager content)
    {
        backgroundSprite = new Background(content);

        resumeButton = new Button(content,
                        "Resume",
                        new Vector2(30, 200),
                        Color.BurlyWood);

        exitButton = new Button(content,
                        "Exit",
                        new Vector2(30, 350),
                        Color.BurlyWood);
    }

    public override void Activate()
    {
    }

    protected override void UpdateScreen(GameTime gameTime,
                                         DisplayOrientation
                                             displayOrientation)
    {
        if (input.IsPressed(ActionResume))
```

```
            {
                changeScreenDelegate(ScreenState.PreviousScreen);
            }

            if (input.IsPressed(ActionExit))
            {
                changeScreenDelegate(ScreenState.Exit);
            }
        }

        protected override void DrawScreen(SpriteBatch batch,
                                            DisplayOrientation
                                                displayOrientation)
        {
            backgroundSprite.Draw(batch);
            resumeButton.Draw(batch);
            exitButton.Draw(batch);
        }
    }
}
```

The `InGameMenu` screen has two options for the user when the game is paused: Resume and Exit. These options are presented as buttons, so to do that, you define some button objects and a background object at the top of the class. You will also define the keys for your inputs.

The `InGameMenu()` class constructor doesn't do anything special, other than passing information to the base screen constructor.

`SetupInputs()` just creates the inputs defined for each button that will be displayed on the screen. For each of the buttons, you will look for a `Tap` gesture as input to be detected by your input classes.

`LoadScreenContent()` creates the background sprite and the two button objects.

The `Activate()` method is empty, because the `InGameMenu` screen doesn't need to do anything special when being activated.

The `UpdateScreen()` method checks the `Input` object for the `Tap` inputs you defined. Then it either returns to the calling screen (`MainGame`) or tells the `ScreenStateSwitchboard` to exit the game.

Finally, the `DrawScreen()` method handles drawing the background and the button images to the screen. This is a fairly basic screen, but a really useful one for most games you'll be making. Giving your players a way to pause the game play and exit quickly is a good practice and is a part of the Windows Phone 7 Application Certification Requirements.

GameOver.cs

The final screen that Drive & Dodge needs is the `GameOver` screen. At this point, when a crash is detected, all the player sees is a Cornflower Blue screen with no way to do anything. The code you are about to add to the `GameOver` class will change that.

Modify the `GameOver` class file to look like Listing 8-39.

LISTING 8-39: GameOver.cs

```csharp
using Microsoft.Xna.Framework;
using Microsoft.Xna.Framework.Content;
using Microsoft.Xna.Framework.Graphics;
using Microsoft.Xna.Framework.Input.Touch;

using DriveAndDodge.Texts;
using DriveAndDodge.Sprites;

namespace DriveAndDodge.Screens
{
    class GameOver : Screen
    {
        Background background;
        Text gameOverText;
        Button playAgainButton;
        Button exitGameButton;

        const string ActionPlayAgain = "PlayAgain";
        const string ActionExitGame = "ExitGame";

        public GameOver(Game game,
                        SpriteBatch batch,
                        ChangeScreen changeScreen)
            : base(game, batch, changeScreen)
        {
        }

        protected override void SetupInputs()
        {
            input.AddTouchGestureInput(ActionPlayAgain,
                                       GestureType.Tap,
                                       playAgainButton.CollisionRectangle);
            input.AddTouchGestureInput(ActionExitGame,
                                       GestureType.Tap,
                                       exitGameButton.CollisionRectangle);
        }

        public override void Activate()
        {
        }

        protected override void LoadScreenContent(ContentManager content)
        {
            background = new Background(content);
            gameOverText = new Text(font,
                                    "Game Over!",
                                    new Vector2(100, 50),
                                    Color.BurlyWood,
                                    Color.Beige,
                                    Text.Alignment.Horizontal,
                                    new Rectangle(0,
```

```
                                                0,
                                                ScreenWidth,
                                                0));
            playAgainButton = new Button(content,
                                    "Play Again",
                                    new Vector2(30, 500),
                                    Color.BurlyWood);
            exitGameButton = new Button(content,
                                    "Exit",
                                    new Vector2(30, 650),
                                    Color.BurlyWood);
        }

        protected override void UpdateScreen(GameTime gameTime,
                                        DisplayOrientation
                                            displayOrientation)
        {
            if (input.IsPressed(ActionPlayAgain))
            {
                soundEffects.PlaySound("SoundEffects/Select");
                changeScreenDelegate(ScreenState.MainGame);
            }
            else if (input.IsPressed(ActionExitGame))
            {
                changeScreenDelegate(ScreenState.Exit);
            }
        }

        protected override void DrawScreen(SpriteBatch batch,
                                        DisplayOrientation
                                            displayOrientation)
        {
            background.Draw(batch);
            gameOverText.Draw(batch);
            playAgainButton.Draw(batch);
            exitGameButton.Draw(batch);
        }
    }
}
```

The `GameOver` screen class looks really similar to the `InGameMenu` class that you just coded. You have some buttons to display on the screen, and the user can choose to either replay the game or exit the game.

You'll add some more functionality to this screen later (primarily dealing with scoring and displaying those scores), but for now, there's not much this class does differently.

The buttons are created, and the inputs are set up. The `Update()` method checks for the inputs and acts accordingly if any are detected. The `Draw()` method displays everything to the user. A lot of the repetitive plumbing is tucked safely away in the base class, making this screen very easy to set up.

With the `GameOver` screen coded, the game is now playable, and you are almost done! The only thing left to handle at this point is wiring the in-game menu and keeping the score.

You'll postpone implementing the in-game menu until the next section, when you learn to properly handle the Back button to conform to Microsoft's guidelines for application certification.

Keeping Score

One thing that keeps gamers coming back for more is keeping track of scores. You learned about saving files to local storage in Chapter 6. You will use that knowledge in Drive & Dodge to persist the high scores.

The scoring system you'll use in Drive & Dodge is stored and retrieved via XML serialization. Windows Phone Game projects don't have a reference to the `System.Xml.Serialization` namespace by default, so you need to add one.

The scoring system used in Drive & Dodge is fairly generic (one that you could use again in future projects). The game has four classes: `Score`, `ScoreList`, `Scores`, and `SerializableDictionary`. Each class plays a different role in making scoring easy to work with and capable of working on the Windows Phone 7 device.

Score.cs

Once you have added the reference, create a new folder called `Scoring` under the `DriveAndDodge` project, and add the `Score` class (used to track an individual score) shown in Listing 8-40 under the `Scoring` folder.

LISTING 8-40: Score.cs

```csharp
namespace DriveAndDodge.Scoring
{
    public class Score
    {
        public string Name;
        public int Value;

        public Score()
        {
        }

        public Score(string name, int value)
        {
            Name = name;
            Value = value;
        }
    }
}
```

The `Score` class is intentionally simple. It holds two key pieces of information — a name and a value. If you've ever looked at any kind of High Score screen, that tends to be the information that is displayed. The `Score` class represents a single element in the High Score list.

ScoreList.cs

Next up is the `ScoreList` class. Add the class shown in Listing 8-41 to the `DriveAndDodge` project under the `Scoring` folder.

LISTING 8-41: ScoreList.cs

```
using System.Collections.Generic;

namespace DriveAndDodge.Scoring
{
    public class ScoreList
    {
        List<Score> scores = new List<Score>();
        int maxScoredStored = 10;

        public ScoreList()
        {
        }

        public void AddScore(Score newScore)
        {
            scores.Add(newScore);

            if (scores.Count <= maxScoredStored)
            {
                return;
            }
            else
            {
                scores.Sort((scoreOne, scoreTwo)
                    => (scoreTwo.Value.CompareTo(scoreOne.Value)));
                scores.RemoveRange(maxScoredStored,
                            scores.Count - maxScoredStored);
            }
        }

        public List<Score> Scores
        {
            get
            {
                scores.Sort((scoreOne, scoreTwo)
                    => (scoreTwo.Value.CompareTo(scoreOne.Value)));
                return scores;
            }
        }
    }
}
```

The `ScoreList` class represents a single High Score list. It keeps track of the highest scores achieved and keeps that list ordered and limited to just the top ten highest scores.

The `maxScoredStored` variable is what dictates that only the ten highest scores are tracked.

The `AddScore()` method is how external classes add a score to an instantiated `ScoreList` object. This method adds the score and then performs some basic list maintenance to ensure that only the top ten scores are being tracked.

`Scores` is the property that external callers would use to get an ordered list (highest to lowest) of their score values being stored in the list.

Scores.cs

Now, let's move on to the `Scores` class. Add the class shown in Listing 8-42 to your `DriveAndDodge` project under the `Scoring` folder.

LISTING 8-42: Scores.cs

```csharp
using System.Collections.Generic;

using System.IO;
using System.IO.IsolatedStorage;

using System.Xml;
using System.Xml.Serialization;

namespace DriveAndDodge.Scoring
{
    class Scores
    {
        private static SerializableDictionary<string, ScoreList> highScores
            = new SerializableDictionary<string,ScoreList>();

        public void AddScore(string type, string name, int value)
        {
            if (!highScores.ContainsKey(type))
            {
                highScores.Add(type, new ScoreList());
            }

            highScores[type].AddScore(new Score(name, value));
        }

        public List<Score> HighScores(string type)
        {
            return highScores[type].Scores;
        }

        public int CurrentHighScore(string type)
        {
            if (highScores.ContainsKey(type))
            {
                return highScores[type].Scores[0].Value;
            }
            return 0;
        }
```

```csharp
        public void Load()
        {
            using (IsolatedStorageFile storage
                = IsolatedStorageFile.GetUserStoreForApplication())
            {
                if (!storage.FileExists("HighScores.xml"))
                {
                    return;
                }

                using (IsolatedStorageFileStream file
                    = storage.OpenFile("HighScores.xml", FileMode.Open))
                {
                    using (XmlReader reader = XmlReader.Create(file))
                    {
                        highScores.ReadXml(reader);
                    }
                }
            }
        }

        public void Save()
        {
            using (IsolatedStorageFile storage
                = IsolatedStorageFile.GetUserStoreForApplication())
            {
                using (IsolatedStorageFileStream file
                    = storage.CreateFile("HighScores.xml"))
                {
                    using (XmlWriter writer = XmlWriter.Create(file))
                    {
                        highScores.WriteXml(writer);
                    }
                }
            }
        }
    }
}
```

The `Scores` class is responsible for maintaining and keeping track of all the various score lists your game might have. It's been generalized so that you can keep track of all kinds of different scores, such as "most kills" or "fastest time." The `Scores` class can add those types of score lists and keep track of those rankings for you. Drive & Dodge stores only the highest number of hazards passed, but it's not a bad idea to plan for the future!

The `SerializableDictionary` object at the top of the class is where all the various score lists are being stored.

You haven't created the `SerializableDictionary` class yet, but you will do that in a moment.

`AddScore()` is what external classes will use to add a new score to an existing `ScoreList`, or to start tracking a score for a new `ScoreList`. The `type` variable passed in to that method is the name of the score list that the score is being added to. All scores added with the same type name are added to the same list. The name is the player name (or maybe some other creative name) of who or what made the score, and the value is the score that person achieved. If the type passed in doesn't exist, a new type of `ScoreList` is created, and the player name and value are then added.

The `HighScores()` method gives external classes a means of accessing the top scores for a particular score list. Just pass in the type of `ScoreList` your object needs, and it retrieves the ordered scores from the dictionary object.

`CurrentHighScore()` is a helper method used to quickly retrieve the top score from any `ScoreList` stored. This is useful if you're interested in whether the player has achieved a new high score.

Next up are the `Load()` and `Save()` methods. These use the `IsolatedStorage` functionality discussed in Chapter 6 to load XML files to and from your phone's storage area.

SerializableDictionary.cs

Now it's time to add the `SerializableDictionary` class discussed previously. The .NET framework doesn't automatically serialize dictionaries out of the box, but with a little coding, you can create a wrapper that will.

First, you need to add a reference in your `DriveAndDodge` project to the `System.XML.Serialization` namespace. Then you add the `SerializableDictionary` class shown in Listing 8-43 to the `Scoring` folder.

LISTING 8-43: SerializableDictionary.cs

```csharp
using System.Collections.Generic;

using System.IO;
using System.Xml;
using System.Xml.Serialization;
using System.Xml.Schema;

namespace DriveAndDodge.Scoring
{
    [XmlRoot("dictionary")]
    public class SerializableDictionary<DKey, DValue>
        : Dictionary<DKey, DValue>, IXmlSerializable
    {
        const string ItemTag = "item";
        const string KeyTag = "key";
        const string ValueTag = "value";

        public XmlSchema GetSchema()
        {
            return null;
        }

        public void ReadXml(XmlReader reader)
        {
            if (IsEmpty(reader))
            {
```

```csharp
            return;
        }

        XmlSerializer keySerializer = new XmlSerializer(typeof(DKey));
        XmlSerializer valueSerializer
            = new XmlSerializer(typeof(DValue));

        while (reader.NodeType != XmlNodeType.EndElement)
        {
            if (reader.NodeType == XmlNodeType.None)
            {
                return;
            }
            ReadItem(reader, keySerializer, valueSerializer);
            reader.MoveToContent();
        }
        reader.ReadEndElement();
    }

    private bool IsEmpty(XmlReader reader)
    {
        bool isEmpty = reader.IsEmptyElement;
        reader.Read();
        return isEmpty;
    }

    private void ReadItem(XmlReader reader,
                          XmlSerializer keySerializer,
                          XmlSerializer valueSerializer)
    {
        reader.ReadStartElement(ItemTag);
        this.Add(ReadKey(reader, keySerializer),
                 ReadValue(reader, valueSerializer));
        reader.ReadEndElement();
    }

    private DKey ReadKey(XmlReader reader, XmlSerializer keySerializer)
    {
        reader.ReadStartElement(KeyTag);
        DKey key = (DKey)keySerializer.Deserialize(reader);
        reader.ReadEndElement();
        return key;
    }

    private DValue ReadValue(XmlReader reader,
                             XmlSerializer valueSerializer)
    {
        reader.ReadStartElement(ValueTag);
        DValue value = (DValue)valueSerializer.Deserialize(reader);
        reader.ReadEndElement();
        return value;
    }

    public void WriteXml(XmlWriter writer)
```

continues

LISTING 8-43 *(continued)*

```csharp
    {
        XmlSerializer keySerializer = new XmlSerializer(typeof(DKey));
        XmlSerializer valueSerializer
            = new XmlSerializer(typeof(DValue));

        foreach (DKey key in this.Keys)
        {
            WriteItem(writer, keySerializer, valueSerializer, key);
        }
    }

    private void WriteItem(XmlWriter writer,
                           XmlSerializer keySerializer,
                           XmlSerializer valueSerializer,
                           DKey key)
    {
        writer.WriteStartElement(ItemTag);
        WriteKey(writer, keySerializer, key);
        WriteValue(writer, valueSerializer, key);
        writer.WriteEndElement();
    }

    private void WriteKey(XmlWriter writer,
                          XmlSerializer keySerializer,
                          DKey key)
    {
        writer.WriteStartElement(KeyTag);
        keySerializer.Serialize(writer, key);
        writer.WriteEndElement();
    }

    private void WriteValue(XmlWriter writer,
                            XmlSerializer valueSerializer,
                            DKey key)
    {
        writer.WriteStartElement(ValueTag);
        valueSerializer.Serialize(writer, this[key]);
        writer.WriteEndElement();
    }
  }
}
```

The whole purpose of this class is just to provide the capability to easily serialize (and deserialize) dictionary objects. Basically, it just cycles through the key and value pairs and writes out the XML files that represent the dictionary.

Now that you have the Scoring classes added, it's time to modify the base Screen class, the MainGame class, and the GameOver class to start working with these new objects.

Screen.cs

Start by modifying the base Screen class. Open the Screen class and add the following using statement to the top of the class so that you can start working with the Scoring objects:

```
using DriveAndDodge.Scoring;
```

Next, add the following two variables at the class level:

```
protected static Scores highScores = new Scores();
private static bool isHighScoresLoaded = false;
```

Add the following block of code to the Screen() class constructor:

```
if (!isHighScoresLoaded)
{
    highScores.Load();
    isHighScoresLoaded = true;
}
```

This ensures that the Scores are loaded off the disk when the game is run and the first screen is created. The isHighScoresLoaded variable ensures that the scores are loaded only once and that they won't be loaded again by the construction of any other screens.

That's it for modifications to the base Screen class. With the addition of the highScores object to the Screen base class, now it is available for use in all your screens. You can start modifying the MainGame and GameOver screens to access that object and use it to keep track of the scores.

MainGame.cs

Before jumping in to modify the MainGame class, you must add another SpriteFont to display the scores you are tracking. Add a new SpriteFont called scoreFont.spritefont to the Fonts folder in the DriveAndDodge Content project, and change its Size property to 20.

You must also add HighScore.wav from the book files at www.wrox.com into the SoundEffects folder of the DriveAndDodge Content project.

Next, add the following class-level variables to your MainGame class:

```
SpriteFont scoreFont;
Text scoreText;
bool isHighScoreAchieved = false;
int currentHighScore;
```

These will be used to display the score and to help notify the player when he or she has achieved a new high score.

Modify the LoadScreenContent() method to look like Listing 8-44.

LISTING 8-44: The LoadScreenContent() Method of the MainGame Class

```
protected override void LoadScreenContent(ContentManager content)
{
    background = new Background(content);
    road = new Road(content);
    car = new Car(new Vector2(120, 599),
                  content,
                  soundEffects,
                  input,
                  ActionMoveLeft,
                  ActionMoveRight,
                  120,
                  280);
    hazards = new Hazards(content, 5, 120, 280);

    scoreFont = content.Load<SpriteFont>("Fonts/scoreFont");
    scoreText = new Text(scoreFont,
                         "Hazards Passed: 0",
                         new Vector2(0, 35),
                         Color.White,
                         Text.Alignment.Horizontal,
                         new Rectangle(0, 0, ScreenWidth, 0));
}
```

Next, modify the `Activate()` method to look like Listing 8-45.

LISTING 8-45: The Activate() Method of the MainGame Class

```
public override void Activate()
{
    car.Reset();
    hazards.Reset();
    road.Reset();

    isHighScoreAchieved = false;
    currentHighScore = highScores.CurrentHighScore("Hazards");
}
```

This retrieves the current high score and resets the `HighScore` achieved tracking variable when a player returns to the `MainGame` screen from the exit screen.

Modify the `UpdateScreen()` method to look like Listing 8-46.

LISTING 8-46: The UpdateScreen() Method of the MainGame Class

```
protected override void UpdateScreen(GameTime gameTime,
                                     DisplayOrientation displayOrientation)
{
    road.Update(gameTime);
    car.Update(gameTime);
```

```
        hazards.Update(gameTime,
                       car,
                       new Sprite.CollisionDelegate(HandleCarCollision));

        if (previousHazardCount != hazards.HazardCount)
        {
            soundEffects.PlaySound("SoundEffects/HazardPass");
            previousHazardCount = hazards.HazardCount;
            scoreText.ChangeText("Hazards Passed: "
                                 + hazards.HazardCount.ToString());
        }

        if (!isHighScoreAchieved && hazards.HazardCount > currentHighScore)
        {
            scoreText.DisplayColor = Color.Blue;
            soundEffects.PlaySound("SoundEffects/HighScore");
            isHighScoreAchieved = true;
        }
    }
```

The new code here updates the `ScoreText` variable to display the current score the player has achieved, and then it checks to see if the player has achieved a new high score. If so, the score text color is changed, and a sound effect is played, letting the player know that he or she broke his or her previous record.

Modify the `HandleCarCollision()` method to look like Listing 8-47.

LISTING 8-47: The HandleCarCollision() Method of the MainGame Class

```
    private void HandleCarCollision()
    {
        soundEffects.PlaySound("SoundEffects/Crash");

        VibrateController vibrate = VibrateController.Default;
        vibrate.Start(TimeSpan.FromSeconds(1));

        highScores.AddScore("Hazards", "", hazards.HazardCount);
        changeScreenDelegate(ScreenState.GameOver);
    }
```

Here, just one new line of code was added. After the car has crashed, you must add the new score the player has achieved to the `HighScore` list. If the score is within the top ten, it is stored; if not, it is discarded.

Finally, change the `DrawScreen()` method to look like the method shown in Listing 8-48.

LISTING 8-48: The DrawScreen() Method of the MainGame Class

```
    protected override void DrawScreen(SpriteBatch batch,
                                       DisplayOrientation displayOrientation)
```

continues

LISTING 8-48 *(continued)*

```
{
    background.Draw(batch);
    road.Draw(batch);
    car.Draw(batch);
    hazards.Draw(batch);
    scoreText.Draw(batch);
}
```

Here you just add a line to draw the `scoreText` to the screen. This gives the player a nice visual display of his or her current score. Now, compile and run the game. As `Hazards` move off the screen, you should see the score appear and increase.

GameOver.cs

The only thing left to do at this point is to show the player his or her top ten scores. The `GameOver` screen would be a great place to do that.

Open the `GameOver` class, and add the following `using` statement to the top of the class file:

```
using DriveAndDodge.Scoring;
```

Next, add the following variables at the class level:

```
SpriteFont scoreFont;
Text scoreText;
Text highScoreTitleText;
```

These will be used to display the `Scores` on the `GameOver` screen. Now, modify the `Activate()` method to look like Listing 8-49.

LISTING 8-49: The Activate() Method of the GameOver Class

```
public override void Activate()
{
    highScores.Save();
}
```

Since at some point you need to save the scores the player has achieved, do it every time the `GameOver` screen is displayed.

The `LoadScreenContent()` method needs to load your new font and text objects, so modify it to look like Listing 8-50.

LISTING 8-50: The LoadScreenContent() Method of the GameOver Class

```
protected override void LoadScreenContent(ContentManager content)
{
    background = new Background(content);
    gameOverText = new Text(font,
```

```
                                "Game Over!",
                                new Vector2(100, 50),
                                Color.BurlyWood,
                                Color.Beige,
                                Text.Alignment.Horizontally,
                                new Rectangle(0, 0, ScreenWidth, 0));

    playAgainButton = new Button(content,
                                "Play Again",
                                new Vector2(30, 500),
                                Color.BurlyWood);

    exitGameButton = new Button(content,
                                "Exit",
                                new Vector2(30, 650),
                                Color.BurlyWood);

    scoreFont = content.Load<SpriteFont>("Fonts/scoreFont");
    scoreText = new Text(scoreFont, "Total Hazards: ", new Vector2(30, 0));
    highScoreTitleText = new Text(scoreFont,
                                ":::High Scores:::",
                                new Vector2(33, 130),
                                Color.White,
                                Text.Alignment.Horizontal,
                                new Rectangle(0, 0, ScreenWidth, 0));
}
```

You don't need to change anything in the `UpdateScreen()` method, but you need to change the `DrawScreen()` method so that the scores are displayed on the screen. Modify the `DrawScreeen()` method to look like Listing 8-51.

LISTING 8-51: The DrawScreen() Method of the GameOver Class

```
protected override void DrawScreen(SpriteBatch batch,
                                   DisplayOrientation displayOrientation)
{
    background.Draw(batch);
    gameOverText.Draw(batch);
    playAgainButton.Draw(batch);
    exitGameButton.Draw(batch);

    highScoreTitleText.Draw(batch);

    scoreText.Position.Y = 150;
    int topScorePosition = 1;
    foreach (Score score in highScores.HighScores("Hazards"))
    {
        scoreText.Position.Y += 30;
        string name = score.Name + "                    ";
        scoreText.ChangeText(topScorePosition.ToString("00")
                            + "  "
                            + name.Substring(0, 15)
```

continues

LISTING 8-51 *(continued)*

```
                                + "  "
                                + score.Value.ToString("000")
                                + " hazards");
            scoreText.Draw(batch);
            topScorePosition += 1;
        }
    }
```

That's it for the `GameOver` screen changes and for the scoring changes in general. Now when you run the game, the scores from previously played games are loaded from disk, and the current score is displayed on the screen while the player is playing. The top ten scores are displayed on the `GameOver` screen, as shown in Figure 8-6.

FIGURE 8-6: The high score screen in action

 Keep in mind that if you are working in the Emulator, your scores are persisted only while the Emulator is running. If you close the Emulator between debugging sessions, it will be like you are starting with a fresh phone each time.

Press F5 to build and run the game so that you can see all the lovely scoring work in action. The only thing left at this point is to implement the in-game menu, and then you'll be done!

Proper Care and Feeding of the Back Button

If you want to make Microsoft happy (and, more importantly, get your application or game accepted into the Windows Marketplace), you need to learn to handle the Back button properly.

In section 5.2.4 of the "Windows Phone 7 Application Certification Requirements" document, Microsoft has laid out some very precise guidelines for how it expects the Back button to behave on each type of screen within a game:

> *5.2.4 Use of Back Button in Games*
>
> *a. Pressing the Back button from the first screen of a game must exit the application.*
>
> *b. During gameplay, pressing the Back button in games must present an in-game menu. This menu must offer the option to resume the game. Pressing the Back button while this menu is up must exit the game. Microsoft recommends that you save the user game state or warn them of possible progress loss before exiting the game.*
>
> *c. Outside gameplay (for example, when the user is viewing the options or help menu), pressing the Back button must return to the previous menu or page.*

Got those rules memorized? It's time to make the Drive & Dodge game compliant with Section 5.2.4. The best way to handle this is by allowing each screen to declare its type, and then the base `Screen` class will act appropriately when the Back button is pressed.

Screen.cs

To get started, you must modify the base `Screen` class. Add this `using` statement to your `Screen` class:

```
using Microsoft.Xna.Framework.Input;
```

Now, add the following enumeration and variables at the class level:

```
public enum BackButtonScreenType
{
    First,
    Gameplay,
    InGameMenu,
    Other
}

private BackButtonScreenType backButtonScreenType;
const string ActionBack = "Back";
```

The `BackButtonScreenType` enumeration sets up the different screen types and creates a key for the `Input` class.

Next, change the `Screen` constructor to look like Listing 8-52.

LISTING 8-52: The Screen() Class Constructor

```
public Screen(Game game,
              SpriteBatch batch,
              ChangeScreen changeScreen,
              BackButtonScreenType backButtonScreenType)
{
    Screen.game = game;
    Screen.content = game.Content;
    Screen.batch = batch;

    changeScreenDelegate = changeScreen;
    touchIndicator = new TouchIndicatorCollection();

    if (music == null)
    {
        music = new Music(content);
    }

    if (soundEffects == null)
    {
        soundEffects = new SoundEffects(content);
    }

    if (!isHighScoresLoaded)
    {
        highScores.Load();
        isHighScoresLoaded = true;
    }

    this.backButtonScreenType = backButtonScreenType;
}
```

This will be a breaking change to the game, because you've added another parameter to the base screen constructor. It now expects all screens that are created to declare their screen type when they're created. The `Screen` class then stores this information to be used later.

Next, you must detect Back button presses with the `Input` class, so modify the `LoadContent()` method to look like Listing 8-53.

LISTING 8-53: The LoadContent() Method of the Screen Class

```
public void LoadContent()
{
    font = content.Load<SpriteFont>("Fonts/screenFont");
    LoadScreenContent(content);

    input.AddGamePadInput(ActionBack, Buttons.Back, true);
    SetupInputs();
}
```

In this method, you are adding the capability to detect the Back button. Now that you can detect it, you need to check it and handle it properly. To do that, modify the `Update()` method to look like Listing 8-54.

LISTING 8-54: The Update() Method of the Screen Class

```
public void Update(GameTime gameTime)
{
    input.BeginUpdate();
    HandleBackButtonInput();

    if (IsTouchIndicatorEnabled)
    {
        touchIndicator.Update(gameTime, content);
    }

    UpdateScreen(gameTime,
                 game.GraphicsDevice
                     .PresentationParameters
                     .DisplayOrientation);
    input.EndUpdate();
}
```

The only change here is a call to the `HandleBackButtonInput()` method, which you haven't created yet. As you might have guessed from the name, this method handles what happens when the Back button is pressed during your game.

Add the `HandleBackButtonInput()` shown in Listing 8-55 to the base `Screen` class.

LISTING 8-55: The HandleBackButtonInput() Method of the Screen Class

```
private void HandleBackButtonInput()
{
    if (input.IsPressed(ActionBack))
    {
        switch (backButtonScreenType)
        {
            case BackButtonScreenType.First:
            {
                game.Exit();
                break;
            }

            case BackButtonScreenType.Gameplay:
            {
                changeScreenDelegate(ScreenState.InGameMenu);
                break;
            }

            case BackButtonScreenType.InGameMenu:
            {
```

continues

LISTING 8-55 *(continued)*

```
            SaveState();
            game.Exit();
            break;
        }

        case BackButtonScreenType.Other:
        {
            changeScreenDelegate(ScreenState.PreviousScreen);
            break;
        }
    }
}
```

At this point, you've implemented the logic that complies with Microsoft's guidelines for the Back button. To recap, if the Back button is pressed, the following actions occur:

➤ When a screen is declared to be the first screen of the game, exit the game.

➤ When the `GamePlay` screen is displayed, show the `InGameMenu` screen.

➤ When the `InGameMenu` screen is displayed, exit the game.

➤ When any other screen in the game is displayed, move back to the previous screen.

So, that's it for the base `Screen` class. It now correctly manages the Back button handling for the game. But now you must fix those breaking changes in the code. Each screen now must pass in the screen type when it's being created.

If you rebuild your project now, you should get four errors, one for each screen in your game.

Title.cs

Start by fixing the `Title` screen. Open the `Title` class and make the following change (shown in bold) to the signature of the `Title` class constructor:

```
public Title(Game game, SpriteBatch batch, ChangeScreen changeScreen)
    : base(game, batch, changeScreen, BackButtonScreenType.First)
{
}
```

Notice that the `Title` screen constructor now passes into the base `Screen` constructor that this is the first screen of the game. Now, if the player presses Back while on the `Title` screen, the game exits, as it's supposed to on that type of screen.

MainGame.cs

Now, make a similar change to the signature of the class constructor for your `MainGame` screen:

```
public MainGame(Game game, SpriteBatch batch, ChangeScreen screenEvent)
    : base(game, batch, screenEvent, BackButtonScreenType.Gameplay)
```

```
{
    IsTouchIndicatorEnabled = true;
}
```

Here you indicate that this is a `Gameplay`-type screen, meaning that if the Back button is pressed, a game menu should open.

InGameMenu.cs

It's time to fix the `InGameMenu` class. Make the following change to the signature of the class constructor:

```
public InGameMenu(Game game, SpriteBatch batch, ChangeScreen changeScreen)
    : base(game, batch, changeScreen, BackButtonScreenType.InGameMenu)
{
}
```

The `InGameMenu` class constructor tells the `Screen` base class that it is an `InGameMenu` screen type. So now if the Back button is pressed while the menu is the current screen, the game exits.

GameOver.cs

Finally, open the `GameOver` class and make the following change to the signature of the class constructor:

```
public GameOver(Game game, SpriteBatch batch, ChangeScreen changeScreen)
    : base(game, batch, changeScreen, BackButtonScreenType.Other)
{
}
```

Here you declare the `GameOver` screen to be an `Other` screen type. Therefore, if the Back button is pressed, the game just moves back to the previous screen.

That's it! The game is now coded to the correct Back button standards, giving you one less thing to worry about when going through the certification process for the Windows Phone 7 Marketplace.

Drive & Dodge is now complete (at least as far as the example in this book will take you), but one last thing will make it much easier to work on the remaining games covered in this book.

CREATING A BASE GAME TEMPLATE

A lot of setup and preparation work was done for all the base classes in this project. Most of them are fairly generic by design and are intended for you to be able to use repeatedly.

To help speed things along the next time, you will create a new `XNAPhoneGame` template project that you can use as a starting point with each new project. This will allow you to focus more on the meat of your game and the cool phone-specific stuff (which is way more interesting than the basic plumbing code) next time.

Any time you want to refresh your memory on some of these base classes, you can always come back to this chapter and read about them again.

Start by ensuring that you save your `DriveAndDodge` game, and then make a copy of the top-level folder. You will be working off the copy of your project and the `Content` project.

Stripping Down to the Essentials

Open the project from the copied folder, and get ready to do some demolition. Not all the classes are generic enough to be part of the template project, so you'll remove those.

Follow these steps:

1. Expand the `Content References` folder, and remove `DriveAndDodgeContent` from the list of references.
2. Expand the `Screens` folder and delete the `GameOver.cs` and `MainGame.cs` classes from the project.
3. Expand the `Sprites` folder and delete the `Car.cs`, `Hazard.cs`, and `Road.cs` classes from the project.
4. Expand the `Images` folder in the `Content` project and delete the `Car.png`, `Hazard.png`, and `Road.png` files.
5. Expand the `Music` folder and delete `RaceSong.wav`.
6. Expand the `SoundEffects` folder and delete the `ChangeLane.wav`, `Crash.wav`, `HazardPass.wav`, and `HighScore.wav` files.

That's it for the deletions. Now you will make some changes to make it easier to work with the template. Start by changing the namespace from `DriveAndDodge` to `XNAPhoneGame`. You can do a "find and replace all" to make that happen quickly. Do that now, and you'll be ready for the next step.

 Pressing Ctrl+H brings up the Find/Replace dialog in Visual Studio.

Next, you must modify a few of the classes to remove some of their game-specific code.

Title.cs

Start with the `Title` screen, and make the following change to the `Activate()` method of the `Title` class:

```
public override void Activate()
{
}
```

Here you remove the line of code that starts the background music playing. Future games might not have music, and they certainly won't be playing the same song as Drive & Dodge.

Next, modify the `LoadScreenContent()` method to look like the following:

```
protected override void LoadScreenContent(ContentManager content)
{
```

```
        background = new Background(content);
        titleText = new Text(font,
                            "Game!",
                            new Vector2(0, (int)(ScreenHeight / 3)),
                            Color.BurlyWood,
                            Color.Beige,
                            Text.Alignment.Horizontally,
                            new Rectangle(0, 0, ScreenWidth, 0));
        startButton = new Button(content, "Start Game", new Vector2(30, 500),
            Color.BurlyWood);
        exitButton = new Button(content, "Exit", new Vector2(30, 650),
            Color.BurlyWood);
    }
```

This is just a minor change to that method. You change the title text from "Drive & Dodge!" to "Game!".

Now remove the following line from the `UpdateScreen()` method in the same class:

```
changeScreenDelegate(ScreenState.MainGame);
```

This way, if the `ActionStart` input is pressed, there's no longer a call to `changeScreenDelegate`. In a different game, you might not go directly to the `MainGame` screen. This will have to be modified for each game.

ScreenStateSwitchboard.cs

Next, dig into the `ScreenStateSwitchboard` class and remove the `MainGame` and `GameOver` lines from the `ScreenState` enumeration so that it looks like the following:

```
public enum ScreenState
{
    Title,
    InGameMenu,
    PreviousScreen,
    Exit
}
```

These are the base screens that every game should have. More screens will be added when new projects are created from this XNA phone game template.

Next, modify the `ChangeScreen()` method to look like the following:

```
private void ChangeScreen(ScreenState screenState)
{
    switch (screenState)
    {
        case ScreenState.Title:
        {
            ChangeScreen(screenState, new CreateScreen(CreateTitleScreen));
            break;
        }

        case ScreenState.InGameMenu:
```

```
            {
                ChangeScreen(screenState, new CreateScreen(CreateInGameMenuScreen));
                break;
            }

            case ScreenState.PreviousScreen:
            {
                currentScreen = previousScreen;
                currentScreen.Activate();
                break;
            }

            case ScreenState.Exit:
            {
                game.Exit();
                break;
            }
        }
    }
```

The `case` statements for handling the screens you removed have been deleted. New cases will be added for each individual new project, so this method will be enhanced then.

Next, delete the `CreateMainGameScreen()` and `CreateGameOverScreen()` methods.

Creating the Templates

That's it! You're now ready to create your base game template for both the game and the content projects. Click the File menu in Visual Studio and select Export Template. This brings up the Export Template Wizard. Ensure that Project Template is selected (it is by default). Select DriveAndDodge from the drop-down menu as the first project you will be exporting, and then click the Next button.

Name the template `XNAPhoneGame`, and then give it a short description, such as "base template for making Windows Phone 7 games."

Leave the defaults for everything else (or find preview and icon images if you'd like), and then click the Finish button.

Next, you will repeat the process for the `Content` project. Click the File menu and select Export Template. This time, select DriveAndDodge Content from the drop-down menu. Name the template `XNAPhoneGameContent`, and give it a description of "base content template for making Windows Phone 7 games." Then click the Finish button.

Using the Templates

Now, it's time to try out the templates to see how they work. Start by opening Visual Studio (close it first if your template project is still open).

Click the File menu and select New Project.

Next, in the New Project dialog, select Visual C# from the languages tree, and choose `XNAPhoneGame` from the available templates. This is the template you just created.

Accept the default name for now (since you won't actually be starting a new game), and click the OK button.

This gives you all the base classes you created and used for your game, but you still need to add the base content project as well. To do that, right-click the solution name in the Solution Explorer and choose Add New Project.

In the New Project dialog, select `XNAPhoneGameContent` as your template project. Leave the default name again, and click OK.

Now your base `Content` project is ready. You can start your project as soon as you add a reference to it from the `Game` project. Right-click the `Content References` folder and select Add Content Reference from the menu.

Next, select your `Content` project name from the Content References dialog that pops up.

At this point, if you press F5 to build and run the project, you will see that you already have the basics for a new game just waiting for you to code the game play.

This approach makes starting new game projects much easier. The authors strongly encourage you to use this technique for sharing base functionality between your games.

SUMMARY

In this chapter, you built a complete game from scratch and learned a number of handy new techniques, including background scrolling and collision detection. You also revisited concepts introduced in earlier chapters.

You also learned how to extract the core classes from your game project and create a basic template that you can use on future game projects.

In Chapter 9, you will learn about working with three-dimensional (3D) models in your games, as well as how to do basic 3D animations and transformations.

Whoa! The World Isn't Flat After All

WHAT'S IN THIS CHAPTER?

- ➤ Using Blender to create 3D models
- ➤ Getting your models from Blender to XNA
- ➤ Using 3D models in your game
- ➤ Texturing your 3D models in Blender
- ➤ Understanding 3D transformations and animations
- ➤ Learning about prebuilt effects in XNA 4.0

In this chapter, you will discover how to create, skin, animate, and use three-dimensional (3D) models in your XNA games. You also will read about the prebuilt effects classes provided by XNA 4.0.

3D GRAPHICS

Not every game needs 3D graphics, but sometimes it makes sense to include them. Imagine a first-person shooter or a high-speed racing game without 3D graphics. It just wouldn't be the same.

Fortunately, your Windows Phone 7 device has excellent support for 3D graphics, including support for DirectX 9 acceleration and Shader Model 3 (with a minimum of Shader Model 2.0).

Creating 3D Models for Your Game

To start creating 3D models, first you must download and install some 3D modeling software. Numerous 3D modeling packages are available, ranging from free to expensive.

Sadly, not everyone is capable of creating good-looking models. Sites like `http://www.turbosquid.com/xna` *offer some excellent free or inexpensive models.*

Even at a basic level, becoming familiar with 3D modeling makes it much easier to get placeholder content working in your game. And knowing some 3D terminology means fewer communication barriers with any 3D modelers you might work with in the future.

For the examples in this chapter, you'll use a free 3D modeling package called Blender that has a fairly large user base, as well as numerous samples and tutorials. Blender can also be used relatively easily to create models for your XNA game.

Most 3D modeling packages are designed for much more than making game models. Many of them have functionality you will never need or touch. In this chapter, you will stick to the relevant parts. A comprehensive overview of Blender (or any 3D modeling package) is beyond the scope of this book.

Getting the Bits

To get started, you will download and install the current version of Blender, which you can grab (for free!) at `http://www.blender.org`.

This book uses version 2.49b. If you download a newer version that looks substantially different from the figures in this chapter, feel free to hit the release archive at `http://download.blender.org/release` and grab the right version so that the interface looks similar.

Once you have everything installed, it's time to launch Blender and get started making your first 3D model.

Getting Started with Blender

When you open Blender, you are greeted with a gray grid on a gray background, some gray menus and panels, and a gray square (which is actually one side of a 3D cube) in the center of the screen.

The first step in this process is to delete the cube. To delete this or any model, right-click the square to select it, and then press the Delete key on the keyboard. The delete confirmation window appears. Click Erase Selected Objects, and the default square model is removed from your 3D workspace.

Creating Primitive Shapes

If you look closely, you see a green vertical line and a red horizontal line running through the workspace. Click where the lines intersect. This is where you will add your first model: a simple cylinder.

Press the spacebar on the keyboard to bring up the Add Model menu. Select Add ➪ Mesh ➪ Cylinder, as shown in Figure 9-1.

Next, you are asked to define a few properties for your cylinder. The only one you'll adjust for now is Depth. Change that to 4.00, and then click the OK button to generate the cylinder model.

It may look like just a circle (as shown in Figure 9-2), but it really is a 3D cylinder. You're just looking straight down on it from above.

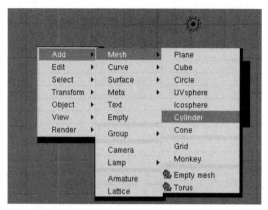

FIGURE 9-1: The Add Mesh menu selection

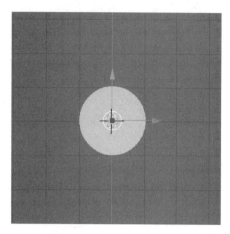

FIGURE 9-2: The top-down view of your cylinder shape

Changing Your Point of View

Using the numeric keypad to switch the camera view is something you'll need to do often in Blender. NumPad 1, 3, and 7 are the keys used often to switch from side, front, and top views. NumPad 2 is used to rotate your 3D models in the world.

 Blender is very keyboard-driven and doesn't necessarily conform to many of the conventions you are used to with Windows-based software. There is a difference between pressing 3 on the top row of the keyboard and pressing 3 on the numeric keypad. Wherever you see NumPad in the text, use the numeric keypad.

Press NumPad 3 to change your view of the cylinder to a side view (as shown in Figure 9-3) and to stage the workspace for adding the next model to the scene.

Combining Shapes

Next, you will add a sphere to sit on top of the cylinder. Begin by clicking near the top of the cylinder to indicate where you want to add a new model.

Next, press the spacebar to open the Add Model menu. Select Add ➪ Mesh ➪ UVsphere. This opens the UVSphere properties dialog.

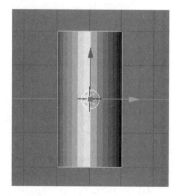

FIGURE 9-3: The side view of your cylinder model

Change the radius of the sphere to 2, just to make it a little larger, and then click the OK button to generate the sphere model. You should now be looking at a sphere sitting on top of a cylinder, similar to a board-game token.

 This is the simple 3D model you'll be working with in these chapters. It's useful as a developer to understand how this process works so that you can adjust your own work flow accordingly when working with a 3D animator on your team.

Just a bit of work is left, and then you will be done setting up and creating the pieces of your 3D model. You just need to position the pieces so that the "head" sits on the "body" in a way that is pleasing to the eye.

Bringing It All Together

To move a model around in the Blender workspace, right-click (to select) and drag (to move) the model around on the screen. Once you have it in position, left-click to drop the model in that location.

Since this is a 3D environment, you must ensure that the models are positioned correctly in all three views. To change your viewpoint, use the NumPad keys mentioned earlier to switch to the side, front, and top views.

Movement in all three views works exactly the same, so just keep switching views and positioning the model until the sphere is sitting on top of the cylinder. It's okay if the cylinder is somewhat inside of the sphere.

Once you have the models positioned the way you want them, it's time to export this model and get it displaying in an XNA game on Windows Phone 7.

Exporting Your Shapes

First, save your Blender file. You will return to add textures and animations later, so saving the base image now gives you a good starting point. To save your work file, select File ➪ Save As and name it LittleGuy.blend.

Now that your work is saved, it's time to export the model so that you can use it in a Windows Phone Game project.

To export your model, you use the FBX file format, which the XNA Content Pipeline recognizes by default. Start by selecting File ➪ Export ➪ Autodesk FBX (.fbx) as your export type.

Next, you must select your Export options, as shown in Figure 9-4. Click the Scene Objects button to ensure that all the objects in the current scene are exported. You must do that since you have both a cylinder and a sphere in your workspace.

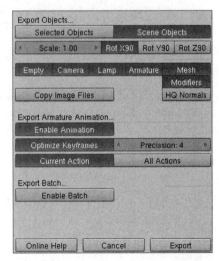

FIGURE 9-4: The Export Objects screen in Blender

Once you've done that, click the Export button. This brings up the Save dialog. Name the file `LittleGuy.fbx`, and click the Export FBX button.

You're done with Blender for now. That wasn't too scary, right? Some developers break into a cold sweat when you mention having to work in a 3D modeling tool, but now you can just nod and smile with no worries.

Using 3D Models in Your Game

Creating a model in Blender was half the battle. Now it's time to bring the model into your XNA game. This section covers adding the model to your project and displaying it onscreen. Then we'll discuss texturing the model.

Adding Models to Your Project

Start by creating a new Windows Phone Game project and naming it `3DSample`. Next, add your `LittleGuy.fbx` model to the `3DSampleContent` project.

> *The complete code for this project is available for download at the book's companion website (www.wrox.com).*

Take a look at the Properties window for the `LittleGuy` model. You see that the Content Importer has defaulted to Autodesk FBX – XNA Framework.

Displaying the Models Onscreen

Now, let's create a little model class to do all the work for you. Add a new class to the `3DSample` game project. Name it `LittleGuy.cs` and add the code shown in Listing 9-1.

LISTING 9-1: LittleGuy.cs in the 3DSample Project

```
using System;
using Microsoft.Xna.Framework;
using Microsoft.Xna.Framework.Content;
using Microsoft.Xna.Framework.Graphics;

namespace 3DSample
{
    class LittleGuy
    {
        public Model model;

        float aspectRatio;

        Vector3 modelPosition = Vector3.Zero;
        Vector2 modelRotation = Vector2.Zero;
        Vector3 cameraPosition = new Vector3(50.0f, 0.0f, 1200.0f);
```

continues

LISTING 9-1 *(continued)*

```csharp
    public LittleGuy(ContentManager content, float ratio)
    {
        model = content.Load<Model>("LittleGuy");
        aspectRatio = ratio;

        modelPosition.X = 80;
        modelPosition.Y = 50;
    }

    public void Draw()
    {
        Matrix[] transforms = new Matrix[model.Bones.Count];
        model.CopyAbsoluteBoneTransformsTo(transforms);

        foreach (ModelMesh mesh in model.Meshes)
        {
            foreach (BasicEffect effect in mesh.Effects)
            {
                effect.EnableDefaultLighting();
                effect.World = transforms[mesh.ParentBone.Index]
                    * Matrix.CreateRotationY(modelRotation.Y)
                    * Matrix.CreateRotationX(modelRotation.X)
                    * Matrix.CreateTranslation(modelPosition);

                effect.View = Matrix.CreateLookAt(cameraPosition,
                    Vector3.Zero, Vector3.Up);

                effect.Projection = Matrix.CreatePerspectiveFieldOfView(
                    MathHelper.ToRadians(45.0f), aspectRatio,
                    1.0f, 10000.0f);
            }
            mesh.Draw();
        }
    }
}
```

The bulk of the work is being done in the `Draw` method. That's where you loop through all the objects and meshes that make up your model and draw them in the XNA world.

With the `LittleGuy` class created, it's time to hook it up in the main game loop. Add the following class-level variable to the `Game1.cs` class:

```csharp
LittleGuy littleGuy;
```

Next, create and load the model by modifying the `LoadContent()` method in the `Game1.cs` class to look like Listing 9-2.

LISTING 9-2: The LoadContent() Method of the Game1 Class

```
protected override void LoadContent()
{
    // Create a new SpriteBatch, which can be used to draw textures.
    spriteBatch = new SpriteBatch(GraphicsDevice);

    // TODO: use this.Content to load your game content here
    littleGuy = new LittleGuy(Content,
                        graphics.GraphicsDevice.Viewport.AspectRatio);
}
```

Finally, you must draw the model onscreen. Modify the Draw() method in the Game1.cs class to look like Listing 9-3.

LISTING 9-3: The Draw() Method of the Game1 Class

```
protected override void Draw(GameTime gameTime)
{
    GraphicsDevice.Clear(Color.CornflowerBlue);

    // TODO: Add your drawing code here
    spriteBatch.Begin();
    littleGuy.Draw();
    spriteBatch.End();

    base.Draw(gameTime);
}
```

That's it! Press F5 to build and run the example so that you can see the model you made displayed in the Emulator or on your device, as shown in Figure 9-5.

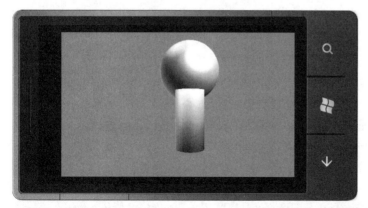

FIGURE 9-5: The LittleGuy model, as displayed on the Windows Phone Emulator

Now it is time to make your LittleGuy model a bit more interesting.

Texturing a Basic 3D Model in Blender

With your model loaded and displaying on your Windows Phone 7 device (or in the Emulator), it's time for you to start making it a little prettier. You do that by texturing or "skinning" the model in Blender.

Start by double-clicking the `LittleGuy.blend` file you saved earlier when creating the model. This launches Blender and restores your 3D workspace to where you left it when you saved. (Or, if you want the practice, go back and repeat the steps from before and re-create the model from scratch.)

Next, download the `HeadTexture.jpg` and `BodyTexture.jpg` image files from this book's website (www.wrox.com). You'll cheat a little by using images that have already been created for you. Trying to walk through using even more artist tools would make this chapter (and this book) a bit too heavy. The two image files you have will be used to texture `LittleGuy`'s head and body.

Configuring Your Workspace

Since you will be texturing, you want to adjust the Blender workspace accordingly. Start by right-clicking the line that separates the top menus from the work area. This brings up the menu for splitting/joining work areas, as shown in Figure 9-6.

Select Split Area from the menu, and then click the right side of the screen to split the area vertically.

Now, for the work area on the right, switch the mode to UV/Image Editor. You do this by clicking the Window type drop-down at the bottom left of the work area and selecting UV/Image Editor from that menu. (Note that the Window Type drop-down displays the icon of the current window type, so currently it looks like a 3D grid, as shown in Figure 9-7.)

FIGURE 9-6: The Area menu at the top of the Blender workspace

Your work area should now be split in two, with the familiar model work area on the left and the UV Image/Editor work area on the right.

Texturing the Model

You have to start texturing somewhere, so let's start with the head. Right-click the sphere to make it the actively selected item.

Press the Tab key to enter Edit mode in the model space work area. While in Edit mode, press the U key to bring up the Unwrap menu, and select Sphere from View (since you are working with a sphere).

> *Think of this as basically taking the outer layer off of a baseball so that you can draw on it, and then rewrapping it when you're done. In the simplest terms, that is what you are seeing in the UV Editor work area. There is a bit more to it than that, but you won't get the deep dive in a simple 3D chapter.*

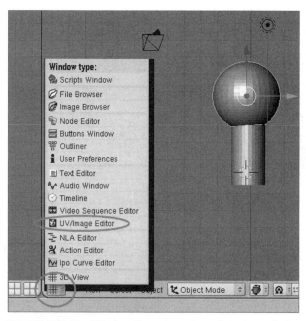

FIGURE 9-7: The Window Type drop-down list, expanded

In the UV Editor work area on the right, select Image ⇨ Open, as shown in Figure 9-8. Navigate to the `HeadTexture.jpg` file you downloaded previously. Doing this places the `HeadTexture.jpg` image onto the UV map you've created for the sphere.

Next, you must tell the sphere to use that texture. Do this by selecting (right-clicking) the sphere in the work area on the left and then pressing the Tab key to take the sphere from Edit mode back into Object mode.

Press the F5 key to enter Shading mode, and then click the Add New button that's under the Link to Object label in the lower panel, as shown in Figure 9-9. This allows you to link a texture to the sphere.

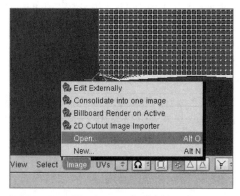

FIGURE 9-8: The Image ⇨ Open menu selection

FIGURE 9-9: The Link to Object dialog

Now, click the Texture Buttons icon (the circled button in Figure 9-10) or press the F6 key. Then click the Texture Type drop-down list (where you see the word None) and select Image.

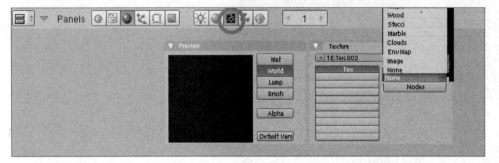

FIGURE 9-10: The Texture Buttons menu, with the Texture Type drop-down list expanded

Selecting this brings up a load file dialog where you can navigate to the `HeaderTexture.jpg` file you downloaded earlier and select it. Now, click the Auto Link button (the car icon circled in Figure 9-11) in the Texture tab to give the texture the name of the image file and complete the linking.

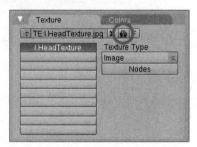

Finally, click the Material Buttons icon (the red ball next to the Texture Buttons icon) and look to the far right of the properties panel. You see that the Texture tab is currently selected. Switch that tab to Map Input and click the UV button. Your texture is now officially UV-mapped.

FIGURE 9-11: The Texture tab with the Auto Link button circled

With the texture UV-mapped and associated with the sphere, you are ready to repeat the same basic steps to texture the cylinder.

Start by right-clicking the cylinder to select it. Next, press the Tab key to put the cylinder into Edit mode. While in Edit mode, press the U key and select Cylinder from View to unwrap the cylinder.

It may look kind of strange at this point because, in the work area to your right, you are still seeing the texture you used for the head. In the UVEditor workspace, select Image ⇨ Open to navigate to and select `BodyTexture.jpg`.

With the image loaded, you need to map it to the cylinder. Select the cylinder by right-clicking it and then pressing the Tab key to switch from Edit mode back to Object mode. Press the F5 key to go into Shading mode, and click the Add New button to start creating the texture link for your cylinder.

Click the Add New button in the Texture panel on the far right of that new properties dialog, and click the Texture Buttons icon to adjust the texture properties. Change the Texture Type to Image, and then click the Load button that appears. Navigate to and select `BodyTexture.jpg`.

After you click the Auto Link button in the Texture panel, the texture is officially linked to the cylinder.

Finally, click the Material Buttons icon, and then select the Map Input tab on the far right of that properties panel. Select UV to indicate you're setting up a UV texture mapping, and you're done!

Save your `.blend` file, and then export it to a `.fbx` file called `LittleGuy.fbx`.

3D Graphics | 257

In the next section, you will learn how to display and rotate your newly textured model on your Windows Phone 7 device or in the Emulator.

Performing 3D Transformations

In this section, you will build upon the `3DSample` project you created earlier in the chapter.

Start by re-adding the `LittleGuy.fbx` file to the `3DSampleContent` project. You are asked if you want to replace the existing image, so say "Yes." Next, add the `BodyTexture.jpg` and `HeaderTexture.jpg` images to the `3DSampleContent` project as well.

You don't have to include these images in your solution, but it's easier to keep them all together.

At this point, you must edit the `LittleGuy.fbx` file. When Blender does the export, it uses the full path to link to the textures, but those paths have changed since you added them to the project. And they need to change, because you'll be releasing this game onto the phone.

It's All Relative

Double-click the `LittleGuy.fbx` file inside the Solution Explorer to open it. Then search for the text `RelativeFilename`.

There should be four occurrences of this text in the file — two for each of the textures you used for modeling. Change the path that is given for each of those properties from the (now-incorrect) exact path to just the filename instead, as shown here:

```
RelativeFilename: "BodyTexture.jpg"
```

This corrects the paths so that the model loads the files from within the project. In the next section, you will rotate `LittleGuy` onscreen.

Rotating Your 3D Object

Open the `LittleGuy.cs` class you coded for the first example, and add the `Update()` method shown in Listing 9-4.

LISTING 9-4: The Update() Method of the LittleGuy Class

```
public void Update(GameTime gameTime)
{
    modelRotation.Y += 0.1f;
    modelRotation.X += 0.01f;
}
```

This method is pretty straightforward. You are adjusting the X and Y values of the *modelRotation* variable, which is used in the `Draw()` method of your `LittleGuy` class as part of the model transformation.

Now, go to the `Game1` class and modify the `Update()` method to look like Listing 9-5.

> **LISTING 9-5:** The Update() Method of the Game1 Class

```
protected override void Update(GameTime gameTime)
{
    // Allows the game to exit
    if (GamePad.GetState(PlayerIndex.One).Buttons.Back
                                        == ButtonState.Pressed)
        this.Exit();

    // TODO: Add your update logic here
    littleGuy.Update(gameTime);

    base.Update(gameTime);
}
```

There's not much to see here. You are just adding a call to the `Update()` method of your `LittleGuy` class.

That's it. You now have a rotating textured model in your XNA game, along the lines of Figure 9-12.

FIGURE 9-12: The fully skinned LittleGuy model, being rotated

In the next section, you will head back into Blender and learn about bones and animations.

Creating 3D Animations

So far, you have created a model and skinned it, but unless you are creating a tree simulation, you probably want to see some movement onscreen. This is accomplished by adding *bones* to your 3D model and applying force to those bones.

Adding Bones to Your Model

Start by loading your `LittleGuy` model into Blender.

Now, rearrange the workspace by right-clicking the vertical line separating the Model workspace and the UV Texture Editor workspace. Select Join Areas from the menu, and then click the area you want to remove, which is the UV Texture Editor workspace on the right.

Now that you're looking at only the 3D model again, press the Tab key to switch from Edit mode back to Object mode.

 If you see a bunch of purple dots around the sphere, you're in Edit mode. Press the Tab key again to get to Object mode.

It's time to give your model some bones, so click in the open space next to the model to move the cursor there. Press the spacebar to add a new type of model to the workspace. In Blender, bones are called *armatures*, so select Add ⇨ Armature.

At the cursor position, you see a triangle-shaped transparent armature. Switch to Edit mode by pressing the F9 key, and then click the X-Ray button (located under Editing Options) so that you can actually see your bones through the model as you place them.

With the armature still selected, press Tab to be able to manipulate the bones. Right-click the tip of the triangle to select it. Press the G key on the keyboard (G for *grab*) so that you can move the mouse to make the armature larger. Make it about half the size of the model's body, and then click to stop.

Press the Tab key to switch back to Object mode. Right-click in the center of the armature to select it, and then press G to grab it. Move the armature to the base of the cylinder and, using the different views (front, side, and top), position the bone so that it's in the center of the `LittleGuy` body.

With the armature positioned in the middle of the cylinder (and still selected), press the Tab key to switch back to Edit mode. Press the E key to extend the armature. This adds a new "bone" or armature and says that the first bone is the parent. Use the mouse to grow the bone from the first one to the base of the sphere so that it looks like Figure 9-13.

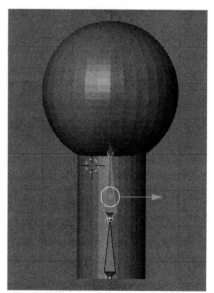

FIGURE 9-13: Two bones inside the LittleGuy model

 Growing bones can be tricky business, and you may not get it right the first time. If things start getting out of hand, don't get frustrated. Simply press Ctrl+Z (undo) a few times and try again.

Finally, it's time to give the two bones you've provided the `LittleGuy` (he's just a little guy, so he doesn't need a lot of bones) some better names.

Select the armature. Go into Edit mode and press the F9 key to select the Editing panel. Look all the way to the right, and you see a section titled Armature Bones.

By default, Blender calls these `Bone` and `Bone.001`. Select the two bones and rename them `TopBone` and `BottomBone`. This is not so important with your smaller model, but just imagine how difficult things might become if you were rigging a human being and trying to hunt for each particular bone you wanted with names such as `Bone.217`. So, do yourself a favor and give your bones logical names.

Calling them "bones" is misleading. They actually work more like muscles, pulling and pushing the model into different positions and poses. Much like your muscles, how they act on the body has a lot to do with how and where they're attached.

In Blender, you attach bones by *weight painting*. This is a way of saying how strong the relationship is between this armature and that vertex in the model. In other words, when the armature moves, it has *X* amount of impact force.

Now that the bones have been added, you will link them to the appropriate meshes. Right-click to select the cylinder model. (You may need to press the Tab key to switch to Object mode.)

Next, press the F9 key to display the editing panel at the bottom of the screen. Look for the Modifiers tab. Select Add Modifier ➪ Armature, as shown in Figure 9-14.

Next, in the Object name box, type the name of the armature you added (most likely you left it with the default name "Armature"). Then click to deselect the Envelopes button (it's pressed by default).

With that modifier added, your cylinder now has the bones attached. Repeat the same steps to add an armature modifier to the sphere. Once that is completed, it's time to tell Blender how those bones will affect the cylinder and sphere meshes.

Weight Painting

For your model, you will not do intricate weight painting. The important lesson here is that, in order for your model to work correctly with the XNA Content Pipeline, every vertex must have some type of weight associated with it.

Before you start painting, you need to make your cylinder a bit more flexible in the middle. You can do this by adding a horizontal cut to the model shape.

First, select the cylinder. Go into Edit mode by pressing the Tab key. Press Ctrl+R to make a horizontal cut on your model. When you click the cylinder, a dashed line appears. Position that line up or down to match where your two bones meet, and then click again to set it in place. This allows your cylinder to bend more in the middle when the armatures are acting on it.

It's time to get to the weight painting! (The authors apologize for adding an exclamation point to make it sound more exciting than it is, and misleading you. Unfortunately, it really *isn't* very exciting.)

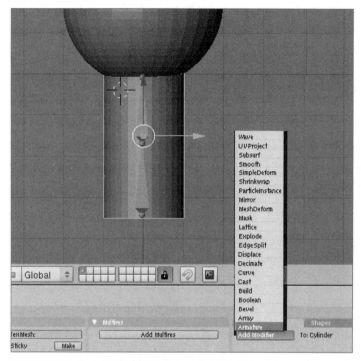

FIGURE 9-14: The Add Modifier list on the Modifiers tab

Next, right-click the cylinder to select it. Change the mode to Weight Paint via the Mode drop-down list, as shown in Figure 9-15.

Your cylinder should now be painted a cool shade of blue. This is the current "weight." Blue means that the armature isn't acting upon the cylinder at all, and red means that the armature is acting upon the cylinder very strongly. Since this rigging is extremely simple, you'll keep things equally simple and weight-paint everything red.

Begin by right-clicking `TopBone` and then clicking the Add button on the Paint tab. You will be painting the top of the cylinder red. That's the area that the top bone will affect. Be sure to switch views and rotate the cylinder to ensure that you've covered all of it.

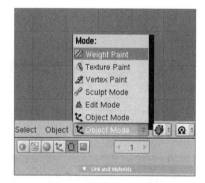

FIGURE 9-15: The Mode drop-down list

Right-click `BottomBone` and paint the entire cylinder red. You won't move the bottom bone, but if you did, it would impact the entire cylinder.

Finally, right-click to select the sphere. By painting the sphere, you are associating the top bone with the sphere. When the top bone moves and bends, the sphere should move along with it.

Now your model is weight-painted. If you were doing this on a more detailed level, you could have gotten pretty granular with just how much a particular armature's moving would have affected a particular area on a mesh.

You can now switch back to Object mode (via the Mode drop-down) and then right-click to select the armatures. With the armatures selected, a new mode is available via the drop-down called Pose Mode. Select Pose mode now, and then right-click to select the top bone in the armature. Press the R key to rotate the bone, and watch the cylinder bend and twist.

If parts of the mesh are staying in place and are stretching and pulling, you missed some areas when you were painting. You can correct this by going back into Weight Paint mode (as you did earlier) and doing some touch-ups.

There's a chance that when you try to import the model into your XNA game, you'll be told that not all bones have weights associated with them. To correct that error, just reopen your Blender file and do some more weight painting.

When you're satisfied with how your model is bending with the bones, it's time to move on to creating the animation.

Animating in Blender

To begin animating in Blender, you must first change your workspace again.

Start by right-clicking at the top of the screen. Split the areas vertically. Then move the mouse to the right edge of the screen and click the middle (or right) mouse button. Split the area on the right horizontally to make your workspace look like Figure 9-16.

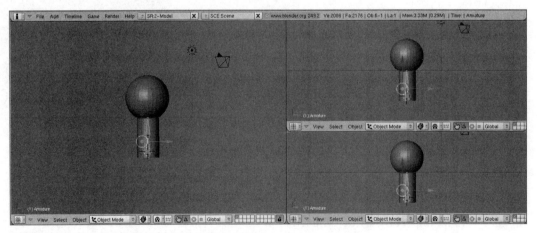

FIGURE 9-16: The Blender workspace in three views

Now, change the workspace type of the top area on the right to Action Editor (by clicking the Window Type drop-down in the lower left of the workspace). Change the bottom area on the right to Timeline the same way. Now you are ready to begin animating the model.

3D Graphics | 263

The animation you will create isn't very fancy — just a simple bowing animation. The purpose is to help you understand how animations are done and, hopefully, get you thinking about even more things you can do in the future.

You'll start in the Action Editor (top-right) workspace. Click the down-arrow button on the right of the Editing Modes box. There are no existing choices, so the only menu option present should be Add New.

 Getting confused by the numerous controls with no discernable name or icon? Just place the cursor over the various buttons and drop-down lists to get a better idea of their names.

Select Add New to create a new action, and give it the name Bow, since that's how you'll refer to it in the XNA example.

Now, you must create a *baseline pose* for your model. This will be the start of how the animation looks. Standing upright is a good way to start a bow, so you will work with that.

In the model space work area on the left, select the armature you created, and switch to Pose mode. Now press the I key and select `LocRotScale` from the menu as the key you want to insert. This adds information about the Location, Rotation, and Scale of each bone as a key in your animation. You've now created your first frame.

Next, click and drag the green line in the Action Editor work area to the 10 marker. This is where you will add the second marker for your animation.

Move back over to the model work area. While still in Pose mode, right-click to select the top bone. Press the R key to start rotating it, and rotate it slightly to the right, as though your character is beginning a bowing motion.

Select both the bones. Press the I key and again choose to insert `LocRotScale` as a key in your animation.

Move the green marker to 20, and make the bow go even deeper. Again, insert the key at that new movement position. Repeat this action, making the bow go as deep as you'd like, and then back up again as your character resumes a full standing position. A good suggestion is to make a full bow by entering 30 and to back up again by entering 60 in the Action Editor markers.

Once you're finished creating the frames of your animation, you can play them back. Move the green marker all the way to the first animation point, and then click the Play icon in the Timeline workspace. If you did things correctly, when you click Play, your character should do a slow, deep, and respectful bow. How polite. And look at you, becoming a 3D animator!

Next, you will learn how to export the model with the animations.

Adding the FBX for XNA Script

Before you can start using animation in XNA, you must download and add a new FBX export script to Blender.

A member of the XNA community realized that the normal `FBX` export script for Blender was not completely compatible with the `SkinnedModelProcessor` that you will use to load your model. Fortunately, this same community member also fixed that for you. All you need to do is add the script and then use it when exporting models with animations.

Start by following this link to download the script file:

`http://www.triplebgames.com/export_fbx__for_xna.py`

Just add that file to your Blender `Scripts` folder, and then restart Blender to make the script available for exporting.

Once the script has been added, you are ready to export the model you created. Select File ➪ Export, and then pick your new export script, which is called Autodesk FBX (.fbx) Modified for XNA.

From the properties window that appears, select Scene Objects ➪ All Actions to make sure everything you created will be exported. After you've selected those options, click the Export button.

Name the export file `LittleGuy.fbx` to stay consistent, and then click Export to complete the process.

The Microsoft Skinning Sample

Now that your model is animated, you must abandon the simple samples you have been working with. Getting animations to work properly takes a bit more work, but luckily, Microsoft has placed a tremendously helpful sample on the Creators website to help you along.

Download the Microsoft Skinning Sample from the Creators website at this link:

`http://creators.xna.com/en-US/sample/skinnedmodel`

The skinned model sample has been updated for XNA 4.0 and Windows Phone 7 and is a great example to work from. It's also one of the reasons the authors chose to focus on creating models in Blender and getting them working on the phone.

Microsoft samples blow away almost anything else you can find on the web. So, instead of drafting a new complex sample from scratch, the authors of this book focused this chapter on making it easier for you to understand all those great 3D samples that already exist.

After you have downloaded and extracted the file, launch `Skinning Sample (Phone).sln`, which opens the Windows Phone 7 version of the project for you to work on and modify.

You can run and see the sample as it is from Microsoft. Don't be too envious of the beautiful model. The one you made is still pretty cool because you are the one who made it.

Now it's time to start modifying the sample so that you can see your animation working on the phone.

Start by adding `LittleGuy.fbx` to the `SkinningSampleContent` project found in the solution. After you've added it, be sure to switch its content processor to the `SkinnedModelProcessor`. After that, add your `HeadTexture.jpg` and `BodyTexture.jpg` files to the content project as well.

Next, open the `SkinningSample` class. This is the only file you must change to see your animation working on the phone.

Modify the *cameraRotation* and *cameraDistance* class-level variables to have the following default values:

```
float cameraRotation = 90;
float cameraDistance = 10;
```

Your `LittleGuy` model is, well, a little guy, and the dude model used originally in the sample is much larger, so you must adjust some of the positioning and distance values.

Change the `LoadContent()` method to look like Listing 9-6.

LISTING 9-6: The LoadContent() Method of the Game Class

```
protected override void LoadContent()
{
    // Load the model.
    currentModel = Content.Load<Model>("LittleGuy");

    // Look up our custom skinning information.
    SkinningData skinningData = currentModel.Tag as SkinningData;

    if (skinningData == null)
        throw new InvalidOperationException
            ("This model does not contain a SkinningData tag.");

    // Create an animation player, and start decoding an animation clip.
    animationPlayer = new AnimationPlayer(skinningData);

    AnimationClip clip = skinningData.AnimationClips["Bow"];

    animationPlayer.StartClip(clip);
}
```

In this method, you load your `LittleGuy` model and then tell the `AnimationClip` class to play the `Bow` action you created in Blender.

Next, in the `Draw()` method, change how the *view* variable is created so that it looks like the following:

```
// Compute camera matrices.
Matrix view = Matrix.CreateTranslation(-20, 5, -10) *
              Matrix.CreateRotationY(MathHelper.ToRadians(cameraRotation)) *
              Matrix.CreateRotationX(MathHelper.ToRadians(cameraArc)) *
              Matrix.CreateLookAt(new Vector3(0, 0, -cameraDistance),
                                  new Vector3(0, 0, 0),
                                  Vector3.Up);
```

All you are doing here is adjusting some of the positioning values so that the `LittleGuy` model is properly centered on the screen.

That's it! You can now build and run the sample to see your little guy bowing to you.

If you run into trouble building or running the sample, and you get an error along the lines of `Error normalizing vertex bone weights. BoneWeightCollection does not contain any weighting values,` *just go back into Blender and do some weight-painting touch-ups until you're sure you've painted every vertex. (It's pretty easy to miss them!)*

WORKING WITH EFFECTS

If you're familiar with XNA 3.x and how shaders worked, you're in for a bit of a surprise. In an effort to get rid of duplicate functionality, and because of some differences between DirectX 9, DirectX 10, and DirectX 11, the following low-level shader APIs have been removed:

- `VertexShader`
- `PixelShader`
- `SetVertexShaderConstant`
- `SetPixelShaderConstant`
- `GetVertexShaderConstant`
- `GetPixelShaderConstant`
- `ShaderConstantTable`
- `ShaderProfile`
- `ShaderRegisterSet`
- `ShaderSemantic`

In addition, the following APIs were removed because of redundancy, poor performance, confusion, or lack of use:

- `EffectPool`
- `EffectParameterBlock`
- `EffectFunction`
- `Effect.Creator`
- `EffectParameter.SetArrayRange`
- `EffectTechnique.IsParameterUsed`

Fortunately, the XNA team has provided a collection of prebuilt effects classes that are easy to use and should cover most cases.

Stock Effects

Primarily because of hardware limitations on the phone hardware, Windows Phone 7 does not support custom shaders. Therefore, Microsoft provides the following five stock effects classes in XNA 4.0 instead:

➤ `BasicEffect` includes transformations and basic lighting for shading. It has optional support for additional lighting, fog, and texturing. The `BasicEffect` API has not changed since XNA 3.1, but significant performance optimizations have been made.

Using lighting can greatly enhance the look of your game, but comes with a cost. When using lights, stick to one light for best performance, or use up to three directional lights to create some interesting 3D effects.

➤ `SkinnedEffect` uses up to 72 bones and four weights (per bone) to move an object by influencing the vertex positions. Use this class for character animations.

➤ `EnvironmentMapEffect` uses a diffuse texture to detail an object and a cube map texture containing an environment map to shade the object because of the environment. This causes the object to reflect the surrounding scene. Additionally, the `fresnel` parameter controls the object's shininess based on the surface's geometry.

Environment mapping renders a cube map of the scene in the six cardinal directions from any point in 3D space. When the cube map is then mapped back onto an object, it creates the visual complexity that the eye expects to see from shiny reflections.

➤ `DualTextureEffect` uses two individual textures, each with its own set of texture coordinates. This technique can be used to generate visually complex imagery if the first texture contains the basic color or detail and the second texture contains complex lighting.

➤ `AlphaTestEffect` can greatly improve rendering performance by updating only pixels where objects are being drawn in a scene. This is performed by setting a test function and a reference alpha level. Any pixel that fails the test is killed off and doesn't get shaded.

Using the Reach Graphics Demo

To get a really good look at all five of the previously mentioned stock effects in action, visit Microsoft's Create site on MSDN and download the Reach Graphics Demo at `http://create.msdn.com/en-US/education/catalog/sample/reach_graphics_demo`.

Interestingly, most of the code in that demo came from other samples also available on the Create site. If you haven't browsed the samples library yet, do so. It contains an incredible amount of useful information.

Once you have the demo downloaded and running, take a look at each of the five configurable effects, and experiment with the settings to get an idea of what they all mean.

SUMMARY

In this chapter, you learned how to use Blender to create and skin a 3D model, as well as how to rig the model with bones for an animation. (You can download Blender at www.Blender.org.) After creating and rigging your model in Blender, you also learned how to import that model into your XNA game and animate it.

Windows Phone 7 does not allow you to create custom shaders, but you have been given a set of configurable effects that will cover most cases. These include `BasicEffect`, `SkinnedEffect`, `EnvironmentMapEffect`, `DualTextureEffect`, and `AlphaTestEffect`.

The Reach Graphics Sample provides an excellent set of examples that you can draw upon when working with the configurable effects.

In Chapter 10, you will learn about the Microsoft Push Notification service and how to alert your players with in-game vibration.

10

It's Your Turn!

WHAT'S IN THIS CHAPTER?

- Understanding Microsoft Push Notifications and how to use pop-up toasts
- Handling in-game notifications
- Using push notifications to update your game's start tile
- Knowing whether your game is running on a device or in emulation
- Vibrating your phone with the VibrateController class

A key aspect of building a great Windows Phone 7 game experience is leveraging the platform's features. Push notifications can be used to send updates and alerts in a variety of ways: in-game (also known as "raw") updates, pop-up toasts, and tile updates.

These types of notifications have many uses, such as informing players when it is their turn, how many active games are waiting for them, or that a message has arrived from another player in a multiplayer game.

In addition to learning about push notifications in this chapter, you will learn how to vibrate the phone and detect your game environment.

UNDERSTANDING PUSH NOTIFICATIONS

The Microsoft Push Notification Service provides a dedicated channel for sending information to a mobile application or game from a web service. This is a significant improvement over having to frequently poll a service to look for updates or notifications, since that would have a negative impact on battery life. Push notifications work the opposite way, allowing you to create cloud services that can push information to your phone, even when your game is not running.

One important thing you need to understand about push notifications as a game developer is that delivery is not guaranteed. This means that you should not be using them to transmit game data or anything essential to game play.

Instead, push notifications are intended for noncritical data, such as turn notifications, game status messages, incoming message alerts, and so on. A best practice for push notifications is to alert your player that something has occurred and provide a way to retrieve the same message manually in the player's game.

Here are some sample scenarios:

- You have created a turn-based, two-player game that allows for up to 32 concurrent games with other players. Each time you or your opponent takes a turn, a message is sent via a push notification to the other player that it is now his or her turn. The total count of games waiting for you to take your turn is displayed as a number on the game's Start tile, via a tile update. Even if push notification fails, you will still be notified of your turn status the next time you launch the game, because the game would check a service to fetch the latest game state.

- You have created a game that allows players to pass short messages back and forth when they submit a turn. A pop-up toast could be used to alert the other player that a message has been received, rather than carrying (and possibly losing) the contents of the message. Even if this notification never makes it, and the pop-up toast never displays, the other player sees the new message the next time he or she starts the game.

- As you play your new Frontier Wars game, raw notifications provide information ("Bessie Mae done got a new cow!") about the actions of other players playing the same game. These do not affect game play, and the player is not impacted if the message is missed. However, seeing the actions of others provides a feeling of interaction and makes the game more interesting.

As you can see, you have a variety of ways to use push notifications in your games. In the following sections, you will learn how to create and consume each of the three types: raw, toast, and tile updates.

Raw Notifications

In-game or "raw" notifications are received only when your game is running, and they can be processed or displayed in the context of the game. How you display them is up to you, of course, but the possibilities are endless.

To demonstrate how raw notifications work, let's create two projects instead of one. In addition to a Windows Phone Game project, let's create a Windows Forms project to push the raw notifications to your phone game.

The complete code for these projects is available for download at the book's companion web site (www.wrox.com).

Understanding Push Notifications | 271

If you don't have an actual device, it's okay. This demo works equally well in the Emulator without any changes.

PushItRawSample

First, create the Windows Phone Game project and name it `PushItRawSample`.

Add a `SpriteFont` to the `PushItRawSampleContent` project, and accept the default name. Set the size to `20`.

Next, open the `References` section in Solution Explorer, and add a reference to `Microsoft.Phone`. This gives you access to the contents of the `Microsoft.Phone.Notification` namespace, which contains the `HttpNotification` class used in this sample.

Add the following `using` statements to the top of the `Game1` class:

```
using Microsoft.Phone.Notification;
using System.Diagnostics;
```

You already know what the first statement is for. The reference to `System.Diagnostics` isn't something you would use in a production application, but it's a necessary part of this sample, as you will see shortly.

All applications or games that use push notifications need an entry for `Publisher` in the `WMApp Manifest`. In Solution Explorer, expand the Properties section and open the `WMAppManifest.xml` file.

The `App` node has a series of attributes that define your game. Scroll all the way to the right, and edit the `Publisher` attribute. You can put anything you like between the quotes, so enter `PushItRaw` there.

You can put whatever you like in the `Publisher` attribute, as long as you put something there. Otherwise, it won't work. When actually publishing to the Marketplace, you are encouraged to put your company name or website name as `Publisher`.

In your `Game1` class, add the following class-level variables:

```
SpriteFont font;
string notificationMessage = "No message received";
```

Scroll down to the `LoadContent()` method, and add this line to load your `SpriteFont` into memory:

```
font = Content.Load<SpriteFont>("SpriteFont1");
```

You will now use the `HttpNotificationChannel` class to create a notification channel between the Microsoft Push Notification Service and your game. This also creates a new subscription for your raw notifications.

Before adding any code, take a look at Listing 10-1 to see the members of the `HttpNotificationChannel` class.

LISTING 10-1: The HttpNotificationChannel Class

```csharp
// Creates a notification channel between the Push Notification Service and
// the Push Client and creates a new subscription for raw notifications.
public class HttpNotificationChannel : IDisposable
{
    public HttpNotificationChannel(string channelName);
    public HttpNotificationChannel(string channelName, string serviceName);

    // The name of the notification channel.
    public string ChannelName { get; }

    // The current active notification channel URI.
    public Uri ChannelUri { get; }

    // Returns true if the notification channel is currently bound to a
    // tile notification subscription and false if not.
    public bool IsShellTileBound { get; }

    // Returns true if the notification channel is currently bound to a
    // toast notification subscription and false if not.
    public bool IsShellToastBound { get; }

    // Returns the URI associated with the notification channel.
    public event EventHandler<NotificationChannelUriEventArgs>
                            ChannelUriUpdated;

    // This exception is thrown when something unexpected happens when
    // using the HttpNotificationChannel class.
    public event EventHandler<NotificationChannelErrorEventArgs>
                            ErrorOccurred;

    // The event raised when the application receives a raw notification.
    public event EventHandler<HttpNotificationEventArgs>
                            HttpNotificationReceived;

    // The event raised when the application receives a toast notification.
    public event EventHandler<NotificationEventArgs>
                            ShellToastNotificationReceived;

    // The method the application uses to bind its default tile with
    // a notification subscription. The tile can only contain local
    // references for resources.
    public void BindToShellTile();

    // Binds the tile passed as the input parameter with a notification
    // subscription. The tile can contain either a local or remote
    // resource reference.
    public void BindToShellTile(Collection<Uri> baseUri);

    // The method used to bind a toast notification subscription
    // to the HttpNotificationChannel class instance.
    public void BindToShellToast();
```

```
    // Closes a notification channel and disassociates all of the
    // subscriptions associated with this instance of the
    // HttpNotificationChannel class.
    public void Close();

    // Used to find a previously created notification channel.
    public static HttpNotificationChannel Find(string channelName);

    // Opens a notification channel with the Push Notification Service.
    public void Open();

    // Unbinds the active tile notification subscription from the
    // notification channel.
    public void UnbindToShellTile();

    // Unbinds the active toast notification subscription from the
    // notification channel.
    public void UnbindToShellToast();
}
```

Using this class, you can create and open a notification channel named `RawNotificationSample` and use that to receive push notifications in this sample project.

Start by adding a class-level variable to contain the notification channel:

```
HttpNotificationChannel channel;
```

Next, create a new method called `CreateNotificationChannel()`, as shown in Listing 10-2.

LISTING 10-2: The CreateNotificationChannel() Method of the Game1 Class

```
void CreateNotificationChannel()
{
    channel = HttpNotificationChannel.Find("RawNotificationSample");

    if (channel == null)
    {
        channel = new HttpNotificationChannel("RawNotificationSample");
        SetupDelegates();
        channel.Open();
    }
    else
    {
        SetupDelegates();
        Debug.WriteLine("Copy URI for Push Tool: "
                        + channel.ChannelUri.ToString());
    }
}
```

This method contains a fair amount of activity. The `Find()` method is a static method that checks to see if the `RawNotificationSample` channel has already been created, and it returns the `HttpNotificationChannel` object if it has.

If you get back a `null`, your channel must not exist, so you create one by calling the constructor and passing in the name you want to use. Then you set up some delegates (which you will look at shortly) and open the newly created channel.

If you did not get back a `null`, you must have an active channel. You'll set up those delegates as before, and then write a message containing the channel URI to the Output window in Visual Studio 2010.

You haven't heard about creating services yet (that's in Chapter 11). So, for now you will simulate the service by copying the URI from the Output window and pasting it into the Windows program you will create in the second part of this sample.

With your `CreateNotificationChannel()` method complete, add a call to your `LoadContent()` method.

Right now, Visual Studio should be complaining about the lack of a `SetupDelegates()` method, so add the one shown in Listing 10-3.

LISTING 10-3: The SetupDelegates() Method of the Game1 Class

```
void SetupDelegates()
{
    channel.ChannelUriUpdated +=
        new EventHandler<NotificationChannelUriEventArgs>
            (channel_ChannelUriUpdated);

    channel.HttpNotificationReceived +=
        new EventHandler<HttpNotificationEventArgs>
            (channel_HttpNotificationReceived);
}
```

In this method, you set up two event handlers. The first is in response to a change in the URI for your notification channel.

Occasionally, your URI changes and the `ChannelUriUpdated` event fires. This typically doesn't happen while your game is actively running, but in rare cases it can. More likely, your game will be suspended as a result of the phone's locking because of inactivity, and you will get a new URI when it resumes.

When this event occurs, the `channel_ChannelUpdated()` method is called. You can see the method in Listing 10-4, so add it to your `Game1` class now.

LISTING 10-4: The channel_ChannelUriUpdated() Method of the Game1 Class

```
void channel_ChannelUriUpdated(object sender,
                               NotificationChannelUriEventArgs e)
{
    Debug.WriteLine("Copy URI for Push Tool: " + e.ChannelUri.ToString());
}
```

As you can see, it is very similar to the `else` clause of Listing 10-2, with one exception. This time, you are passing in the event argument as `e` and pulling the `ChannelUri` property from there.

The second event handler is triggered in response to receiving the actual HTTP notification, which contains your raw information. When this occurs, the `channel_HttpNotificationReceived()` method is called. Take a look at Listing 10-5 and add it to your `Game1` class.

LISTING 10-5: The channel_HttpNotificationReceived() Method of the Game1 Class

```
void channel_HttpNotificationReceived(object sender,
                                    HttpNotificationEventArgs e)
{
    if (e.Notification.Body != null && e.Notification.Headers != null)
    {
        System.IO.StreamReader reader =
            new System.IO.StreamReader(e.Notification.Body);
        notificationMessage = reader.ReadLine();
    }
}
```

When this method is called, you do a quick check to ensure that you have a valid notification. Then, you set up a `StreamReader` object to pull out the body of the notification and store it in the *notificationMessage* string you created earlier. This will be used in the `Draw()` method to display the raw notification.

At this point, you're almost finished with the phone half of the sample. The only thing remaining is to add some code to your `Draw()` method to actually display the contents of the raw notification. Add the following block of code just before the call to the `base.Draw()` method:

```
spriteBatch.Begin();
spriteBatch.DrawString(font, notificationMessage, new Vector2(50,200),
    Color.White);
spriteBatch.End();
```

That's it for the phone part of the sample. Before you move on to the next step, take a moment to build and run the `PushItRawSample` project. You can deploy to either the Emulator or the phone at this point; it doesn't really matter.

On the phone's screen, you see the text "No message received"; it will stay that way until the phone receives a raw notification.

Now, take a look at the Output window in Visual Studio 2010. At the very bottom, you should see a message containing the URI for sending raw notification data to your phone (or the Emulator).

 Depending on whether you are running Visual Studio 2010 Express or a different SKU, such as Professional or Ultimate, you may not see the Output window. If you are running Express, make sure you are set for Expert mode. If you still don't see it, try pressing Ctrl+W and then O to open the Output window manually.

This URI will be different every time your game is run, or if it gets suspended and resumed. Normally, you would have a cloud service in place through which you could send that URI

information. That way, if any notifications need to be sent to the phone, the service would have the proper URI for each active player.

In this case, you are the service. You will take the URI from the Output window and paste it into the Windows form you are about to create, along with a message for the phone.

PushItRawWindows

Welcome to the second half of the raw-notifications sample. You'll create a Windows client program that accepts two inputs: the URI from your phone application, and a message to send. When you click the "Push it Raw" button, `HttpWebRequest` creates and sends a stream to the Push Notification Service via the URI specified.

> You can't do this next part in the Windows Phone edition of Visual Studio 2010 Express. You need either a full version of Visual Studio 2010 or the freely downloadable Visual C# 2010 Express to have access to the correct project types. The Express edition of C# is available for download at www.microsoft.com/express.

Start by creating a new Windows Forms application and naming it `PushItRawWindows`.

On your `Form1` design surface, drag two labels, two textboxes, and a button. Configure them as shown in Table 10-1.

TABLE 10-1: PushItRawWindows Form1 Controls and Properties

CONTROL NAME	PROPERTY	VALUE
Form1	Text	Push it Raw
label1	Text	Phone URI
label2	Text	Message
txtPhoneUri	Size	681, 22
txtMessage	Size	681, 22
btnRaw	Text	Push it Raw

The end result doesn't have to be a perfect match with Figure 10-1, but it should look reasonably close. Be sure to name your textbox and button controls correctly, or the code you are about to write won't work properly.

Once you have the design surface finished, double-click the button control to create your `Click` event. In the handler for the `Click` event, add the following line of code:

```
SendRawNotification(txtPhoneUri.Text, txtMessage.Text);
```

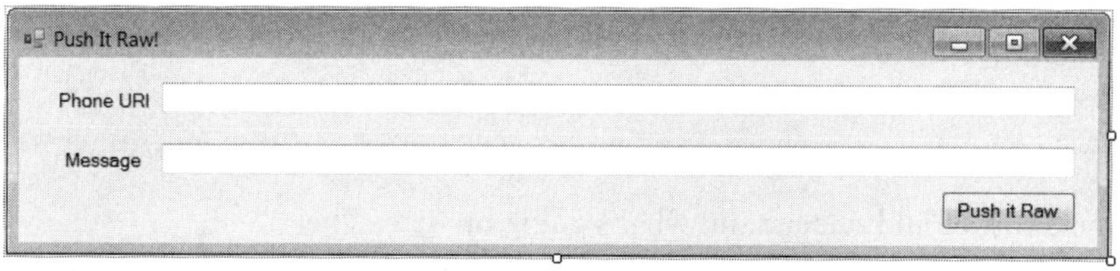

Understanding Push Notifications | 277

FIGURE 10-1: The PushItRaw Windows Forms design surface

If only it were that simple! Right about now, Visual Studio is telling you that you don't have a `SendRawNotification()` method defined yet. Of course, that's where the real action is.

At the top of the class file, add the following two `using` statements:

```
using System.Net;
using System.IO;
```

Add the code shown in Listing 10-6 to your `Form1` class, right after the `Click` event handler.

LISTING 10-6: The SendRawNotification() Method of the Form1 Class

```
private void SendRawNotification(string uri, string message)
{
    var sendNotificationRequest = (HttpWebRequest)WebRequest.Create(uri);

    sendNotificationRequest.Method = "POST";
    sendNotificationRequest.Headers.Add("X-NotificationClass", "3");

    byte[] notificationMessage = new UTF8Encoding().GetBytes(message);
    sendNotificationRequest.ContentLength = notificationMessage.Length;

    using (Stream requestStream = sendNotificationRequest.GetRequestStream())
    {
        requestStream.Write(notificationMessage,
                            0,
                            notificationMessage.Length);
    }

    var response = (HttpWebResponse)sendNotificationRequest.GetResponse();

    string notificationStatus = response.Headers["X-NotificationStatus"];
    string subscriptionStatus = response.Headers["X-SubscriptionStatus"];
    string connectionStatus = response.Headers["X-DeviceConnectionStatus"];
}
```

Take a moment to go through this method. First you take the URI you pasted into the textbox and create your `HttpWebRequest` object.

Next, you set your request method to `"POST"` and add a notification class with a value of `"3"` to the `Headers` collection of the request.

Be sure you use `"POST"` *for your request method, or you will get a 405 "Method Not Allowed" response code.*

Before you go any further, you should understand what's going on here. The `"X-NotificationClass"` header is treated like a priority by the Push Notification Service, and a value of `"3"` means to send the message immediately.

A quick trip to the MSDN documentation reveals three possible values:

- 3 — The Push Notification Service delivers the message immediately.
- 13 — The message is delivered within 450 seconds (7.5 minutes).
- 23 — The message is delivered within 900 seconds (15 minutes).

Next, you set up a byte array called *notificationMessage* to hold the contents of the message textbox. The length of this array is then used to set the length of the `HttpWebRequest`.

After that, you create a stream and feed it to the `HttpWebRequest`, sending it to the specified URI.

Finally, using the same `HttpWebRequest` object, you fetch the response information and dump it into the variables at the end.

Even though you don't actually display the contents of those variables on your form, they can provide useful diagnostic information that you can see by adding some `Debug.WriteLine()` statements, or by placing a breakpoint and examining each one individually.

Don't just discard the response codes when building your game, because they contain some important information. If, after sending your notification, you get a value of `QueueFull` in the `X-NotificationStatus` response, you may want to resend your notification later.

On the other hand, a value of `Received` doesn't actually mean the phone received your notification — only that the Push Notification Service received it. A quick check of the `X-DeviceConnectionStatus` may reveal a value of `Connected` or `Temporarily Disconnected`. The former means your notification was accepted and queued for delivery. The latter means the notification is in the queue, but the device is currently disconnected.

At this point, you're ready to test your raw notifications. The easiest way to do this is to have two copies of Visual Studio running at the same time. Have your XNA project in one and the Windows form you just created in the other.

Build and run your XNA project on either the Emulator or the phone. Keep an eye on the Output window in Visual Studio. After 2 to 3 seconds (sometimes longer), you see the URI. Copy the URI (not the whole message, just the URI).

On your phone's screen (or the Emulator) you see the message "No message received," indicating that the phone is ready to get a raw notification.

Now, in the other copy of Visual Studio, build and run your Windows Forms application. Paste the URI into the top box, type a message in the bottom box, and press the button.

After a couple seconds, the message on your phone changes to match the message you typed into the Windows form.

When you are running on an actual device, you should be aware of one more thing. The Emulator never "goes idle," but if your phone goes back to the lock screen after an idle period, your game is suspended. When your game resumes, you get a new URI, and the `ChannelUriUpdated` event fires. If you have a phone, let it go idle while running this sample, and keep an eye on the Output window in Visual Studio as you resume.

Pop-Up Toasts

Toast notifications are system-wide notifications that do not disrupt active games or applications and that require no user intervention. They hang around the top of the screen for 10 seconds and then vanish.

If you want to get rid of a toast sooner, a `Flick` gesture will do the trick. If you tap the toast, the sending application or game is launched. For an example of a toast notification, look at the upper area of Figure 10-2.

FIGURE 10-2: A sample toast notification

Toasts contain two properties you can manipulate: a title and a subtitle. The title is displayed in bold text, and the subtitle is displayed in regular text, immediately following the title.

In addition to the title and subtitle, a toast notification displays a tiny version of your game icon to the left. There is no method for passing a different icon.

PassTheToastSample

To help you understand how all this works, it's time to do another sample.

This sample is conceptually similar to the `PushItRawSample` from the preceding section. However, in addition to receiving raw notifications in your game, you will receive toast notifications outside of your game.

For toast notifications to work, you need a URI. To get a URI, your game must be run at least once. Much like in the preceding sample, you will act as the intermediary service that communicates with the Push Notification Service.

As soon as you have a URI, you can continue sending toasts to the same URI until it changes. Several things can cause a URI to change, including receiving malformed messages. After the URI has changed, your players will be unable to receive any more toasts related to your game until they run it again.

Start by creating a new Windows Phone Game project, and name it `PassTheToastSample`.

Next, open the `References` section in Solution Explorer, and add a reference to `Microsoft.Phone`. This gives you access to the contents of the `Microsoft.Phone.Notification` namespace, which contains the `HttpNotification` class used in this sample.

Add the following `using` statements to the top of the `Game1` class:

```
using Microsoft.Phone.Notification;
using System.Diagnostics;
```

As mentioned in the preceding section, if you want to use Push Notifications in your game, it must have an entry for `Publisher` in the `WMAppManifest`.

In Solution Explorer, expand the `Properties` section and open the `WMAppManifest.xml` file.

The `App` node has a series of attributes that define your game. Scroll all the way to the right, and edit the `Publisher` attribute. You can put anything you like between the quotes, so enter `PassTheToast` there.

Add a class-level variable to store your `HttpNotificationChannel` object:

```
HttpNotificationChannel channel;
```

Next, add the `CreateNotificationChannel()` method, as shown in Listing 10-7.

LISTING 10-7: The CreateNotificationChannel() Method of the Game1 Class

```
void CreateNotificationChannel()
{
    channel = HttpNotificationChannel.Find("PassTheToastSample");

    if (channel == null)
    {
        channel = new HttpNotificationChannel("PassTheToastSample");
        SetupDelegates();
        channel.Open();
    }
    else
    {
        SetupDelegates();
        Debug.WriteLine("Copy URI for Push Tool: "
                    + channel.ChannelUri.ToString());
    }
}
```

When you have this method in place, add the following line to your `LoadContent()` method:

```
CreateNotificationChannel();
```

Now add the `SetupDelegates()` method, as shown in Listing 10-8.

Understanding Push Notifications | 281

LISTING 10-8: The SetupDelegates() Method of the Game1 Class

```
void SetupDelegates()
{
    channel.ChannelUriUpdated +=
        new EventHandler<NotificationChannelUriEventArgs>
            (channel_ChannelUriUpdated);
}
```

Much like the raw sample, this code binds the `ChannelUriUpdated` event to an event handler named `channel_ChannelUriUpdated()`. Add the method shown in Listing 10-9 to your class.

LISTING 10-9: The channel_ChannelUriUpdated() Method of the Game1 Class

```
void channel_ChannelUriUpdated(object sender,
                               NotificationChannelUriEventArgs e)
{
    Debug.WriteLine("Copy URI for Push Tool: "
                    + channel.ChannelUri.ToString());
}
```

This outputs the URI for you to copy and paste into the Windows Forms program you will create in the second half of this sample.

You're almost done. You have only one more method to update. Ironically, it's the `Update()` method. Add the following block of code to your `Update()` method, before the call to `base.Update()`:

```
// Bind the channel to toast notifications if it's open but still unbound
if (channel != null && !channel.IsShellToastBound)
{
    channel.BindToShellToast();
}
```

This code ensures that you have an open channel and binds it to toast notifications if it's not already bound. Without this functionality, your game would not know that it has received any toast notifications.

At this point, you have everything you need in XNA to find or create a notification channel and to send toast notifications to your players when they are out of your game.

PassTheToastWindows

In this part of the sample, you will create a Windows Forms program to push a toast notification to the phone or the Emulator (wherever you ran the XNA to generate the URI).

This time, you must accept three inputs: the URI from your phone application, a title for your toast, and a subtitle. When you click the Pass The Toast! button, `HttpWebRequest` creates and sends a stream to the Push Notification Service via the URI specified.

Just like in the previous sample, you can't do this next part in the Windows Phone edition of Visual Studio 2010 Express. If you don't have a full version of Visual Studio 2010, you can download Visual C# 2010 Express at www.microsoft.com/express.

Start by creating a new Windows Forms Application and naming it `PassTheToastWindows`.

On your `Form1` design surface, drag three labels, three textboxes, and a button. Configure them as shown in Table 10-2.

TABLE 10-2: PassTheToastWindows Form1 Controls and Properties

CONTROL NAME	PROPERTY	VALUE
Form1	Text	Pass The Toast!
label1	Text	Phone URI
label2	Text	Title
label3	Text	Subtitle
txtPhoneUri	Size	681, 22
txtTitle	Size	681, 22
txtSubtitle	Size	681, 22
btnRaw	Text	Pass The Toast!

The end result doesn't have to be a perfect match with Figure 10-3, but it should look reasonably close. Be sure to name your textbox and button controls correctly, or the code you are about to write won't work properly.

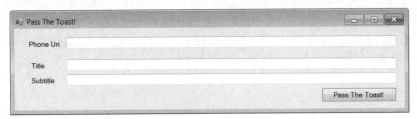

FIGURE 10-3: The PassTheToast Windows Forms design surface

When you have the design surface finished, double-click the button control to create your `Click` event. In the handler for the `Click` event, add the following line of code:

```
SendToastNotification(txtPhoneUri.Text, txtTitle.Text, txtSubtitle.Text);
```

Before you start writing the `SendToastNotification()` method, add these two `using` statements to the top of the class file:

```
using System.Net;
using System.IO;
```

Of course, you don't actually have a `SendToastNotification()` method defined yet, so add the code shown in Listing 10-10 to your `Form1` class, right after the `Click` event handler.

LISTING 10-10: The SendToastNotification() Method of the Form1 Class

```
private void SendToastNotification(string uri, string title, string subtitle)
{
    var sendToast = (HttpWebRequest)WebRequest.Create(uri);

    sendToast.Method = "POST";
    sendToast.ContentType = "text/xml";
    sendToast.Headers.Add("X-WindowsPhone-Target", "toast");
    sendToast.Headers.Add("X-NotificationClass", "2");

    string toastXML = "<?xml version=\"1.0\" encoding=\"utf-8\"?>" +
                    "<wp:Notification xmlns:wp=\"WPNotification\">" +
                        "<wp:Toast>" +
                            "<wp:Text1>" + title + "</wp:Text1>" +
                            "<wp:Text2>" + subtitle + "</wp:Text2>" +
                        "</wp:Toast>" +
                    "</wp:Notification>";

    byte[] toastMessage = new UTF8Encoding().GetBytes(toastXML);
    sendToast.ContentLength = toastMessage.Length;

    using (Stream requestStream = sendToast.GetRequestStream())
    {
        requestStream.Write(toastMessage,
                            0,
                            toastMessage.Length);
    }

    var response = (HttpWebResponse)sendToast.GetResponse();

    string notificationStatus = response.Headers["X-NotificationStatus"];
    string subscriptionStatus = response.Headers["X-SubscriptionStatus"];
    string connectionStatus = response.Headers["X-DeviceConnectionStatus"];
}
```

Take a moment to go through this method. First you take the URI you pasted into the textbox and create your `HttpWebRequest` object.

Next, you set your request method to `"POST"` and set the content type to XML. In the `Headers` collection, you specify that you are sending a toast to the phone. Finally, you add a notification class with a value of `"2"`, which tells the Push Notification Service to send the message immediately.

This is a little different from the raw notifications, where you used a 3 to send immediately. Here are the values for toast notifications:

- 2 — The Push Notification Service delivers the message immediately.
- 12 — The message is delivered within 450 seconds (7.5 minutes).
- 22 — The message is delivered within 900 seconds (15 minutes).

You must send your toast information as XML, as defined by the previous `ContentType` property, so you create a notification message containing two pieces of text: a title and subtitle.

Next, you set up a byte array called *toastMessage* to hold the XML message. The length of this array is then used to set the length of your `HttpWebRequest` object.

Finally, you create a stream and feed the XML to the `HttpWebRequest` (which is pointed at the URI you specified), fetch the response information, and dump it into the variables at the end.

Take a look at the previous sample (`PushItRawSample`) for an explanation of what the response information means and how you can work with it in your service.

You're finally ready to test your toast notifications. The easiest way to do this is to have two copies of Visual Studio running at the same time. Have your XNA project in one and the Windows form you just created in the other.

Build and run your XNA project on either the Emulator or the phone. Keep an eye on the Output window in Visual Studio. After 2 to 3 seconds (sometimes longer), you see the URI. Copy the URI (not the whole message, just the URI).

At this point, you can end your game. If you were using the Emulator, be sure to keep it running (the Emulator, not the game).

Now, in the other copy of Visual Studio, build and run your Windows Forms application. Paste the URI you just copied into the Phone URI textbox, type a title and subtitle into the corresponding boxes, and press the Pass the Toast! button.

After a (hopefully) brief wait, your phone or the Emulator displays a toast message containing the title and subtitle you typed into the Windows form.

Toasts will not pop up while your game is running, regardless of orientation or whether you have it set to full screen. Fortunately, there is a way to consume toast (Get it? Consume toast?) data in your game, so keep reading!

Consuming Toasts as Raw Notifications in Your Game

With a little extra code, it is possible to display information received as a toast within the context of your game, just like a raw notification.

Go back into your `PassTheToastSample` example (XNA) and add a `SpriteFont` to the `PassTheToastSampleContent` project. Just accept the default name and set the size property to 30.

Next, add these two class-level variables:

Understanding Push Notifications | 285

```
SpriteFont font;
string notificationMessage = "No message received";
```

You don't need to add anything to the `Game` class constructor or the `Initialize()` method. So, skip both of those and add the following to the `LoadContent()` method:

```
font = Content.Load<SpriteFont>("SpriteFont1");
```

There is nothing to change in the `CreateNotificationChannel()` method, so skip that as well.

In the `SetupDelegates()` method, add the following line to add an event handler for the `ShellToastNotificationReceived` event:

```
channel.ShellToastNotificationReceived +=
    new EventHandler<NotificationEventArgs>
        (channel_ShellToastNotificationReceived);
```

This allows you to receive toast notification data that would otherwise be ignored while your game is running.

> *This still doesn't give you the ability to have toast notifications pop up onscreen while your game is running, but you can use the toast data just like raw data.*

Now, add the `channel_ShellToastNotificationReceived()` method shown in Listing 10-11 to your `Game1` class.

LISTING 10-11: The channel_ShellToastNotificationReceived() Method of the Game1 Class

```
void channel_ShellToastNotificationReceived(object sender,
                                            NotificationEventArgs e)
{
    if (e.Collection != null)
    {
        notificationMessage = "";

        var collection = (Dictionary<string, string>)e.Collection;
        var messageBuilder = new System.Text.StringBuilder();

        foreach (string elementName in collection.Values)
        {
            notificationMessage += elementName;
        }
    }
}
```

When this method executes, it means that your game has received a toast notification. The `NotificationEventArgs` object (named e) gets converted to a string dictionary with two keys and two values. This method iterates through the values and builds the *notificationMessage* string, which you will write onscreen in the `Draw()` method.

The last thing to update is the `Draw()` method. Add this next block of code to write to the screen the text of the toast notification you have received:

```
spriteBatch.Begin();
spriteBatch.DrawString(font, notificationMessage, new Vector2(50, 200),
    Color.White);
spriteBatch.End();
```

Now, run both the `PassTheToastSample` game and the `PassTheToastWindows` form as before. Copy the URI over to the form, and enter a title and subtitle.

Press the Pass The Toast! button. Shortly thereafter you will see the title and subtitle appear on your game screen.

Press the Back button on the phone (or the Emulator), and click the Pass The Toast! button again without changing any other data. This time you see a toast notification at the top of your phone.

Tile Notifications

The final notification to discuss in this section is the tile notification. Every game has an assigned tile that your players can pin to the Start screen if they choose.

Tiles are more than just launch icons, though. They can display information about the state of your game, received via push notifications or updated by a schedule.

Tiles can be updated at any time in the following three ways:

- *Background image* — This can be updated using an image stored either locally or remotely, based on the path you provide.
- *Title* — The title is a string that is set via the project Properties screen in Visual Studio 2010. Titles must fit on a single line and cannot extend past the tile's width.
- *Count* — You can display an integer value with a range of 1 to 99. If you do not provide a new value, the current value continues to display. Sending a 0 clears the count and removes the circle image from the tile.

Even though you can modify the values of these items, you do not have any control over their placement at this time. Count values (if any) are displayed on the top right, and Title values (if any) are displayed on the bottom left, as shown in Figure 10-4.

FIGURE 10-4: Tile notifications and their updatable properties

When creating your own tiles, keep in mind that they must have a file size of 80 KB or less and dimensions of 173 pixels wide by 173 pixels high.

PushingTileSample

The best way to learn is by doing, so start by creating a Windows Phone Game project, and name it `PushingTileSample`.

Like you've done in the other two samples so far in this chapter, you also will create a Windows Forms program to send information to the phone or the Emulator via the URI generated by your game project.

After your project has been created, open the Properties window by right-clicking the project name in Solution Explorer and selecting Properties.

On the XNA Game Studio tab of the Properties window, find the "Tile title" and "Tile image" fields, as shown in Figure 10-5.

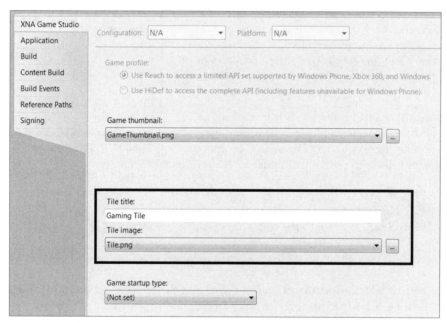

FIGURE 10-5: The XNA Game Studio project Properties window

Now, change the "Tile title" field to `Pushing Tile`. Before you can set the "Tile image" field to anything other than one of the default values, you must add some tile images to your project.

Grab the images for this section from this book's website, located at www.wrox.com. After you have downloaded the tile images, you must add them to your `PushingTileSampleContent` project. Don't create a separate folder for the images, because that will change the path and cause the sample code to break.

If you provide an invalid path, the Windows Phone 7 operating system defaults to the previous good tile background image so that your users won't see a broken image. This is a good thing, although it can make debugging a little trickier at times.

At this point, you should have six tile images in your content project, named `Tile.png` and `Tile10.png` to `Tile14.png`. The images for `Tile1` to `Tile9` are hosted online for you, but more on that in a bit.

When pushing a tile update that includes a background change, you aren't sending the new image to the phone as part of the notification. Instead, you send a path to the new image, which may be local or on the web.

If the path provided is for a web-hosted image, the phone downloads it. The image should be less than 80 KB in size. For best results, include images locally (as part of the game installation) where possible. Image downloads that take longer than 15 seconds may time out.

In Solution Explorer, click each of the six images in your `PushingTileSampleContent` project and look at the Properties window. Change the "Copy to Output Directory" property of each image from "Do not copy" to "Copy always," as shown in Figure 10-6.

After you have added all the images and set their properties, go back to the project Properties screen and select the default tile image by clicking the ellipses next to the "Tile image" drop-down list. This allows you to browse to the content folder where your images are stored.

FIGURE 10-6: Tile properties

> By default, the first folder to open is the project folder, so you need to navigate up one folder and then down into the `PushingTileSampleContent` folder to find the tile images you seek.

Once you have the correct folder, select the `TILE.PNG` image and click the Open button. (If you get an error saying that the file already exists, don't worry. You're good to go.) You can close the project Properties window now.

Before jumping into the `Game1` class, you must do a couple more things. In Solution Explorer, under the `Properties` folder, open the `WMAppManifest.xml` file and modify the `Publisher` attribute, just like you did for the previous samples. You can put anything you like here, as long as you put something. Ordinarily, this would be where you would put the name of your company or your website URL.

Return to Solution Explorer and expand the `References` folder. Add a reference to `Microsoft.Phone`.

At the top of your `Game1.cs` class file, add the following `using` statements:

```
using Microsoft.Phone.Notification;
using System.Diagnostics;
using System.Collections.ObjectModel;
```

Add a class-level variable to store your `HttpNotificationChannel` object:

```
HttpNotificationChannel channel;
```

Next, add the now-familiar `CreateNotificationChannel()` method to your `Game1` class, as shown in Listing 10-12.

LISTING 10-12: The CreateNotificationChannel() Method of the Game1 Class

```
void CreateNotificationChannel()
{
    channel = HttpNotificationChannel.Find("PushingTile");

    if (channel == null)
    {
        channel = new HttpNotificationChannel("PushingTile");
        SetupDelegates();
        channel.Open();
    }
    else
    {
        SetupDelegates();
        Debug.WriteLine("Copy URI for Push Tool: "
                        + channel.ChannelUri.ToString());
    }
}
```

This version is identical to the method of the same name in the previous two samples, with the exception of the channel name.

With this method in place, you can now add the following line to the end of your `LoadContent()` method:

```
CreateNotificationChannel();
```

The `SetupDelegates()` method is up next, so take a look at the code in Listing 10-13 and add it to your `Game1` class.

LISTING 10-13: The SetupDelegates() Method of the Game1 Class

```
void SetupDelegates()
{
    channel.ChannelUriUpdated +=
        new EventHandler<NotificationChannelUriEventArgs>
            (channel_ChannelUriUpdated);
}
```

Unlike the previous notification types, no raw data is associated with tile updates, so the `SetupDelegates()` method in this sample is pretty sparse by comparison.

Now, add the event handler method for the `ChannelUriUpdated` event, as shown in Listing 10-14.

> **LISTING 10-14:** The channel_ChannelUriUpdated() Method of the Game1 Class

```
void channel_ChannelUriUpdated(object sender,
                            NotificationChannelUriEventArgs e)
{
    Debug.WriteLine("Copy URI for Push Tool:" + e.ChannelUri.ToString());
}
```

Again, nothing is new here. You will copy the URI from the Output window in Visual Studio to the Windows program (which you will create shortly).

Next, you will add the following block of code to your `Update()` method, just before the call to the `base.Update()` method:

```
if (channel != null && !channel.IsShellTileBound)
{
    Collection<Uri> ListOfAllowedDomains =
        new Collection<Uri> { new Uri("http://www.xnadevelopment.com") };
    channel.BindToShellTile(ListOfAllowedDomains);
}
```

This should be a familiar pattern, with a slight twist. As in the other samples, you are checking the channel to ensure that it is not `null` and is not already bound to a tile notification subscription.

On the inside, you are creating a collection of URI objects and adding the `xnadevelopment.com` domain, finally binding that list to the channel. This allows you to specify a safe list of domains from which to pull tile background images.

That's it for the first half of the sample. If you run it at this point, you'll get the usual URI in the Output window, but nowhere to use it.

PushingTileWindows

You know what happens next. You will create a Windows Forms program to push a tile notification to the phone or the Emulator (wherever you ran the XNA to generate the URI). This time, you need only two inputs: the URI from your XNA game, and the title to appear on the tile.

When you click the Push The Tile! button, a stream is created and is sent by `HttpWebRequest` to the Push Notification Service via the URI specified.

> *Just like with the previous two samples, you can't do this next part in the Windows Phone edition of Visual Studio 2010 Express. If you don't have a full version of Visual Studio 2010, you can download Visual C# 2010 Express at www .microsoft.com/express.*

Start by creating a new Windows Forms application and naming it `PushingTileWindows`.

On your `Form1` design surface, drag two labels, two textboxes, and a button. Configure them as shown in Table 10-3.

TABLE 10-3: PushingTileWindows Form1 Controls and Properties

CONTROL NAME	PROPERTY	VALUE
Form1	Text	Push The Tile!
label1	Text	Phone URI
label2	Text	Title
txtPhoneUri	Size	681, 22
txtTitle	Size	681, 22
btnRaw	Text	Push The Tile!

The end result doesn't have to be a perfect match with Figure 10-7, but it should look reasonably close. Be sure to name your textbox and button controls correctly, or the code you are about to write won't work properly.

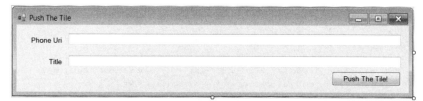

FIGURE 10-7: The PushTheTile Windows Forms design surface

When the design surface is finished, double-click the button control to create your `Click` event. Inside the handler for the `Click` event, add the following line of code:

```
SendTileNotification(txtPhoneUri.Text, txtTitle.Text);
```

Add these two `using` statements to the top of your class file:

```
using System.Net;
using System.IO;
```

Next up is the method where all the important stuff happens. Add the `SendTileNotification()` method shown in Listing 10-15 to your `Game1` class.

LISTING 10-15: The SendTileNotification() Method of the Game1 Class

```
void SendTileNotification(string uri, string title)
{
    var sendTile = (HttpWebRequest)WebRequest.Create(uri);

    sendTile.Method = "POST";
```

continues

LISTING 10-15 *(continued)*

```
        sendTile.ContentType = "text/xml";
        sendTile.Headers.Add("X-WindowsPhone-Target", "token");
        sendTile.Headers.Add("X-NotificationClass", "1");

        // Choose a random tile number to push and a random count value.
        // Normally you would want this to make some kind of sense in the
        // context of your game.
        var random = new Random();
        var count = random.Next(0, 15);
        var background = String.Empty;

        if (count < 10)
        {
            background = "http://www.xnadevelopment.com/wp7Tiles/Tile"
                        + count.ToString()
                        + ".jpg";
        }
        else
        {
            backgroundImage = "/Content/Tile" + count.ToString() + ".png";
        }

        string tileMessage =
            "<?xml version=\"1.0\" encoding=\"utf-8\"?>"
            + "<wp:Notification xmlns:wp=\"WPNotification\">"
                + "<wp:Tile>"
                    "<wp:BackgroundImage>" + background + "</wp:BackGroundImage>"
                    + "<wp:Count>" + count.ToString() + "<wp:Count>"
                    + "<wp:Title>" + title + "</wp:Title>"
                + "</wp:Tile>"
            + "</wp:Notification>";

        byte[] notificationMessage = new UTF8Encoding().GetBytes(tileMessage);
        sendTile.ContentLength = notificationMessage.Length;

        using (Stream requestStream = SendTile.GetRequestStream())
        {
            requestStream.Write(notificationMessage,
                                0,
                                notificationMessage.Length);
        }

        var response = (HttpWebResponse)sendTile.GetResponse();

        string notificationStatus = response.Headers["X-NotificationStatus"];
        string subscriptionStatus = response.Headers["X-SubscriptionStatus"];
        string connectionStatus = response.Headers["X-DeviceConnectionStatus"];
    }
```

Some of this method should be fairly familiar to you by now, but a few key pieces need to be covered, so take a good look.

In the `Headers` collection, you specify that you are sending a tile update (token) to the phone and setting the notification class "to `"1"`, which tells the Push Notification Service to send the message immediately.

This is a little different from the raw and toast notifications. Here are the values for tile notifications:

- `1` — The Push Notification Service delivers the message immediately.
- `11` — The message is delivered within 450 seconds (7.5 minutes).
- `21` — The message is delivered within 900 seconds (15 minutes).

Next, you create a random number between 0 and 14 and grab a remote image if the number is between 0 and 9. Otherwise, you use a local image for numbers between 10 and 14. There's really no reason to do this other than to demonstrate how to grab images from either source. You will also use the random number as your count value.

You are sending your tile message as XML, so you create a notification message containing three pieces of text: a background path, a count value, and a title.

Next, you set up a byte array called *tileMessage* to hold the XML message. The array length is used to set the length of your `HttpWebRequest`.

Finally, you create a stream and feed the XML to the `HttpWebRequest` (which is pointed at the URI you specified), fetch the response information, and dump it into the variables at the end.

Take a look at the first sample (`PushItRawSample`) for an explanation of what the response information means, and how you can work with it in your service.

You're finally ready to test your tile notifications. The easiest way to do this is to have two copies of Visual Studio running at the same time. Have your XNA project in one and the Windows form you just created in the other.

Build and run your XNA project on either the Emulator or the phone. Keep an eye on the Output window in Visual Studio. After 2 to 3 seconds (sometimes longer), you see the URI. Copy the URI so that you can paste it into the `PushingTileWindows` program.

Now, you can end your game since you have what you need. If you are using the Emulator instead of a phone, be sure to only shut down the game.

At this point, you have the URI on your clipboard but you don't actually have a tile to update. Tap the right-arrow icon on the top right of your Start screen (this applies to the phone or the Emulator) to open the application list.

To pin the `PushingTile` sample to the Start screen, tap and hold the entry in the program list until you see a context menu giving you the option to "pin to start" or uninstall your game. Tap the "pin to start" option, and then go back to the Start screen.

Now, in the other copy of Visual Studio, press F5 to build and run your `PushingTileWindows` application. Paste the URI you just copied into the Phone URI textbox, provide a title in the Title textbox, and press the Push The Tile! button.

After a (hopefully) brief wait, the tile on your phone or the Emulator changes to a randomly selected background image, and a corresponding count number appears in the top-right corner.

Images pulled from local storage will have the word LOCAL! in the middle of the tile. If you get an image with no number, don't panic. That just means a 0 was sent, which removes the count from the tile.

That's it for the push notification types. Next, you will learn another way to get your player's attention.

GOOD VIBRATIONS

Vibrating the phone is an excellent way to notify your players that something important is happening in your game. It can be used for everything from a subtle nag (along the lines of "Hey, buddy, it's still your turn") to adding a little extra punch to explosions and collisions.

Generally speaking, vibrating the phone should be used in moderation. It's a drain on the battery, and, of course, it loses significance if it's used all the time. Save it for things that warrant extra attention. Also, some folks don't like vibrating alerts (or want to preserve battery life), so be sure to give your players the option to turn them off in your game.

The Microsoft.Devices Namespace

Regardless of whether you are using Silverlight or XNA, everything you need to vibrate the phone can be found in the `Microsoft.Devices` namespace.

To see how this works, create a new Windows Phone Game project, and name it `VibrationSample`.

Add a new `SpriteFont` to your `VibrationSampleContent` project, and call it `VibrationFont.spritefont`. Set the size to 20.

Add a class-level variable to hold your font:

```
SpriteFont vibrationFont;
```

Now, load it into memory via the `LoadContent()` method:

```
vibrationFont = Content.Load<SpriteFont>("VibrationFont");
```

At this point, you're ready to do something a little more interesting, so expand the `References` section and add a reference to the `Microsoft.Phone` namespace.

Now, at the top of your `Game1` class, add the following `using` statement:

```
using Microsoft.Devices
```

The `Microsoft.Devices` namespace you just added contains the `VibrateController` class, which enables you to vibrate your phone. But it also has another very useful class called `Environment`, which you will look at next.

Environment

The `Environment` class provides a single property called `DeviceType` that returns an enumeration of the same name. The `DeviceType` enumeration contains two possible values:

- `Device`
- `Emulator`

Checking this property in your game tells you whether you are running on an actual device or in the Emulator, which can be pretty handy in certain cases.

You already have your project started and a `SpriteFont` loaded, so go ahead and add the following block of code to your `Draw()` method:

```
spriteBatch.Begin();
spriteBatch.DrawString(vibrationFont,
                "Device Type: " + Microsoft.Devices
                    .Environment.DeviceType.ToString(),
                new Vector2(25,25),
                Color.Crimson);
spriteBatch.End();
```

To see this in action, press F5 to build and run the `VibrationSample`. If you have a phone, run it there first and observe the device type being displayed onscreen. Next, select the Windows Phone 7 Emulator from the XNA Game Studio Deployment Device drop-down box, and run it again.

Where this really becomes valuable is when you are building games that depend on phone features that aren't in the Emulator, such as GPS or the camera. You need to simulate input from those features when running in the Emulator, and that means the game must know whether you are running on actual hardware.

VibrateController

This class exposes a single property named `Default` that you must use to obtain an instance of the `VibrateController` object. Once you have an instance, two methods are available for controlling vibrations on your device: `Start()` and `Stop()`.

The `Start()` method accepts a `TimeSpan` parameter, which allows you to specify how long (in seconds, minutes, or hours) the device will vibrate. Calling this method typically looks like this:

```
VibrateController.Default.Start(new TimeSpan(0, 0, 5));
```

This code tells the phone to vibrate for 5 seconds and then stop. The `TimeSpan` class constructor accepts three parameters in the following order: hours, minutes, and seconds.

If you want your gamers to hate you, set the vibration duration to minutes or hours. After they finish recharging their phone batteries, you can expect a few nasty calls. Seriously, don't ever do this.

The `Stop()` method does exactly what you would expect. It stops the vibration, even if the duration has not elapsed yet.

Before you implement this in the `VibrationSample` project, you must add a few control variables. At the class level, add the following two variables:

```
int CurrentCount;
string VibrationStatus;
```

`CurrentCount` is used for timer control. `VibrationStatus` indicates whether the phone should be currently vibrating, which is handy when running in the Emulator.

Next, in the `Update()` method, you will add the following block of code, after the `if` block that checks for input from the Back button, and before the call to the `base.Update()` method:

```
VibrationStatus = "vibrating.";

// The vibrations start after 4 seconds, so the starting status is "not
// vibrating"
if ((gameTime.TotalGameTime.Seconds < 2)
|| (gameTime.TotalGameTime.Seconds >= CurrentCount + 2))
    VibrationStatus = "not vibrating.";

// Every 4 seconds, vibrate for 2 seconds
if (gameTime.TotalGameTime.Seconds >= CurrentCount + 4)
{
    VibrateController.Default.Start(new TimeSpan(0, 0, 2));
    CurrentCount = gameTime.TotalGameTime.Seconds;
}
```

Unfortunately, the `VibrateController` class doesn't expose any properties to report whether the phone is actively vibrating, so you have to resort to a little timing trickery in this code. You know when the vibrations start and end, so you can change the value of `VibrationStatus` on a timer.

In the `Draw()` method, add this line inside the `SpriteBatch` block to show the vibration status:

```
spriteBatch.DrawString(vibrationFont,
                "Device is " + VibrationStatus,
                new Vector2(25, 50),
                Color.Crimson);
```

Set your XNA Game Studio Deployment Device drop-down box to Windows Phone 7 Device (if you have one), and press F5 to build and run. After a 4-second pause, your phone alternates vibrating and not vibrating in 2-second intervals.

If you do not have a phone, you can still run this code in the Emulator. The Emulator safely ignores the call to start vibrating, and the `VibrationStatus` variable is displayed so that you can tell when the phone would be vibrating.

The last thing to cover in this sample is stopping the vibration before the duration has elapsed. You do this by calling the `Stop()` method. Change the `if` block to look like this:

```
// Allows the game to exit
if (GamePad.GetState(PlayerIndex.One).Buttons.Back == ButtonState.Pressed)
{
```

```
        VibrateController.Default.Stop();
        this.Exit();
}
```

While you are in there, temporarily comment out the call to the `this.Exit()` method. Now whenever you press the Back button, the vibration stops, even if time remains.

Let the application keep running (since you commented out the line to kill the app). After a few seconds, the vibration restarts. The `Stop()` method doesn't disable vibration; it only kills the current duration.

You can call the `Stop()` method from within the `OnDeactivated()` event to stop any active vibrations after your game loses focus (such as when you receive a notification or incoming call).

Along the same lines, if your game terminates normally, any active vibrations stop when your game does. So, you don't need to put anything special in the `OnExiting()` event.

Unfortunately, if your game terminates unexpectedly while a vibration is running, the vibration may continue indefinitely after the game ends. The only way to get it to stop at that point is by turning off the phone (or letting the battery drain) or by running your game again so that the `VibrateController` instance receives a new duration.

To simulate this, run your code on a device and wait for it to vibrate. While it is vibrating, click the Stop Debugging icon in Visual Studio 2010. The code stops executing, your phone returns to the Start screen, and the vibration continues. Just run the code again and press the Back button on your phone to stop it.

That's all there is to know about the code necessary to vibrate the phone in your game. But one last concept must be addressed.

If you've spent much time in the Xbox Live Indie Games channel, you've probably seen the various "massager" applications that are available. Many of them tout various features such as "strongest vibrations available" or various settings for vibration patterns. After reading this section, you should understand that those claims are patently false. There's no way to control any aspect of the vibrations other than duration. You also can't do subsecond vibrations. The minimum duration is 1 second.

Nothing is stopping you from taking the knowledge you have gained in this section and creating the Super Deluxe Massager App for Windows Phone 7 (that is, other than integrity and good taste). However, the authors of this book sincerely hope you'll use your newly acquired powers for good and make some interesting and compelling games instead.

SUMMARY

Raw notifications can be used while your game is running to let your players know what other players are doing, or when updates are available for your game.

Pop-up toast notifications are sent when your game is not running. They can be used to alert players when it is their turn or when something requires their attention in the game.

Tile notifications can be used to update your game's Start tile by changing the icon or overlaying additional information on top of the tile, such as the number of active games awaiting your turn.

Push notifications are not guaranteed delivery and thus should not be used to transmit any personal information or game-critical data.

The `Microsoft.Devices` namespace contains methods and properties for controlling phone vibrations and determining whether your game is running on an actual device or in emulation.

In Chapter 11, you will learn about creating and consuming web services for use in your game. You will also learn how to create two very important services — global scoreboards and matchmaking.

11

The World Outside Your Window(s)

WHAT'S IN THIS CHAPTER?

- Understanding the concepts behind working with HTTP requests
- Creating a web service to track high scores for your game
- Building a matchmaking service for your games
- Understanding the principles behind RSS and REST service calls

In addition to the push notifications covered in Chapter 10, you will likely want to connect to other remote services. In this chapter, you will learn how to connect to (and consume) Simple Object Access Protocol (SOAP) and Representational State Transfer (REST) web services to extend the reach of your game beyond just the phone.

One key difference between a good game and a great one is the ability to compete with others. Matchmaking services give your players an opportunity to find opponents, whether by random matchups or from a friends list they can create and manage themselves. Even if your players aren't actively playing against each other at the same time, high-score boards provide an opportunity for bragging rights at the global level.

In addition to player services such as high score and matchmaking, you can consume RSS news feeds (perhaps for display in your game's Start screen) and even push information to a social medium, such as Twitter or Facebook.

Of course, your phone can do only so much. So, to make all these wonderful ideas come to life, you need to know how to use services.

CONSUMING WEB SERVICES

You may have heard people talk about using (or, more properly, *consuming*) XML web services in their applications or games. They are referring to SOAP web services. SOAP serves as the container for an XML request/response from your application or game to your web service and back. Fortunately, that's pretty much all you need to know about SOAP.

Web services are actually pretty cool, because they are designed to work as though they were a class local to your project, rather than sitting on a server halfway across the world (which they just might be). Before you can use a service in your code, you must create one (or find an existing one that does what you need).

In the following example, you start by creating a simple service that returns some data to your game, just so you can get a feel for how it works.

Live to Serve You

Start by creating a Windows Communication Foundation (WCF) service application named `LiveToServeYou`. You can find this project type under the WCF section of the New Project window in Visual Studio 2010, as shown in Figure 11-1.

FIGURE 11-1: The Visual Studio 2010 New Project window

> *If you are using Microsoft Visual Studio 2010 Express for Windows Phone, you won't find the WCF Service Application project type. To work along with this example, you must download and use the free Visual Web Developer 2010 Express (or use the full version of Visual Studio 2010).*

Once you have created the project, open the `Service1.svc.cs` file and take a look. Microsoft provides two sample methods. Listing 11-1 shows the entire code file.

> *The complete code for this project is available for download at the book's companion website (www.wrox.com).*

LISTING 11-1: The Service1.svc.cs Code File

```csharp
using System;
using System.Collections.Generic;
using System.Linq;
using System.Runtime.Serialization;
using System.ServiceModel;
using System.ServiceModel.Web;
using System.Text;

namespace LiveToServeYou
{
    // NOTE: You can use the "Rename" command on the "Refactor" menu to
    // change the class name "Service1" in code, svc and config file
    // together.
    public class Service1 : IService1
    {
        public string GetData(int value)
        {
            return string.Format("You entered: {0}", value);
        }

        public CompositeType
            GetDataUsingDataContract(CompositeType composite)
        {
            if (composite == null)
            {
                throw new ArgumentNullException("composite");
            }
            if (composite.BoolValue)
            {
                composite.StringValue += "Suffix";
            }
```

continues

LISTING 1-1 *(continued)*

```
            return composite;
        }
    }
}
```

You won't be using either of these methods, but it's a good idea to understand their purpose anyway.

The first method, `GetData()`, is rather simple. It illustrates how you would create a method that accepts and returns the standard data types in .NET — in this case, accepting an integer and returning a string. The method you will create for your service will follow the same concept.

The second method, `GetDataUsingDataContract()`, uses a composite data type and is a little more involved. To get a better idea of what's going on, take a look at the `IService1.cs` file, shown in Listing 11-2. It contains the interface definition for your service, as well as the class definition for the `CompositeType`.

LISTING 11-2: The IService1.cs Code File

```
using System;
using System.Collections.Generic;
using System.Linq;
using System.Runtime.Serialization;
using System.ServiceModel;
using System.ServiceModel.Web;
using System.Text;

namespace LiveToServeYou
{
    // NOTE: You can use the "Rename" command on the "Refactor" menu to
    // change the interface name "IService1" in both code and config file
    // together.
    [ServiceContract]
    public interface IService1
    {

        [OperationContract]
        string GetData(int value);

        [OperationContract]
        CompositeType GetDataUsingDataContract(CompositeType composite);

        // TODO: Add your service operations here
    }


    // Use a data contract as illustrated in the sample below to add
    // composite types to service operations.
    [DataContract]
```

```
public class CompositeType
{
    bool boolValue = true;
    string stringValue = "Hello ";

    [DataMember]
    public bool BoolValue
    {
        get { return boolValue; }
        set { boolValue = value; }
    }

    [DataMember]
    public string StringValue
    {
        get { return stringValue; }
        set { stringValue = value; }
    }
}
```

As you can see, interface definitions exist for both methods. When you create your own methods for your service, you must update the interface definition as well. Be sure to decorate any method signatures with the [OperationContract] attribute to indicate that the method is part of a service contract in your application or game.

In addition to the interface, you have the definition for the CompositeType class. This class has two public members: a bool and a string. When you need to use a homemade composite data type, you must decorate the class with the [DataContract] attribute (which marks your class as serializable). Also, each of your public members must be decorated with the [DataMember] attribute (again specifying that the individual members are serializable).

Being serializable is a pretty big deal. Serializing (and deserializing) is how XML web services can pass data back and forth between your game and the web service.

 Serializing *is the process of converting the state of your object into XML — or sometimes another format, such as JavaScript Object Notation (JSON), but, in this case, it's XML.* Deserializing *is the process of taking that same XML and using it to create an in-memory object containing the same state as the original object.*

Sometimes you will need to write code to handle the serialization and deserialization of XML. But, when using an XML web service, this is handled for you under the hood. Once you have a reference to the service, you can treat it as if it were like any other class local to your solution.

Now that you have created the WCF Service Application project, it's time to make it do something. Start by changing the IService1 interface (conveniently located in the IService1.cs file) to look like Listing 11-3.

LISTING 11-3: The Modified IService1.cs Code File

```
using System;
using System.Collections.Generic;
using System.Runtime.Serialization;
using System.ServiceModel;
using System.ServiceModel.Web;
using System.Text;

namespace LiveToServeYou
{
    // NOTE: You can use the "Rename" command on the "Refactor" menu to
    // change the interface name "IService1" in both code and config file
    // together.
    [ServiceContract]
    public interface IService1
    {
        [OperationContract]
        string CurrentTime();
    }
}
```

In this code, you are creating the interface definition for your service contract and stubbing out the `CurrentTime()` method. This method will be called remotely via your XNA game to fetch the current time from "the server" (which, in this case, is your own computer).

Next, update the `Service1` class (located in the `Service1.svc.cs` file) to look like Listing 11-4.

LISTING 11-4: The Modified Service1.svc.cs Code File

```
using System;
using System.Collections.Generic;
using System.Linq;
using System.Runtime.Serialization;
using System.ServiceModel;
using System.ServiceModel.Web;
using System.Text;

namespace LiveToServeYou
{
    // NOTE: You can use the "Rename" command on the "Refactor" menu to
    // change the class name "Service1" in code, svc and config file
    // together.
    public class Service1 : IService1
    {
        public string CurrentTime()
        {
            return DateTime.Now.ToString();
        }
    }
}
```

In the `Service1` class, you can see the `CurrentTime()` method, which returns a string containing the current date and time.

In a real-world scenario, you would deploy this service somewhere other than your local PC, since you want your game to be able to access it over the Internet. Pretty much any web-hosting company that supports .NET would be suitable for this purpose.

At this point, your very simple service is complete, so press F6 to build it and get ready to move on to the second half of this example — building a game to consume your service.

Serve Me

For the second half of this example, you will create an XNA game to consume the service you created. Start a new Windows Phone Game project, and name it `ServeMe`.

You'll need a `SpriteFont` to display the results of your service call, so add one to the `ServeMeContent` project and accept the default name of `SpriteFont1`. Set the `Size` property to `20` to make it readable.

> *The complete code for this project is available for download at the book's companion website (www.wrox.com).*

Adding a Service Reference

Before you start writing code, you might as well get this part out of the way. To use your newly created service, you must set a reference to it. This works a little differently from adding namespace references, since you actually need the service's address to add the reference.

To get this address, you must switch back to the service project and run it. This launches the WCF Test Client, shown in Figure 11-2, which contains the information you need.

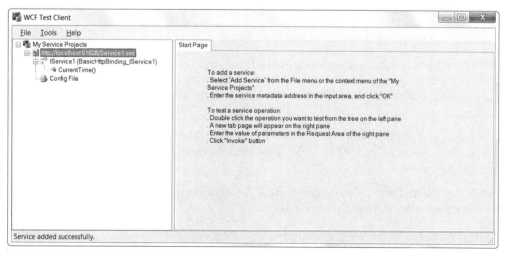

FIGURE 11-2: The WCF Test Client

As long as you are looking at the Test Client, take a moment and expand the node under `IService1` (if it isn't already expanded). Look familiar? That's where you will find any methods you created for the web service.

Double-click the `CurrentTime()` method and look at the test pane to the right, as shown in Figure 11-3. You can see multiple tabs by double-clicking the entry for `CurrentTime()` again.

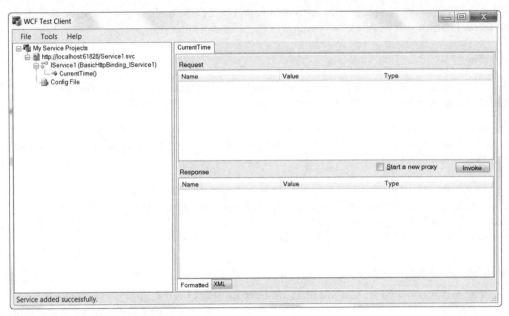

FIGURE 11-3: The CurrentTime() test panel

Your method doesn't accept any parameters, but if it did, you could enter them here in the Request pane.

Click the Invoke button to actually make a call to the web service and invoke the `CurrentTime()` method. The results are displayed in the Response pane, along with the data type of the returned value, as shown in Figure 11-4.

If you are curious as to what the resulting XML from your service call looks like, click the XML tab at the bottom of the window to shift from formatted view to XML view. This isn't necessary for this example, but it does provide some insight into what is being sent back to your game.

Right now, the piece of information you need is the service address, or Uniform Resource Indicator (URI). You often see the terms URI and URL used interchangeably, and that's fine, since they are basically the same thing.

Right-click the URI and select Copy Address from the context menu. You will use this address to create a service reference in your `ServeMe` project.

Back in the `ServeMe` project, in the Solution Explorer window, right-click Service References and select Add Service Reference from the context menu.

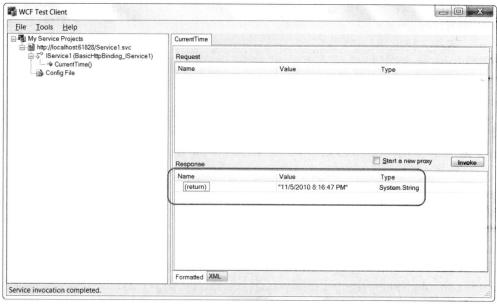

FIGURE 11-4: The results of calling the CurrentTime() method

With the Add Service Reference window open, paste the address you just copied into **the Address** drop-down list and click Go. This queries the service contract and returns a list **of operations** (methods) you can use in your project, as shown in Figure 11-5.

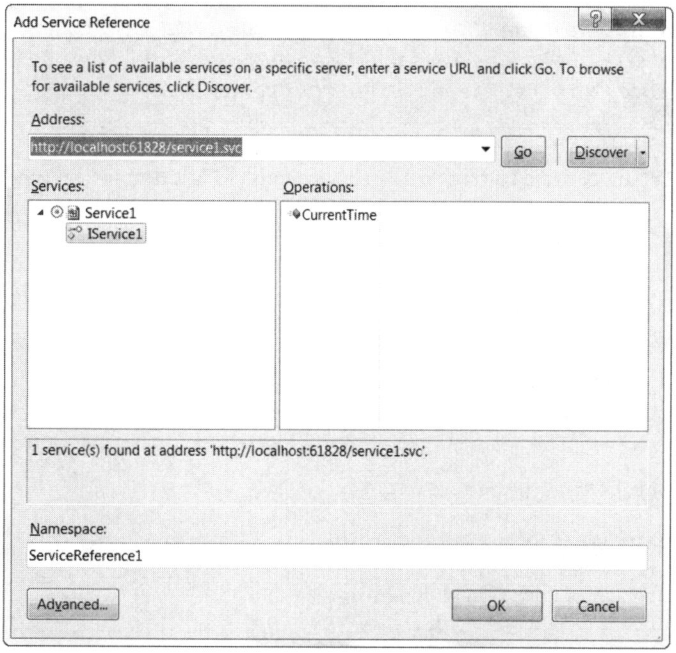

FIGURE 11-5: The Add Service Reference window

With the service selected, click the OK button to accept the default name (ServiceReference1), and add this service reference to your ServeMe project.

Game1.cs

At this point, you've added a SpriteFont and a service reference, so you're almost ready to start adding some code to the project. You need to add a few more references. Expand the References section in the Solution Explorer, and make sure that you have the System.Net, System.Runtime.Serialization, and System.Servicemodel namespace references.

Now you're ready to write some code. Open the Game1.cs file and add the following using statement to the top:

```
using ServeMe.ServiceReference1;
```

Now, add the following class-level variables to your Game1 class:

```
SpriteFont spriteFont;
Service1Client service1Client;
string CurrentTime;
```

The first variable declaration requires no explanation at this point. The last one stores the string value of the call to the CurrentTime() method of your service.

The *service1Client* variable exposes a class that provides methods for handling the asynchronous WCF call.

If Service1Client has you scratching your head, that's okay. It's not actually part of the .NET Framework, nor is it something you created, except that technically it's both. This is one of several partial classes that were autogenerated when you added the service reference (ServiceReference1) to your game.

In this sample, you will use a DoubleTap gesture to trigger the service call, so add the following line in the Initialize() method:

```
TouchPanel.EnabledGestures = GestureType.DoubleTap;
```

As you saw in Chapter 4, you must declare what gestures your game will support. So, you do that here and then check for whichever ones you declared in the Update() method.

Inside your LoadContent() method, add the following code to load your SpriteFont into memory, create an instance of the Service1Client class, and set an event handler for when your service call completes:

```
spriteFont = Content.Load<SpriteFont>("SpriteFont1");

service1Client = new Service1Client();
service1Client.CurrentTimeCompleted
    += new EventHandler<CurrentTimeCompletedEventArgs>
        (service1Client_CurrentTimeCompleted);
```

Now, add the method shown in Listing 11-5, which you previously named as the event handler.

LISTING 11-5: The service1Client_CurrentTimeCompleted() Method

```
void service1Client_CurrentTimeCompleted(object sender,
                                         CurrentTimeCompletedEventArgs e)
{
    currentTime = e.Result.ToString();
}
```

Whenever your service eventually returns a value from the call to the `CurrentTime()` method, this method fires and assigns the returned value to the local *currentTime* variable.

As mentioned earlier, you will make the call to your service whenever a `DoubleTap` gesture is performed, so add the following block of code to your `Update()` method:

```
while (TouchPanel.IsGestureAvailable)
{
    GestureSample gesture = TouchPanel.ReadGesture();
    if (gesture.GestureType == GestureType.DoubleTap)
    {
        Service1Client.CurrentTimeAsync();
        Break;
    }
}
```

One thing you should definitely notice here is that you don't actually call the `CurrentTime()` method directly and wait for an answer before your game can continue. You actually call the method asynchronously via one of the helper methods in the generated `Service1Client` class.

> If you have worked with web services in the past in Windows or web applications, the asynchronous call may be new to you. This way may seem more complex at first, but once you've done it a couple times, you'll see it's a piece of cake. It's so much better than having your game effectively frozen while waiting for an answer from the service that, once you get it, you'll never want to do it any other way.

Doing this allows your game loop to continue — well, looping — while keeping an eye out for an answer from the service. When that answer comes in, the event handler you defined previously (for the `CurrentTimeCompleted` event) gets called.

The only thing left at this point is to add the next few lines of code to your `Draw()` method to display the results on the screen:

```
spriteBatch.Begin();
spriteBatch.DrawString(spriteFont,
                    "Current Time: " + currentTime,
                    new Vector2(50, 200),
                    Color.White);
spriteBatch.End();
```

That's it for the coding. It's time to run this sample.

If the `LiveToServeYou` service isn't already running, you need to open that project first and run it so that your game can hit it.

Switch back to the `ServeMe` project, and press F5 to build and run the game. (This will work just as well in the Emulator as on a Windows phone.)

When you see the Current Time: message, double-tap the screen. After a second or two, you should see the message update with the current date and time.

> **When** working with services that return some form of "local" information, such as time, remember that they pull that data from wherever it's being hosted, not from your phone. You'll always get the correct time when running the service on your local developer machine, but the server you use for hosting your service may be in a different time zone or even a different country.

Congratulations! You just built and consumed your first WCF service from an XNA game running on Windows Phone 7. Not too shabby.

Now you're ready for something a little more challenging — a global high-scores service for your game.

I GET HIGH SCORES WITH A LITTLE HELP FROM MY FRIENDS

In this section, you will take what you've learned about interacting with services and build a functional global high-scores system that can track the top ten high scores from all phones playing your game.

In addition to creating and consuming another WCF service, you will leverage your knowledge of push notifications (from Chapter 10) to let people know when a new high score has been set. You will also learn how to obtain your user's anonymous Live ID (this sounds like a contradiction, we know) from the `UserExtendedProperties` class.

This sample requires three separate projects:

- `HighScoreService` (WCF service)
- `ScoreMe` (XNA Windows Phone Game)
- `HighScoreTester` (Windows Forms application)

There's no sense in delaying things any further. It's time to get started. First is the high-scores service.

HighScoreService

Start by creating a WCF Service Application named `HighScoreService`. The steps for creating this service are the same as the previous example, so feel free to flip back and refer to that as necessary.

This service uses a couple of custom classes to keep track of player and score information, so you'll create those first.

Add a new class called `Score` to your `HighScoreService` project, and add the code shown in Listing 11-6.

> *The complete code for this project is available for download at the book's companion website (www.wrox.com).*

LISTING 11-6: The Score Class

```
using System;
using System.Collections.Generic;
using System.Linq;
using System.Web;

namespace HighScoreService
{
    public class Score
    {
        public string Name;
        public int Value;

        public Score(string Name, int value)
        {
            this.Name = name;
            this.Value = value;
        }
    }
}
```

As you can see, there's not a whole lot to it. You simply store a player name and a value (specifically, a high score). You will use this class as the data type for a generic `List` object (that stores the high scores) maintained by `HighScoreService`.

Next, add another class to your project and name it `Player`. Use the code shown in Listing 11-7.

LISTING 11-7: The Player Class

```
using System;
using System.Collections.Generic;
using System.Linq;
using System.Web;

namespace HighScoreService
{
    public class Player
```

continues

LISTING 11-7 *(continued)*

```
    {
        public string PhoneUri;
        public string PhoneID;
        public string PassCode;

        public Player(string phoneURI, string phoneID)
        {
            this.PhoneUri = phoneURI;
            this.PhoneID = phoneID;
        }
    }
}
```

The `Player` class exposes three properties. The `PhoneUri` variable contains the phone URI for the named player. This will be used to send a push notification to players when a new high score is posted. `PhoneID` is used to identify (anonymously) where the high score came from, and `PassCode` stores a bit of security to help prevent people from gaming the high-score boards.

The `Player` class is used in a `Dictionary` object, along with a `string` representing the anonymous Live ID generated by the player's phone (more on that in a bit).

With `Score` and `Player` classes added to your project, it's time to do some housekeeping. Right now, you have a service named `Service1.svc` and a matching interface named `IService1.cs`.

Rename the `Service1.svc` file by right-clicking it in the Solution Explorer and selecting Rename. Name it `HighScore.svc` and then do the same thing for the `IService1.cs` file, naming it `IHighScore.cs`. Be sure to answer "Yes" when asked if you want to rename any references to the interface in your project.

The last thing to do here is to change the name of your service class from `Service1` to `HighScore`, so that the class definition line looks like this:

```
public class HighScore : IHighScore
```

Now, open the `IHighScore` interface and add definitions for the methods you will implement in your service. It should resemble Listing 11-8 when you are done.

LISTING 11-8: The IHighScore Interface

```
using System;
using System.Collections.Generic;
using System.Linq;
using System.Runtime.Serialization;
using System.ServiceModel;
using System.ServiceModel.Web;
using System.Text;

namespace HighScoreService
{
```

```csharp
[ServiceContract]
public interface IHighScore
{
    [OperationContract]
    string Identify(string phoneURI, string phoneID);

    [OperationContract]
    string CurrentHighScores();

    [OperationContract]
    void AddScore(string phoneURI,
                  string phoneID,
                  string name,
                  int score,
                  string passcode);
}
```

With the definitions complete, it's time to focus on the implementation of the service. Switch to the `HighScore` class (located in the `HighScore.svc.cs` file) and add the following `using` statements:

```csharp
using System.Net;
using System.IO;
```

Inside the `HighScore` class, add the following class-level variables to hold your scores and players, respectively:

```csharp
static List<Score> scores = new List<Score>();
static Dictionary<string, Player> players = new Dictionary<string, Player>();
```

In your `IHighScore` interface, you defined three methods. The first of these is the `Identify()` method, shown in Listing 11-9.

LISTING 11-9: The Identify() Method of the HighScore Service

```csharp
public string Identify(string phoneURI, string phoneID)
{
    if (!players.ContainsKey(phoneID))
    {
        players.Add(phoneID, new Player(phoneURI, phoneID));
    }

    players[phoneID].PassCode = DateTime.Now.ToUniversalTIme().ToString();
    return players[phoneID].PassCode;
}
```

This method accepts a string containing the phone URI (you learned about this in Chapter 10) and a string containing the phone ID (technically, it's an anonymous Live ID — more on that later in this chapter).

If the phone ID is not already in the *players* list, it is added, and a passcode is generated and returned to the caller.

Next on the list is the `CurrentHighScores()` method, which is shown in Listing 11-10. Add this to your `HighScore` service.

LISTING 11-10: The CurrentHighScores() Method

```
public string CurrentHighScores()
{
    var scoreList = (from score in scores
                     orderby score.Value descending
                     select score).ToList();

    var topTenHighScores = string.Empty;
    var count = 0;

    foreach (Score score in scoreList)
    {
        topTenHighScores += score.Name + " " + score.Value.ToString() + ":";
        count += 1;

        if (count > 9)
            break;
    }

    return topTenHighScores;
}
```

In this method, you use a LINQ statement to query the contents of the *scores* list, returning a collection ordered from highest to lowest. You then loop through that to generate a delimited string containing names and scores, which you return to the caller.

The third and final method in your interface is `AddScore()`, which is shown in Listing 11-11.

LISTING 11-11: The AddScore() Method

```
public void AddScore(string phoneURI,
                     string phoneID,
                     string name,
                     int score,
                     string passcode)
{
    string Title = "New High Score!";
    string Message = "A new high score has been set! Can you beat it?";

    // You may want to implement something more robust than a simple
    // passcode to make sure people aren't gaming your high score service!
    if (passcode == players[phoneID].PassCode)
    {
        players[phoneID].PhoneUri = phoneURI;

        // Find the current high score
        var highScoreList = (from highScore in scores
```

```
                        orderby highScore.Value descending
                        select highScore).ToList();

        scores.Add(new Score(name, score));

        // Find the new high score list
        var newScoreList = (from highScore in scores
                            orderby highScore.Value descending
                            select highScore).ToList();

        // Check to see if the new score is in the number one spot; if so,
        // notify all players that a new high score has been set!
        if (highScoreList.Count == 0
        || (highScoreList[0].Value != newScoreList[0].Value))
        {
            foreach (Player player in players.Values)
            {
                // No need to send the notification to the player that
                // just set the score; they already KNOW they're awesome
                if (player.PhoneID != phoneID)
                {
                    SendToastNotification(player.PhoneUri, Title, Message);
                }
            }
        }
    }
}
```

A few things are going on in this method, so let's break them down.

First, you check the *passcode* provided by the caller. You saw this being generated in the `Identify()` method of your service and then passed back to the caller (your phone game). In the `AddScore()` method, your game gives back the same *passcode* to the service when it's time to update the high score.

This action provides some simple (but effective) authentication to make sure you are who you say you are. It's not impenetrable, since a brute-force hack could get past it, but it provides a good foundation to start from.

Assuming that the provided *passcode* matches the one your service has stored for that player (which is indexed by *phoneID*), you are good to go.

First, you update the phone's URI with the one provided, in case it has changed since the last time you updated. This doesn't happen often, but it's always best to be safe.

Next, you fetch the current high-scores list, ordered from highest to lowest. You then add your new score to the list and fetch it again into a separate variable so that you can compare the top score between the two collections.

Finally, if this is the first-ever high-score entry, or if it's a new top high score (meaning the very top of the list, not just any high score), loop through each *player* in the *players* list and send a toast notification using the URI stored for each phone.

The last method in this class service isn't public, and it is called only from the `AddScore()` method. Add the `SendToastNotification()` method shown in Listing 11-12 to your `HighScore` service class.

LISTING 11-12: The SendToastNotification() Method

```csharp
private void SendToastNotification(string uri, string title, string message)
{
    try
    {
        HttpWebRequest notificationRequest
            = (HttpWebRequest)WebRequest.Create(uri);

        notificationRequest.Method = "POST";
        notificationRequest.ContentType = "text/xml";
        notificationRequest.Headers.Add("X-WindowsPhone-Target",
                                        "toast");
        notificationRequest.Headers.Add("X-NotificationClass",
                                        "2");

        // From the MSDN documentation, possible batching interval values:
        // 2: Message is delivered immediately.
        // 12: Message is delivered within 450 seconds.
        // 22: Message is delivered within 900 seconds.

        string toastMessage =
            "<?xml version=\"1.0\" encoding=\"utf-8\"?>" +
            "<wp:Notification xmlns:wp=\"WPNotification\">" +
              "<wp:Toast>" +
                "<wp:Text1>" + title + "</wp:Text1>" +
                "<wp:Text2>" + message + "</wp:Text2>" +
              "</wp:Toast>" +
            "</wp:Notification>";

        var notificationMessage = new UTF8Encoding().GetBytes(toastMessage);
        notificationRequest.ContentLength = notificationMessage.Length;

        using (Stream requestStream = notificationRequest.GetRequestStream())
        {
            requestStream.Write(notificationMessage,
                                0,
                                notificationMessage.Length);
        }

        // Sends the notification and gets the response.
        var response = (HttpWebResponse)notificationRequest.GetResponse();
        var notificationStatus = response.Headers["X-NotificationStatus"];

        var notificationChannelStatus
            = response.Headers["X-SubscriptionStatus"];
        var deviceConnectionStatus
            = response.Headers["X-DeviceConnectionStatus"];
```

```
            }
            catch (Exception ex)
            {
                string error = ex.Message;
                // ToDo: add code to email or log error
            }
        }
    }
```

A lot of this code should look familiar to you, since it's covered in detail in Chapter 10. There really isn't much new going on here. You're creating a toast notification based on the *title* and *message* provided and then sending it to the *uri* for the phone that called the service.

One thing worth noting in this method is the exception handling. If the URI is malformed in some way, an exception could be thrown. Being able to look at the exception can help you figure out just what is going on. If you're publishing your service somewhere other than your local machine, you will want a way to log exceptions or possibly have them e-mailed to you so that you can track down issues and get them addressed quickly.

That's it for the *HighScore* service. Next up, you will build the Windows Phone Game part of the example.

ScoreMe

Now it's time to create a new Windows Phone Game project to take advantage of your *HighScore* service. Name it *ScoreMe*.

If you are using the Express versions of Visual Studio 2010, you need to switch back to the Windows Phone edition and create a new solution.

As usual, you will want to add a *SpriteFont* to your *ScoreMeContent* project so that you can display the results on screen. Accept the default name, and set the size to *25*.

The complete code for this project is available for download at the book's companion website (www.wrox.com).

Next, you must add a service reference to your *HighScore* service in your project. For a refresher on how to do this, look back to the *ServeMe* project earlier in this chapter. Make sure your service has been built and run at least once before trying to add a reference to it.

With that taken care of, open your *Game1* class and add the following *using* statements at the top:

```
using Microsoft.Phone.Notification;
using Microsoft.Phone.Info;
using ScoreMe.HighScores;
using System.ComponentModel;
```

Inside the `Game1` class, add the following class-level variable declarations:

```
SpriteFont displayFont;
HighScoreClient highScores;

string[] highScoresList;
int submittedScore;

string passcode;
string phoneURI;
string userID;
string notificationMessage = string.Empty;
```

The first two variables should be familiar. You've seen *displayFont* before, and the *highScores* variable contains your reference to the service. The *highScoresList* variable is returned from the service, along with *passcode*, and the rest are populated locally and sent to your service.

The `Game1` constructor doesn't have anything new, so skip it and take a look at the `Initialize()` method. Like the previous example, you will use a `DoubleTap` gesture to act as your triggering event, so add the following line of code:

```
TouchPanel.EnabledGestures = GestureType.DoubleTap;
```

In your `LoadContent()` method, you will load your `SpriteFont`, acquire the anonymous Live ID, and define some event handlers for your service. Make your `LoadContent()` method look like Listing 11-13.

LISTING 11-13: The LoadContent() Method of the Game1 Class

```
protected override void LoadContent()
{
    spriteBatch = new SpriteBatch(GraphicsDevice);
    displayFont = Content.Load<SpriteFont>("SpriteFont1");

    // Get the user's unique anonymous Live ID
    string anid = UserExtendedProperties.GetValue("ANID") as string;
    if (anid == null)
    {
        anid = "##123456789123456789123456789123345";
    }
    userID = anid.Substring(2, 32);

    highScores = new HighScoreClient();
    highScores.IdentifyCompleted
        += new EventHandler<IdentifyCompletedEventArgs>
            (highScores_IdentifyCompleted);

    highScores.AddScoreCompleted
        += new EventHandler<AsyncCompletedEventArgs>
            (highScores_AddScoreCompleted);

    highScores.CurrentHighScoresCompleted
        += new EventHandler<CurrentHighScoresCompletedEventArgs>
```

```
            (highScores_CurrentHighScoresCompleted);

        CreateNotificationChannel();
    }
```

The first couple of lines in this method are pretty standard stuff that you've seen before. Where it starts to get interesting is in the next code block, where you acquire the unique Anonymous Live ID.

Anonymous Live ID

The Anonymous Live ID is a Guaranteed Unique Identifier (GUID) that is generated by a Windows Phone device for the purpose of uniquely identifying the user without actually revealing any personal information. You generate the Anonymous Live ID (ANID) by calling the `GetValue()` method of the `UserExtendedProperties` class and passing in a string containing ANID as a parameter.

> *In the current release of the* `Microsoft.Phone.Info` *namespace, the only supported property of* `UserExtendedProperties.GetValue()` *is* ANID.

Because it's based on a Live ID, this works only on an actual Windows Phone device. Calling this code in the Emulator always returns a `null`, so you need to cover this possibility by providing a made-up ANID for testing purposes.

Once you have the ANID, you must strip the string to just the GUID by using the `SubStr()` method shown in the code.

> *GUIDs are always 32 characters. The ANID returns some additional information before and after the GUID you need.*

HighScoreClient

The next block of code in your `LoadContent()` method deals with instantiating the `HighScoreClient` class generated when you added the service reference to your project. It also maps the event handlers for the completion events for each of the three methods you exposed in the service.

> *This is pretty cool stuff. When you added the service reference, it generated not only the client class, but also all the events for asynchronously working with your service. All you have to do is map your own methods as event handlers.*

Let's step out of the `LoadContent()` method for a moment (you already added all the code) and take a look at the event handlers.

The first handler points to the `highScores_IdentifyCompleted()` method, so add the code shown in Listing 11-14 to your class.

LISTING 11-14: The highScores_IdentifyCompleted() Method

```
void highScores_IdentifyCompleted(object sender,
                                  IdentifyCompletedEventArgs e)
{
    passcode = e.Result;
    highScores.CurrentHighScoresAsync();
}
```

This subroutine receives the *passcode* initially generated by your service during the `Identify` process and stores it locally to use for authentication later.

Next, an asynchronous call is made to fetch the high-scores list, which, in turn, triggers the `highScores_CurrentHighScoresCompleted()` method when an answer is returned from the service.

Add the `highScores_CurrentHighScoresCompleted()` method to your class, as shown in Listing 11-15.

LISTING 11-15: The highScores_CurrentHighScoresCompleted() Method

```
void highScores_CurrentHighScoresCompleted(object sender,
                                           CurrentHighScoresCompletedEventArgs e)
{
    highScoresList = e.Result.Split(":".ToCharArray());
}
```

This method takes the colon-delimited string of high scores returned from the service and splits them into a char array before assigning them to the *highScoresList* (technically, a string array).

The third event handler is the `highScores_AddScoreCompleted()` method, which is fired after a call to `AddScoreAsync()` has completed. Add the `highScores_AddScoreCompleted()` method to your class, as shown in Listing 11-16.

LISTING 11-16: The highScores_AddScoreCompleted() Method

```
void highScores_AddScoreCompleted(object sender,
                                  AsyncCompletedEventArgs e)
{
    highScores.CurrentHighScoresAsync();
}
```

Once this handler is called, signifying that the new score was added, it immediately requests the most up-to-date high-scores list.

Now, let's get back to the `LoadContent()` method.

Push Notifications

The last line of the `LoadContent()` method should look familiar. You saw `CreateNotificationChannel()` in Chapter 10 when you dealt with push notifications.

Add the following class-level variable to store your notification channel:

```
HttpNotificationChannel channel;
```

Next, add the `CreateNotificationChannel()` method, shown in Listing 11-17, to your class.

LISTING 11-17: The CreateNotificationChannel() Method

```
void CreateNotificationChannel()
{
    channel = HttpNotificationChannel.Find("HighScores");

    if (channel == null)
    {
        channel = new HttpNotificationChannel("HighScores");
        SetupDelegates();
        channel.Open();
    }
    else
    {
        SetUpDelegates();
    }
}
```

In this method, you check to see if the `HighScores` channel already exists, and you create/open it if it does not. The `SetUpDelegates()` method assigns event handlers specific to push notifications. Add the `SetUpDelegates()` method shown in Listing 11-18.

LISTING 11-18: The SetUpDelegates() Method

```
void SetUpDelegates()
{
    channel.ChannelUriUpdated
        += new EventHandler<NotificationChannelUriEventArgs>
            (channel_ChannelUriUpdated);

    channel.ShellToastNotificationReceived
        += new EventHandler<NotificationEventArgs>
            (channel_ShellToastNotificationReceived);
}
```

These events fire whenever you get a new Channel URI and when a toast notification is received. For a refresher on these, flip back to Chapter 10.

Remember, toast notifications pop up only when your game is not running. But toasts received while your game is running can (and should) be treated as raw notifications.

You've mapped the event handlers, so now you must add the methods they point to. The `channel_ChannelUriUpdated()` method, shown in Listing 11-19, is first, so add that to your class now.

LISTING 11-19: The channel_ChannelUriUpdated() Method

```
void channel_ChannelUriUpdated(object sender,
                               NotificationChannelUriEventArgs e)
{
    phoneURI = e.ChannelUri.ToString();
    highScores.IdentifyAsync(phoneURI, userID);
}
```

This method is called whenever a new URI is generated for the phone. The new URI is passed back to the service, along with the anonymous Live ID, so the service is always up to date.

The next event handler in `SetUpDelegates()` is mapped to the `channel_ShellToastNotificationReceived()` method, which is shown in Listing 11-20. Add this method to your class.

LISTING 11-20: The channel_ShellToastNotificationReceived() Method

```
void channel_ShellToastNotificationReceived(object sender,
                                            NotificationEventArgs e)
{
    if (e.Collection != null)
    {
        var collection = (Dictionary<string, string>)e.Collection;

        foreach (string elementValue in collection.Values)
        {
            notificationMessage += " " + elementValue;
        }
    }
}
```

This method gets called whenever a toast notification is received while your game is running. Since toasts don't pop up when you have a game running, you can choose to ignore them or process them as raw notifications.

The toast notification always contains a title and a message. So, you dump the contents of the toast into a dictionary and then loop through it to construct a string (*notificationMessage*), which you will display during the `Draw()` method.

Next, you must change the `Update()` method, which is shown in Listing 11-21. The new or changed lines are in bold.

LISTING 11-21: The Update() Method

```
protected override void Update(GameTime gameTime)
{
    // Allows the game to exit
    if (GamePad.GetState(PlayerIndex.One).Buttons.Back
        == ButtonState.Pressed)
        this.Exit();

    // Bind the channel to Toast notifications if it's open
    // and hasn't already been bound
    if (channel != null && !channel.IsShellToastBound)
        channel.BindToShellToast();

    // Accept gesture input
    while (TouchPanel.IsGestureAvailable)
    {
        GestureSample gesture = TouchPanel.ReadGesture();
        if (gesture.GestureType == GestureType.DoubleTap)
        {
            Random random = new Random();
            submittedScore = random.Next(0, 1000000000);
            highScores.AddScoreAsync(phoneURI,
                            userID,
                            "Georgie",
                            submittedScore,
                            passcode);
        }
    }

    base.Update(gameTime);
}
```

The `Update()` method has two significant additions, but neither of them is anything you haven't seen before. The first new block of code ensures that the notification channel is bound to receiving toast notifications.

The other new block of code waits for a `DoubleTap` gesture and generates a random "score" between 1 and 1,000,000,000. Then it takes the locally stored phone URI, the anonymous Live ID, the name of the high scorer, the score to be submitted, and the passcode generated by the service in the `Identify()` method and passes them all into the asynchronous `AddScoreAsync()` method.

 "Georgie" refers to your loveable coauthor George Clingerman. He'll deny it, but he really prefers to be called Georgie ... honest! You may want to substitute your own players' names, though.

The `AddScoreAsync()` method stores the updated phone URI when you pass it in. Chances are it probably won't have changed between identifying yourself to the service and posting a score, but it is possible — so better safe than sorry.

The last method to update in your game is the `Draw()` method. It's shown in Listing 11-22, with the changed parts in bold.

LISTING 11-22: The Draw() Method

```
protected override void Draw(GameTime gameTime)
{
    GraphicsDevice.Clear(Color.CornflowerBlue);

    spriteBatch.Begin();

    if (highScoresList != null)
    {
        int YOffset = 0;
        foreach (string score in highScoresList)
        {
            spriteBatch.DrawString(displayFont,
                        score,
                        new Vector2(50, 50 + YOffset),
                        Color.White);
            YOffset += 25;
        }
    }

    spriteBatch.DrawString(displayFont,
                "New Score: " + submittedScore.ToString(),
                new Vector2(50, 400),
                Color.White);

    if (passcode == null)
    {
        spriteBatch.DrawString(displayFont,
                    "Not Identified by Service Yet...",
                    new Vector2(50, 430), Color.White);
    }
    else
    {
        spriteBatch.DrawString(displayFont,
                    notificationMessage,
                    new Vector2(50, 430),
                    Color.White);
    }

    spriteBatch.End();

    base.Draw(gameTime);
}
```

The first new block of code in the `Draw()` method checks to see if the high-scores list has any entries and displays them if it does. The second block displays the most recent score submitted to the high-scores service from that device or the Emulator. The third and final new block displays the text of any toast notifications that are received while the game is running.

Notice the phrase "displays ... any toast notifications that are received." The way this code is written, no matter what game or application sent the toast, you will see it in this game. That's something to think about when you're deciding how to react to push notifications in your game.

That's it for the `ScoreMe` project. Only one more to go, and then you will be done with the global high-scores system. Up next is a Windows Forms project that will serve as your test application for the high-scores service.

HighScoreTester

In this project, which is the third piece of the high-scores system, you build a Windows Forms application to help test the `HighScores` service. You will be able to submit high scores as if you were a second phone (or the Emulator).

Why do this? You can have only a single instance of the Windows Phone Emulator running, and most developers are unlikely to have multiple phone devices handy for testing purposes.

Create a new Windows Forms Application project, and name it `HighScoreTester`.

The complete code for this project is available for download at the book's companion website (www.wrox.com).

Next, set a service reference to the `HighScores` service. For a refresher on how to do this, look back to the `ServeMe` project earlier in this chapter. Make sure your service has been built and run at least once before you try to add a reference to it.

Open `Form1.cs` in Design view and add the controls shown in Table 11-1. Be sure to set the properties listed for each control.

TABLE 11-1: Form1 Controls and Properties

CONTROL	PROPERTY	VALUE
Form1	Size	591, 332
	Text	High Score Tester
label1	Text	PhoneID:

continues

TABLE 11-1 *(continued)*

CONTROL	PROPERTY	VALUE
label2	Text	Name:
label3	Text	Score:
txtPhoneID	Size	132, 22
txtName	Size	132, 22
txtScore	Size	132, 22
btnIdentify	Text	Identify
btnAddScore	Text	Add Score
btnRefresh	Text	Refresh
lstHighScores	ItemHeight	16
	Size	335, 228

When you are finished, you should have something that looks like Figure 11-6. The exact placement of the controls isn't critical, but make sure you name them correctly, or your code won't work.

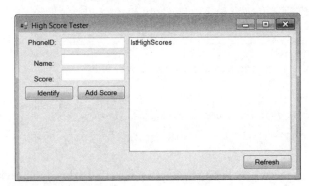

FIGURE 11-6: The High Score Tester form

Switch to the code-behind for your form, and add the following `using` statement to the top:

```
using HighScoreTester.HighScores;
```

Next, add the following class-level variables to your `Form1` class:

```
HighScoreClient highScores;
string passcode;
```

In your class constructor, add these four lines to instantiate the service client and set up your event handlers:

```
highScores = new HighScoreClient();

highScores.IdentifyCompleted
```

```
        += new EventHandler<IdentifyCompletedEventArgs>(highScores_IdentifyCompleted);
highScores.AddScoreCompleted
        += new EventHandler<AsyncCompletedEventArgs>(highScores_AddScoreCompleted);
highScores.CurrentHighScoresCompleted
        += new EventHandler<CurrentHighScoresCompletedEventArgs>
            (highScores_CurrentHighScoresCompleted);
```

There's nothing here you haven't seen before. You set up the asynchronous completion event handlers for each of the three methods you defined in your high-scores service.

Now you must create the methods for these event handlers. So, first add the `highScores_CurrentHighScoresCompleted()` method, shown in Listing 11-23.

LISTING 11-23: The highScores_CurrentHighScoresCompleted() Method

```
void highScores_CurrentHighScoresCompleted(object Sender,
                                CurrentHighScoresCompletedEventArgs e)
{
    lstHighScores.Items.Clear();
    string[] highScores = e.Result.Split(":".ToCharArray());
    foreach (string score in highScores)
    {
        lstHighScores.Items.Add(score);
    }
}
```

Next up is the `highScores_AddScoreCompleted()` method. Add the code shown in Listing 11-24 to your class.

LISTING 11-24: The highScores_AddScoreCompleted() Method

```
void highScores_AddScoreCompleted(object sender, AsyncCompletedEventArgs e)
{
    highScores.CurrentHighScoresAsync();
}
```

Just like in your XNA game, after you post a new high score, you request the newly updated list of scores.

Now add the `highScores_IdentifyCompleted()` method, shown in Listing 11-25.

LISTING 11-25: The highScores_IdentifyCompleted() Method

```
void highScores_IdentifyCompleted(object sender,
                                IdentifyCompletedEventArgs e)
{
    passcode = e.Result;
    highScores.CurrentHighScoresAsync();
}
```

Just like the previous method, this one wraps up with a call to fetch the most recent high-scores list.

Now, create a click event handler for your `btnRefresh` control. The easiest and quickest way to do this is to switch back to the designer and double-click the button. Once you have done that, add the bold code shown in Listing 11-26.

LISTING 11-26: The btnRefresh_Click() Event Handler

```
void btnRefresh_Click(object sender, EventArgs e)
{
    highScores.CurrentHighScoresAsync();
}
```

Add click event handlers for the `btnIdentify` and `btnAddScore` controls. Once those are in place, add the bold code shown in Listings 11-27 and 11-28 to their respective event handlers.

LISTING 11-27: The btnIdentify_Click() Event Handler

```
void btnIdentify_Click()
{
    highScores.IdentifyAsync
}
```

LISTING 11-28: The btnAddScore_Click() Event Handler

```
void btnAddScore_Click(object sender, EventArgs e)
{
    int score;
    int.TryParse(txtScore.Text, out score);
    highScores.AddScoreAsync("12345",
                            txtPhoneID.Text,
                            txtName.Text,
                            score,
                            passcode);
}
```

One thing worth highlighting is that you don't actually pass in a URI to the `AddScoreAsync()` method in this case. There is no way for your Windows Forms application to receive a push notification, so it doesn't matter that you are just putting in `"12345"` instead of an actual URI.

That's it for the `HighScoreTester` part of the example. Now you're ready to test everything.

Testing the High-Score Service

Start by running your `HighScoreService` project. When the WCF Test Client window is visible, it's ready to start receiving requests.

Next, run your `ScoreMe` project. When the game starts, you see the message "Not Identified by Service Yet." This message disappears after a couple of seconds, after the service returns a passcode to the game.

Double-tap your phone (or double-click in the Emulator) to submit a score to the service. After a pause, you see Georgie's latest randomly generated high score.

In the High Score Tester application, click the Refresh button; you see the same score appear in the window to the right. While you are still in the High Score Tester application, type in a `PhoneID` of your choice (four to six characters is fine) and click the Identify button.

Now, with the same `PhoneID`, type in your name and a score and click the Add Score button. You see your score show up in the list on the right side of the form. Do this a couple more times, with various scores.

Now go back to the `ScoreMe` game, and double-tap to submit a new score. You see the score, along with all the scores submitted via the High Score Tester.

Double-tap a few more times on the `ScoreMe` game to get at least ten scores on the list. Then go back into the High Score Tester and submit a score that is higher than anything in the list.

Keep an eye on the `ScoreMe` game. After a brief delay, you see a message proclaiming that a new high score has been set.

Now, press the Start button to close the `ScoreMe` game, and go back to the main screen. Switch back over to the High Score Tester and enter another highest score. You see a toast (with the same message) pop up on the phone or the Emulator.

That's it for this example, but you could enhance it in a number of ways if you choose. You could have the service send all submitted high scores (in the top ten) as raw data to the phones, to capture as needed. So, the high-scores screen would always be up to date whenever new high scores are submitted.

In the next section, you will learn how to create a matchmaking system for your games. Like the high-scores system you just completed, this example uses a WCF service, a Windows Phone Game, and a Windows Form for testing.

GOT A MATCH?

A critical part of networked gaming is finding opponents (or teammates) to play with. In this section, you will build a matchmaking service for your game.

MatchMaker

Start by creating a WCF Service Application named `MatchMaker`. The steps for creating this service are the same as for the first example in this chapter, so feel free to flip back and refer to that as necessary.

This service uses a couple of custom classes (`Gamer` and `GameRequest`) to keep track of gamer and request information. `Gamer` uses `GameRequest`, so you will implement `GameRequest` first.

The complete code for this project is available for download at the book's companion website (www.wrox.com).

GameRequest.cs

Add a new class to your `MatchMaker` project, and name it `GameRequest.cs`. This class contains three public properties (`ID`, `Name`, and `CurrentStatus`), as well as a class constructor to populate those properties.

Start by adding the properties to your class:

```
public string ID;
public string Name;
public Status CurrentStatus;
```

Visual Studio should be complaining about the `Status` type right about now. This is a public enumeration that contains the values `Open`, `WaitingResponse`, `NewRequest`, and `InGame`. Add the `Status` enumeration to your class, as shown here:

```
public enum Status
{
    Open,
    WaitingResponse,
    NewRequest,
    InGame
}
```

Finally, add the class constructor:

```
public GameRequest(string id, string name, Status status)
{
    this.ID = id;
    this.Name = name;
    this.CurrentStatus = status;
}
```

That's it for the `GameRequest` class. Now it's time for the `Gamer` class.

Gamer.cs

Add a new class to your `MatchMaker` project, and name it `Gamer.cs`. This class provides three public properties (*ID*, *Name*, and *GameRequests*), as well as three methods (`SendRequest()`, `AcceptRequest()`, and `DeclineRequest()`).

Start by adding the properties:

```
public string ID;
public string Name;
public Dictionary<string, GameRequest>
    GameRequests = new Dictionary<string, GameRequest>();
```

Next, add the class constructor:

```
public Gamer(string id, string name)
{
    this.ID = id;
    this.Name = name;
}
```

Now, add the three methods contained in this class. First is the `SendRequest()` method, as shown in Listing 11-29.

LISTING 11-29: The SendRequest() Method of the Gamer Class

```
public void SendRequest(Gamer gamer)
{
    // We arbitrarily limit the number of requests a gamer can have
    // to five, just to show how it might be done. Feel free to change
    // this in your game, or remove it altogether.
    if (gamer.GameRequests.Count > 5
    && !GameRequests.ContainsKey(gamer.ID)
    && !gamer.GameRequests.ContainsKey(ID))
    {
        GameRequests.Add(gamer.ID,
                        new GameRequest(gamer.ID,
                                        gamer.Name,
                                        GameRequest.Status.WaitingResponse));
        gamer.GameRequests.Add(ID,
                        new GameRequest(ID,
                                        Name,
                                        GameRequest.Status.NewRequest));
    }
}
```

In this method, you are passing in a `gamer` object, representing the person you want to send a request to. If that person has fewer than five requests, your request is added to his or her *GameRequests* collection as "waiting for a response" and to yours as a new request.

Next, add the `AcceptRequest()` method shown in Listing 11-30.

LISTING 11-30: The AcceptRequest() Method of the Gamer Class

```
public void AcceptRequest(Gamer gamer)
{
    if (GameRequests[gamer.ID].CurrentStatus = GameRequest.Status.NewRequest)
    {
        GameRequests[gamer.ID].CurrentStatus = GameRequest.Status.InGame;
        gamer.GameRequests[ID].CurrentStatus = GameRequest.Status.InGame;
    }
}
```

This is pretty straightforward, so let's keep moving. Add the `DeclineRequest()` method shown in Listing 11-31 to your class.

LISTING 11-31: The DeclineRequest() Method of the Gamer Class

```
public void DeclineRequest(Gamer gamer)
{
    GameRequests.Remove(gamer.ID);
    gamer.GameRequests.Remove(ID);
}
```

Like the one before it, this method updates the status of the passed-in `gamer` object and then updates the local `game` object.

That's all there is for the `Gamer` class. Next, you will code the interface and the related service. But first, you must do some renaming. Right now, you have a service named `Service1.svc` and a matching interface named `IService1.cs`.

Rename the `Service1.svc` file by right-clicking it in the Solution Explorer and selecting Rename. Name it `MatchMakerService.svc` and then do the same thing for the `IService1.cs` file, naming it `IMatchMaker.cs`. Be sure to answer "Yes" when asked if you want to rename any references to the interface in your project.

The last thing to do here is to change the name of your service class from `Service1` to `MatchMakerService` so that the class definition line looks like this:

```
public class MatchMakerService : IMatchMaker
```

IMatchMaker.cs

Now, open the `IMatchMaker` interface and add definitions for the methods you will implement in your service, as shown in Listing 11-32.

LISTING 11-32: The IMatchMaker Interface File

```csharp
using System;
using System.Collections.Generic;
using System.Linq;
using System.Runtime.Serialization;
using System.ServiceModel;
using System.ServiceModel.Web;
using System.Text;

namespace MatchMaker
{
    [ServiceContract]
    public interface IMatchMaker
    {
        [OperationContract]
        string AvailableGames(string myID, string myName);

        [OperationContract]
        void RequestGame(string myID, string theirID);

        [OperationContract]
        void AcceptGameRequest(string myID, string theirID);

        [OperationContract]
        void DeclineGameRequest(string myID, string theirID);
    }
}
```

You will implement these four methods in the next section.

MatchMakerService.svc.cs

In your `MatchMakerService` class, add the following class-level variable:

```
static Dictionary<string, Gamer> gamers = new Dictionary<string, Gamer>();
```

This dictionary stores all your `Gamer` objects as they access the service to request or accept games.

The first method to implement is the `AvailableGames()` method. It adds the gamer to the collection if it isn't already present and then returns a string containing a list of currently available games to the gamer, in four types:

- Games the gamer is playing
- Game invites the gamer is waiting on a response for
- Game invites the gamer must respond to
- Games the gamer can create invites for

Add the `AvailableGames()` method, shown in Listing 11-33.

LISTING 11-33: The AvailableGames() Method of the MatchMakerService Class

```csharp
public string AvailableGames(string myID, string myName)
{
    // Add gamer to list if not already present
    if (!gamers.ContainsKey(myID))
    {
        gamers.Add(myID, new Gamer(myID, myName));
    }

    // Create list of currently available games (all types) by gamer
    string availableGames = string.Empty;
    foreach (GameRequest request in gamers[myID].GameRequests.Values)
    {
        availableGames += "@"
                    + request.ID
                    + ":"
                    + request.Name + ";"
                    + request.CurrentStatus.ToString()
                    + "-";
    }

    // Add some open games to the list as well
    int gamesToAdd = 4 - gamers[myID].GameRequests.Count;
    for (int openGames = 0; openGames <= gamesToAdd; openGames++)
    {
        foreach (Gamer gamer in gamers.Values)
        {
```

continues

LISTING 11-33 *(continued)*

```
            if (gamer.GameRequests.Count < 5
            && gamer.ID != myID
            && !availableGames.Contains("@" + gamer.ID + ":"))
            {
                availableGames += "@"
                            + gamer.ID
                            + ":"
                            + gamer.Name
                            + ";"
                            + GameRequest.Status.Open.ToString()
                            + "-";
                break;
            }
        }
    }

    return availableGames;
}
```

This method accepts an `ID` and `Name` to add to the `gamers` collection. Next, you iterate over the `GameRequests` collection (of the specified `gamer` object) and build a string containing the `ID`, `Name`, and `CurrentStatus` of each request, eventually returning it to the calling code.

The next method to add is `RequestGame()`, as shown in Listing 11-34.

LISTING 11-34: The RequestGame() Method of the MatchMakerService Class

```
public void(string myID, string theirID)
{
    gamers[myID].SendRequest(gamers[theirID]);
}
```

This calls the `SendRequest()` method of the local `Gamer` object (as determined by `myID`) and passes in the target `Gamer` object (as determined by `theirID`).

The next method to add is `AcceptGameRequest()`, as shown in Listing 11-35.

LISTING 11-35: The AcceptGameRequest() Method of the MatchMakerService Class

```
public void AcceptGameRequest(string myID, string theirID)
{
    gamers[myID].AcceptRequest(gamers[theirID]);
}
```

This method calls the `AcceptRequest()` method of the local `Gamer` object (as determined by `myID`) and passes in the target `Gamer` object (as determined by `theirID`).

The next method to add is `DeclineGameRequest()`, as shown in Listing 11-36.

LISTING 11-36: The DeclineGameRequest() Method of the MatchMakerService Class

```
public void DeclineGameRequest(string myID, string theirID)
{
    gamers[myID].DeclineRequest(gamers[theirID]);
}
```

This method calls the `DeclineRequest()` method of the local `Gamer` object (as determined by `myID`) and passes in the target `Gamer` object (as determined by `theirID`).

In the next section, you will build a Windows Phone Game to use in your `MatchMaker` service.

MatchMe

Start by creating a new Windows Phone Game project with the name `MatchMe`. Also add a `SpriteFont` to the `MatchMeContent` project. Give it a size of 25.

> *The complete code for this project is available for download at the book's companion website (www.wrox.com).*

Next, add a service reference to the `MatchMaking` service you created earlier in this example. Refer to the `LiveToServeYou` example if you need a refresher on how to do this.

At the top of your `Game1` class file, add the following `using` statements:

```
using Microsoft.Phone.Info;
using MatchMe.MatchMaking;
```

Now add the following class-level variables to your `Game1` class:

```
Rectangle requestGame = new Rectangle(50, 400,  200, 100);
Rectangle acceptGame  = new Rectangle(50, 400,  200, 100);
Rectangle declineGame = new Rectangle(50, 400,  200, 100);
```

This block of variables is responsible for defining the touch areas mapped to the Request, Accept, and Decline commands, as shown in Figure 11-7.

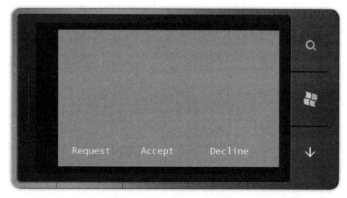

FIGURE 11-7: The starting MatchMe screen, with no requests

Now, add the following as well, also at the class level:

```
MatchMakerClient matchMaker;
List<string> games = new List<string>();
SpriteFont display;
string userID;
string selectedID;
```

In your `Initialize()` method, add a line to enable the `DoubleTap` gesture, as follows:

```
TouchPanel.EnabledGestures = GestureType.DoubleTap;
```

Next, add the following code to your `LoadContent()` method:

```
Display = Content.Load<SpriteFont>("SpriteFont1");
```

No explanation is needed for that line, since you've seen it a few dozen times by now. Add the following block next:

```
string anid = UserExtendedProperties.GetValue("ANID") as string;
if (anid == null)
{
    anid = "##1234567891234567891234567891232345";
}
userID = anid.Substring(2, 32);
```

This code retrieves (or fakes, in the case of the Emulator) the anonymous Live ID for each phone running your game.

Now add the code to instantiate the `MatchMaker` service client and set up the various event handlers:

```
matchMaker = new MatchMakerClient();
matchMaker.AvailableGamesCompleted
    += new EventHandler<AvailableGamesCompletedEventArgs>
        (matchMaker_AvailableGamesCompleted);

matchMaker.RequestGameCompleted
    += new EventHandler<System.ComponentModel.AsyncCompletedEventArgs>
        (matchMaker_RequestGameCompleted);

matchMaker.AcceptGameRequestCompleted
    += new EventHandler<System.ComponentModel.AsyncCompletedEventArgs>
        (matchMaker_AcceptGameRequestCompleted);

matchMaker.DeclineGameRequestCompleted
    += new EventHandler<System.ComponentModel.AsyncCompletedEventArgs>
        (matchMaker_DeclineGameRequestCompleted);

matchMaker.AvailableGamesAsync(userID, "Georgie");
```

This block of code instantiates the `MatchMaker` service client and maps the `AvailableGames()` method of your service, along with the `AcceptGame()`, `RequestGame()`, and `DeclineGame()` methods.

You also make your first call to the `AvailableGames()` method and pass in the user ID (the anonymous Live ID) and a name. With that, you are done with the `LoadContent()` method.

With the four event handlers mapped, Visual Studio should be complaining about not having the methods you defined, so add those next:

```
void matchMaker_DeclineGameRequestCompleted(object sender,
        System.ComponentModel.AsyncCompletedEventArgs e)
{
    matchMaker.AvailableGamesAsync(userID, SelectedPlayerID());
}

void matchMaker_AcceptGameRequestCompleted(object sender,
        System.ComponentModel.AsyncCompletedEventArgs e)
{
    matchMaker.AvailableGamesAsync(userID, SelectedPlayerID());
}

void matchMaker_RequestGameCompleted(object sender,
        System.ComponentModel.AsyncCompletedEventArgs e)
{
    matchMaker.AvailableGamesAsync(userID, SelectedPlayerID());
}
```

These three methods all do the same thing. After a request has been created, accepted, or denied, they request the available games. Now, add the final event handler, which fires as soon as the `AvailableGames()` request has completed:

```
void matchMaker_AvailableGamesCompleted(object sender,
                                        AvailableGamesCompletedEventArgs e)
{
    games.Clear();
    string[] availableGames = e.Result.ToString().Split("-".ToArray());
    foreach (string game in availableGames)
    {
        games.Add(game);
    }
}
```

This method clears the local list of games and rebuilds it with the data returned from the `MatchMaker` service.

In your `Update()` method, add the following `while()` loop:

```
while (TouchPanel.IsGestureAvailable)
{
    GestureSample gesture = TouchPanel.ReadGesture();
    if (gesture.GestureType == GestureType.DoubleTap)
    {
        var gestureCollision = new Rectangle((int)gesture.Position.X,
                                             (int)gesture.Position.Y,
                                             15,
                                             15);
        if (gestureCollision.Intersects(requestGame))
        {
            matchMaker.RequestGameAsync(userID, SelectedPlayerID());
        }
```

```
            else if (gestureCollision.Intersects(acceptGame))
            {
                matchMaker.AcceptGameRequestAsync(userID, SelectedPlayerID());
            }
            else if (gestureCollision.Intersects(declineGame))
            {
                matchMaker.DeclineGameRequestAsync(userID, SelectedPlayerID());
            }

            int YOffset = 0;
            foreach (string game in games)
            {
                if (gestureCollision.Intersects(new Rectangle
                    (0, 50 + YOffset, 350, 50)))
                {
                    selectedID = game;
                    break;
                }
                YOffset += 75;
            }
        }
    }
}
```

In this code, you are checking to see if a `DoubleTap` gesture has occurred on any of the three commands (as defined by the rectangles you created earlier) at the bottom of the screen. The appropriate request is made asynchronously.

You also check for any double-taps on the individual games listed and set the *selectedID* variable to the ID of whichever game was selected. This is used in the `SelectedPlayerID()` method to determine the player ID of the selected game.

Now you will create the `SelectedPlayerID()` method from the code shown in Listing 11-37.

LISTING 11-37: The SelectedPlayerID() Method of the Game1 Class

```
public string SelectedPlayerID()
{
    if (selectedID == string.Empty)
    {
        return string.Empty;
    }

    return selectedID.Substring(1, selectedID.IndexOf(":") - 1);
}
```

This method picks apart the game string (*selectedID*), which looks like `"@gamerID:gamerName;requestStatus"` and returns the gamer ID to the calling code.

You're almost finished with this project! The last thing to update is your `Draw()` method so that it looks like Listing 11-38.

LISTING 11-38: The Update() Method of the Game1 Class

```
protected override void Draw(GameTime gameTime)
{
    GraphicsDevice.Clear(Color.CornflowerBlue);
    spriteBatch.Begin();

    int YOffset = 0;
    foreach (string game in games)
    {
        if (selectedID == game)
        {
            spriteBatch.DrawString(display,
                                   game,
                                   new Vector2(50, 50 + YOffset),
                                   Color.Yellow);
        }
        else
        {
            spriteBatch.DrawString(display,
                                   game,
                                   new Vector2(50, 50 + YOffset),
                                   Color.White);
        }
        YOffset += 75;
    }

    spriteBatch.DrawString(display,
                           "Request",
                           new Vector2(requestGame.X, requestGame.Y),
                           Color.White);

    spriteBatch.DrawString(display,
                           "Accept",
                           new Vector2(acceptGame.X, acceptGame.Y),
                           Color.White);

    spriteBatch.DrawString(display,
                           "Decline",
                           new Vector2(declineGame.X, declineGame.Y),
                           Color.White);
    spriteBatch.End();
    base.Draw(gameTime);
}
```

In your `Draw()` method, you write out the game string of any active gamer, as returned from the `MatchMaker` service. You also draw the three Request, Accept, and Decline buttons at the bottom of the screen.

That's it for the `MatchMe` project. Next, you will create the third and final part of the example and then test everything.

MatchMakerTester

This project will be used to test the `MatchMaker` service and serve as a second device for creating matchups.

Start by creating a Windows Forms project and naming it `MatchMakerTester`.

Next, set a service reference to the `MatchMaking` service. For a refresher on how to do this, look back at the `MatchMe` project earlier in this chapter. Make sure your service has been built and run at least once before trying to add a reference to it.

> *The complete code for this project is available for download at the book's companion website (www.wrox.com).*

Form1

Open `Form1.cs` in Design view and add the controls shown in Table 11-2. Be sure to set the properties listed for each control.

TABLE 11-2: Form1 Controls and Properties

CONTROL	PROPERTY	VALUE
Form1	Size	667, 452
	Text	Match Maker Tester
label1	Text	PhoneID:
label2	Text	Name:
txtPhoneID	Size	132, 22
txtName	Size	132, 22
btnRefresh	Text	Refresh
btnRequest	Text	Request
btnAccept	Text	Accept
btnDecline	Text	Decline
lstAvailableGames	ItemHeight	16
	Size	507, 292

When you are done, you should have something that looks like Figure 11-8. The exact placement of the controls isn't critical, but make sure that you name them correctly, or your code won't work.

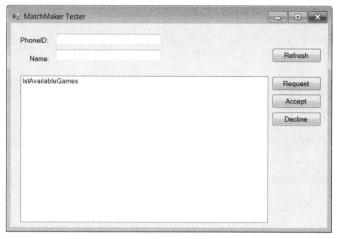

FIGURE 11-8: The MatchMakerTester Windows Form

Now that you have created the test form, switch to code-behind view and add the following `using` statement:

```
using MatchMakerTester.MatchMaker;
```

At the class level, add the following variable to store the `MatchMaker` service client:

```
MatchMakerClient client;
```

In the `Form1` constructor, instantiate the client and set up the various event handlers, as shown in Listing 11-39.

LISTING 11-39: The Form1() Constructor

```
public Form1()
{
    InitializeComponent()

    client = new MatchMakerClient();

    client.AvailableGamesCompleted
        += new EventHandler<AvailableGamesCompletedEventArgs>
            (client_AvailableGamesCompleted);

    client.RequestGameCompleted
        += new EventHandler<AsyncCompletedEventArgs>
            (client_RequestGameCompleted);

    client.AcceptGameRequestCompleted
        += new EventHandler<AsyncCompletedEventArgs>
            (client_AcceptGameRequestCompleted);

    client.DeclineGameRequestCompleted
        += new EventHandler<AsyncCompletedEventArgs>
            (client_DeclineGameRequestCompleted);
}
```

Just like in the `MatchMe` game, you are setting up the event handlers for the various states of requests (Requested, Accepted, and Declined).

Now you set up the methods those event handlers are pointing to, starting with Listings 11-40 through 11-43.

LISTING 11-40: The client_DeclineGameRequestCompleted() Method of the Game1 Class

```
void client_DeclineGameRequestCompleted(object sender,
                                        AsyncCompletedEventArgs e)
{
    client.AvailableGamesAsync(txtPhoneID.Text, txtName.Text);
}
```

LISTING 11-41: The client_AcceptGameRequestCompleted() Method of the Game1 Class

```
void client_AcceptGameRequestCompleted(object sender,
                                       AsyncCompletedEventArgs e)
{
    client.AvailableGamesCompleted(txtPhoneID.Text, txtName.Text);
}
```

LISTING 11-42: The client_RequestGameCompleted() Method of the Game1 Class

```
void client_RequestGameCompleted(object sender,
                                 AsyncCompletedEventArgs e)
{
    client.AvailableGamesAsync(txtPhoneID.Text, txtName.Text);
}
```

LISTING 11-43: The client_AvailableGamesCompleted() Method of the Game1 Class

```
void client_AvailableGamesCompleted(object sender,
                                    AvailableGamesCompletedEventArgs e)
{
    string availableGames = e.Result.ToString();
    string[] games = availableGames.Split("-".ToCharArray());

    lstAvailableGames.Items.Clear();
    foreach (string game in games)
    {
        lstAvailableGames.Items.Add(game);
    }
}
```

In the `AvailableGamesCompleted()` method, you take the result string and split it into an array. Then you clear the list box and iterate through the array to populate the list of game requests.

Next, add the event handler for your form controls. The quickest way to do this is to switch to Design view and double-click each of the four buttons.

With the four `Click` events in place, it's time to add the code. Start with the `btnRefresh_Click()` method, as shown in Listing 11-44.

LISTING 11-44: The btnRefresh_Click() Method of the Game1 Class

```
void btnRefresh_Click(object sender, EventArgs e)
{
    client.AvailableGamesAsync(txtPhoneID.Text, txtName.Text);
}
```

This method takes the `PhoneID` and `Name` provided by the tester and passes them to the `AvailableGames()` method of your service.

Next, add the `btnRequestGame_Click()` method, as shown in Listing 11-45.

LISTING 11-45: The btnRequestGame_Click() Method of the Game1 Class

```
void btnRequestGame_Click(object sender, EventArgs e)
{
    client.RequestGameAsync(txtPhoneID.Text, SelectedPlayerID());
}
```

The next two methods are very similar to this one, and they pass in the same criteria, just to a different method call on the service. First, you add the `btnAcceptRequest_Click()` method shown in Listing 11-46, and then the `btnDeclineRequest_Click()` method shown in Listing 11-47.

LISTING 11-46: The btnAcceptRequest_Click() Method of the Game1 Class

```
void btnAcceptRequest_Click(object sender, EventArgs e)
{
    client.AcceptGameRequestAsync(txtPhoneID.Text, SelectedPlayerID());
}
```

LISTING 11-47: The btnDeclineRequest_Click() Method of the Game1 Class

```
void btnDeclineRequest_Click(object sender, EventArgs e)
{
    client.DeclineGameRequest(txtPhoneID.Text, SelectedPlayerID());
}
```

Finally, you add the `SelectedPlayerID()` method shown in Listing 11-48 to your `Game1` class.

> **LISTING 11-48:** The SelectedPlayerID() Method of the Game1 Class
>
> ```
> string SelectedPlayerID()
> {
>     return lstAvailableGames.SelectedItem.ToString()
>         .Substring(1, lstAvailableGames.SelectedItem.ToString()
>                       .IndexOf(":") - 1);
> }
> ```

This method returns the player ID from the gamer string used with the Available Games list box control.

That's it for this project. Now it's time to test everything.

Testing the MatchMaker Service

At this point, you have three projects: a `MatchMaker` service, a test form called `MatchMakerTester`, and an XNA game called `MatchMe`.

To test this sample and to see how everything works together, do the following:

1. Start your `MatchMaker` service if it's not already running.
2. Start the `MatchMakerTester` Windows Forms application.
3. In the test application, enter **123** in the Phone ID field and **Joe** in the Name field. Click the Refresh button. This registers Joe (and his phone) with the service.
4. Repeat step 3, this time adding another Phone ID of **124**. Put **Frank** in the Name field, and click the Refresh button. You see the list of available players Frank can request a match with.
5. Re-enter **123**, and click the Refresh button to see the available matches to Joe. If the status is "open," you can request a match.
6. Select Frank in the list box, and click the Request button. The service sends back the list. The status is "WaitingResponse."
7. Type in the Phone ID of the other player (**124**), and click the Refresh button. Frank now displays a status of NewRequest, which he can accept or decline.
8. Accept the request. The status switches to InGame.
9. Start the `MatchMe` game on your phone or the Emulator. You see the status of various matches on the screen.
10. Switch back to the test application and create a new person, with a Phone ID of **125** and a Name of **Amy**.
11. Request a match with Georgie (the person created by your phone).

Feel free to experiment with accepting and declining different requests to get a feel for how the system works. You will see it in action again (with more features) in Chapter 12 as part of the Poker Dice game you will build.

WORKING WITH HTTP REQUESTS

In addition to WCF services, there is another way to get calls from the Internet. The `HttpWebRequest` class allows you to call exposed services directly and consume the data they return (typically in XML or JSON format).

JavaScript Notation (JSON) is a more object-oriented markup than XML. As a result, it's slightly less human-readable when you're looking at the raw data.

Another cool thing is that these types of calls do not require a service reference in your project. As long as your phone or device has an active Internet connection, you're all set!

WeatherWitch

In this section, you will build a simple XNA game that talks to the Google Application Programming Interface (API) and returns weather information to your game. Weather data may seem like an odd choice for an example, but it does illustrate the concept of how to use these types of service calls. Maybe you can come up with a cool way to use real weather data in your game.

Start by creating a Windows Phone Game project and naming it `WeatherWitch`. Add a `SpriteFont` to your `WeatherWitchContent` project, and give it a size of 25.

The complete code for this project is available for download at the book's companion website (www.wrox.com).

Inside the `Game1.cs` class file, add the following `using` statements:

```
using System.Text;
using System.Xml;
using System.Xml.Linq;
```

Now add the following class-level variables:

```
string cityData;
string conditionData;
string temperatureData;
Texture2D conditionTexture;
SpriteFont displayFont;
```

The three strings store city and weather information, and `Texture2D` stores the image that is returned as part of the `WeatherImage` callback you will see shortly.

There is nothing new for you to add in your `Game1()` constructor or the `Initialize()` method, so skip both of those.

In your `LoadContent()` method, load your `SpriteFont` into memory and make a call to the `GetWeather()` method, as shown here:

```
displayFont = Content.Load<SpriteFont>("SpriteFont1");
GetWeather();
```

Now, add the `GetWeather()` method shown in Listing 11-49 to your `Game1` class.

LISTING 11-49: The GetWeather() Method of the Game1 Class

```
void GetWeather()
{
    var req =
        HttpWebRequest.Create(@"http://www.google.com/ig/api?weather=98682");
    req.Method = "GET";
    IAsyncResult token
        = req.BeginGetResponse(new AsyncCallback(GetWeatherCallBack), req);
}
```

This method creates a new `HttpWebRequest` object and passes in the API call. The API requires that the request be in the form of a `GET` (rather than a `POST`).

Finally, an asynchronous callback is defined that points to the `GetWeatherCallBack()` method, defined in Listing 11-50, which you add next.

LISTING 11-50: The GetWeatherCallBack() Method of the Game1 Class

```
void GetWeatherCallBack(IAsyncResult result)
{
    var response =
        ((HttpWebRequest)result.AsyncState).EndGetResponse(result);

    var reader = new StreamReader(response.GetResponseStream());
    var responseString = reader.ReadToEnd();
    reader.Close();

    cityData = SubString(responseString, "<city data=\"", "/>");
    conditionData = SubString(responseString, "<condition data=\"", "/>");
    temperatureData = SubString(responseString, "<temp_f data=\"", "/>");

    string image = SubString(responseString, "<icon data=\"", "/>");
    var req = HttpWebRequest.Create(@"http://www.google.com" + image);

    req.Method = "GET";
    IAsyncResult token
        = req.BeginGetResponse(new AsyncCallback(GetWeatherImageCallBack),
                               req);
}
```

This method begins by accepting an asynchronous result from the API call. The `EndGetResponse()` method returns a `WebRequest` result, which is dumped into the `streamreader` object (`reader`) and is read into the `responseString` variable.

The `cityData`, `conditionData`, and `temperatureData` are then parsed from the XML in the `responseString`, along with the path of the weather icon, which is stored in the `image` variable.

A second `WebRequest` is formed to fetch the image from the constructed path, and a new callback is designated to receive the image.

Add the `GetWeatherImageCallBack()` method shown in Listing 11-51 to your `Game1` class.

LISTING 11-51: The GetWeatherImageCallBack() Method of the Game1 Class

```
void GetWeatherImageCallBack(IAsyncResult result)
{
    var response
        = ((HttpWebRequest)result.AsyncState).EndGetResponse(result);
    conditionTexture = Texture2D.FromStream(graphics.GraphicsDevice,
                                            response.GetResponseStream());
{
```

This method is called when the API returns a response to the request for the weather image. The `FromStream()` method of the `Texture2D` class is used to take in the stream and cast it to the `Texture2D` object, `conditionTexture`.

Next, add the `SubString()` helper method shown in Listing 11-52 (which you used in the `GetWeatherCallBack()` method).

LISTING 11-52: The SubString() Method of the Game1 Class

```
string SubString(string original, string start, string end)
{
    int startIndex = original.IndexOf(start) + start.Length;
    return original.SubString(startIndex,
                         original.IndexOf(end, startIndex)
                            - startIndex - 1);
}
```

This extremely handy helper method can be used to parse values by looking for a start and end string (chunk of text), rather than requiring a positional index that might be different from one run to the next.

No changes are required for the `UnloadContent()` or `Update()` methods, so you can skip both of those.

The only thing left in this example is to update the `Draw()` method with the bold code shown in Listing 11-53.

LISTING 11-53: The Draw() Method of the Game1 Class

```
protected override void Draw(GameTime gameTime)
{
    GraphicsDevice.Clear(Color.CornflowerBlue);

    spriteBatch.Begin();

    if (conditionTexture != null)
    {
        spriteBatch.DrawString(displayFont,
                               cityData,
                               new Vector2(100, 100),
                               Color.White);

        spriteBatch.Draw(conditionTexture,
                         new Vector2(100, 150),
                         Color.White);

        spriteBatch.DrawString(displayFont,
                               conditionData,
                               new Vector2(150, 150),
                               Color.White);

        spriteBatch.DrawString(displayFont,
                               temperatureData + " degrees",
                               new Vector2(100, 200),
                               Color.White);
    }

    spriteBatch.End();

    base.Draw(gameTIme);
}
```

That's it for this example. It's time to build and run the `WeatherWitch` application (you can't really call it a game) on your device or the Emulator.

If you run it several times and it always says the weather is "rainy," don't worry. This isn't a bug; it's Vancouver. Try changing the zip code from `98682` to somewhere sunnier, such as `29687`.

Pulling an RSS Feed into Your Game

When consuming an RSS feed, the same principles apply as in the previous section. Since the content of the RSS feed is essentially XML referenced by a URI, you can fetch it just as you would the weather data in the previous example.

Once you have the resulting XML, you can parse it and consume some or all of the data however you see fit.

RSS is a great way to share information with people who have your game. Some typical uses are alerting your users to new content for your game, introducing users to other games you have developed, and informing users of things such as game-server downtime for maintenance.

Time for a REST(ful) Web Service

In addition to WCF services and RSS feeds, you have one more area to cover. Representational State Transfer (REST) Services work much like the Google API calls in the `WeatherWitch` example.

You just fire up the `HttpWebRequest` class and pass in the URI of the REST call you want to make. The key difference here is that REST calls typically support multiple return formats, such as XML or JSON. To specify which format to receive, the path of the service includes the format either as part of the folder structure leading up to the call or as the call's extension.

Several popular services on the web use a REST API, such as Eventbrite or Twitter.

SUMMARY

This chapter covered WCF web services and how to set references to them in your project. Setting a reference creates a proxy client class that enables you to make service calls as though they are local to your project.

You learned how to create a high-scores system that is shared between all users of your game. You also learned how to create a matchmaking system, which will be expanded upon further in Chapter 12.

Finally, you learned how to use the `HttpWebRequest` class to access APIs, REST services, and RSS feeds all over the Internet to add more content to your game.

In Chapter 12, you will take what you have learned and build the second game of this book — Poker Dice.

12
Putting It All Together: Poker Dice with Friends

WHAT'S IN THIS CHAPTER?

➤ Using everything you've learned thus far and making a game called "Poker Dice with Friends"

It's time to take everything you have learned in the previous chapters and make your second complete game for Windows Phone 7.

> *The examples provided in the "Putting it All Together" chapters (Chapters 8, 12, and 15) assume knowledge of C#. Without that, the sample projects may be a bit overwhelming and confusing. These chapters are not for beginners, but for experienced developers who are familiar with C# and somewhat familiar with the XNA framework and game-development concepts.*

"Poker Dice with Friends" (or Poker Dice, for short) is a turn-based dice game where you and your opponent attempt to make poker hands. This chapter walks you through the development of the game to teach you how to create a turn-based service game for Windows Phone 7.

TAKING CARE OF THE PRELIMINARIES

In "Poker Dice with Friends," you can request games with your friends and then roll the dice to see who comes up with the best Poker Dice hand. The best hand wins the game.

Poker Dice is a lot like regular poker, only played with dice. The closest poker variant to this would be Five Card Draw. Following is a ranking of hands to determine the best hand:

- *Five of a kind*, such as 5 5 5 5 5
- *Four of a kind*, such as 4 4 4 4
- *Full house*, such as 5 5 5 4 4
- *Three of a kind*, such as 3 3 3
- *Two pairs*, such as 3 3 2 2
- *One pair*, such as 2 2
- *High die*, such as 6

Win or lose, you can keep playing as long as you have people to challenge!

Service Flow versus Screen Flow

Normally in game development, you start by thinking about the game-screen flow. This time, though, you start by thinking about just what the service needs to do for the game. Your service must be ready to chat with your game before you can really dive in and write your Poker Dice game.

This game consists of challenges between players, so it probably needs a way to identify just who is available to play. An identify method would be useful.

A player also needs to be able to see what current games he or she is involved in, so that also sounds like a good method. The player can query the service by providing some sort of identification, and the service can then return a list of games that the provided ID currently has stored.

Other features also would be useful. A player needs a way to start a new game, accept game requests from someone else, decline game requests from someone he doesn't want to play with, and so on.

What else? Players will need to take turns. That's a good thing to do. If the player is waiting for his or her opponent to take a turn, the player probably needs some way to remind the opponent to do that, so some kind of "nudge" method would be a good idea.

Players also need some way to forfeit a game. Additionally, after they've won or lost they need a way to prune their list of games, so there should be a remove method.

That sounds like a pretty good list. Let's recap:

- Identify who is available to play
- Identify current games
- Request a game
- Accept a game request
- Decline a game request
- Take a turn
- Nudge a player who is slow to respond

➤ Forfeit a game

➤ Remove a game

This seems like a pretty functional list of methods for the `PokerDiceService`. Now that you have thought about what the service should do, it's time to get coding!

Creating the Poker Dice Service

Before you can start playing "Poker Dice with Friends," you must be able to let those "friends" know that you want to play. This means that you must create some kind of service to handle that communication.

In Chapter 11, you learned how to create a web service to handle the matchmaking duties. The Poker Dice service you're about to create is based on that example, and it adds some extra functionality.

> *The complete code for this project is available for download at the book's companion website (www.wrox.com).*

Start by creating a new WCF Service Application, and name it `PokerDiceService`. This creates a basic service application project with some base classes. You'll start by modifying the interface for your service.

First, you should give it a more descriptive name than `IService`. So, right-click the `IService1.cs` file in Solution Explorer and select Rename. Name it `IPokerDice.cs` and say "Yes" to the dialog that asks if you would like to rename internal references as well.

IPokerDice.cs

Now that your interface is properly named, modify `IPokerDice` to look like Listing 12-1.

LISTING 12-1: The Modified IPokerDice Interface of the PokerDiceService

```
using System.ServiceModel;

namespace PokerDiceService
{
    [ServiceContract]
    public interface IPokerDice
    {
        [OperationContract]
        void Identify(string playerID, string phoneUri, string playerName);

        [OperationContract]
        string CurrentGames(string playerID);

        [OperationContract]
```

continues

LISTING 12-1 *(continued)*

```
        void RequestGame(string playerID);

        [OperationContract]
        void AcceptGameRequest(string playerID, string opponentID);

        [OperationContract]
        void DeclineGameRequest(string playerID, string opponentID);

        [OperationContract]
        void TakeTurn(string playerID, string opponentID, string roll);

        [OperationContract]
        void Nudge(string playerID, string opponentID);

        [OperationContract]
        void RemoveGame(string playerID, string opponentID);

        [OperationContract]
        void Forfeit(string playerID, string opponentID);
    }
}
```

These methods represent the ones that any application/game that wants to talk to the service will have available.

Now that the interface is created, it's time to start building the rest of the functionality. The service will manage games, so you will create a game class to represent that object.

Game.cs

Add a new class to the `PokerDiceService` project, and call it `Game`. Modify the `Game.cs` class file to look like Listing 12-2.

LISTING 12-2: The Game Class of the PokerDiceService

```
namespace PokerDiceService
{
    public class Game
    {
        public string ID;
        public string Name;
        public string Roll;

        public enum Status
        {
            WaitingResponse,
            NewRequest,
            YourTurn,
            TheirTurn,
            Win,
```

```
                Lose
        }
        public Status CurrentStatus;

        public Game(string id, string name, Status status)
        {
            this.ID = id;
            this.Name = name;
            this.CurrentStatus = status;
            this.Roll = string.Empty;
        }
    }
}
```

The Game object will be used to represent the game being played between two gamers. It keeps track of the status, the opponent, and what Poker Dice roll the player got.

With the Game object created, it's time for you to create the Gamer class.

Gamer.cs

Add a new class to the PokerDiceService, and call it Gamer. Modify it to look like Listing 12-3.

LISTING 12-3: The Gamer Class of the PokerDiceService

```
using System;
using System.Collections.Generic;
using System.Linq;
using System.Web;
using System.Net;
using System.IO;
using System.Text;

namespace PokerDiceService
{
    public class Gamer
    {
        public string ID;
        public string Name;
        public string PhoneURI;

        public Dictionary<string, Game> Games
            = new Dictionary<string, Game>();

        public Gamer(string id, string name, string phoneURI)
        {
            this.ID = id;
            this.Name = name;
        }

        public void SendRequest(Gamer gamer)
        {
            // If the gamer the player wants to send a request to
```

continues

LISTING 12-3 *(continued)*

```csharp
            // has less than 5 current games (just to keep things
            // from getting out of control) then add the new game
            // requests to both gamers
            if (gamer.Games.Count < 5
                && !Games.ContainsKey(gamer.ID)
                && !gamer.Games.ContainsKey(ID))
            {
                Games.Add(gamer.ID,
                        new Game(gamer.ID,
                                 gamer.Name,
                                 Game.Status.WaitingResponse));
                gamer.Games.Add(ID,
                            new Game(ID,
                                     Name,
                                     Game.Status.NewRequest));
            }
        }

        public void AcceptRequest(Gamer opponent)
        {
            if (Games[opponent.ID].CurrentStatus == Game.Status.NewRequest)
            {
                Games[opponent.ID].CurrentStatus = Game.Status.TheirTurn;
                opponent.Games[ID].CurrentStatus = Game.Status.YourTurn;
            }
        }

        public void DeclineRequest(Gamer gamer)
        {
            Games.Remove(gamer.ID);
            gamer.Games.Remove(ID);
        }

        public void TakeTurn(Gamer opponent, string roll)
        {
            if (Games[opponent.ID].CurrentStatus == Game.Status.YourTurn)
            {
                Games[opponent.ID].Roll = roll;

                //Check to see if the game is over
                if (opponent.Games[ID].Roll != string.Empty)
                {
                    if (HandRank.IsWinningRoll(roll,
                                            opponent.Games[ID].Roll))
                    {
                        Games[opponent.ID].CurrentStatus = Game.Status.Win;
                        opponent.Games[ID].CurrentStatus = Game.Status.Lose;
                    }
                    else
                    {
                        Games[opponent.ID].CurrentStatus = Game.Status.Win;
                        opponent.Games[ID].CurrentStatus = Game.Status.Lose;
```

```csharp
            }
        }
        else
        {
            Games[opponent.ID].CurrentStatus = Game.Status.TheirTurn;
            opponent.Games[ID].CurrentStatus = Game.Status.YourTurn;
        }
    }
}

public void Nudge(Gamer opponent)
{
    if (Games[opponent.ID].CurrentStatus == Game.Status.TheirTurn)
    {
        SendToastNotification(opponent.PhoneURI,
            "Remember, it's your turn... Let's roll already!");
    }
}

public void RemoveGame(Gamer opponent)
{
    // If the game is over then it can be removed from the list
    if (Games[opponent.ID].CurrentStatus == Game.Status.Win
        || Games[opponent.ID].CurrentStatus == Game.Status.Lose)
    {
        Games.Remove(opponent.ID);
    }
    else if (Games[opponent.ID].CurrentStatus
        == Game.Status.WaitingResponse)
    {
        Games.Remove(opponent.ID);
        opponent.Games.Remove(ID);
    }
}

public void Forfeit(Gamer opponent)
{
    if (Games[opponent.ID].CurrentStatus == Game.Status.YourTurn
        || Games[opponent.ID].CurrentStatus == Game.Status.TheirTurn)
    {
        Games[opponent.ID].CurrentStatus = Game.Status.Lose;
        opponent.Games[ID].CurrentStatus = Game.Status.Win;
    }
}

private void SendToastNotification(string uri, string message)
{
    try
    {
        HttpWebRequest sendNotificationRequest
            = (HttpWebRequest)WebRequest.Create(uri);

        sendNotificationRequest.Method = "POST";
        sendNotificationRequest.ContentType = "text/xml";
        sendNotificationRequest.Headers.Add("X-WindowsPhone-Target",
```

continues

LISTING 12-3 *(continued)*

```
                                                "toast");
        sendNotificationRequest.Headers.Add("X-NotificationClass",
                                            "2");

        // Possible batching interval values:
        // 2: message delivered immediately.
        // 12: message delivered within 450 seconds.
        // 22: message delivered within 900 seconds.

        string toastMessage
            = "<?xml version=\"1.0\" encoding=\"utf-8\"?>" +
                "<wp:Notification xmlns:wp=\"WPNotification\">" +
                    "<wp:Toast>" +
                        "<wp:Text1>Poker Dice!</wp:Text1>" +
                        "<wp:Text2>" + message + "</wp:Text2>" +
                    "</wp:Toast>" +
                "</wp:Notification>";

        byte[] notificationMessage
            = new UTF8Encoding().GetBytes(toastMessage);
        sendNotificationRequest.ContentLength
            = notificationMessage.Length;

        using (Stream requestStream
            = sendNotificationRequest.GetRequestStream())
        {
            requestStream.Write(notificationMessage,
                                0,
                                notificationMessage.Length);
        }

        //Sends the notification and gets the response.
        HttpWebResponse response
            = (HttpWebResponse)sendNotificationRequest.GetResponse();
        string notificationStatus
            = response.Headers["X-NotificationStatus"];
        string notificationChannelStatus
            = response.Headers["X-SubscriptionStatus"];
        string deviceConnectionStatus
            = response.Headers["X-DeviceConnectionStatus"];
    }
    catch (Exception ex)
    {
        string error = ex.Message;
    }
}
```

The `Gamer` class does a lot of work. It manages all the games a player might be involved in and helps move a game through its various states.

Notice that the `Gamer` class calls a `HandRank.IsWinningRoll()` method. The `IsWinningRoll()` method and the `HandRank` class help with all the Poker Dice logic, but you still haven't created them. Let's do that next.

HandRank.cs

Add a new class to the `PokerDiceService` project, and call it `HandRank`. Add the code shown in Listing 12-4 to your `HandRank` class.

LISTING 12-4: The HandRank Class of the PokerDiceService

```
using System.Collections.Generic;

namespace PokerDiceService
{
    public class HandRank
    {
        public static bool IsWinningRoll(string roll, string opponentsRoll)
        {
            // Populate the dictionaires with the values (1, 6) and how
            // many times they're found in the roll. These will be used
            // to determine the hand rank.
            Dictionary<int, int> playerOne = new Dictionary<int, int>();
            Dictionary<int, int> playerTwo = new Dictionary<int, int>();

            for (int value = 6; value >= 1; value--)
            {
                playerOne.Add(value, StringCount(roll,
                                                value.ToString()));
                playerTwo.Add(value, StringCount(opponentsRoll,
                                                value.ToString()));

                // Check to see if the player has 5 of a kind; if they do
                // and the other player does not, they are the winning roll
                if (playerOne[value] == 5 && playerTwo[value] != 5)
                {
                    return true;
                }
                else if (playerOne[value] != 5 && playerTwo[value] == 5)
                {
                    return false;
                }
                else if (playerOne[value] == 5 && playerTwo[value] == 5)
                {
                    return false;
                }
            }

            // Check to see if either play has 4 of a kind
            if (playerOne.ContainsValue(4) || playerTwo.ContainsValue(4))
            {
                return IsHigherOfKind(4, playerOne, playerTwo);
```

continues

LISTING 12-4 *(continued)*

```
        }

        // Check for Full House
        bool isPlayerOneFullHouse = playerOne.ContainsValue(3)
                                 && playerOne.ContainsValue(2);

        bool isPlayerTwoFullHouse = playerTwo.ContainsValue(3)
                                 && playerTwo.ContainsValue(2);

        if (isPlayerOneFullHouse || isPlayerTwoFullHouse)
        {
            return IsHigherFullHouse(playerOne, playerTwo);
        }

        // Check to see if either player has 3 of a kind
        if (playerOne.ContainsValue(3) || playerTwo.ContainsValue(3))
        {
            return IsHigherOfKind(3, playerOne, playerTwo);
        }

        // Check for two pairs or a single pair
        if (playerOne.ContainsValue(2) || playerTwo.ContainsValue(2))
        {
            return IsHighPairsOrPair(playerOne, playerTwo);
        }

        // Who has high card
        return IsHighCard(playerOne, playerTwo);
    }

    private static bool IsHigherOfKind(int valueToCheck,
                                       Dictionary<int, int> playerOne,
                                       Dictionary<int, int> playerTwo)
    {
        // If playerTwo does have the valueToCheck then player one wins
        if (!playerTwo.ContainsValue(valueToCheck))
        {
            return true;
        }

        // Check to see if Player 1 has the higher value to check
        for (int value = 6; value >= 1; value--)
        {
            if (playerOne[value] == valueToCheck
                && playerTwo[value] != valueToCheck)
            {
                return true;
            }
        }

        // Player two had a higher value to check
        return false;
```

```csharp
    }

    private static bool IsHigherFullHouse(Dictionary<int, int> playerOne,
                                          Dictionary<int, int> playerTwo)
    {
        // Player Two doesn't have a full house so Player One wins
        if (!playerTwo.ContainsValue(3))
        {
            return true;
        }

        // Check for higher 3 of a kind in their full house
        for (int value = 6; value >= 1; value--)
        {
            if (playerOne[value] == 3 && playerTwo[value] != 3)
            {
                return true;
            }
            else if (playerOne[value] != 3 && playerTwo[value] == 3)
            {
                return false;
            }
        }

        // Check to see who has the higher 2 of a kind
        // (since they had the same 3 of a kind)
        for (int value = 6; value >= 1; value--)
        {
            if (playerOne[value] == 2 && playerTwo[value] != 2)
            {
                return true;
            }
            else if (playerOne[value] != 2 && playerTwo[value] == 2)
            {
                return false;
            }
        }

        // They've got the same full house, so make player one lose...
        return false;
    }

    private static bool IsHighPairsOrPair(Dictionary<int, int> playerOne,
                                          Dictionary<int, int> playerTwo)
    {
        // Check if player has two pairs
        int playerOneCount = 0;
        int playerTwoCount = 0;
        int playerOneHighPair = 0;
        int playerTwoHighPair = 0;
        for (int value = 6; value >= 1; value--)
        {
            if (playerOne[value] == 2)
            {
                playerOneCount += 1;
```

continues

LISTING 12-4 *(continued)*

```
                if (value > playerOneHighPair)
                {
                    playerOneHighPair = value;
                }
            }

            if (playerTwo[value] == 2)
            {
                playerTwoCount += 1;
                if (value > playerTwoHighPair)
                {
                    playerTwoHighPair = value;
                }
            }
        }

        if (playerOneCount == 2 && playerTwoCount != 2)
        {
            return true;
        }
        else if (playerOneCount != 2 && playerTwoCount == 2)
        {
            return false;
        }
        else if (playerOneCount == 2 && playerTwoCount == 2)
        {
            return playerOneHighPair > playerTwoHighPair;
        }

        return IsHigherOfKind(2, playerOne, playerTwo);
    }

    private static bool IsHighCard(Dictionary<int, int> playerOne,
                                   Dictionary<int, int> playerTwo)
    {
        for (int value = 6; value >= 1; value--)
        {
            // If the player has the current card value and
            // the opponent does not then the player has the
            // high card
            if (playerOne[value] != 0 && playerTwo[value] == 0)
            {
                return true;
            }
            else if (playerOne[value] == 0 && playerTwo[value] != 0)
            {
                return false;
            }
        }

        return false;
    }
```

```
            private static int StringCount(string text, string pattern)
            {
                int count = 0;
                int index = 0;
                while ((index = text.IndexOf(pattern, index)) != -1)
                {
                    count++;
                    index += pattern.Length;
                }
                return count;
            }
        }
    }
```

The `HandRank` class analyzes the die results and determines the hand rank, comparing it to the opponent's hand.

Now that you have created the `Game` and `Gamer` classes, as well as the `HandRank` class to help determine which Poker Dice roll is a winning roll, it's time to add the code to the service class and make it functional.

PokerDice.svc

First, you should give the service a better name than `Service1.svc`. Right-click the file and select Rename. Name the file `PokerDice.svc` and press Enter.

Now, modify the `PokerDice.svc` file to look like Listing 12-5.

LISTING 12-5: The PokerDice Service

```
using System;
using System.Collections.Generic;
using System.Linq;

namespace PokerDiceService
{
    public class PokerDiceService : IPokerDice
    {
        static Dictionary<string, Gamer> gamers
            = new Dictionary<string, Gamer>();

        public void Identify(string playerID,
                             string phoneURI,
                             string playerName)
        {
            if (!gamers.ContainsKey(playerID))
            {
                gamers.Add(playerID,
                        new Gamer(playerID,
                                  playerName, phoneURI));
            }
```

continues

LISTING 12-5 *(continued)*

```csharp
        else
        {
            gamers[playerID].PhoneURI = phoneURI;
        }
    }

    public string CurrentGames(string playerID)
    {
        if (!gamers.ContainsKey(playerID))
        {
            return "";
        }

        // Create the list of currently available games to the gamer
        // (ones they're playing, ones they're waiting on a response
        // for, ones they need to respond to and ones they can request)
        string currentGames = string.Empty;
        foreach (Game request in gamers[playerID].Games.Values)
        {
            currentGames += "@"
                        + request.ID
                        + ":"
                        + request.Name
                        + ";"
                        + request.CurrentStatus.ToString()
                        + "-";
        }

        return currentGames;
    }

    public void RequestGame(string playerID)
    {
        // If there aren't any other gamers yet then just return
        if (gamers.Count <= 1)
        {
            return;
        }

        // Find a random gamer who doesn't currently have 5 games
        // and send them a game request
        Random random = new Random();
        if (gamers.ContainsKey(playerID)
            && gamers[playerID].Games.Count < 5)
        {
            for (int gameRequestAttempt = 0;
                    gameRequestAttempt < 100;
                    gameRequestAttempt++)
            {
                int randomPlayerIndex = random.Next(0, gamers.Count - 1);
                if (gamers.ElementAt(randomPlayerIndex).Key != playerID
                    && gamers.ElementAt(randomPlayerIndex)
                        .Value.Games.Count < 5)
```

```
                    {
                        gamers[playerID].SendRequest(gamers
                            .ElementAt(randomPlayerIndex).Value);
                        return;
                    }
                }
            }
        }

        public void AcceptGameRequest(string playerID, string opponentID)
        {
            gamers[playerID].AcceptRequest(gamers[opponentID]);
        }

        public void DeclineGameRequest(string playerID, string opponentID)
        {
            gamers[playerID].DeclineRequest(gamers[opponentID]);
        }

        public void TakeTurn(string playerID,
                             string opponentID,
                             string score)
        {
            gamers[playerID].TakeTurn(gamers[opponentID], score);
        }

        public void Nudge(string playerID, string opponentID)
        {
            gamers[playerID].Nudge(gamers[opponentID]);
        }

        public void RemoveGame(string playerID, string opponentID)
        {
            gamers[playerID].RemoveGame(gamers[opponentID]);
        }

        public void Forfeit(string playerID, string opponentID)
        {
            gamers[playerID].Forfeit(gamers[opponentID]);
        }
    }
}
```

With that, your `PokerDiceService` is complete and ready to interact with any client that subscribes to it. In most cases, that would be your Windows Phone 7 game. But to help with development (and testing!), it would also be useful to have a Windows Forms application that could simulate other users also playing your Poker Dice game.

Let's tackle that next.

Creating the Poker Dice Tester

The `PokerDiceTester` application isn't fancy. It's important during development that you put only as much work and time into your tools as necessary.

Because you will use this tool only to test your Poker Dice game, you don't need to spend too much time making it pretty and polished. It's rough, but it gets the job done. More importantly, it saves you the time and money it would cost to have multiple phones available for testing.

PokerDiceTest

Start by creating a new Windows Forms application, and name it `PokerDiceTest`.

In Solution Explorer, under the Service References section, add a reference to your `PokerDiceService`. Table 12-1 lists the controls to add (and what to name them), along with any specific property values.

TABLE 12-1: PokerDiceTest Controls

CONTROL	PROPERTY	VALUE
lblPlayerID	Text	PlayerID:
lblPhoneUri	Text	PhoneURI:
lblName	Text	Name:
txtPlayerID	Size	359, 22
txtPhoneUri	Size	359, 22
txtName	Size	359, 22
lstCurrentGames	Size	283, 292
btnIdentify	Text	Identify
btnCurrentGames	Text	Current Games
btnRequestGames	Text	Request Games
btnAcceptGameRequest	Text	Accept Request
btnDeclineGameRequest	Text	Decline Request
btnTakeTurn	Text	Take Turn
btnNudge	Text	Nudge
btnRemoveGame	Text	Remove Game
btnForfeit	Text	Forfeit

You want your form to look roughly like Figure 12-1 when you are finished.

With the design concerns out of the way, it's time to switch to code view (by pressing F7) and add the code shown in Listing 12-6 to your `PokerDiceTest` Windows Forms class.

FIGURE 12-1: The completed PokerDiceTest form

LISTING 12-6: The PokerDiceTest Form Class

```
using System;
using System.Collections.Generic;
using System.ComponentModel;
using System.Data;
using System.Drawing;
using System.Linq;
using System.Text;
using System.Windows.Forms;

using PokerDiceTester.PokerDiceService;

namespace PokerDiceTester
{
    public partial class Form1 : Form
    {
        PokerDiceClient pokerDiceClient;

        public Form1()
        {
            InitializeComponent();

            pokerDiceClient = new PokerDiceClient();
            pokerDiceClient.IdentifyCompleted
                += new EventHandler<AsyncCompletedEventArgs>
                    (pokerDiceClient_IdentifyCompleted);
            pokerDiceClient.CurrentGamesCompleted
                += new EventHandler<CurrentGamesCompletedEventArgs>
                    (pokerDiceClient_CurrentGamesCompleted);
```

continues

LISTING 12-6 *(continued)*

```csharp
            pokerDiceClient.RequestGameCompleted
                += new EventHandler<AsyncCompletedEventArgs>
                    (pokerDiceClient_RequestGameCompleted);
            pokerDiceClient.AcceptGameRequestCompleted
                += new EventHandler<AsyncCompletedEventArgs>
                    (pokerDiceClient_AcceptGameRequestCompleted);
            pokerDiceClient.DeclineGameRequestCompleted
                += new EventHandler<AsyncCompletedEventArgs>
                    (pokerDiceClient_DeclineGameRequestCompleted);
            pokerDiceClient.TakeTurnCompleted
                += new EventHandler<AsyncCompletedEventArgs>
                    (pokerDiceClient_TakeTurnCompleted);
            pokerDiceClient.NudgeCompleted
                += new EventHandler<AsyncCompletedEventArgs>
                    (pokerDiceClient_NudgeCompleted);
            pokerDiceClient.RemoveGameCompleted
                += new EventHandler<AsyncCompletedEventArgs>
                    (pokerDiceClient_RemoveGameCompleted);
            pokerDiceClient.ForfeitCompleted
                += new EventHandler<AsyncCompletedEventArgs>
                    (pokerDiceClient_ForfeitCompleted);

        btnCurrentGames.Enabled = false;
        btnRequestGames.Enabled = false;
        btnAcceptGameRequest.Enabled = false;
        btnDeclineGameRequest.Enabled = false;
        btnTakeTurn.Enabled = false;
        btnNudge.Enabled = false;
        btnRemoveGame.Enabled = false;
        btnForfeit.Enabled = false;
    }

    void pokerDiceClient_IdentifyCompleted(object sender,
                                        AsyncCompletedEventArgs e)
    {
        btnCurrentGames.Enabled = true;
    }

    void pokerDiceClient_CurrentGamesCompleted(object sender,
                                CurrentGamesCompletedEventArgs e)
    {
        string availableGames = e.Result.ToString();
        string[] games = availableGames.Split("-".ToCharArray());

        lstCurrentGames.Items.Clear();
        foreach (string game in games)
        {
            lstCurrentGames.Items.Add(game);
        }

        btnRequestGames.Enabled = true;
        btnAcceptGameRequest.Enabled = true;
```

```csharp
        btnDeclineGameRequest.Enabled = true;
        btnTakeTurn.Enabled = true;
        btnNudge.Enabled = true;
        btnRemoveGame.Enabled = true;
        btnForfeit.Enabled = true;
    }

    void pokerDiceClient_RequestGameCompleted(object sender,
                                           AsyncCompletedEventArgs e)
    {
        pokerDiceClient.CurrentGamesAsync(txtPlayerID.Text);
    }

    void pokerDiceClient_AcceptGameRequestCompleted(object sender,
                                           AsyncCompletedEventArgs e)
    {
        pokerDiceClient.CurrentGamesAsync(txtPlayerID.Text);
    }

    void pokerDiceClient_DeclineGameRequestCompleted(object sender,
                                           AsyncCompletedEventArgs e)
    {
        pokerDiceClient.CurrentGamesAsync(txtPlayerID.Text);
    }

    void pokerDiceClient_TakeTurnCompleted(object sender,
                                           AsyncCompletedEventArgs e)
    {
        pokerDiceClient.CurrentGamesAsync(txtPlayerID.Text);
    }

    void pokerDiceClient_NudgeCompleted(object sender,
                                         AsyncCompletedEventArgs e)
    {
        pokerDiceClient.CurrentGamesAsync(txtPlayerID.Text);
    }

    void pokerDiceClient_RemoveGameCompleted(object sender,
                                           AsyncCompletedEventArgs e)
    {
        pokerDiceClient.CurrentGamesAsync(txtPlayerID.Text);
    }

    void pokerDiceClient_ForfeitCompleted(object sender,
                                          AsyncCompletedEventArgs e)
    {
        pokerDiceClient.CurrentGamesAsync(txtPlayerID.Text);
    }

    private void btnIdentify_Click(object sender, EventArgs e)
    {
        pokerDiceClient.IdentifyAsync(txtPlayerID.Text,
                              txtPhoneURI.Text,
                              txtName.Text);
```

continues

LISTING 12-6 *(continued)*

```csharp
        btnRequestGames.Enabled = false;
        btnAcceptGameRequest.Enabled = false;
        btnDeclineGameRequest.Enabled = false;
        btnTakeTurn.Enabled = false;
        btnNudge.Enabled = false;
        btnRemoveGame.Enabled = false;
        btnForfeit.Enabled = false;
    }

    private void btnCurrentGames_Click(object sender, EventArgs e)
    {
        pokerDiceClient.CurrentGamesAsync(txtPlayerID.Text);
    }

    private void btnRequestGames_Click(object sender, EventArgs e)
    {
        pokerDiceClient.RequestGameAsync(txtPlayerID.Text);
    }

    private void btnAcceptGameRequest_Click(object sender, EventArgs e)
    {
        pokerDiceClient.AcceptGameRequestAsync(txtPlayerID.Text,
                                        SelectedOpponentID());
    }

    private void btnDeclineGameRequest_Click(object sender, EventArgs e)
    {
        pokerDiceClient.DeclineGameRequestAsync(txtPlayerID.Text,
                                        SelectedOpponentID());
    }

    private void btnTakeTurn_Click(object sender, EventArgs e)
    {
        Random random = new Random();
        string diceRolled = string.Empty;
        for (int die = 1; die <= 5; die++)
        {
            diceRolled += random.Next(1, 7).ToString();
        }

        pokerDiceClient.TakeTurnAsync(txtPlayerID.Text,
                                 SelectedOpponentID(),
                                 diceRolled);
    }

    private void btnNudge_Click(object sender, EventArgs e)
    {
        pokerDiceClient.NudgeAsync(txtPlayerID.Text,
                            SelectedOpponentID());
    }

    private void btnRemoveGame_Click(object sender, EventArgs e)
```

```
            {
                pokerDiceClient.RemoveGameAsync(txtPlayerID.Text,
                                                SelectedOpponentID());
            }

            private void btnForfeit_Click(object sender, EventArgs e)
            {
                pokerDiceClient.ForfeitAsync(txtPlayerID.Text,
                                             SelectedOpponentID());
            }

            string SelectedOpponentID()
            {
                return lstCurrentGames.SelectedItem
                    .ToString().Substring(1,
                                    lstCurrentGames.SelectedItem
                                        .ToString().IndexOf(„:") - 1);
            }
        }
    }
```

You can now compile and run the `PokerDiceTester`. (Just make sure that the `PokerDiceService` is running first!)

Using the PokerDiceTester

To use the tester, start by entering a player ID. This can be any string value you want to identify as a player. The Windows Phone will use the ANID (the Anonymous ID associated with a phone user) for this value. Enter **123** in the PlayerID textbox.

Next, you must enter a phone URI. Again, this is just a made-up value in the tester. The Windows Phone Device will actually get a URI from the Microsoft Notification Service. So, enter **45678** in the PhoneURI textbox.

In the tester, the name is just a visual aid to show who you might be playing against, so any name will work fine. Enter **Frank** in the Name textbox.

Once you've entered the player ID, phone URI, and name, click the Identify button. The Identify button sends a message to the `PokerDiceService` saying, "Here I am. Add me to your list!" You can add new players to the service this way.

Also, you will enter a previously entered player ID (and associated information) and click the Identify button to switch between impersonating those players from within the `PokerDiceTester`.

Now that you have been identified by the service, click the Current Games button. This asks the service to return a list of all the games the currently identified player ID is engaged in and to display them in the Current Games listbox.

Click the Request Games button to ask the service to randomly pick another player and ask that player for a game. This game will be added to the Current Games list for the requesting player.

Once a player has games in the Current Games list, he or she can select them and then click the Accept Request, Decline Request, Take Turn, Nudge, Remove Game, or Forfeit buttons as appropriate. The status is updated in the Current Games list depending on the action taken (that is, if the action taken was valid for the selected game's current status).

Now that the `PokerDiceTester` is complete, you can create multiple opponents for your Windows Phone device to play against. You also can switch between them to test various statuses and ensure that the Poker Dice game you're about to write behaves appropriately. This is quite a useful testing tool!

With the service and the testing application created, you are ready to start making the "Poker Dice with Friends" Windows Phone 7 game.

CREATING "POKER DICE WITH FRIENDS"

With the service code out of the way, you can now focus on creating the "Poker Dice with Friends" game for Windows Phone. The work will be made easier by leveraging the template you created in Chapter 8.

Setting Up the Game Project Template

At the end of Chapter 8, you created a game project template you can use to get up and running with the Poker Dice example in this chapter. If you're having trouble remembering or you skipped that chapter, now would be a good time to revisit it. In this chapter, you use the `XNAPhoneGame` and `XNAPhoneGameContent` templates you created in Chapter 8 so that you can focus more on the game screens and game play and less on all the supporting classes and infrastructure.

Launch Visual Studio, and select New Project. In the New Project dialog, select Visual C# under the Installed Templates section on the left. This allows you to see all the templates you have installed.

Now, select `XNAPhoneGame`. This is the template you created previously, and you will use it as the base `Game` template. This will save you a lot of work and allow you to get your game up and running fairly quickly.

Name your new project `PokerDice`.

With the base `Game` project created, you need to create the base `Content` project. Right-click the `PokerDice` solution, and add a new project. Select the `XNAPhoneGameContent` template, and name it `PokerDiceContent`. Click OK.

Now that the `Game` and `Content` projects are in the solution, you must link the two. Expand the `Content References` folder found under the `PokerDice` game project, and delete any reference links that might currently exist there. (To delete them, simply select them and press the Delete key.)

After deleting any existing references, right-click and select Add Content Reference. Select your `Poker Dice Content` project, and click OK.

That's all there is to creating a link between the `Game` and `Content` projects. This is a very useful thing to remember if you ever need to add multiple `Content` projects to a game.

It's now time to start writing your "Poker Dice with Friends" game!

Modifying the Templates

In this section, you will modify some of the existing template files and add new functionality. The first class to modify is `Title`.

Title.cs

The `Title` screen was part of the base `Game` project, so all you must do now is modify it to match your Poker Dice game.

First, you need to add a new background image to the `Content` project. Add the `Background.png` file from the code files on this book's companion website (www.wrox.com) to the `Images` folder found in the `PokerDiceContent` project, and replace the existing image already there.

Next, open the `Title.cs` file and modify it to look like Listing 12-7.

LISTING 12-7: The Title Class of "Poker Dice with Friends"

```
using Microsoft.Xna.Framework;
using Microsoft.Xna.Framework.Graphics;
using Microsoft.Xna.Framework.Content;
using Microsoft.Xna.Framework.Input.Touch;

using XNAPhoneGame.Sprites;
using XNAPhoneGame.Texts;

namespace XNAPhoneGame.Screens
{
    class Title : Screen
    {
        Background background;
        Button startButton;
        Button exitButton;

        const string ActionStart = "Start";
        const string ActionExit = "Exit";

        public Title(Game game, SpriteBatch batch, ChangeScreen changeScreen)
            : base(game, batch, changeScreen, BackButtonScreenType.First)
        {
        }

        protected override void SetupInputs()
        {
            input.AddTouchGestureInput(ActionStart,
                                      GestureType.Tap,
                                      startButton.CollisionRectangle);
            input.AddTouchGestureInput(ActionExit,
                                      GestureType.Tap,
                                      exitButton.CollisionRectangle);
        }

        protected override void LoadScreenContent(ContentManager content)
```

continues

LISTING 12-7 *(continued)*

```
        {
            background = new Background(content);
            startButton = new Button(content,
                                "Start Game",
                                new Vector2(30, 500),
                                Color.LightBlue);
            exitButton = new Button(content,
                                "Exit",
                                new Vector2(30, 650),
                                Color.LightBlue);
        }

        protected override void UpdateScreen(GameTime gameTime,
                                    DisplayOrientation displayOrientation)
        {
            if (input.IsPressed(ActionStart))
            {
                soundEffects.PlaySound("SoundEffects/Select");
            }
            else if (input.IsPressed(ActionExit))
            {
                changeScreenDelegate(ScreenState.Exit);
            }
        }

        protected override void DrawScreen(SpriteBatch batch,
                                    DisplayOrientation displayOrientation)
        {
            background.Draw(batch);
            startButton.Draw(batch);
            exitButton.Draw(batch);
        }
    }
}
```

Build and run the project (press F5) to see your pretty `Title` screen. If all goes well, you should see the screen shown in Figure 12-2 on your device or the Emulator.

Now it's time to add some real functionality.

Enhancing the ScreenStateSwitchboard Class

With a new game come new screens. This means that the `ScreenStateSwitchboard` class (the class in your framework responsible for routing and switching between screens) must be updated to know about those screens and to know how to create and manage them.

Creating "Poker Dice with Friends" | 375

FIGURE 12-2: The "Poker Dice with Friends" start screen

ScreenStateSwitchboard.cs

Open the `ScreenStateSwitchboard.cs` class file, and modify it to look like Listing 12-8.

LISTING 12-8: The ScreenStateSwitchboard Class of Poker Dice

```
using System.Collections.Generic;

using Microsoft.Xna.Framework;
using Microsoft.Xna.Framework.Graphics;
using Microsoft.Phone.Notification;
using System;

namespace XNAPhoneGame.Screens
{
    public enum ScreenState
    {
        Title,
        InGameMenu,
        GameLobby,
```

continues

LISTING 12-8 *(continued)*

```
            RequestGame,
            GameInfo,
            Nudge,
            Forfeit,
            RemoveGame,
            MainGame,
            DiceSelect,
            PreviousScreen,
            Exit
    }

    class ScreenStateSwitchboard
    {
        static Game game;
        static SpriteBatch batch;
        static Screen previousScreen;
        static Screen currentScreen;
        static Dictionary<ScreenState, Screen> screens
            = new Dictionary<ScreenState, Screen>();

        private HttpNotificationChannel channel;
        private Uri currentUri;
        private delegate Screen CreateScreen();

        public ScreenStateSwitchboard(Game game, SpriteBatch batch)
        {
            ScreenStateSwitchboard.game = game;
            ScreenStateSwitchboard.batch = batch;
            ChangeScreen(ScreenState.Title);

            CreateNotificationChannel();
        }

        public void CreateNotificationChannel()
        {
            channel = HttpNotificationChannel.Find("PokerDice");

            if (channel == null)
            {
                channel = new HttpNotificationChannel("PokerDice");
                SetUpDelegates();
                channel.Open();
            }
            else
            {
                currentScreen.ChannelUriUpdated
                    (channel.ChannelUri.ToString());
                SetUpDelegates();
            }
        }

        public void SetUpDelegates()
        {
```

```csharp
            channel.ChannelUriUpdated
            += new EventHandler<NotificationChannelUriEventArgs>
                (channel_ChannelUriUpdated);

            channel.ShellToastNotificationReceived
            += new EventHandler<NotificationEventArgs>
                (channel_ShellToastNotificationReceived);
        }

        void channel_ShellToastNotificationReceived(object sender,
                                            NotificationEventArgs e)
        {
            if (e.Collection != null)
            {
                var collection = (Dictionary<string, string>)e.Collection;
                var messageBuilder = new System.Text.StringBuilder();

                var notificationMessage = string.Empty;
                foreach (string elementName in collection.Keys)
                {
                    notificationMessage += elementName;
                }

                currentScreen.ShellToastNotificationReceived
                    (notificationMessage);
            }
        }

        void channel_ChannelUriUpdated(object sender,
                                    NotificationChannelUriEventArgs e)
        {
            currentUri = e.ChannelUri;
            currentScreen.ChannelUriUpdated(e.ChannelUri.ToString());
        }

        private void ChangeScreen(ScreenState screenState)
        {
            switch (screenState)
            {
                case ScreenState.Title:
                    {
                        ChangeScreen(screenState,
                                new CreateScreen(CreateTitleScreen));
                        break;
                    }

                case ScreenState.GameLobby:
                    {
                        ChangeScreen(screenState,
                                new CreateScreen(CreateGameLobbyScreen));
                        break;
                    }

                case ScreenState.RequestGame:
                    {
```

continues

LISTING 12-8 *(continued)*

```
            ChangeScreen(screenState,
                    new CreateScreen(CreateRequestGameScreen));
            break;
        }

    case ScreenState.MainGame:
        {
            ChangeScreen(screenState,
                    new CreateScreen(CreateMainGameScreen));
            break;
        }

    case ScreenState.DiceSelect:
        {
            ChangeScreen(screenState,
                    new CreateScreen(CreateDiceSelectScreen));
            break;
        }

    case ScreenState.Forfeit:
        {
            ChangeScreen(screenState,
                    new CreateScreen(CreateForfeitScreen));
            break;
        }

    case ScreenState.GameInfo:
        {
            ChangeScreen(screenState,
                    new CreateScreen(CreateGameInfoScreen));
            break;
        }

    case ScreenState.Nudge:
        {
            ChangeScreen(screenState,
                    new CreateScreen(CreateNudgeScreen));
            break;
        }

    case ScreenState.RemoveGame:
        {
            ChangeScreen(screenState,
                    new CreateScreen(CreateRemoveGameScreen));
            break;
        }

    case ScreenState.InGameMenu:
        {
            ChangeScreen(screenState,
```

```csharp
                              new CreateScreen(CreateInGameMenuScreen));
                    break;
                }

            case ScreenState.PreviousScreen:
                {
                    currentScreen = previousScreen;
                    currentScreen.Activate();
                    break;
                }

            case ScreenState.Exit:
                {
                    game.Exit();
                    break;
                }
        }
    }

    private void ChangeScreen(ScreenState screenState,
                              CreateScreen createScreen)
    {
        previousScreen = currentScreen;

        if (!screens.ContainsKey(screenState))
        {
            screens.Add(screenState, createScreen());
            screens[screenState].LoadContent();
        }
        currentScreen = screens[screenState];
        currentScreen.Activate();
    }

    private Screen CreateTitleScreen()
    {
        return new Title(game,
                         batch,
                         new Screen.ChangeScreen(ChangeScreen));
    }

    private Screen CreateInGameMenuScreen()
    {
        return new InGameMenu(game,
                              batch,
                              new Screen.ChangeScreen(ChangeScreen));
    }

    private Screen CreateGameLobbyScreen()
    {
        return null;
    }

    private Screen CreateMainGameScreen()
    {
        return null;
```

continues

LISTING 12-8 *(continued)*

```
    }

    private Screen CreateGameInfoScreen()
    {
        return null;
    }

    private Screen CreateRequestGameScreen()
    {
        return null;
    }

    private Screen CreateRemoveGameScreen()
    {
        return null;
    }

    private Screen CreateNudgeScreen()
    {
        return null;
    }

    private Screen CreateForfeitScreen()
    {
        return null;
    }

    private Screen CreateDiceSelectScreen()
    {
        return null;
    }

    public void Update(GameTime gameTime)
    {
        currentScreen.Update(gameTime);

        // Bind the channel to Toast notifications if
        // it's open and hasn't been already bound
        if (channel != null && !channel.IsShellToastBound)
        {
            channel.BindToShellToast();
        }
    }

    public void Draw()
    {
        currentScreen.Draw();
    }
    }
}
```

Even with these changes to the `ScreenStateSwitchboard` class, a couple of errors still remain. You may have noticed that you hook up to receive some toast notifications. (Remember how the `PokerDiceService` sends notifications to players to "nudge" them?) To finish all the setup for keeping the latest values of the PhoneURI and to notify a screen that a toast notification arrived, some changes need to be made to the base `Screen` class.

Let's go back to the `Screen` class and make some changes. First, add the following `using` statement to the top of the `Screen` class:

```
using Microsoft.Phone.Info;
```

Then, add the following `static` objects at the class level:

```
protected static string PhoneUri = string.Empty;
protected static string PhoneAnonymousID = "123";
```

These will be used to keep track of the ANID retrieved for the phone (the unique identification value that each phone user has), as well as the current value for the phone URI.

Next, modify the `Screen` constructor to look like Listing 12-9.

LISTING 12-9: The Screen Class Constructor

```
public Screen(Game game,
              SpriteBatch batch,
              ChangeScreen changeScreen,
              BackButtonScreenType backButtonScreenType)
{
    Screen.game = game;
    Screen.content = game.Content;
    Screen.batch = batch;

    changeScreenDelegate = changeScreen;
    touchIndicator = new TouchIndicatorCollection();

    if (music == null)
    {
        music = new Music(content);
    }

    if (soundEffects == null)
    {
        soundEffects = new SoundEffects(content);
    }

    if (!isHighScoresLoaded)
    {
        highScores.Load();
        isHighScoresLoaded = true;
    }

    if (PhoneAnonymousID == string.Empty)
```

continues

LISTING 12-9 *(continued)*

```
    {
        object ANID;
        if (UserExtendedProperties.TryGetValue("ANID", out ANID))
        {
            if (ANID != null && ANID.ToString().Length >= 34)
            {
                PhoneAnonymousID = ANID.ToString().Substring(2, 32);
            }
        }
    }

    this.backButtonScreenType = backButtonScreenType;
}
```

The significant change here is the addition of loading the ANID from the phone. It's important to note that if you're testing in the Emulator, you can't get an ANID. That's why you use the default value of `"123"` for testing purposes.

Finally, add the following methods to the `Screen` class:

```
public void ChannelUriUpdated(string newChannelUri)
{
    PhoneUri = newChannelUri;
    ChannelUriUpdatedNotification(PhoneUri);
}

protected virtual void ChannelUriUpdatedNotification(string newChannelUri)
{
}

public virtual void ShellToastNotificationReceived(string toastMessage)
{
}
```

These will be used to update the URI and to notify the screens that the URI has been updated or that a new shell toast notification has been received.

Next, since you're setting up your `PokerDice` game to receive notifications, you must edit the `WMAppManifest.xml` file to have a publisher name. In Solution Explorer, expand the `Properties` folder to see the `WMAppManifest.xml` file. Open the file, and for the `Publisher` attribute, fill in something like the following:

```
Publisher="XNADevelopment.com">
```

With all these changes to the `Screen` class, and the addition of the `Publisher`, your compile errors should now be gone. Rebuild the project (press F6) just to make sure.

Adding the PokerDiceService

Before you can progress much further with making Poker Dice, you have to add a reference to the `PokerDiceService` that the game will use. Luckily, this part is relatively easy.

First open the `PokerDiceService` project, and then open the `PokerDice.svc` file in that project.

 It's important to make sure that the `.svc` file is open because what happens when you run the project changes based on what file is currently open and has the cursor focus in the IDE. If other classes are open, your service might open in a web page. But if you have the `.svc` file open, the WCF Test Client launches and runs.

With the WCF Test Client running, right-click the web address for your service and select Copy Address. This is the address you will use in the Windows Phone 7 game so that it knows how to add the service reference.

To add the service reference to your Poker Dice game, right-click the `Game` project in Solution Explorer and select Add Service Reference. In the Service Reference dialog, paste the address you copied previously and then click the Go button. This searches for and discovers your service and then downloads the interface information your project needs to subscribe to this service.

Change the namespace to `PokerDiceService`, and click the Add button.

After the service reference has been added, you must add a DLL reference to the `System.NET` DLL for the `PokerDice` game project. It's not clear why that reference isn't added automatically, but if you don't add it manually, multiple compile errors will result.

Creating the GameInformation and DiceGame Supporting Classes

Now that the `PokerDiceService` reference has been added, you're ready for the next step. It's time to create some more supporting classes. Unfortunately, after adding these supporting classes you still won't see anything new, but you will be prepared for that to happen very soon.

DiceGame.cs

Start by adding the `DiceGame` class to the `PokerDice` project. After you've added the class file, modify the `DiceGame.cs` file to look like Listing 12-10.

LISTING 12-10: The DiceGame Class of Poker Dice

```
using System.Collections.Generic;

namespace XNAPhoneGame
{
    class DiceGame
    {
        public enum Status
        {
            Waiting,
            New,
```

continues

LISTING 12-10 *(continued)*

```
            YourTurn,
            TheirTurn,
            Win,
            Lose
        }

        private string gameID;
        public string ID
        {
            get { return gameID; }
        }

        private string playerName;
        public string PlayerName
        {
            get { return playerName; }
        }

        private Status currentStatus;
        public Status CurrentStatus
        {
            get { return currentStatus; }
        }

        public List<int> DiceRoll = new List<int>();
        public int CurrentRoll = 0;

        public DiceGame(string gameID, string playerName, string status)
        {
            this.gameID = gameID;
            this.playerName = playerName;

            switch (status)
            {
                case "WaitingResponse":
                    {
                        currentStatus = Status.Waiting;
                        break;
                    }

                case "NewRequest":
                    {
                        currentStatus = Status.New;
                        break;
                    }

                case "TheirTurn":
                    {
                        currentStatus = Status.TheirTurn;
                        break;
                    }
```

```
            case "YourTurn":
                {
                    currentStatus = Status.YourTurn;
                    break;
                }

            case "Win":
                {
                    currentStatus = Status.Win;
                    break;
                }

            case "Lose":
                {
                    currentStatus = Status.Lose;
                    break;
                }
            }
        }
    }
}
```

The `DiceGame` class manages information about a single Poker Dice game that the player might be involved in. It keeps track of the state, as well as the dice rolls the player makes.

GameInformation.cs

Next, add a new class to the `PokerDice` game project, and name it `GameInformation`. After you've added the class, open it and modify it to look like Listing 12-11.

LISTING 12-11: The GameInformation Class of Poker Dice

```
using System.Collections.Generic;

namespace XNAPhoneGame
{
    class GameInformation
    {
        public static List<DiceGame> Games = new List<DiceGame>();
        public static DiceGame CurrentGame = null;
    }
}
```

There's not a lot to the `GameInformation` class. It just contains some variables to keep track of the games a player is involved in and the current game that the person is viewing or playing.

Button.cs

Finally, you must make some enhancements to the `Button` class. The Poker Dice game does something a little different with buttons that the base framework wasn't originally designed to do.

Open the `Button.cs` class file, and begin making the following changes. First, change the `DisplayText` property so that it's a read/write property:

```
string displayText;
public string DisplayText
{
    get { return displayText; }
    set
    {
        displayText = value;
        buttonText.ChangeText(displayText);
    }
}
```

This allows the text for the buttons to be dynamically changed to different values while the game is running.

Now, add a new property called `Enabled` to the `Button` class:

```
bool isEnabled = true;
public bool Enabled
{
    get { return isEnabled; }
    set { isEnabled = value; }
}
```

This gives you a way of knowing whether a button should be enabled. In the future, this could be useful for drawing the button in a disabled way. But for now, it's just a state-tracking variable.

Now it's time to make something visual happen on the screen.

Creating the Game Lobby

With the `ScreenStateSwitchboard` class and the supporting classes ready to go, you can begin adding some more screens to the Poker Dice game.

Since this is a multiplayer game (that's the "friends" part of the title), a game lobby is a good screen to create.

GameLobby.cs

Add a new class to the `Screens` folder in the `PokerDice` game project, and call it `GameLobby`. Modify the `GameLobby.cs` file to match Listing 12-12.

LISTING 12-12: The GameLobby Class of Poker Dice

```
using Microsoft.Xna.Framework;
using Microsoft.Xna.Framework.Graphics;
using Microsoft.Xna.Framework.Content;
using Microsoft.Xna.Framework.Input.Touch;

using XNAPhoneGame.Sprites;
using XNAPhoneGame.Texts;
```

```csharp
using PokerDice.PokerDiceService;
using System.Collections.Generic;

namespace XNAPhoneGame.Screens
{
    class GameLobby : Screen
    {
        Text currentGamesTitle;
        Button requestGameButton;
        Button gameOneButton;
        Button gameTwoButton;
        Button gameThreeButton;
        Button gameFourButton;
        Button gameFiveButton;

        const string ActionRequestGame = "Request";
        const string ActionGameOne = "GameOne";
        const string ActionGameTwo = "GameTwo";
        const string ActionGameThree = "GameThree";
        const string ActionGameFour = "GameFour";
        const string ActionGameFive = "GameFive";

        bool isCurrentlyAbleToRequest = false;
        bool isCurrentlyPlayingGameOne = false;
        bool isCurrentlyPlayingGameTwo = false;
        bool isCurrentlyPlayingGameThree = false;
        bool isCurrentlyPlayingGameFour = false;
        bool isCurrentlyPlayingGameFive = false;

        PokerDiceClient pokerDiceClient;

        public GameLobby(Game game,
                        SpriteBatch batch,
                        ChangeScreen changeScreen)
            : base(game,
                   batch,
                   changeScreen,
                   BackButtonScreenType.Other)
        {
            pokerDiceClient = new PokerDiceClient();

            pokerDiceClient.IdentifyCompleted
                += new System.EventHandler
                    <System.ComponentModel.AsyncCompletedEventArgs>
                        (pokerDiceClient_IdentifyCompleted);

            pokerDiceClient.CurrentGamesCompleted
                += new System.EventHandler
                    <CurrentGamesCompletedEventArgs>
                        (pokerDiceClient_CurrentGamesCompleted);

            pokerDiceClient.RequestGameCompleted
                += new System.EventHandler
                    <System.ComponentModel.AsyncCompletedEventArgs>
                        (pokerDiceClient_RequestGameCompleted);
```

continues

LISTING 12-12 *(continued)*

```csharp
    }

    void pokerDiceClient_RequestGameCompleted(object sender,
                System.ComponentModel.AsyncCompletedEventArgs e)
    {
        changeScreenDelegate(ScreenState.RequestGame);
    }

    void pokerDiceClient_IdentifyCompleted(object sender,
                System.ComponentModel.AsyncCompletedEventArgs e)
    {
        pokerDiceClient.CurrentGamesAsync(PhoneAnonymousID);
    }

    void pokerDiceClient_CurrentGamesCompleted(object sender,
                            CurrentGamesCompletedEventArgs e)
    {
        isCurrentlyAbleToRequest = false;
        isCurrentlyPlayingGameOne = false;
        isCurrentlyPlayingGameTwo = false;
        isCurrentlyPlayingGameThree = false;
        isCurrentlyPlayingGameFour = false;
        isCurrentlyPlayingGameFive = false;

        string results = e.Result.ToString();
        string[] currentGames = results.Split("-".ToCharArray());

        GameInformation.Games.Clear();
        foreach (string game in currentGames)
        {
            if (game.Contains(":") && game.Contains(";"))
            {
                int idIndex = game.IndexOf(":") - 1;
                int nameIndex = game.IndexOf(";") - 1;
                int statusIndex = game.Length - 1;

                string gameID = game.Substring(1, idIndex);
                string name = game.Substring(idIndex + 2,
                                        nameIndex - idIndex - 1);
                string status = game.Substring(nameIndex + 2,
                                        statusIndex - nameIndex - 1);
                GameInformation.Games.Add(new DiceGame(gameID,
                                                    name,
                                                    status));
            }
        }

        if (GameInformation.Games.Count < 5)
        {
            isCurrentlyAbleToRequest = true;
        }
```

```csharp
        if (GameInformation.Games.Count >= 1)
        {
            gameOneButton.DisplayText =
                GameInformation.Games[0].PlayerName
                + " "
                + GameInformation.Games[0].CurrentStatus.ToString();

            isCurrentlyPlayingGameOne = true;
        }

        if (GameInformation.Games.Count >= 2)
        {
            gameTwoButton.DisplayText =
                GameInformation.Games[1].PlayerName
                + " "
                + GameInformation.Games[1].CurrentStatus.ToString();

            isCurrentlyPlayingGameTwo = true;
        }

        if (GameInformation.Games.Count >= 3)
        {
            gameThreeButton.DisplayText =
                GameInformation.Games[2].PlayerName
                + " "
                + GameInformation.Games[2].CurrentStatus.ToString();

            isCurrentlyPlayingGameThree = true;
        }

        if (GameInformation.Games.Count >= 4)
        {
            gameFourButton.DisplayText =
                GameInformation.Games[3].PlayerName
                + " "
                + GameInformation.Games[3].CurrentStatus.ToString();

            isCurrentlyPlayingGameFour = true;
        }

        if (GameInformation.Games.Count >= 5)
        {
            gameFiveButton.DisplayText =
                GameInformation.Games[4].PlayerName
                + " "
                + GameInformation.Games[4].CurrentStatus.ToString();

            isCurrentlyPlayingGameFive = true;
        }
    }

    protected override void SetupInputs()
    {
```

continues

LISTING 12-12 *(continued)*

```
        input.AddTouchGestureInput(ActionRequestGame,
                                   GestureType.Tap,
                                   requestGameButton.CollisionRectangle);

        input.AddTouchGestureInput(ActionGameOne,
                                   GestureType.Tap,
                                   gameOneButton.CollisionRectangle);

        input.AddTouchGestureInput(ActionGameTwo,
                                   GestureType.Tap,
                                   gameTwoButton.CollisionRectangle);

        input.AddTouchGestureInput(ActionGameThree,
                                   GestureType.Tap,
                                   gameThreeButton.CollisionRectangle);

        input.AddTouchGestureInput(ActionGameFour,
                                   GestureType.Tap,
                                   gameFourButton.CollisionRectangle);

        input.AddTouchGestureInput(ActionGameFive,
                                   GestureType.Tap,
                                   gameFiveButton.CollisionRectangle);
    }

    public override void Activate()
    {
        pokerDiceClient.IdentifyAsync(PhoneAnonymousID,
                                      PhoneUri,
                                      "Georgie");
    }

    protected override void LoadScreenContent(ContentManager content)
    {
        currentGamesTitle = new Text(font,
                                     "Current Games",
                                     Vector2.Zero,
                                     Color.White,
                                     Text.Alignment.Horizontally,
                                     new Rectangle(0, 20, 480, 50));

        requestGameButton = new Button(content,
                                       "Request Game",
                                       new Vector2(30, 100),
                                       Color.LightBlue);

        gameOneButton = new Button(content,
                                   "Game One",
                                   new Vector2(30, 210),
                                   Color.LightBlue);

        gameTwoButton = new Button(content,
```

```csharp
                                    "Game Two",
                                    new Vector2(30, 320),
                                    Color.LightBlue);

        gameThreeButton = new Button(content,
                                    "Game Three",
                                    new Vector2(30, 430),
                                    Color.LightBlue);

        gameFourButton = new Button(content,
                                    "Game Four",
                                    new Vector2(30, 540),
                                    Color.LightBlue);

        gameFiveButton = new Button(content,
                                    "Game Five",
                                    new Vector2(30, 650),
                                    Color.LightBlue);

        // Note: Ideally you would have a screen for the
        // user to enter their name, but for the sake of time
        // and brevity (and because this game is already
        // getting too many screens) we've just hardcoded
        // a name for now.
        pokerDiceClient.IdentifyAsync(PhoneAnonymousID,
                                    PhoneUri,
                                    "Georgie");
    }

    protected override void UpdateScreen(GameTime gameTime,
                        DisplayOrientation displayOrientation)
    {
        if (isCurrentlyAbleToRequest
            && input.IsPressed(ActionRequestGame))
        {
            soundEffects.PlaySound("SoundEffects/Select");
            pokerDiceClient.RequestGameAsync(PhoneAnonymousID);
        }
        else if (isCurrentlyPlayingGameOne
            && input.IsPressed(ActionGameOne))
        {
            soundEffects.PlaySound("SoundEffects/Select");
            GameInformation.CurrentGame = GameInformation.Games[0];
            changeScreenDelegate(ScreenState.GameInfo);
        }
        else if (isCurrentlyPlayingGameTwo
            && input.IsPressed(ActionGameTwo))
        {
            soundEffects.PlaySound("SoundEffects/Select");
            GameInformation.CurrentGame = GameInformation.Games[0];
            changeScreenDelegate(ScreenState.GameInfo);
        }
        else if (isCurrentlyPlayingGameThree
            && input.IsPressed(ActionGameThree))
        {
```

continues

LISTING 12-12 *(continued)*

```
            soundEffects.PlaySound("SoundEffects/Select");
            GameInformation.CurrentGame = GameInformation.Games[0];
            changeScreenDelegate(ScreenState.GameInfo);
        }
        else if (isCurrentlyPlayingGameFour
            && input.IsPressed(ActionGameFour))
        {
            soundEffects.PlaySound("SoundEffects/Select");
            GameInformation.CurrentGame = GameInformation.Games[0];
            changeScreenDelegate(ScreenState.GameInfo);
        }
        else if (isCurrentlyPlayingGameFive
            && input.IsPressed(ActionGameFive))
        {
            soundEffects.PlaySound("SoundEffects/Select");
            GameInformation.CurrentGame = GameInformation.Games[0];
            changeScreenDelegate(ScreenState.GameInfo);
        }
    }

    protected override void DrawScreen(SpriteBatch batch,
                        DisplayOrientation displayOrientation)
    {
        currentGamesTitle.Draw(batch);

        if (isCurrentlyAbleToRequest)
        {
            requestGameButton.Draw(batch);
        }

        if (isCurrentlyPlayingGameOne)
        {
            gameOneButton.Draw(batch);
        }

        if (isCurrentlyPlayingGameTwo)
        {
            gameTwoButton.Draw(batch);
        }

        if (isCurrentlyPlayingGameThree)
        {
            gameThreeButton.Draw(batch);
        }

        if (isCurrentlyPlayingGameFour)
        {
            gameFourButton.Draw(batch);
        }

        if (isCurrentlyPlayingGameFive)
        {
```

```
                gameFiveButton.Draw(batch);
            }
        }

        protected override void ChannelUriUpdatedNotification
            (string newChannelUri)
        {
            pokerDiceClient.IdentifyAsync(PhoneAnonymousID,
                                          newChannelUri,
                                          "Georgie");
        }
    }
}
```

With the `GameLobby` class created, you can hook it up in the `ScreenStateSwitchboard` class and enhance the `Title` class to navigate to the `GameLobby` screen when the Start Game button is pressed.

Go back to the `ScreenStateSwitchboard` class, and modify the `CreateGameLobbyScreen()` method to look like Listing 12-13.

LISTING 12-13: The CreateGameLobbyScreen() Method of the ScreenStateSwitchboard Class

```
private Screen CreateGameLobbyScreen()
{
    return new GameLobby(game,
                         batch,
                         new Screen.ChangeScreen(ChangeScreen));
}
```

Next, open the `Title` class and modify the `UpdateScreen()` method to look like Listing 12-14.

LISTING 12-14: The UpdateScreen() Method of the Title Class

```
protected override void UpdateScreen(GameTime gameTime,
                                     DisplayOrientation displayOrientation)
{
    if (input.IsPressed(ActionStart))
    {
        soundEffects.PlaySound("SoundEffects/Select");
        changeScreenDelegate(ScreenState.GameLobby);
    }
    else if (input.IsPressed(ActionExit))
    {
        changeScreenDelegate(ScreenState.Exit);
    }
}
```

At this point, you should be able to compile and deploy (by pressing F5) Poker Dice to your phone or the Emulator. If the service isn't running, you'll get "endpoint not found" errors, so be sure the service is running first.

If you prefer to deploy to your Windows Phone device via WiFi rather than over the cable, you need to change the `ServiceReferences.ClientConfig` file to point to the computer on your network where the service is running, instead of just using the default of localhost. Here's an example of `ServiceReferences.ClientConfig` changed in the `PokerDice` game project to point to a PC called George-PDC:

```
<client>
    <endpoint address="http://George-PDC:56827/PokerDice.svc"
        binding="basicHttpBinding"
        bindingConfiguration="BasicHttpBinding_IPokerDice"
        contract="PokerDiceService.IPokerDice"
        name="BasicHttpBinding_IPokerDice" />
</client>
```

Hopefully your computer is somewhat beefy if you're running the service and the game on the same PC. If not, things can get a little bogged down.

Once you are up and running, your game should look like Figure 12-3.

As exciting as the new `GameLobby` screen may be, work still needs to be done. It's time to add some more to this game. Next you will tackle the `Message` class.

Message.cs

This class is used by quite a few of the screens in Poker Dice. It's a way to tell the user that something has occurred. Examples of such messages might be that a game has been removed from a player's list, or that a nudge has been sent to an opponent.

Start by adding the `Message` class to the `Screens` folder, and then modify it to look like Listing 12-15.

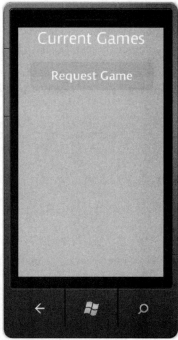

FIGURE 12-3: The Current Games screen

LISTING 12-15: The Message Class of Poker Dice

```
using Microsoft.Xna.Framework;
using Microsoft.Xna.Framework.Graphics;
using Microsoft.Xna.Framework.Content;
using Microsoft.Xna.Framework.Input.Touch;

using PokerDice.Sprites;
using PokerDice.Texts;

namespace PokerDice.Screens
{
    class Message : Screen
```

```csharp
{
    string displayText;
    Text message;
    Button gameLobbyButton;
    Button exitButton;

    const string ActionGameLobby = "Lobby";
    const string ActionExit = "Exit";

    public Message(string message,
                   Game game,
                   SpriteBatch batch,
                   ChangeScreen changeScreen)
        : base(game,
               batch,
               changeScreen,
               BackButtonScreenType.First)
    {
        this.displayText = message;
    }

    protected override void SetupInputs()
    {
        input.AddTouchGestureInput(ActionGameLobby,
                                   GestureType.Tap,
                                   gameLobbyButton.CollisionRectangle);

        input.AddTouchGestureInput(ActionExit,
                                   GestureType.Tap,
                                   exitButton.CollisionRectangle);
    }

    public override void Activate()
    {
    }

    protected override void LoadScreenContent(ContentManager content)
    {
        gameLobbyButton = new Button(content,
                                     "Current Games",
                                     new Vector2(30, 540),
                                     Color.LightBlue);

        exitButton = new Button(content,
                                "Exit",
                                new Vector2(30, 650),
                                Color.LightBlue);

        message = new Text(font,
                           displayText,
                           new Vector2(0, 0),
                           Color.White,
                           Text.Alignment.None,
                           new Rectangle(0, 0, 480, 500));
    }
```

continues

LISTING 12-15 *(continued)*

```
protected override void UpdateScreen(GameTime gameTime,
                        DisplayOrientation displayOrientation)
{
    if (input.IsPressed(ActionGameLobby))
    {
        soundEffects.PlaySound("SoundEffects/Select");
        changeScreenDelegate(ScreenState.GameLobby);
    }
    else if (input.IsPressed(ActionExit))
    {
        changeScreenDelegate(ScreenState.Exit);
    }
}

protected override void DrawScreen(SpriteBatch batch,
                        DisplayOrientation displayOrientation)
{
    message.Draw(batch);
    gameLobbyButton.Draw(batch);
    exitButton.Draw(batch);
}
    }
}
```

The `Message` screen is fairly simple. It just takes in some text and displays it on the screen. It then gives the user the option of exiting the game or returning to the game lobby. It's simple, but very useful.

Next, go back to the `ScreenStateSwitchboard` class and modify the `CreateRequestGameScreen()`, `CreateRemoveGameScreen()`, `CreateNudgeScreen()`, and `CreateForfeitScreen()` methods to look like Listings 12-16, 12-17, 12-18, and 12-19, respectively.

LISTING 12-16: The CreateRequestGameScreen() Method of the ScreenStateSwitchboard Class

```
private Screen CreateRequestGameScreen()
{
    return new Message(" A game request    \n" +
                       " has been sent.    \n\n" +
                       " You will be notified \n" +
                       " when the challenge \n" +
                       " is accepted!      \n" ,
                       game,
                       batch,
                       new Screen.ChangeScreen(ChangeScreen));
}
```

LISTING 12-17: The CreateRemoveGameScreen() Method of the ScreenStateSwitchboard Class

```
        private Screen CreateRemoveGameScreen()
        {
```

```
                return new Message(" The game has been  \n" +
                                   " removed and you    \n" +
                                   " are ready for new  \n" +
                                   " challenges!        \n",
                                   game,
                                   batch,
                                   new Screen.ChangeScreen(ChangeScreen));
        }
```

LISTING 12-18: The CreateNudgeScreen() Method of the ScreenStateSwitchboard Class

```
        private Screen CreateNudgeScreen()
        {
                return new Message(" A 'nudge' message  \n" +
                                   " has been sent.     \n\n" +
                                   " Hopefully they take\n" +
                                   " their turn soon!   \n" ,
                                   game,
                                   batch,
                                   new Screen.ChangeScreen(ChangeScreen));
        }
```

LISTING 12-19: The CreateForfeitScreen() Method of the ScreenStateSwitchboard Class

```
        private Screen CreateForfeitScreen()
        {
                return new Message(" You have ended the \n" +
                                   " match.             \n\n" +
                                   " Ready for a new    \n" +
                                   " challenger?        \n",
                                   game,
                                   batch,
                                   new Screen.ChangeScreen(ChangeScreen));
        }
```

These methods create a new `Message` screen and pass it in a message. (Often, including some carriage returns and spacing makes them look prettier.)

Creating the GameInfo Screen

At this stage, you have some new screens but you don't really have any way of navigating to them. So, you need to create the `GameInfo` screen. The player sees this screen when he or she looks at a particular game from the `GameLobby` list.

The `GameInfo` screens give the opponent's name and the game's current status. Then they give the player a few options from which to choose, based on that current status. For example, if it's currently an opponent's turn, the player might want to send a "nudge" to remind the opponent that he or she still must take a turn.

GameInfo.cs

To get started creating the `GameInfo` screen, right-click the `Screens` folder in the `PokerDice` game project, and add a new class called `GameInfo`. Open it and modify it to look like Listing 12-20.

LISTING 12-20: The GameInfo Class of Poker Dice

```csharp
using Microsoft.Xna.Framework;
using Microsoft.Xna.Framework.Graphics;
using Microsoft.Xna.Framework.Content;
using Microsoft.Xna.Framework.Input.Touch;

using XNAPhoneGame.Sprites;
using XNAPhoneGame.Texts;
using PokerDice.PokerDiceService;

namespace XNAPhoneGame.Screens
{
    class GameInfo : Screen
    {
        Text name;
        Text status;

        Button acceptRequestButton;
        Button declineRequestButton;
        Button takeTurnButton;
        Button nudgeButton;
        Button forfeitButton;
        Button removeButton;
        Button gameLobbyButton;

        const string ActionAcceptRequest = "Accept";
        const string ActionDeclineRequest = "Decline";
        const string ActionTakeTurn = "TakeTurn";
        const string ActionNudge = "Nudge";
        const string ActionForfeit = "Forfeit";
        const string ActionRemove = "Remove";
        const string ActionGameLobby = "GameLobby";

        PokerDiceClient pokerDiceClient;

        public GameInfo(Game game,
                        SpriteBatch batch,
                        ChangeScreen changeScreen)
            : base(game,
                   batch,
                   changeScreen,
                   BackButtonScreenType.First)
        {
        }

        protected override void SetupInputs()
        {
            input.AddTouchGestureInput(ActionAcceptRequest,
                                       GestureType.Tap,
                                       acceptRequestButton.CollisionRectangle);

            input.AddTouchGestureInput(ActionDeclineRequest,
                                       GestureType.Tap,
```

```csharp
                                    declineRequestButton.CollisionRectangle);

            input.AddTouchGestureInput(ActionTakeTurn,
                                       GestureType.Tap,
                                       takeTurnButton.CollisionRectangle);

            input.AddTouchGestureInput(ActionNudge,
                                       GestureType.Tap,
                                       nudgeButton.CollisionRectangle);

            input.AddTouchGestureInput(ActionForfeit,
                                       GestureType.Tap,
                                       forfeitButton.CollisionRectangle);

            input.AddTouchGestureInput(ActionRemove,
                                       GestureType.Tap,
                                       removeButton.CollisionRectangle);

            input.AddTouchGestureInput(ActionGameLobby,
                                       GestureType.Tap,
                                       gameLobbyButton.CollisionRectangle);
        }
        public override void Activate()
        {
            name = new Text(font,
                            "Name: "
                                + GameInformation.CurrentGame.PlayerName,
                            new Vector2(50, 0));

            status = new Text(font,
                              "Status: "
                                  + GameInformation.CurrentGame
                                      .CurrentStatus.ToString(),
                              new Vector2(50, 50));

            switch (GameInformation.CurrentGame.CurrentStatus)
            {
                case DiceGame.Status.New:
                    {
                        acceptRequestButton.Enabled = true;
                        declineRequestButton.Enabled = true;
                        takeTurnButton.Enabled = false;
                        nudgeButton.Enabled = false;
                        forfeitButton.Enabled = false;
                        removeButton.Enabled = false;
                        break;
                    }

                case DiceGame.Status.Waiting:
                    {
                        acceptRequestButton.Enabled = false;
                        declineRequestButton.Enabled = false;
                        takeTurnButton.Enabled = false;
                        nudgeButton.Enabled = false;
```

continues

LISTING 12-20 *(continued)*

```
                    forfeitButton.Enabled = false;
                    removeButton.Enabled = true;
                    break;
                }

            case DiceGame.Status.YourTurn:
                {
                    acceptRequestButton.Enabled = false;
                    declineRequestButton.Enabled = false;
                    takeTurnButton.Enabled = true;
                    nudgeButton.Enabled = false;
                    forfeitButton.Enabled = true;
                    removeButton.Enabled = false;
                    break;
                }

            case DiceGame.Status.TheirTurn:
                {
                    acceptRequestButton.Enabled = false;
                    declineRequestButton.Enabled = false;
                    takeTurnButton.Enabled = false;
                    nudgeButton.Enabled = true;
                    forfeitButton.Enabled = true;
                    removeButton.Enabled = true;
                    break;
                }

            case DiceGame.Status.Win:
                {
                    acceptRequestButton.Enabled = false;
                    declineRequestButton.Enabled = false;
                    takeTurnButton.Enabled = false;
                    nudgeButton.Enabled = false;
                    forfeitButton.Enabled = false;
                    removeButton.Enabled = true;
                    break;
                }

            case DiceGame.Status.Lose:
                {
                    acceptRequestButton.Enabled = false;
                    declineRequestButton.Enabled = false;
                    takeTurnButton.Enabled = false;
                    nudgeButton.Enabled = false;
                    forfeitButton.Enabled = false;
                    removeButton.Enabled = true;
                    break;
                }
        }
    }

    protected override void LoadScreenContent(ContentManager content)
```

```csharp
{
    pokerDiceClient = new PokerDiceClient();

    pokerDiceClient.AcceptGameRequestCompleted
        += new System.EventHandler
            <System.ComponentModel.AsyncCompletedEventArgs>
                (pokerDiceClient_AcceptGameRequestCompleted);

    pokerDiceClient.DeclineGameRequestCompleted
        += new System.EventHandler
            <System.ComponentModel.AsyncCompletedEventArgs>
                (pokerDiceClient_DeclineGameRequestCompleted);

    pokerDiceClient.NudgeCompleted
        += new System.EventHandler
            <System.ComponentModel.AsyncCompletedEventArgs>
                (pokerDiceClient_NudgeCompleted);

    pokerDiceClient.ForfeitCompleted
        += new System.EventHandler
            <System.ComponentModel.AsyncCompletedEventArgs>
                (pokerDiceClient_ForfeitCompleted);

    pokerDiceClient.RemoveGameCompleted
    += new System.EventHandler
        <System.ComponentModel.AsyncCompletedEventArgs>
            (pokerDiceClient_RemoveGameCompleted);

    name = new Text(font,
                    "Name: "
                        + GameInformation.CurrentGame.PlayerName,
                    new Vector2(50, 0));

    status = new Text(font,
                    "Status: "
                        + GameInformation.CurrentGame
                            .CurrentStatus.ToString(),
                    new Vector2(50, 50));

    acceptRequestButton = new Button(content,
                                    "Accept Request",
                                    new Vector2(30, 300),
                                    Color.LightBlue);

    declineRequestButton = new Button(content,
                                    "Decline Request",
                                    new Vector2(30, 420),
                                    Color.LightBlue);

    takeTurnButton = new Button(content,
                                "Take Turn",
                                new Vector2(30, 300),
                                Color.LightBlue);

    nudgeButton = new Button(content,
```

continues

LISTING 12-20 *(continued)*

```
                                    "Nudge",
                                    new Vector2(30, 300),
                                    Color.LightBlue);

        forfeitButton = new Button(content,
                                    "Forfeit",
                                    new Vector2(30, 420),
                                    Color.LightBlue);

        removeButton = new Button(content,
                                    "Remove",
                                    new Vector2(30, 420),
                                    Color.LightBlue);

        gameLobbyButton = new Button(content,
                                    "Current Games",
                                    new Vector2(30, 540),
                                    Color.LightBlue);
    }

    void pokerDiceClient_RemoveGameCompleted(object sender,
                System.ComponentModel.AsyncCompletedEventArgs e)
    {
        changeScreenDelegate(ScreenState.RemoveGame);
    }

    void pokerDiceClient_ForfeitCompleted(object sender,
                System.ComponentModel.AsyncCompletedEventArgs e)
    {
        changeScreenDelegate(ScreenState.Forfeit);
    }

    void pokerDiceClient_NudgeCompleted(object sender,
                System.ComponentModel.AsyncCompletedEventArgs e)
    {
        changeScreenDelegate(ScreenState.Nudge);
    }

    void pokerDiceClient_DeclineGameRequestCompleted(object sender,
                System.ComponentModel.AsyncCompletedEventArgs e)
    {
        changeScreenDelegate(ScreenState.GameLobby);
    }

    void pokerDiceClient_AcceptGameRequestCompleted(object sender,
                System.ComponentModel.AsyncCompletedEventArgs e)
    {
        changeScreenDelegate(ScreenState.GameLobby);
    }

    protected override void UpdateScreen(GameTime gameTime,
                        DisplayOrientation displayOrientation)
```

```csharp
{
    if (takeTurnButton.Enabled && input.IsPressed(ActionTakeTurn))
    {
        soundEffects.PlaySound("SoundEffects/Select");
        changeScreenDelegate(ScreenState.MainGame);
    }
    else if (acceptRequestButton.Enabled
        && input.IsPressed(ActionAcceptRequest))
    {
        soundEffects.PlaySound("SoundEffects/Select");
        pokerDiceClient.AcceptGameRequestAsync(PhoneAnonymousID,
                            GameInformation.CurrentGame.ID);
    }
    else if (declineRequestButton.Enabled
        && input.IsPressed(ActionDeclineRequest))
    {
        soundEffects.PlaySound("SoundEffects/Select");
        pokerDiceClient.DeclineGameRequestAsync(PhoneAnonymousID,
                            GameInformation.CurrentGame.ID);
    }
    else if (nudgeButton.Enabled && input.IsPressed(ActionNudge))
    {
        soundEffects.PlaySound("SoundEffects/Select");
        pokerDiceClient.NudgeAsync(PhoneAnonymousID,
                            GameInformation.CurrentGame.ID);
    }
    else if (forfeitButton.Enabled && input.IsPressed(ActionForfeit))
    {
        soundEffects.PlaySound("SoundEffects/Select");
        pokerDiceClient.ForfeitAsync(PhoneAnonymousID,
                            GameInformation.CurrentGame.ID);
    }
    else if (removeButton.Enabled && input.IsPressed(ActionRemove))
    {
        soundEffects.PlaySound("SoundEffects/Select");
        pokerDiceClient.RemoveGameAsync(PhoneAnonymousID,
                            GameInformation.CurrentGame.ID);
    }
    else if (gameLobbyButton.Enabled
        && input.IsPressed(ActionGameLobby))
    {
        soundEffects.PlaySound("SoundEffects/Select");
        changeScreenDelegate(ScreenState.GameLobby);
    }
}

protected override void DrawScreen(SpriteBatch batch,
                        DisplayOrientation displayOrientation)
{
    name.Draw(batch);
    status.Draw(batch);

    DrawButton(acceptRequestButton, batch);
    DrawButton(declineRequestButton, batch);
    DrawButton(takeTurnButton, batch);
```

continues

LISTING 12-20 *(continued)*

```
            DrawButton(nudgeButton, batch);
            DrawButton(forfeitButton, batch);
            DrawButton(removeButton, batch);
            gameLobbyButton.Draw(batch);
        }

        private void DrawButton(Button button, SpriteBatch batch)
        {
            if (button.Enabled)
            {
                button.Draw(batch);
            }
        }
    }
}
```

One interesting thing about the `GameInfo` screen is that it displays or hides the button based on the current state of the Poker Dice game.

Now that the `GameInfo` screen is created, it's time to add some code to navigate to and display the screen. Open the `ScreenStateSwitchboard` class, and modify the `CreateGameInfo()` method to look like the following:

```
private Screen CreateGameInfoScreen()
        {
            return new GameInfo(game,
                               batch,
                               new Screen.ChangeScreen(ChangeScreen));
        }
```

Build and deploy the game. (Don't forget to have the `PokerDiceService` running!)

You will probably want to launch the `PokerDiceTester` as well to create some opponents to play. After you've created some players using the `PokerDiceTester`, you can request games with them and then view the status of the games via the `GameLobby`.

As you forfeit, nudge, and so on from the new `GameInfo` screen you created (see Figure 12-4), you should also be notified via the `Message` screen as each of those actions happens.

Only one little piece remains. You still must be able to take your turn! But before you can do that, you must add some dice to roll.

Adding the Dice Model

Since you can do three-dimensional (3D) modeling on the phone and dice are a fairly simple 3D object to work with, the dice you'll roll in Poker Dice will be 3D models.

Creating "Poker Dice with Friends" | **405**

FIGURE 12-4: The GameInfo Screen of Poker Dice

 The authors would like to thank Glenn Wilson for creating the 3D dice models used in this project.

To begin, start by adding a new folder called `Models` to the `PokerDiceContent` project. Next, add to the `Models` folder the `SimpleDice.fbx` and `SimpleDice_Texture.png` files from the files on this book's companion website (www.wrox.com).

Die.cs

Once the content has been added, add a new folder to the `PokerDice` game project, and call it `Models` as well. Next, add a new class called `Die` to that folder. This class represents a single six-sided die model in your game. Open the `Die.cs` file, and modify it to look like Listing 12-21.

LISTING 12-21: The Die Class of Poker Dice

```
using System;
using Microsoft.Xna.Framework;
using Microsoft.Xna.Framework.Content;
```

continues

LISTING 12-21 *(continued)*

```
using Microsoft.Xna.Framework.Graphics;

namespace XNAPhoneGame
{
    class Die
    {
        public BoundingSphere collisionSphere;
        public int FaceValue = 100;

        Model myModel;

        float aspectRatio;
        float modelRotationX;
        float modelRotationY;
        float movementX;
        float movementY;

        float elapsedRollTime = 0.0f;
        double maxRollTime;

        Vector3 modelPosition = Vector3.Zero;
        Vector3 cameraPosition = new Vector3(50.0f, 0.0f, 2500.0f);

        int NonMovingCollisions = 0;

        public Die(ContentManager content,
                   float ratio,
                   Random random,
                   double rollTime)
        {
            myModel = content.Load<Model>("Models/SimpleDice");
            aspectRatio = ratio;

            modelPosition.X = random.Next(-400, 400);
            modelPosition.Y = random.Next(-700, 700);

            movementX = 10;
            if (random.Next(-5, 5) < 0)
            {
                movementX = -10;
            }

            movementY = 5;
            if (random.Next(-5, 5) < 0)
            {
                movementY = -5;
            }

            maxRollTime = rollTime;
        }

        public void Roll(double theMaxRollTime)
```

```csharp
{
    maxRollTime = theMaxRollTime;

    Random random = new Random();

    movementX = 20;
    if (random.Next(-5, 5) < 0)
    {
        movementX = -20;
    }

    movementY = 10;
    if (random.Next(-5, 5) < 0)
    {
        movementY = -10;
    }

    elapsedRollTime = 0.0f;
    NonMovingCollisions = 0;
}

public void Collision(Die collidingDie, GameTime gameTime)
{
    movementX *= -1;
    movementY *= -1;

    if (elapsedRollTime > maxRollTime)
    {
        collidingDie.elapsedRollTime -= 0.5f;
        elapsedRollTime -= 0.5f;
        NonMovingCollisions += 1;
        if (NonMovingCollisions > 5)
        {
            modelPosition.X = 0;
            modelPosition.Y = 0;
        }
    }
    else
    {
        do
        {
            MoveDie(gameTime);
            collisionSphere
                = new BoundingSphere(new Vector3(modelPosition.X,
                                                modelPosition.Y,
                                                modelPosition.Z),
                                     130);

        } while (collidingDie.collisionSphere
                    .Intersects(collisionSphere));
    }
}

private void MoveDie(GameTime gameTime)
{
```

continues

LISTING 12-21 *(continued)*

```
            if (movementY > 0)
            {
                // Move up the screen
                modelRotationX
                    -= (float)(20 * gameTime.ElapsedGameTime.TotalSeconds);
            }
            else if (movementY < 0)
            {
                // Move down the screen
                modelRotationX
                    += (float)(20 * gameTime.ElapsedGameTime.TotalSeconds);
            }

            if (movementX > 0)
            {
                // Move to the right of the screen
                modelRotationY
                    += (float)(2 * gameTime.ElapsedGameTime.TotalSeconds);
            }
            else if (movementX < 0)
            {
                // Move to the left of the screen
                modelRotationY
                    -= (float)(2 * gameTime.ElapsedGameTime.TotalSeconds);
            }


            if (MathHelper.ToDegrees(modelRotationX) > 360)
            {
                modelRotationX = 0;
            }

            if (MathHelper.ToDegrees(modelRotationY) > 360)
            {
                modelRotationY = 0;
            }

            modelPosition.X += movementX;
            if (modelPosition.X >= 480 || modelPosition.X < -480)
            {
                if (modelPosition.X >= 480)
                {
                    modelPosition.X = 400;
                }

                if (modelPosition.X < -480)
                {
                    modelPosition.X = -400;
                }

                movementX *= -1;
            }
```

```
            modelPosition.Y += movementY;
            if (modelPosition.Y >= 800 || modelPosition.Y < -800)
            {
                if (modelPosition.Y >= 800)
                {
                    modelPosition.Y = 720;
                }

                if (modelPosition.Y < -800)
                {
                    modelPosition.Y = -720;
                }
                movementY *= -1;
            }
        }

        public void Update(GameTime gameTime)
        {
            if (elapsedRollTime < maxRollTime)
            {
                elapsedRollTime += gameTime.ElapsedGameTime.TotalSeconds;
                MoveDie(gameTime);
            }
            else
            {
                float currentRotationValueX = 0;
                float currentRotationValueY = 0;

                if (movementY > 0)
                {
                    if (MathHelper.ToDegrees(modelRotationX) < 90)
                    {
                        modelRotationX -= (float)(25 *
                            gameTime.ElapsedGameTime.TotalSeconds);
                        modelRotationX = MathHelper.Clamp(modelRotationX,
                            MathHelper.ToRadians(0),
                            MathHelper.ToRadians(90));
                        currentRotationValueX = 0;
                    }
                    else if (MathHelper.ToDegrees(modelRotationX) < 180)
                    {
                        modelRotationX -= (float)(25 *
                            gameTime.ElapsedGameTime.TotalSeconds);
                        modelRotationX = MathHelper.Clamp(modelRotationX,
                            MathHelper.ToRadians(90),
                            MathHelper.ToRadians(180));
                        currentRotationValueX = 90;
                    }
                    else if (MathHelper.ToDegrees(modelRotationX) < 270)
                    {
                        modelRotationX -= (float)(25 *
                            gameTime.ElapsedGameTime.TotalSeconds);
                        modelRotationX = MathHelper.Clamp(modelRotationX,
                            MathHelper.ToRadians(180),
```

continues

LISTING 12-21 *(continued)*

```
                    MathHelper.ToRadians(270));
                currentRotationValueX = 180;
            }
            else if (MathHelper.ToDegrees(modelRotationX) < 360)
            {
                modelRotationX -= (float)(25 *
                    gameTime.ElapsedGameTime.TotalSeconds);
                modelRotationX = MathHelper.Clamp(modelRotationX,
                    MathHelper.ToRadians(270),
                    MathHelper.ToRadians(360));
                currentRotationValueX = 270;
            }
        }
        else if (movementY < 0)
        {
            if (MathHelper.ToDegrees(modelRotationX) <= 90)
            {
                modelRotationX += (float)(25 *
                    gameTime.ElapsedGameTime.TotalSeconds);
                modelRotationX = MathHelper.Clamp(modelRotationX,
                    MathHelper.ToRadians(0),
                    MathHelper.ToRadians(90));
                currentRotationValueX = 90;
            }
            else if (MathHelper.ToDegrees(modelRotationX) <= 180)
            {
                modelRotationX += (float)(25 *
                    gameTime.ElapsedGameTime.TotalSeconds);
                modelRotationX = MathHelper.Clamp(modelRotationX,
                    MathHelper.ToRadians(91),
                    MathHelper.ToRadians(180));
                currentRotationValueX = 180;
            }
            else if (MathHelper.ToDegrees(modelRotationX) <= 270)
            {
                modelRotationX += (float)(25 *
                    gameTime.ElapsedGameTime.TotalSeconds);
                modelRotationX = MathHelper.Clamp(modelRotationX,
                    MathHelper.ToRadians(181),
                    MathHelper.ToRadians(270));
                currentRotationValueX = 270;
            }
            else if (MathHelper.ToDegrees(modelRotationX) <= 360)
            {
                modelRotationX += (float)(25 *
                    gameTime.ElapsedGameTime.TotalSeconds);
                modelRotationX = MathHelper.Clamp(modelRotationX,
                    MathHelper.ToRadians(271),
                    MathHelper.ToRadians(360));
                currentRotationValueX = 360;
            }
        }
```

```
                if (movementX > 0)
                {
                    if (MathHelper.ToDegrees(modelRotationY) <= 90)
                    {
                        modelRotationY += (float)(25 *
                            gameTime.ElapsedGameTime.TotalSeconds);
                        modelRotationY = MathHelper.Clamp(modelRotationY,
                            MathHelper.ToRadians(0),
                            MathHelper.ToRadians(90));
                        currentRotationValueY = 90;
                    }
                    else if (MathHelper.ToDegrees(modelRotationY) <= 180)
                    {
                        modelRotationY += (float)(25 *
                            gameTime.ElapsedGameTime.TotalSeconds);
                        modelRotationY = MathHelper.Clamp(modelRotationY,
                            MathHelper.ToRadians(91),
                            MathHelper.ToRadians(180));
                        currentRotationValueY = 180;
                    }
                    else if (MathHelper.ToDegrees(modelRotationY) <= 270)
                    {
                        modelRotationY += (float)(25 *
                            gameTime.ElapsedGameTime.TotalSeconds);
                        modelRotationY = MathHelper.Clamp(modelRotationY,
                            MathHelper.ToRadians(181),
                            MathHelper.ToRadians(270));
                        currentRotationValueY = 270;
                    }
                    else if (MathHelper.ToDegrees(modelRotationY) <= 360)
                    {
                        modelRotationY += (float)(25 *
                            gameTime.ElapsedGameTime.TotalSeconds);
                        modelRotationY = MathHelper.Clamp(modelRotationY,
                            MathHelper.ToRadians(271),
                            MathHelper.ToRadians(360));
                        currentRotationValueY = 360;
                    }
                }
                else if (movementX < 0)
                {
                    if (MathHelper.ToDegrees(modelRotationY) < 90)
                    {
                        modelRotationY -= (float)(25 *
                            gameTime.ElapsedGameTime.TotalSeconds);
                        modelRotationY = MathHelper.Clamp(modelRotationY,
                            MathHelper.ToRadians(0),
                            MathHelper.ToRadians(90));
                        currentRotationValueY = 0;
                    }
                    else if (MathHelper.ToDegrees(modelRotationY) < 180)
                    {
                        modelRotationY -= (float)(25 *
```

continues

LISTING 12-21 *(continued)*

```
                gameTime.ElapsedGameTime.TotalSeconds);
        modelRotationY = MathHelper.Clamp(modelRotationY,
            MathHelper.ToRadians(90),
            MathHelper.ToRadians(180));
        currentRotationValueY = 90;
    }
    else if (MathHelper.ToDegrees(modelRotationY) < 270)
    {
        modelRotationY -= (float)(25 *
            gameTime.ElapsedGameTime.TotalSeconds);
        modelRotationY = MathHelper.Clamp(modelRotationY,
            MathHelper.ToRadians(180),
            MathHelper.ToRadians(270));
        currentRotationValueY = 180;
    }
    else if (MathHelper.ToDegrees(modelRotationY) < 360)
    {
        modelRotationY -= (float)(25 *
            gameTime.ElapsedGameTime.TotalSeconds);
        modelRotationY = MathHelper.Clamp(modelRotationY,
            MathHelper.ToRadians(270),
            MathHelper.ToRadians(360));
        currentRotationValueY = 270;
    }
}

if ((currentRotationValueY == 0
&& currentRotationValueX == 0) ||
    (currentRotationValueY == 0
&& currentRotationValueX == 360) ||
    (currentRotationValueY == 360
&& currentRotationValueX == 0) ||
    (currentRotationValueY == 180
&& currentRotationValueX == 180) ||
    (currentRotationValueY == 360
&& currentRotationValueX == 360))
{
    FaceValue = 6;
}
else if ((currentRotationValueY == 270
    && currentRotationValueX == 0) ||
        (currentRotationValueY == 90
    && currentRotationValueX == 180) ||
        (currentRotationValueY == 270
    && currentRotationValueX == 360))
{
    FaceValue = 5;
}
else if ((currentRotationValueY == 0
    && currentRotationValueX == 270) ||
        (currentRotationValueY == 90
    && currentRotationValueX == 270) ||
```

```
                    (currentRotationValueY == 180
                && currentRotationValueX == 270) ||
                    (currentRotationValueY == 270
                && currentRotationValueX == 270) ||
                    (currentRotationValueY == 360
                && currentRotationValueX == 270))
            {
                FaceValue = 4;
            }
            else if ((currentRotationValueY == 0
                && currentRotationValueX == 90) ||
                    (currentRotationValueY == 90
                && currentRotationValueX == 90) ||
                    (currentRotationValueY == 180
                && currentRotationValueX == 90) ||
                    (currentRotationValueY == 270
                && currentRotationValueX == 90) ||
                    (currentRotationValueY == 360
                && currentRotationValueX == 90))
            {
                FaceValue = 3;
            }
            else if ((currentRotationValueY == 90
                && currentRotationValueX == 0) ||
                    (currentRotationValueY == 270
                && currentRotationValueX == 180) ||
                    (currentRotationValueY == 90
                && currentRotationValueX == 360))
            {
                FaceValue = 2;
            }
            else if ((currentRotationValueY == 0
                && currentRotationValueX == 180) ||
                    (currentRotationValueY == 180
                && currentRotationValueX == 0) ||
                    (currentRotationValueY == 360
                && currentRotationValueX == 180) ||
                    (currentRotationValueY == 180
                && currentRotationValueX == 360))
            {
                FaceValue = 1;
            }
            else
            {
                FaceValue = 100;
            }

        }

        //Create a total bounding sphere for the mesh
        collisionSphere = new BoundingSphere(new Vector3(modelPosition.X,
            modelPosition.Y, modelPosition.Z), 130);
    }

    public void Draw(SpriteBatch batch, GraphicsDevice graphics)
```

continues

LISTING 12-21 *(continued)*

```
        {
            Matrix[] transforms = new Matrix[myModel.Bones.Count];
            myModel.CopyAbsoluteBoneTransformsTo(transforms);

            foreach (ModelMesh mesh in myModel.Meshes)
            {
                foreach (BasicEffect effect in mesh.Effects)
                {
                    effect.EnableDefaultLighting();
                    effect.World = transforms[mesh.ParentBone.Index] *
                        Matrix.CreateRotationY(modelRotationY) *
                        Matrix.CreateRotationX(modelRotationX)
                        * Matrix.CreateTranslation(modelPosition);
                    effect.View = Matrix.CreateLookAt(cameraPosition,
                        Vector3.Zero, Vector3.Up);
                    effect.Projection = Matrix.CreatePerspectiveFieldOfView(
                        MathHelper.ToRadians(45.0f), aspectRatio,
                        1.0f, 10000.0f);
                }

                mesh.Draw();
            }
        }
    }
}
```

The `Die` class handles the movement of the dice on the phone screen, simulating the rolling, responding to collisions, and then determining which face value the dice end up displaying when they stop.

A lot of code is involved, but most of it is just brute-force logic to figure out which face value is showing. This is one of those examples that, while correct, may be *too* correct. There is actually a much easier way to do a dice roll: Fake it! Before you start the dice-rolling animation, figure out which face should be shown. Then roll the dice around and just stick on top the texture you want at the end.

That's one of the beautiful things about coding (especially game coding!): You can always do little tricks to help get around the long, complicated ways. But don't you feel better knowing the long, complicated way? It builds character! Or, at least it builds a nice-looking `Die` class!

With the `Die` class built, you're ready to start building the actual Poker Dice game.

Creating the MainGame Screen

The `MainGame` screen is where the dice will roll. When the player comes to this screen, the dice begin their merry 3D animated dance, bouncing off the sides of the screen and each other until each die stops on a face.

MainGame.cs

Start by adding a new class named `MainGame` to the `Screens` folder. Then open the `MainGame` class and modify it to look like Listing 12-22.

LISTING 12-22: The MainGame Class of Poker Dice

```csharp
using System;
using System.Collections.Generic;

using Microsoft.Xna.Framework;
using Microsoft.Xna.Framework.Graphics;
using Microsoft.Xna.Framework.Content;
using Microsoft.Xna.Framework.Input.Touch;

using XNAPhoneGame.Sprites;
using XNAPhoneGame.Texts;

namespace XNAPhoneGame.Screens
{
    class MainGame : Screen
    {
        GraphicsDevice graphics;
        List<Die> die = new List<Die>();
        Random randomRoll = new Random();
        bool isRolling = false;

        public MainGame(Game game,
                       SpriteBatch batch,
                       ChangeScreen changeScreen)
            : base(game,
                  batch,
                  changeScreen,
                  BackButtonScreenType.Gameplay)
        {
            graphics = game.GraphicsDevice;
        }

        protected override void SetupInputs()
        {
            input.AddTouchGestureInput("Select",
                                      GestureType.DoubleTap,
                                      new Rectangle(0, 0, 480, 800));
        }

        public override void Activate()
        {
            die.Clear();
            for (int diceCount = 0;
                diceCount < (5 - GameInformation.CurrentGame.DiceRoll.Count);
                diceCount++)
            {
                die.Add(new Die(content,
                               graphics.Viewport.AspectRatio,
                               randomRoll,
                               (double)randomRoll.Next(2, 5)));
            }

            isRolling = true;
```

continues

LISTING 12-22 *(continued)*

```
        foreach (Die aDie in die)
        {
            aDie.Roll(new Random().Next(2, 5));
        }
    }

    protected override void UpdateScreen(GameTime gameTime,
                            DisplayOrientation displayOrientation)
    {
        if (input.IsPressed("Select") && !isRolling)
        {
            foreach (Die aDie in die)
            {
                GameInformation.CurrentGame.DiceRoll.Add(aDie.FaceValue);
            }

            GameInformation.CurrentGame.CurrentRoll += 1;
            changeScreenDelegate(ScreenState.DiceSelect);
        }

        isRolling = false;
        foreach (Die aDie in die)
        {
            aDie.Update(gameTime);
            if (aDie.FaceValue == 100)
            {
                isRolling = true;
            }
        }

        for (int aIndex = 0; aIndex < die.Count; aIndex++)
        {
            for (int aColllisionIndex = aIndex + 1;
                 aColllisionIndex < die.Count;
                 aColllisionIndex++)
            {
                if (die[aIndex].collisionSphere
                    .Intersects(die[aColllisionIndex].collisionSphere))
                {
                    die[aIndex].Collision(die[aColllisionIndex],
                                    gameTime);
                    isRolling = true;
                }
            }
        }

    }

    protected override void DrawScreen(SpriteBatch batch,
                            DisplayOrientation displayOrientation)
    {
        foreach (Die aDie in die)
```

```
            {
                aDie.Draw(batch, graphics);
            }
        }
    }
}
```

The `MainGame` screen checks the `GameInformation` class to see how many dice should be rolled. It then kicks off that roll and keeps the dice rolling until the dice are no longer colliding. Figure 12-5 shows an example.

When the dice have finished, the player can double-tap the screen to end his or her roll and go to the `DiceSelect` screen.

Creating the DiceSelect Screen

The `DiceSelect` screen is where the player chooses which dice from the roll to keep and which to reroll. The player also ends a turn from this screen.

The `DiceSelect` screen displays the dice the user just rolled, but it uses a two-dimensional (2D) representation of the dice. This means that you must add a new image to the `Content` project. Grab the `Dice.png` file from the files on this book's companion website (www.wrox.com), and add it to the `Images` folder in the `PokerDiceContent` project.

DiceSelect.cs

After the die image has been added, you must add a new class called `DiceSelect` to the `Screens` folder. When you have done that, open the `DiceSelect.cs` file, and modify it to look like Listing 12-23.

FIGURE 12-5: The dice in action on the main screen

LISTING 12-23: The DiceSelect Class of Poker Dice

```
using System.Collections.Generic;

using Microsoft.Xna.Framework;
using Microsoft.Xna.Framework.Graphics;
using Microsoft.Xna.Framework.Content;
using Microsoft.Xna.Framework.Input.Touch;

using XNAPhoneGame.Sprites;
using XNAPhoneGame.Texts;
using PokerDice.PokerDiceService;

namespace XNAPhoneGame.Screens
{
```

continues

LISTING 12-23 *(continued)*

```
class DiceSelect : Screen
{

    Button rollButton;
    Button endTurnButton;

    Texture2D diceImage;

    const string ActionRoll = "Roll";
    const string ActionEndTurn = "EndTurn";
    const string ActionDieOne = "One";
    const string ActionDieTwo = "Two";
    const string ActionDieThree = "Three";
    const string ActionDieFour = "Four";
    const string ActionDieFive = "Five";

    Rectangle dieOne = new Rectangle(0, 0, 118, 124);
    Rectangle dieTwo = new Rectangle(118, 0, 118, 124);
    Rectangle dieThree = new Rectangle(245, 0, 118, 124);
    Rectangle dieFour = new Rectangle(0, 124, 118, 124);
    Rectangle dieFive = new Rectangle(118, 124, 118, 124);

    bool isDieOneSelected = false;
    bool isDieTwoSelected = false;
    bool isDieThreeSelected = false;
    bool isDieFourSelected = false;
    bool isDieFiveSelected = false;

    PokerDiceClient pokerDiceClient;

    public DiceSelect(Game game,
                      SpriteBatch batch,
                      ChangeScreen changeScreen)
        : base(game,
               batch,
               changeScreen,
               BackButtonScreenType.First)
    {
    }

    protected override void SetupInputs()
    {
        input.AddTouchGestureInput(ActionRoll,
                                   GestureType.Tap,
                                   rollButton.CollisionRectangle);

        input.AddTouchGestureInput(ActionEndTurn,
                                   GestureType.Tap,
                                   endTurnButton.CollisionRectangle);

        input.AddTouchGestureInput(ActionDieOne,
                                   GestureType.Tap,
```

```
                            dieOne);

        input.AddTouchGestureInput(ActionDieTwo,
                                    GestureType.Tap,
                                    dieTwo);

        input.AddTouchGestureInput(ActionDieThree,
                                    GestureType.Tap,
                                    dieThree);

        input.AddTouchGestureInput(ActionDieFour,
                                    GestureType.Tap,
                                    dieFour);

        input.AddTouchGestureInput(ActionDieFive,
                                    GestureType.Tap,
                                    dieFive);
    }

    public override void Activate()
    {
    }

    protected override void LoadScreenContent(ContentManager content)
    {
        rollButton = new Button(content,
                                "Roll",
                                new Vector2(30, 500),
                                Color.LightBlue);

        endTurnButton = new Button(content,
                                    "End Turn",
                                    new Vector2(30, 650),
                                    Color.LightBlue);

        diceImage = content.Load<Texture2D>("Images/Dice");

        pokerDiceClient = new PokerDiceClient();
        pokerDiceClient.TakeTurnCompleted
        += new System.EventHandler
            <System.ComponentModel.AsyncCompletedEventArgs>
                (pokerDiceClient_TakeTurnCompleted);
    }

    void pokerDiceClient_TakeTurnCompleted(object sender,
                    System.ComponentModel.AsyncCompletedEventArgs e)
    {
        changeScreenDelegate(ScreenState.GameLobby);
    }

    protected override void UpdateScreen(GameTime gameTime,
                                DisplayOrientation displayOrientation)
    {
        if (GameInformation.CurrentGame.CurrentRoll < 3
        && input.IsPressed(ActionRoll))
```

continues

LISTING 12-23 *(continued)*

```
        {
            List<int> selectedDice = new List<int>();
            if (isDieOneSelected)
            {
                selectedDice.Add(GameInformation.CurrentGame
                    .DiceRoll[0]);
            }

            if (isDieTwoSelected)
            {
                selectedDice.Add(GameInformation.CurrentGame
                    .DiceRoll[1]);
            }

            if (isDieThreeSelected)
            {
                selectedDice.Add(GameInformation.CurrentGame
                    .DiceRoll[2]);
            }

            if (isDieFourSelected)
            {
                selectedDice.Add(GameInformation.CurrentGame
                    .DiceRoll[3]);
            }

            if (isDieFiveSelected)
            {
                selectedDice.Add(GameInformation.CurrentGame
                    .DiceRoll[4])                       }

            GameInformation.CurrentGame.DiceRoll.Clear();
            GameInformation.CurrentGame.DiceRoll = selectedDice;

            soundEffects.PlaySound("SoundEffects/Select");
            changeScreenDelegate(ScreenState.MainGame);
        }
        else if (input.IsPressed(ActionEndTurn))
        {
            string finalRoll =
                GameInformation.CurrentGame.DiceRoll[0].ToString() +
                GameInformation.CurrentGame.DiceRoll[1].ToString() +
                GameInformation.CurrentGame.DiceRoll[2].ToString() +
                GameInformation.CurrentGame.DiceRoll[3].ToString() +
                GameInformation.CurrentGame.DiceRoll[4].ToString();

            pokerDiceClient.TakeTurnAsync(PhoneAnonymousID,
                                        GameInformation.CurrentGame.ID,
                                        finalRoll);
        }
        else if (input.IsPressed(ActionDieOne))
        {
```

```csharp
            isDieOneSelected = !isDieOneSelected;
        }
        else if (input.IsPressed(ActionDieTwo))
        {
            isDieTwoSelected = !isDieTwoSelected;
        }
        else if (input.IsPressed(ActionDieThree))
        {
            isDieThreeSelected = !isDieThreeSelected;
        }
        else if (input.IsPressed(ActionDieFour))
        {
            isDieFourSelected = !isDieFourSelected;
        }
        else if (input.IsPressed(ActionDieFive))
        {
            isDieFiveSelected = !isDieFiveSelected;
        }
    }

    protected override void DrawScreen(SpriteBatch batch,
                            DisplayOrientation displayOrientation)
    {
        DrawDice(new Vector2(0, 0),
                GameInformation.CurrentGame.DiceRoll[0],
                isDieOneSelected);

        DrawDice(new Vector2(118, 0),
                GameInformation.CurrentGame.DiceRoll[1],
                isDieTwoSelected);

        DrawDice(new Vector2(245, 0),
                GameInformation.CurrentGame.DiceRoll[2],
                isDieThreeSelected);

        DrawDice(new Vector2(0, 124),
                GameInformation.CurrentGame.DiceRoll[3],
                isDieFourSelected);

        DrawDice(new Vector2(118, 124),
                GameInformation.CurrentGame.DiceRoll[4],
                isDieFiveSelected);

        if (GameInformation.CurrentGame.CurrentRoll < 3)
        {
            rollButton.Draw(batch);
        }

        endTurnButton.Draw(batch);
    }

    private void DrawDice(Vector2 position,
                        int dieValue,
                        bool isDieSelected)
    {
```

continues

LISTING 12-23 *(continued)*

```
            Rectangle destination = new Rectangle((int)position.X,
                                                  (int)position.Y,
                                                  118,
                                                  124);
            Color color = Color.White;
            if (isDieSelected)
            {
                color = Color.Yellow;
            }

            switch (dieValue)
            {
                case 1:
                    {
                        batch.Draw(diceImage,
                                   destination,
                                   new Rectangle(0, 0, 118, 124),
                                   color);
                        break;
                    }

                case 2:
                    {
                        batch.Draw(diceImage,
                                   destination,
                                   new Rectangle(118, 0, 118, 124),
                                   color);
                        break;
                    }

                case 3:
                    {
                        batch.Draw(diceImage,
                                   destination,
                                   new Rectangle(245, 0, 118, 124),
                                   color);
                        break;
                    }

                case 4:
                    {
                        batch.Draw(diceImage,
                                   destination,
                                   new Rectangle(0, 124, 118, 124),
                                   color);
                        break;
                    }

                case 5:
                    {
                        batch.Draw(diceImage,
                                   destination,
```

```
                            new Rectangle(118, 124, 118, 124),
                            color);
                    break;
                }
                case 6:
                {
                    batch.Draw(diceImage,
                            destination,
                            new Rectangle(245, 124, 118, 124),
                            color);
                    break;
                }
            }
        }
    }
}
```

The player can tap a die to set it aside to keep. After he decides which die to keep, he can either choose to roll again with the remaining dice, or end his turn if he thinks he has the best possible Poker Dice hand.

With the addition of the `DiceSelect` screen, the Poker Dice example is done! You should now have a playable turn-based game.

This demo illustrates the basics of what it will take to make a turn-based game of your own. (In fact, you should find plenty of code you can reuse!)

ENHANCING YOUR GAME

Although the Poker Dice example showcases a lot, it has a long way to go before you can call it a polished game. A few things are missing. Adding them would be an excellent exercise:

➤ What if the player rolls and then immediately quits if he or she doesn't like the dice roll? How do you keep players from "gaming" the game?

➤ What about taking advantage of some of the phone's cooler features, such as allowing players to shake the phone to roll the dice?

Making game samples is easy, but taking extra steps can be challenging. It's important that you put time into thinking through just what extra bits of polish your games need.

Take a look at best-selling games for a good lead in finding the right balance. Pay close attention to how to create an entire experience:

➤ Do the game's menu sounds tie into the game play?

➤ Does the game draw you in from the second it launches?

It's important to note the small things that make a game a hit and to emulate them in your own projects. It's hard work, but you'll get noticed in the end.

SUMMARY

In this chapter, you built a complete game from scratch. You learned a number of handy new techniques, including how to use a matchmaking service, 3D animation, and basic game-play concepts, along with revisiting concepts you learned in earlier chapters.

In Chapter 13, you will learn how to use the Location API to make your games and apps location-aware.

13

Dude, Where's My Car?

WHAT'S IN THIS CHAPTER?

- ➤ Understanding the Location API
- ➤ How to look up your current location with the GeoCoordinateWatcher class
- ➤ How to use the CivicAddressResolver class

Windows Phone 7 offers a Location API that allows you to determine your location in multiple ways, including GPS, WiFi lookup, and cell tower triangulation. This chapter prepares you for using that service.

UNDERSTANDING AND ACCESSING THE LOCATION API

The Location API is provided so that you don't have to worry about customizing your game or application for specific hardware configurations. This includes not needing to worry about the specifics of how the data is acquired (via GPS, cell tower, and so on).

Everything you need to access your phone's location is stored within the `System.Device.Location` namespace. You will be concerned with three types of data in this chapter: `CivicAddress`, `GeoCoordinate`, and `GeoPosition`.

Unfortunately, if you don't have a phone, you'll be unable to test all the examples presented in this chapter as intended. The Emulator has no means of acquiring actual GPS data.

BEST PRACTICES FOR USING LOCATION SERVICES

In this chapter, you will learn several different ways to interact with the Location API inside your game or app. What follows are some best practices when dealing with location data.

Asking Permission

When using any of the methods presented in this chapter in your app or game, you must ask the user's permission to get his or her location. Failure to do so can result in your app or game being rejected during Marketplace Certification.

> *For more information on the certification process as it pertains to Location Services, be sure to take a look at Section 6.1 in the Windows Phone 7 Application Certification Requirements document.*

Power Consumption

One thing you should learn very quickly is that battery consumption is a huge priority for Microsoft (and for your users) and should be a priority for you as well. Overuse of Location Services can rapidly drain the battery of a Windows Phone device. An inverse relationship exists between battery life and accuracy. You must manage this balance carefully to provide the desired functionality of your app or game while being responsible with the device's limited resources.

All the demos in this chapter use `GeoPositionAccuracy.High` for the best possible effect, but this increases battery consumption.

Microsoft recommends using `GeoPositionAccuracy.Default` in most cases and switching to high accuracy only when you absolutely must have the increased precision. It is also recommended that you not turn on the Location Service until you need it, and turn it off when it is no longer necessary.

Level of Accuracy

The Location Service uses multiple sources of data, including GPS and cell tower triangulation, but you don't need to concern yourself with the specifics, because the native code layer handles that for you. All you must do is choose between `GeoPositionAccuracy.High` and the power-optimized `GeoPositionAccuracy.Default` when initializing the `GeoCoordinateWatcher` class.

Movement Threshold

The sensors in your phone are very sensitive. Therefore, setting this property too low can result in signal noise from surface reflection. The examples in this chapter use a much smaller threshold, but for best results you should set the `MovementThreshold` property to `20` (meters) in your apps or games.

USING LOCATION SERVICES IN YOUR GAMES

With the preliminaries out of the way, let's take a closer look at the components you use to incorporate Location Services in your games.

CivicAddress

As you might have guessed from the name, this class represents a civic address, also called a street address. This class contains the following string properties:

- `AddressLine1`
- `AddressLine2`
- `Building`
- `City`
- `CountryRegion`
- `FloorLevel`
- `PostalCode`
- `StateProvince`

In addition to these self-explanatory properties, there is one Boolean property, which doesn't really fit with the others:

- `IsUnknown`

This is a read-only property that returns a `true` or `false` value indicating whether the `CivicAddressResolver` class was able to resolve an address from a `GeoCoordinate` position.

The `CivicAddress()` class constructor has two overloads. One has no parameters and can be used to create an empty instance of `CivicAddress`. The other constructor accepts the eight string properties just listed.

CivicAddressResolver

This class is used to convert a `GeoCoordinate` position (as returned from the `GeoCoordinateWatcher` class) to a `CivicAddress` object. It can do so synchronously or asynchronously. You will learn more about the `GeoCoordinate` and `GeoCoordinateWatcher` classes later in this chapter.

> *When this book was written, the `CivicAddressResolver` class was present but not implemented on Windows Phone 7. Rather than exclude it from this book, we included the following section, which shows how to use it after it has been implemented in a future release.*

Did You Order Pizza?

To test this functionality, create a new Windows Game project and name it `DidYouOrderPizza`. The Location Services API requires a reference to the `System.Device` dynamic link library (DLL), so expand the References section in the Solution Explorer and add it.

The complete code for this project is available for download at the book's companion website (www.wrox.com).

You also need a `SpriteFont` to display information on the phone, so add one of those to your `DidYouOrderPizzaContent` project and leave the name as `SpriteFont1`. Set the `Size` property of your `SpriteFont` to `25` to ensure readability.

At the top of your `Game1` class file, add the following `using` statement:

    using System.Device.Location;

This gives you access to the `System.Device` DLL you added the reference to earlier.

This example shows how to resolve the `Position` data from a `GeoCoordinateWatcher` object both synchronously and asynchronously. First you will learn how to do so synchronously.

Resolving an Address Synchronously

Add the method shown in Listing 13-1 to your `Game1` class.

LISTING 13-1: The ResolveAddressSync() Method of the Game1 Class

```
static CivicAddress ResolveAddressSync()
{
    var gcWatcher = new GeoCoordinateWatcher(GeoPositionAccuracy.High);
    gcWatcher.MovementThreshold = 1.0;
    gcWatcher.TryStart(false, TimeSpan.FromMilliseconds(1000));

    var caResolver = new CivicAddressResolver();

    if (gcWatcher.Position.Location.IsUnknown == false)
    {
        var cAddress
            = caResolver.ResolveAddress(gcWatcher.Position.Location);

        location = watcher.Position.Location.IsUnknown.ToString();

        if (!cAddress.IsUnknown)
        {
            return cAddress;
        }
        else
        {
            // address unknown
            return null;
        }
    }

    return null;
}
```

This method creates a `GeoCoordinateWatcher` object with high accuracy and a movement threshold set to 1 meter. The `TryStart()` method is called with a timeout of 1 second.

The first argument the `TryStart()` method takes is set to `false` to display the permission dialog. The method also returns `true` to indicate whether data acquisition was started before the timeout occurred.

Assuming that your GPS is working, the `Location` property of the *gcWatcher* variable contains a pair of coordinates that are passed into the `CivicAddressResolver` object (named *caResolver*). If the `CivicAddressResolver` can resolve the address, it is returned to the calling code. Otherwise, this method returns a `null`.

Finally, if the GPS isn't working and no location data is returned, this method returns a `null` to the calling code.

To test this, you must add a few more things to the `Game1` class. Start by adding the following class-level variables:

```
SpriteFont font;
CivicAddress address;
string location = "";
```

Next, in the `Initialize()` method, add the following line to support a couple of multitouch gestures to kick off the GPS code:

```
TouchPanel.EnabledGestures = GestureType.DoubleTap | GestureType.Hold;
```

You will use the `DoubleTap` gesture for the synchronous call and implement the `Hold` gesture for the asynchronous call described later in this chapter.

Add the following code to your `LoadContent()` method to load your `SpriteFont` into memory:

```
font = Content.Load<SpriteFont>("SpriteFont1");
```

Now, modify the `Update()` method to look like Listing 13-2. The new code is in bold.

LISTING 13-2: The Update() Method of the Game1 Class

```
protected override void Update(GameTime gameTIme)
{
    if (GamePad.GetState(PlayerIndex.One).Buttons.Back == ButtonState.Pressed)
        this.Exit();

    if (TouchPanel.IsGestureAvailable)
    {
        GestureSample gesture = TouchPanel.ReadGesture();
        switch (gesture.GestureType)
        {
            case GestureType.DoubleTap:
                address = ResolveAddressSync();
                break;

            case GestureType.Hold:

                break;
```

continues

LISTING 13-2 *(continued)*

```
        }
    }
    base.Update(gameTime);
}
```

In the `Update()` method, you check for the `DoubleTap` gesture and then call the `ResolveAddressSync()` method to acquire and process the GPS data.

The last thing you need to touch right now is the `Draw()` method, shown in Listing 13-3.

LISTING 13-3: The Draw() Method of the Game1 Class

```
protected override void Draw(GameTime gameTime)
{
    GraphicsDevice.Clear(Color.CornflowerBlue);

    spriteBatch.Begin();

    if (address != null)
    {
        spriteBatch.DrawString(font,
                               address.AddressLine1,
                               new Vector2(50, 50),
                               Color.White);
        spriteBatch.DrawString(font,
                               address.AddressLine2,
                               new Vector2(50, 75),
                               Color.White);
        spriteBatch.DrawString(font,
                               address.City,
                               new Vector2(50, 100),
                               Color.White);
        spriteBatch.DrawString(font,
                               address.StateProvince,
                               new Vector2(50, 125),
                               Color.White);
        spriteBatch.DrawString(font,
                               location,
                               new Vector2(50, 300),
                               Color.White);
    }
    else
    {
        spriteBatch.DrawString(font,
                               "Address Unknown",
                               new Vector2(50, 100),
                               Color.White);
        spriteBatch.DrawString(font,
                               location,
                               new Vector2(50, 300),
```

```
                    Color.White);
        }

        spriteBatch.End();

    base.Draw(gameTime);
}
```

Not much is going on in this method. Either you have a resolved civic address or you don't. If you do, display it; otherwise, display the "Address Unknown" message. Either way, you display the location data.

You'll return to the code for the asynchronous example later in this chapter. First, you should test what you have in place.

> *This code will run in the Emulator, but it won't produce any meaningful results. You really need to run this on a device to get the full effect.*

Set your XNA Game Studio Deployment Device drop-down to Windows Phone 7 Device. Ensure that your Zune software is running and that your phone is unlocked. Press the F5 key to build and deploy to your phone.

Once the app has loaded and is running on your phone, you should see the "Address Unknown" message.

Double-tap the screen and wait about a second. If your GPS is working properly (and you have a decent signal), you see the location data on the screen.

If you live somewhere that the Civic Address Resolver can recognize, you see a street address in addition to the location data. Otherwise, you see the location data and the "Address Unknown" message.

Resolving an Address Asynchronously

Now it's time to go back into the project and update the Game1 class to support an asynchronous call.

Revisit your Update() method and add the following line under the case statement for Gesture.Hold:

```
ResolveAddressAsync();
```

Next, add the ResolveAddressAsync() method shown in Listing 13-4.

LISTING 13-4: The ResolveAddressAsync() Method of the Game1 Class

```
void ResolveAddressAsync()
{
    var gcWatcher = new GeoCoordinateWatcher(GeoPositionAccuracy.High);

    bool started = false;
    gcWatcher.MovementThreshold = 1.0;
    started = gcWatcher.TryStart(false, TimeSpan.FromMilliseconds(1000));
```

continues

LISTING 13-4 *(continued)*

```
        if (started)
        {
            var caResolver = new CivicAddressResolver();

            caResolver.ResolveAddressCompleted
                += new EventHandler<ResolveAddressCompletedEventArgs>
                    (caResolver_ResolveAddressCompleted);

            if (gcWatcher.Position.Location.IsUnknown == false)
            {
                location = gcWatcher.Position.Location.ToString();
                caResolver.ResolveAddressAsync(watcher.Position.Location);
            }
        }
    }
}
```

This method sets up the `GeoCoordinateWatcher` object with high accuracy, a 1-meter threshold, and a 1-second timeout.

After *gcWatcher* starts, you instantiate the address resolver and set up an event handler for the `ResolveAddressCompleted` event.

Finally, the `GeoLocation` data is captured, stored locally, and passed on to the `ResolveAddressAsync()` call.

Now, add the `caResolver_ResolveAddressCompleted()` method shown in Listing 13-5.

LISTING 13-5: The caResolver_ResolveAddressCompleted() Method

```
    void caResolver_ResolveAddressCompleted(object sender,
                                            ResolveAddressCompletedEventArgs e)
{
    if (!e.Address.IsUnknown)
    {
        address = e.Address;
    }
    else
    {
        address = null;
    }
}
```

This method waits for a response from the asynchronous call to resolve the civic address. It then assigns the `CivicAddress` object to the global *address* variable.

With that in place and nothing to add to the `Draw()` method, you're ready to fire it up and give it a try.

Again, ensure that your Zune software is running and that your device is unlocked. Press F5 to build and deploy. Once it is running, perform a `Hold` gesture. You see the location information and the civic address information, assuming that the resolver can map your coordinates to an actual address.

GeoCoordinate

The `GeoCoordinate` class represents a global location via latitude and longitude coordinates and may additionally include altitude, accuracy, speed, and course information.

The class contains four possible constructors:

- ➤ An empty constructor
- ➤ A constructor that accepts latitude and longitude
- ➤ A constructor that accepts latitude, longitude, and altitude
- ➤ A constructor that accepts the previous parameters, plus horizontal accuracy, vertical accuracy, speed, and course

As you may deduce from the constructors in this list, the `GeoCoordinate` class supports the following properties:

- ➤ Latitude
- ➤ Longitude
- ➤ Altitude
- ➤ HorizontalAccuracy
- ➤ VerticalAccuracy
- ➤ Speed
- ➤ Course

All these properties return a `Double` value.

In addition to these properties is a familiar read-only Boolean property:

- ➤ IsUnknown

The `IsUnknown` property is used as a sanity check to see if the `GeoCoordinate` class contains any location data. You should always check this before trying to work with `GeoCoordinate` data.

Finally, in addition to the usual set of methods inherited from the object class (such as `Equals()`, `Finalize()`, `GetType()`, and so on), you have the `GetDistanceTo()` method. It compares the current `GeoCoordinate` instance to another passed in as a parameter and returns the distance between the two locations, expressed in meters.

To use the `GeoCoordinate` class as part of the Location Service, you need to be familiar with the `GeoCoordinateWatcher` class, which is covered next.

GeoCoordinateWatcher

You already saw this class in action in the `DidYouOrderPizza` example, but there's more to it, as shown in Listing 13-6. The class has been trimmed for readability but is otherwise intact.

LISTING 13-6: The GeoCoordinateWatcher Class

```
public class GeoCoordinateWatcher()
{
    public GeoCoordinateWatcher();
    public GeoCoordinateWatcher(GeoPositionAccuracy desiredAccuracy);

    // The desired accuracy for data returned from the location service.
    public GeoPositionAccuracy DesiredAccuracy { get; }

    // The minimum distance that must be travelled between successive
    // PositionChanged events.
    public double MovementThreshold { get; set; }

    // The application's level of access to the location service.
    public GeoPositionPermission Permission { get; }

    // The most recent position obtained from the location service.
    public GeoPosition<GeoCoordinate> Position { get; }

    // The status of the location service.
    public GeoPositionStatus Status { get; }

    // Occurs when the location service detects a change in position.
    public event EventHandler
        <GeoPositionChangedEventArgs<GeoCoordinate>> PositionChanged;

    // Occurs when the status of the location service changes.
    public event EventHandler
        <GeoPositionStatusChangedEventArgs> StatusChanged;

    // Raises the PositionChanged event.
    protected void
        OnPositionChanged(GeoPositionChangedEventArgs<GeoCoordinate> e);

    // Raises the PositionStatusChanged event.
    protected void
        OnPositionStatusChanged(GeoPositionStatusChangedEventArgs e);

    // Raises the PropertyChanged event for the GeoCoordinateWatcher class.
    protected void OnPropertyChanged(string propertyName);

    // Starts the acquisition of data from the location service.
    public void Start();
    public void Start(bool suppressPermissionPrompt);

    // Stops the acquisition of data from the location service.
    public void Stop();

    // Attempts to start the acquisition of data from the location service.
    // If the provided timeout interval is exceeded before the location
    // service responds, the request for location is stopped and the method
    // returns false.
```

```
    public bool TryStart(bool suppressPermissionPrompt, TimeSpan timeout);
}
```

To get a better feel for this class and the `GeoCoordinate` class, let's create another example.

FindMe

Start by creating a new Windows Phone Game project and naming it `FindMe`.

The complete code for this project is available for download at the book's companion website (www.wrox.com).

You also need a `SpriteFont` (no surprise at this point), so add one to your `FindMeContent` project and keep the default name. Be sure to give it a size of 25 for readability.

In the Solution Explorer, you must add a reference in the `FindMe` project. Expand the References section and add a reference to the `System.Device` DLL.

Now it's time to jump into the `Game1` class. Start by adding the following `using` statement at the top of the `Game1` class file:

```
using System.Device.Location;
```

Add the following class-level variables:

```
GeoCoordinateWatcher locationWatcher;
string locationWatcherStatus;
SpriteFont displayFont;
```

You can skip the constructor and `Initialize()` method, because you have nothing to add in either of them. In your `LoadContent()` method, add the following two lines:

```
displayFont = Content.Load<SpriteFont>("SpriteFont1");
StartLocationWatcher();
```

Since Visual Studio 2010 is likely barking at you about the call to the `StartLocationWatcher()` method, add that next. The complete method is shown in Listing 13-7.

LISTING 13-7: The StartLocationWatcher() Method of the Game1 Class

```
void StartLocationWatcher()
{
    if (locationWatcher == null)
    {
        locationWatcher = new GeoCoordinateWatcher(GeoPositionAccuracy.High);

        locationWatcher.MovementThreshold = 0;

        locationWatcher.StatusChanged
            += new EventHandler<GeoPositionStatusChangedEventArgs>
                (locationWatcher_StatusChanged);
```

continues

LISTING 13-7 *(continued)*

```
    }

    locationWatcher.Start();

    locationWatcherStatus = "Location data initializing...";
}
```

This method sets up the `GeoCoordinateWatcher` object (if it isn't already instantiated) with a high accuracy and a threshold of 0 meters. (The previous example used a threshold of 1 meter.)

Also, the event handler for the `StatusChanged` event is set up to point to the `locationWatcher_StatusChanged()` method.

Finally, the `Start()` method of the `GeoCoordinateWatcher` object is called, and the initial status is set to "initializing," which is displayed onscreen.

Now that you have declared the event handler, you must implement the method to call. Add the `locationWatcher_StatusChanged()` method shown in Listing 13-8.

LISTING 13-8: The locationWatcher_StatusChanged() Method of the Game1 Class

```
void locationWatcher_StatusChanged(object sender,
                            GeoPositionStatusChangedEventArgs e)
{
    switch (e.Status)
    {
        case GeoPositionStatus.Disabled:
            {
                locationWatcherStatus = "Location device disabled. ";
                locationWatcherStatus += "Unable to retrieve location data.";
                break;
            }

        case GeoPositionStatus.Initializing:
            {
                locationWatcherStatus = "Location data initializing...";
                break;
            }

        case GeoPositionStatus.NoData:
            {
                locationWatcherStatus = "No location data available.";
                break;
            }

        case GeoPositionStatus.Ready:
            {
                locationWatcherStatus = "Location data READY!";
                break;
            }
```

        }
    }

This method simply reads the `GeoPositionStatus` returned from the asynchronous call to the `locationWatcher.Start()` method and populates the `locationWatcherStatus` variable with a string to be displayed.

The last method to update in this example is the `Draw()` method. Take a look at Listing 13-9 and add the code in bold.

LISTING 13-9: The Draw() Method of the Game1 Class

```
protected override void Draw(GameTime gameTime)
{
    GraphicsDevice.Clear(Color.CornflowerBlue);

    spriteBatch.Begin();

    spriteBatch.DrawString(displayFont,
                           locationWatcherStatus,
                           new Vector(50, 30),
                           Color.White);

    if (locationWatcher.Status == GeoPositionStatus.Ready)
    {
        spriteBatch.DrawString(displayFont,
                               "Altitude:"
                                   + locationWatcher.Position.Location
                                   .Altitude.ToString(),
                               New Vector2(50,75).
                               Color.White);

        spriteBatch.DrawString(displayFont,
                               "Course:"
                                   + locationWatcher.Position.Location
                                   .Course.ToString(),
                               New Vector2(50,105).
                               Color.White);

        spriteBatch.DrawString(displayFont,
                               "Speed:"
                                   + locationWatcher.Position.Location
                                   .Speed.ToString(),
                               New Vector2(50,135).
                               Color.White);

        spriteBatch.DrawString(displayFont,
                               "HAccuracy:"
                                   + locationWatcher.Position.Location
                                   .HorizontalAccuracy.ToString(),
                               New Vector2(50,165).
                               Color.White);
```

continues

LISTING 13-9 *(continued)*

```
            spriteBatch.DrawString(displayFont,
                            "VAccuracy:"
                                + locationWatcher.Position.Location
                                .VerticalAccuracy.ToString(),
                            New Vector2(50,195).
                            Color.White);

            spriteBatch.DrawString(displayFont,
                            "Latitude:"
                                + locationWatcher.Position.Location
                                .Latitude.ToString(),
                            New Vector2(50,225).
                            Color.White);

            spriteBatch.DrawString(displayFont,
                            "Longitude:"
                                + locationWatcher.Position.Location
                                .Longitude.ToString(),
                            New Vector2(50,255).
                            Color.White);
    }

    spriteBatch.End();

    base.Draw(gameTime);
}
```

In the `Draw()` method you just added, you check the status of the `GeoCoordinateWatcher` object (the *locationWatcher* variable) and display the various properties if the status is Ready.

Depending on where you are geographically when you execute this code, it can take anywhere from 1 second to a couple minutes to get a result. It's also possible you won't get a result (other than "Unable to retrieve location data").

Build and deploy this project, ensuring that your Windows Phone 7 device is selected as the deployment device.

As soon as the app is running and displaying data, go for a walk and see the coordinates change. The `MovementThreshold` property is set artificially low in this demo; it is polling roughly once per second. This is so that you can see results without having to drive around. But normally you would want to use a higher threshold for your app or game for more precise results (and less battery consumption).

 One of the authors had to load this example onto his phone and take a drive to see any results. GPS can be somewhat unpredictable.

The last section of this chapter focuses on the `GeoPosition` class.

GeoPosition

The `GeoPosition<T>` class represents a geographic position made up of a location and time stamp. The `GeoPosition<T>` class exposes two properties:

- `Location`
- `TimeStamp`

This class has no example because you will never use it directly. The `GeoCoordinateWatcher` `.Position` property uses this class to return location data.

The `GeoPosition<T>` class has no methods of its own — only the usual methods inherited from `Object`.

SUMMARY

In this chapter, you learned some best practices for using the Location Services API. The two most important considerations when using Location Services are battery conservation and accuracy. These two factors have an inverse relationship.

The `GeoCoordinateWatcher` class is responsible for acquiring location data and turning the Location Services on and off. The `CivicAddressResolver` class takes geographic coordinates and converts them into a civic address, which includes a street address, city, state, and zip code (among other data).

In Chapter 14, you will learn about tasks and choosers, such as the Camera Capture task and photo chooser.

14

Take a Picture; It'll Last Longer!

WHAT'S IN THIS CHAPTER?

- ➤ Understanding the concept of Launchers and Choosers
- ➤ Using your device's camera and photo features
- ➤ Creating and sending an SMS text message with SMSComposeTask
- ➤ Creating and sending an e-mail with EmailComposeTask
- ➤ Capturing and using photos with CameraCaptureTask and PhotoChooserTask
- ➤ Using MediaPlayerLauncher to play music from the user's collection

Windows Phone 7 offers a variety of Launchers and Choosers to expose basic phone functionality, such as the Camera Capture and Photo Chooser tasks, as well as the SMS Compose and Email Compose tasks and the Email Address Chooser.

In this chapter, you will learn about the various Launchers and Choosers, how they work, and how to implement them in your apps and games.

LAUNCHERS AND CHOOSERS

Launchers and *Choosers* are used by Windows Phone games and applications to enable common tasks such as taking a picture, sending a text or e-mail message, and even making a phone call. The `Microsoft.Phone.Tasks` namespace contains all the Launchers and Choosers for Windows Phone 7. Choosers return some form of data to the calling program, and Launchers do not. Table 14-1 shows some common Launchers and Choosers.

TABLE 14-1: Common Launchers and Choosers

TASK CATEGORY	CLASS	DESCRIPTION
Camera	`CameraCaptureTask`	This allows you to take a picture with the phone camera.
	`PhotoChooserTask`	This allows you to select a picture already taken.
Contacts	`PhoneNumberChooserTask`	This allows you to select a phone number from Contacts.
	`SaveEmailAddressTask`	This allows you to save an e-mail address to the specified contact.
	`SavePhoneNumberTask`	This allows you to save a phone number to the specified contact.
	`EmailAddressChooserTask`	This allows you to select an e-mail address from Contacts.
E-mail and Short Message Service (SMS)	`EmailComposeTask`	This allows you to compose and send an e-mail.
	`SmsComposeTask`	This allows you to compose and send an SMS text message.
Marketplace	`MarketplaceDetailTask`	This allows you to pull up the application detail page in the Windows Phone Marketplace.
	`MarketplaceHubTask`	This allows you to display the Windows Phone Marketplace Hub.
	`MarketplaceReviewTask`	This allows you to retrieve a specific Marketplace review page.
	`MarketplaceSearchTask`	This allows you to search the Windows Phone Marketplace.
Other	`MediaPlayerLauncher`	This allows you to launch the Media Player.
	`PhoneCallTask`	This allows you to make a phone call.
	`SearchTask`	This allows you to launch the Search screen.
	`WebBrowserTask`	This allows you to launch a web browser.

Not all the tasks listed in Table 14-1 are examined in this chapter, so if you need more information, be sure to check out the MSDN reference page at `http://msdn.microsoft.com/en-us/library/ff428753(v=VS.92).aspx`.

Over the following series of examples, you will learn how to use some of the tasks listed in Table 14-1.

NOWPICTURETHIS

To learn how to use the `CameraCaptureTask` and `PhotoChooserTask` classes, start by creating a new Windows Phone Game project. Call it `NowPictureThis`.

> *The complete code for the project in this chapter is available for download at the book's companion website (www.wrox.com).*

You won't need a `SpriteFont` for this one, but you will need to expand the References tab in the Solution Explorer window and add a reference to the `Microsoft.Phone` dynamic link library (DLL).

With your reference in place, open the `Game1.cs` class file and add these two `using` statements at the top:

```
using Microsoft.Phone.Tasks;
using System.IO;
```

First, you'll learn about the `CameraCaptureTask` class. In this example, you will add all the code to get that working, and then you'll return to this project to add support for the `PhotoChooserTask` class.

CameraCaptureTask

The `CameraCaptureTask` class allows your game or application to take a photo using the device camera. This class contains a single parameterless constructor and exposes a single public method called `Show()`.

> *This is one of the classes that you will use in Chapter 15 when you put together the Picture Puzzle game.*

Inside the `Game1` class, add the following class-level variables:

```
CameraCaptureTask camera;
Texture2D selectedPhoto;
```

With this code, you are setting up the `CameraCaptureTask` object and `Texture2D` to store the photo in memory.

You don't need to add anything to the `Game1` constructor, so you can skip over that and open the `Initialize()` method. Add the following line to the `Initialize()` method, just after the TODO comment:

```
TouchPanel.EnabledGestures = GestureType.DoubleTap;
```

You will add another gesture later to trigger `PhotoChooserTask`. However, for now let's focus on the `CameraCaptureTask` class. In your `LoadContent()` method, add the following code:

```
camera = new CameraCaptureTask();
camera.Completed += new EventHandler<PhotoResult>(camera_Completed);
```

With the event handler in place for the *camera.Completed* event, it's time to add the code for the `camera_Completed()` method, as shown in Listing 14-1.

LISTING 14-1: The camera_Completed() Method of the Game1 Class

```
void camera_Completed(object sender, PhotoResult e)
{
    if (e.ChosenPhoto != null)
    {
        selectedPhoto = Texture2D.FromStream(GraphicsDevice,
                                                    e.ChosenPhoto);
    }

    using (MemoryStream = new MemoryStream())
    {
        selectedPhoto.SaveAsJpeg(stream, 480, 800);
        stream.Position = 0;

        MediaLibrary library = new MediaLibrary();
        var picName = DateTime.Now.Year.ToString().Substring(2,2)
                    + DateTime.Now.Month.ToString()
                    + DateTime.Now.Day.ToString()
                    + DateTime.Now.Hour.ToString()
                    + DateTime.Now.Second.ToString()
                    + DateTime.Now.Millisecond.ToString();

        library.SavePicture(picName, stream);
        stream.Close();
    }
}
```

This method starts by accepting a `PhotoResult` object when the `CameraCaptureTask` completes. Assuming that the `ChosenPhoto` property isn't null, you then create a `Texture2D` of the photo from the stream (contained by the `ChosenPhoto` property). Once you have the *selectedPhoto*, you create a `MemoryStream` object and pass it into the `SaveAsJpeg()` method, along with the photo's dimensions.

Next, you will save the picture you created. In order to do this, you must first create a `MediaLibrary` object and then generate a name for your photo from the date and time. You pass the `MemoryStream` object and the photo's name into the `SavePicture()` method of the `MediaLibrary` object.

Last, you close the stream.

In the `Update()` method, add the following block of code after the `TODO` comment:

```
while (TouchPanel.IsGestureAvailable)
{
    GestureSample gesture = TouchPanel.ReadGesture();

    if (gesture.GestureType == GestureType.DoubleTap)
    {
        camera.Show();
        break;
    }
}
```

When your user performs a `DoubleTap` gesture, you call the `Show()` method of your `CameraCaptureTask`.

The last code to add for this example is in the `Draw()` method. Add the following `SpriteBatch` block between the calls to `base.Draw()` and `GraphicsDevice.Clear()`:

```
spriteBatch.Begin();

if (selectedPhoto != null)
{
    spriteBatch.Draw(selectedPhoto, new Rectangle(0, 0, 800, 480), Color.White);
}

spriteBatch.End();
```

At this point, you're ready to build and run the example.

If you have a device to deploy to, you must make a decision. Normally, when deploying to your phone, the Zune software must be running. Unfortunately, it seems that `CameraCaptureTask` (along with `PhotoChooserTask`) does not play well with the Zune software.

In order for these tasks to work properly on your device, you must do one of the following:

➤ Deploy your game the normal way via the Zune software by pressing F5. Once your game is up and running, end the game and disconnect your phone from the cable. Restart your game from within the phone.

➤ Use the Application Deployment tool (described in the next section).

Even if you don't have a phone, you should read this next part, because you can use this tool to deploy to the Emulator as well as the phone.

The Application Deployment Tool

Most of the time, you won't need this tool to push your apps to the phone. But in certain cases (such as now) you may want to keep your phone connected, so you need to run an app on your phone.

The Application Deployment tool is not a part of Visual Studio 2010. Instead, it is found under the Windows Phone Developer Tools item on your Windows Start menu, as shown in Figure 14-1.

To use this tool, you must first create a prepackaged .XAP file. You can do that simply by pressing F6 to build your solution (without deploying anywhere).

After you have built your game, start the Application Deployment tool, shown in Figure 14-2, and browse to your .XAP file.

FIGURE 14-1: Locating the Application Deployment tool on the Windows Start menu

Depending on where you saved your project, your `.XAP` file will be located in the `application name\application name\bin\Windows Phone\debug` path, below the main folder of your app or game solution.

FIGURE 14-2: The Application Deployment tool

 If you are using a full version of Visual Studio 2010, you may have switched from doing debug builds to doing release builds. If so, just change the last part of your path to `release` *instead of* `debug`.

The file you are looking for will have the same name as your solution, and a `.XAP` extension. Select that file and click the Open button.

 If you have Windows set to hide file extensions, it's helpful to know that the `.XAP` *icon is the one that looks like a blank sheet of paper. Fortunately, the Application Deployment tool shows only* `.XAP` *files when you're browsing, so you should be good to go.*

In the Target drop-down menu, select either Windows Phone 7 Emulator or Windows Phone 7 Device, and click the Deploy button. Keep an eye on the Status line. When it says "XAP Deployment Complete," your game has been deployed and you can now test it as usual.

Speaking of testing, let's get back to that.

Testing NowPictureThis

With the `NowPictureThis` game on your phone or in the Emulator, fire it up from within the device. You can access it by opening the Applications menu (use the white arrow inside the circle).

After you launch the game and you see the cornflower blue screen, perform a `DoubleTap` gesture. If you are using a phone, you see whatever your camera is pointing at. If you are using the Emulator, you see something resembling Figure 14-3.

What now? If you are using a phone, take a picture of something by pointing your camera and pressing the camera button on the side of your device.

If you are running in the Emulator, things work a little differently because it has no built-in camera. You see a circular icon in the top right of the Emulator screen. Click it. You see a white background with a black box moving along the edges. It appears for just a moment, and then you hear the "camera click." At that point you can accept or retake the picture.

For now, choose to retake the picture. Repeat this a couple of times. You will notice that the black box keeps moving around the edges of the screen, so you can simulate taking several action shots if you like.

FIGURE 14-3: CameraCaptureTask running in the Windows Phone Emulator

At some point, click or tap the Accept button. The photo is saved to your media library and is displayed onscreen.

Being able to capture an image and use it in your game or app has a lot of potential. With the right code, you can do anything from barcode scanning to facial recognition to using the various images as an in-game representation of the player. For example, you could use avatars (only less animated), or you could crop images and create silly dancing videos (like the ones found on the JibJab website at www.jibjab.com).

Of course, the other half of being able to do all that neat stuff is having the option of loading the images you take from a collection of photos rather than having to rely on good timing to capture the perfect live shot. For this, you have `PhotoChooserTask` at your disposal.

PhotoChooserTask

The `PhotoChooserTask` class allows your app or game to select a photo from your media library or Camera Roll via the Photo Chooser application.

In addition to the parameterless constructor and the `Show()` method, you can use two public integer properties to set the photo's `PixelHeight` and `PixelWidth`. A third property, the `ShowCamera` Boolean, can be used to determine whether the user is given the option of starting the camera app as part of the photo-choosing process.

Go back into your `NowPictureThis` project and open the `Game1` class so that you can add a few things to support `PhotoChooserTask`.

You already have all the references and namespaces you need, so add the following variable at the class level:

```
PhotoChooserTask photoChooser;
```

In your `LoadContent()` method, add the following code after the `CameraCaptureTask` block:

```
photoChooser = new PhotoChooserTask();
photoChooser.Completed += new EventHandler<PhotoResult>(photoChooser_Completed);
```

This pattern should look familiar by now. Instantiate the task, set up an event handler, and add the method shown in Listing 14-2 to support it.

LISTING 14-2: The photoChooser_Completed() Method of the Game1 Class

```
void photoChooser_Completed(object sender, PhotoResult e)
{
    if (e.ChosenPhoto != null)
    {
        selectedPhoto = Texture2D.FromStream(GraphicsDevice,
                                        e.ChosenPhoto)
    }
}
```

With this method you are accepting a `PhotoResult` object from the completion of your `PhotoChooserTask` and making sure it is not `null`. Assuming that a photo is present, the `ChosenPhoto` stream is fed into the `FromStream()` method of the `Texture2D` class to populate the `selectedPhoto` variable with the resulting `Texture2D` object.

Next, you add another code block to the `Update()` method to support this task. Just after the `if` block inside the `while` block, add the following `else` block:

```
else if (gesture.GestureType == GestureType.Hold)
{
    photoChooser.Show();
    break;
}
```

This code is pretty simple. If the user performs a `Hold` gesture, launch the Photo Chooser app from the phone (or the Emulator). Whatever the user selects is returned to the event handler and processed.

The `Draw()` method doesn't require any modification, so you're ready to test the modified `NowPictureThis` game.

Following the deployment instructions outlined earlier, deploy to your phone or the Emulator, and give it a test. Use the `DoubleTap` gesture to launch the camera app, or use the `Hold` gesture to launch the Photo Chooser app.

Pretty awesome, right? One last thing worth mentioning is that with the current code, you must perform separate gestures to call either the camera app or the Photo Chooser app. But with one line of code, your users can pull up the Photo Chooser app and have the option to use the camera or choose an existing picture.

Add the following line of code just above `photoChooser.Show();` in the `else if` block in your `Update()` method:

```
photoChooser.ShowCamera = true;
```

With that in place, build, deploy, and try testing your game again. This time, when you pull up the `PhotoChooserTask`, you see a camera icon at the bottom of the screen. Clicking that launches the camera app.

If you take a picture at this point, it is saved to the media library and displayed onscreen, just as if you had selected an existing picture.

Now let's look at some of the other Tasks available to you as a Windows Phone developer.

CLASSES FOR MESSAGING TASKS

The following classes cover creating and sending messages to other players, specifically SMS text messages and e-mail messages.

SmsComposeTask

The `SmsComposeTask` class is used to create and send an SMS text message via the text messaging app on your phone.

This task is discussed in more detail in Chapter 16. Here you get a preview.

Like the previous tasks in this chapter, this class contains a parameterless constructor and a `Show()` method. It also has two string properties that you will use to populate the `Body` and `To` fields of the text message.

To use this task, create a variable and instantiate the `SmsComposeTask` object:

```
var textMessage = new SmsComposeTask();
```

Next, fill in the properties:

```
textMessage.Body = "Hey Wally! Check me out! I'm a SMS text message!";
textMessage.To = "18657403004";
```

Finally, wrap it up with a call to the `Show()` method:

```
textMessage.Show();
```

Of course, this code won't actually send the message. It only shows the SMS Compose application. You can edit the body of the text before sending it, as shown in Figure 14-4.

FIGURE 14-4: SmsComposeTask in the Emulator

To test this task, grab the previous block of text message code and add it to the `NowPictureThis` example, inside the `GestureType.Hold` code block. Just be sure to comment out the following two lines, or you will get an error:

```
//photoChooser.ShowCamera = true
//photoChooser.Show()
```

Build and deploy your game again. Perform a `Hold` gesture to see the `SmsComposeTask` screen. When your text message is ready, click the send icon (it looks like a word balloon with motion lines), and you're done.

One potential in-game use for this task might be to allow your users to send their friends invites to download and try your awesome game.

EmailComposeTask

The `EmailComposeTask` class is used to launch the phone's Email application with a prepopulated new message that is ready to send. You can use this to allow your users to send an e-mail from your app or game.

This task follows the same pattern as the others you have seen. It includes a parameterless constructor, a `Show()` method, and a handful of properties for prepopulating the `Body`, `Cc`, `To`, and `Subject` fields, respectively.

To use this task, instantiate the `EmailComposeTask` object:

```
var EmailComposeTask email = new EmailComposeTask();
```

Next, fill in the properties:

```
email.Body = "Thanks so much for writing this book. It's awesome and I learned
    SO much!";
```

```
email.Cc = "clingermangw@gmail.com";
email.To = "chrisgwilliams@gmail.com";
email.Subject = "Your book rocks!";
```

Last, call the `Show()` method:

```
email.Show();
```

This displays the application to compose an e-mail. This gives your user an opportunity to edit and send the e-mail.

To test this, return to the `NowPictureThis` project. This time, comment out the `SmsComposeTask` code and add the block of e-mail code just provided. The e-mail message is sent from whatever account you have set up on your phone.

EmailAddressChooserTask

If you don't want to prepopulate the `To` and `Cc` address fields on the `EmailComposeTask` screen, you can use the `EmailAddressChooserTask` class as part of this process.

The `EmailAddressChooserTask` class launches the Contacts application and allows your user to select an e-mail address and return that address as a string to your app or game.

This class does not contain any properties, so you can just instantiate it and call the `Show()` method.

Because it's a Chooser, you return a value to the calling program. So, you must add an event handler to respond to the `Completed` event. Your event handler should go in the `LoadContent()` method and look something like the following code block:

```
eAddressChooser = new EmailAddressChooserTask(); // declare this at the class
                                                 // level
eAddressChooser.Completed += new
    EventHandler<EmailResult>(eAddressChooser_Completed);
```

Your event handler would look like Listing 14-3.

LISTING 14-3: The eAddressChooser_Completed() Method of the Game1 Class

```
void eAddressChooser_Completed(object sender, EmailResult e)
{
    if (e.Email != null)
    {
        emailAddress = e.Email;
        // you declared emailAddress elsewhere (class level)
    }
}
```

With all that set up, it's just a matter of showing it at the right time. Add the following line to the `Hold` gesture block, as before. Be sure to comment out the other Launchers.

```
eAddressChooser.Show();
```

Once this is called and your event handler fires, you have a string containing one or more e-mails in your *emailAddress* variable to use as you see fit. Assuming that you have some contacts defined in your phone, give it a test drive by pressing F5 to build and deploy your `NowPictureThis` game.

The last item to show isn't exactly a Launcher or a Chooser. Instead, it launches the Media Player app.

MEDIAPLAYERLAUNCHER

The `MediaPlayerLauncher` class is included in the `Microsoft.Phone.Tasks` namespace but doesn't actually return any values to your program, fetch pictures, or generate e-mails or text messages. Instead, it allows you to call the Media Player from your application or game.

Like the rest of the Launchers and Choosers described in this chapter, `MediaPlayerLauncher` consists of a single parameterless constructor, along with a `Show()` method and the following three properties:

- Controls
- Location
- Media

The Controls Property

The `Controls` property accepts a bitwise combination of flags that determine which controls are displayed. Listing 14-4 shows all the flags for the `Controls` property.

LISTING 14-4: The MediaPlaybackControls Enumeration

```
public enum MediaPlaybackControls
{
    None = 0,
    Pause = 1,
    Stop = 2,
    FastForward = 4,
    Rewind = 8,
    Skip = 16,
    All = 31,
}
```

The first and last entries in the `MediaPlaybackControls` enumeration are special, since they tell the Media Player to show all or none of the controls. If you specify `None` along with any other controls, you still get whatever other controls you listed. If you specify `All` along with any other controls, you get all controls displayed.

To set the `Controls` property, use a block of code like the following:

```
MediaPlayerLauncher mpl = new MediaPlayerLauncher();
mpl.Controls = MediaPlaybackControls.Stop
             | MediaPlaybackControls.Rewind
             | MediaPlaybackControls.FastForward;
```

This tells the Media Player to display only the `Stop`, `Rewind`, and `FastForward` controls when you call the `Show()` method.

The Location Property

The `Location` property is write-only and sets a `MediaLocationType` value to indicate the location of the media file to be played. Listing 14-5 shows the enumeration of `MediaLocationType`.

LISTING 14-5: The MediaLocationType Enumeration

```
public enum MediaLocationType
{
    None = 0,
    Install = 1,
    Data = 2,
}
```

These may seem like odd values to you, and to a degree you're right. If you assign `MediaLocationType.None` to the `Location` property, the `Show()` method throws a `FileNotFoundException`. If you use `MediaLocationType.Install`, you are telling the Media Player that the file is located in your app or game install directory (on the phone). Finally, if you use `MediaLocationType.Data`, that means the media file is located in the Isolated Storage space for your app or game.

The Media Property

The `Media` property accepts a URI that points to the media file you want to play. It can point to a file that exists on the Internet (provided that your user has an Internet connection) or to a file in the location indicated by the `Location` property.

If you wanted to play a file from isolated storage, the code would look like this:

```
mpl.Location = MediaLocationType.Data;
mpl.Media = new Uri("mymusic.wmv", UriKind.Relative);
```

If you are using the install location or a web-based file, you need to change this block of code accordingly, but you get the idea.

The only thing left is to call the `Show()` method as follows:

```
mpl.Show();
```

> *Some people within the XNA game developer community have criticized and complained about the Media Player's appearance and performance in the Emulator. Don't worry. The experience is significantly better on an actual device.*

That's it for the Launchers and Choosers that are covered in this book. You can check out and learn about several more on the MSDN page at http://msdn.microsoft.com/en-us/library/ff428753(v=VS.92).aspx.

SUMMARY

In this chapter, you learned about the various Launchers and Choosers and how to implement them in your app or game.

The `PhotoChooserTask` and `CameraCaptureTask` classes are meant to be used together, giving your users the option to take a new picture or use an existing one when a photo is required.

The `SmsComposeTask` class makes it easy to compose and send SMS text messages from your game.

The `EmailComposeTask` class is used to create and send e-mails from your game. It can be used in conjunction with `EmailAddressChooserTask` to pull addresses from your Contacts list. You can also use `EmailAddressChooserTask` independently of `EmailComposeTask` to fetch e-mail addresses from the Contacts list for other purposes in your app or game.

`MediaPlayerLauncher` allows you to call the Media Player from within your app or game and lets you play songs stored locally or play them across the Internet.

In Chapter 15, you will take what you have learned over the last few chapters and put together the third and final game of this book — Picture Puzzle.

15

Putting It All Together: Picture Puzzle

WHAT'S IN THIS CHAPTER?

➤ Using everything you've learned thus far to create your third game, Picture Puzzle

You've learned quite a bit thus far. Now it's time to create a third complete game for Windows Phone 7.

The examples provided in the "Putting It All Together" chapters (Chapters 8, 12, and 15) assume knowledge of C#. Without that, the sample projects may seem a bit overwhelming and confusing. These chapters are not for beginners, but for experienced developers who are familiar with C# and who are somewhat familiar with the XNA framework and game development concepts.

The Picture Puzzle game you create in this chapter takes advantage of the Camera Capture and Photo Chooser tasks. This chapter walks you through the development of the game and teaches you how to incorporate concepts such as multitouch and media playback from earlier chapters.

PICTURE PUZZLE

With Picture Puzzle, a player can take a picture of something that is then stored. The picture is turned into a jigsaw puzzle that the player can put together. Not only does Picture Puzzle show you how to use the Camera Task in a game, but the creation of the jigsaw puzzle also takes advantage of some of the "state" objects to create effects in XNA 4.0.

Sounds pretty cool, right? Well, now that you know the basics, it's time to design the screen flow.

DESIGNING THE SCREEN FLOW

When you created the Drive & Dodge game in Chapter 8, you walked through the exercise of designing the screen flow. Before you create a game, it's always a good practice to work out the basic screen flow in your head. This helps you think through the various pieces you might need to start construction (as well as what things you might need to learn because you're unsure how to do them).

Figure 15-1 shows a diagram mapping the screen flow for the Picture Puzzle game.

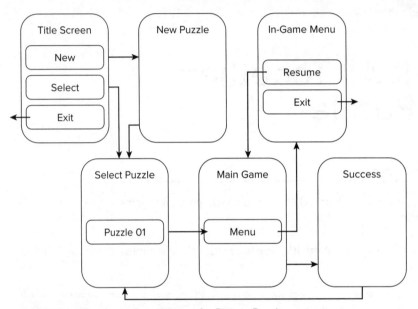

FIGURE 15-1: The screen flow diagram for Picture Puzzle

CREATING PICTURE PUZZLE

After you completed the Drive & Dodge example at the end of Chapter 8, you actually laid the groundwork for getting started with the example in this chapter. To begin creating Picture Puzzle, you will use the Game and Content templates you created at that time.

 The complete code for this project is available for download at the book's companion website (www.wrox.com).

Create a new XNAPhoneGame project from the template. This will be the base Game template for Picture Puzzle, which will save you a lot of work and allow you to get this game up and running fairly quickly.

Type PicturePuzzle as the name, and click OK.

Now that you've added the base `Game` project template, add the `XNAPhoneGameContent` project template as well. Name it `PicturePuzzleContent`, and click OK.

With the `Content` project added to the solution, you now must link the `Game` and `Content` project templates. To do that, within Solution Explorer expand the `Content References` folder found in the `PicturePuzzle` game project. Delete any content references that may exist, and then right-click the `Content References` folder and select Add Content Reference. From this dialog, select your `PicturePuzzleContent` project and click OK.

This links your `Content` project to your `Game` project. (It's also how you would add multiple `Content` projects to a game if you ever find that necessary!)

With the base game already constructed, it's time to get started with creating Picture Puzzle. A great place to begin is the `Title` screen.

Creating the Title Screen

The base project already has a `Title` screen class. You just need to enhance it so that it makes sense for the new game you're working on.

Start by adding the new background image for Picture Puzzle to the Picture Puzzle `Content` folder. Copy the image file from this book's companion website (www.wrox.com), and paste it into the `Images` folder in the `PicturePuzzleContent` project, replacing the existing `Background.png` image found there.

Next, you must add a new `SpriteFont` called `titleFont` to the `Fonts` folder of the `PicturePuzzleContent` project. Change the `FontName` property of your `SpriteFont` to `Kootenay`. Change the Size to `55` and the Style to `Bold`.

Title.cs

Now you must modify the `Title` class file (located in the `Screens` folder) to look like Listing 15-1.

LISTING 15-1: The Title Class of Picture Puzzle

```
using Microsoft.Xna.Framework;
using Microsoft.Xna.Framework.Graphics;
using Microsoft.Xna.Framework.Content;
using Microsoft.Xna.Framework.Input.Touch;

using XNAPhoneGame.Sprites;
using XNAPhoneGame.Texts;

namespace XNAPhoneGame.Screens
{
    class Title : Screen
    {
        Background backgroundSprite;
        Button createNewPuzzleButton;
        Button playExistingPuzzleButton;
```

continues

LISTING 15-1 *(continued)*

```csharp
    Button exitButton;

    Text titleText;
    SpriteFont titleFont;

    const string ActionCreateNewPuzzle = "Create";
    const string ActionPlayExistingPuzzle = "Puzzle";
    const string ActionExit = "Exit";

    public Title(Game game, SpriteBatch batch, ChangeScreen changeScreen)
        : base(game, batch, changeScreen, BackButtonScreenType.First)
    {
    }

    protected override void SetupInputs()
    {
        input.AddTouchGestureInput(ActionCreateNewPuzzle,
                                   GestureType.Tap,
                                   createNewPuzzleButton.TouchArea);

        input.AddTouchGestureInput(ActionPlayExistingPuzzle,
                                   GestureType.Tap,
                                   playExistingPuzzleButton.TouchArea);

        input.AddTouchGestureInput(ActionExit,
                                   GestureType.Tap,
                                   exitButton.TouchArea);
    }

    public override void Activate()
    {
    }

    protected override void LoadScreenContent(ContentManager content)
    {
        backgroundSprite = new Background(content);

        createNewPuzzleButton = new Button(content,
                                           "New Puzzle",
                                           new Vector2(30, 380),
                                           Color.SteelBlue);

        playExistingPuzzleButton = new Button(content,
                                              "Load Puzzle",
                                              new Vector2(30, 500),
                                              Color.SteelBlue);

        exitButton = new Button(content,
                                "Exit",
                                new Vector2(30, 620),
                                Color.SteelBlue);
```

```csharp
            titleFont = content.Load<SpriteFont>("Fonts/TitleFont");
            titleText = new Text(titleFont,
                                 "Picture Puzzle",
                                 new Vector2(0, 150),
                                 Color.SteelBlue,
                                 Color.White,
                                 Text.Alignment.Horizontal,
                                 new Rectangle(0, 0, 480, 800));
        }

        protected override void UpdateScreen(GameTime gameTime,
                                        DisplayOrientation displayOrientation)
        {
            if (input.IsPressed(ActionCreateNewPuzzle))
            {
                soundEffects.PlaySound("SoundEffects/Select");
            }
            else if (input.IsPressed(ActionPlayExistingPuzzle))
            {
                soundEffects.PlaySound("SoundEffects/Select");
            }
            else if (input.IsPressed(ActionExit))
            {
                changeScreenDelegate(ScreenState.Exit);
            }
        }

        protected override void DrawScreen(SpriteBatch batch,
                                      DisplayOrientation displayOrientation)
        {
            backgroundSprite.Draw(batch);

            createNewPuzzleButton.Draw(batch);
            playExistingPuzzleButton.Draw(batch);
            exitButton.Draw(batch);

            titleText.Draw(batch);
        }
    }
}
```

Most of this code should be familiar to you (provided that you created the previous two game projects). The `Background`, `Button`, and `Text` objects were all created previously as part of the template and are available for you to use right away. This allows you to quickly throw together a new `Title` screen and see some progress.

If you build and run the game (by pressing F5) at this point, you should see the start of the Picture Puzzle game, as shown in Figure 15-2. The Exit button already works!

With the `Title` screen constructed, it's time to begin creating some of the other screens and enhancing the `ScreenStateSwitchboard` class to handle the state switching between them.

FIGURE 15-2: The Picture Puzzle Start screen

Enhancing the ScreenStateSwitchboard

Since the `ScreenStateSwitchboard` will direct traffic through your game, it might be best to modify that class next to get all the plumbing in place.

ScreenStateSwitchboard.cs

Modify the `ScreenStateSwitchboard.cs` file to look like Listing 15-2.

LISTING 15-2: The ScreenStateSwitchboard Class of Picture Puzzle

```
using System.Collections.Generic;

using Microsoft.Xna.Framework;
using Microsoft.Xna.Framework.Graphics;

namespace XNAPhoneGame.Screens
{
    public enum ScreenState
    {
        Title,
        InGameMenu,
        PreviousScreen,
        Exit,
        SelectPuzzle,
```

```csharp
        NewPuzzle,
        MainGame,
        PuzzleComplete,
    }

    class ScreenStateSwitchboard
    {
        static Game game;
        static SpriteBatch batch;
        static Screen previousScreen;
        static Screen currentScreen;
        static Dictionary<ScreenState, Screen> screens
            = new Dictionary<ScreenState, Screen>();

        private delegate Screen CreateScreen();

        public ScreenStateSwitchboard(Game game, SpriteBatch batch)
        {
            ScreenStateSwitchboard.game = game;
            ScreenStateSwitchboard.batch = batch;
            ChangeScreen(ScreenState.Title);
        }

        private void ChangeScreen(ScreenState screenState)
        {
            switch (screenState)
            {
                case ScreenState.Title:
                    {
                        ChangeScreen(screenState,
                                new CreateScreen(CreateTitleScreen));
                        break;
                    }

                case ScreenState.InGameMenu:
                    {
                        ChangeScreen(screenState,
                                new CreateScreen(CreateInGameMenuScreen));
                        break;
                    }

                case ScreenState.PreviousScreen:
                    {
                        currentScreen = previousScreen;
                        currentScreen.Activate();
                        break;
                    }

                case ScreenState.Exit:
                    {
                        game.Exit();
                        break;
                    }

                case ScreenState.NewPuzzle:
```

continues

LISTING 15-2 *(continued)*

```csharp
                    {
                        ChangeScreen(screenState,
                                new CreateScreen(CreateNewPuzzleScreen));
                        break;
                    }

                case ScreenState.SelectPuzzle:
                    {
                        ChangeScreen(screenState,
                                new CreateScreen(CreateSelectPuzzleScreen));
                        break;
                    }

                case ScreenState.MainGame:
                    {
                        ChangeScreen(screenState,
                                new CreateScreen(CreateMainGameScreen));
                        break;
                    }

                case ScreenState.PuzzleComplete:
                    {
                        ChangeScreen(screenState,
                            new CreateScreen(CreatePuzzleCompleteScreen));
                        break;
                    }
            }
        }

        private void ChangeScreen(ScreenState screenState,
                            CreateScreen createScreen)
        {
            previousScreen = currentScreen;

            if (!screens.ContainsKey(screenState))
            {
                screens.Add(screenState, createScreen());
                screens[screenState].LoadContent();
            }
            currentScreen = screens[screenState];
            currentScreen.Activate();
        }

        private Screen CreateTitleScreen()
        {
            return new Title(game,
                        batch,
                        new Screen.ChangeScreen(ChangeScreen));
        }

        private Screen CreateInGameMenuScreen()
        {
            return new InGameMenu(game,
```

```
                                    batch,
                                    new Screen.ChangeScreen(ChangeScreen));
            }

            public Screen CreateNewPuzzleScreen()
            {
                return null;
            }

            public Screen CreateSelectPuzzleScreen()
            {
                return null;
            }

            public Screen CreateMainGameScreen()
            {
                return null;
            }

            public Screen CreatePuzzleCompleteScreen()
            {
                return null;
            }

            public void Update(GameTime gameTime)
            {
                currentScreen.Update(gameTime);
            }

            public void Draw()
            {
                currentScreen.Draw();
            }
        }
    }
```

In the `ScreenStateSwitchBoard` class, you added to the `ScreenState` enumeration the screens that will exist in the Picture Puzzle game. (You know what screens should exist from the time you took to design the screen flow earlier.) The `ChangeScreen()` method uses that information to know which screen needs to be created and then switched to.

Notice that several screen-creation methods in `ScreenStateSwitchboard` currently return `null`. That is because you haven't made them yet, so let's do that next.

Creating the NewPuzzle Screen

The `NewPuzzle` screen is where the player can take a picture of whatever he or she sees to create a new image that can be used to make a new puzzle. This operation uses the Camera Task on the phone.

NewPuzzle.cs

To begin creating the `NewPuzzle` screen, right-click the `Screens` folder in Solution Explorer and add a new class named `NewPuzzle`. Then, modify the `NewPuzzle` class to look like Listing 15-3.

LISTING 15-3: The NewPuzzle Class of Picture Puzzle

```csharp
using System;
using System.IO;

using Microsoft.Xna.Framework;
using Microsoft.Xna.Framework.Content;
using Microsoft.Xna.Framework.Graphics;
using Microsoft.Xna.Framework.GamerServices;
using Microsoft.Xna.Framework.Media;

using Microsoft.Phone.Tasks;

using XNAPhoneGame.Sprites;

namespace XNAPhoneGame.Screens
{
    class NewPuzzle : Screen
    {
        Background backgroundSprite;
        CameraCaptureTask camera;
        Texture2D selectedPhoto;
        string puzzleName;
        GraphicsDevice graphicsDevice;

        enum State
        {
            TakingPicture,
            PictureRejected,
            ShowKeyboard,
            NamingPicture,
            PictureNamed,
            PuzzleSaved
        }
        State currentState = State.TakingPicture;

        public NewPuzzle(Game game,
                         GraphicsDevice device,
                         ContentManager content,
                         SpriteBatch batch,
                         ChangeScreen changeScreen)
            : base(game,
                   batch,
                   changeScreen,
                   BackButtonScreenType.Other)
        {
            graphicsDevice = device;

            camera = new CameraCaptureTask();
            camera.Completed
                += new EventHandler<PhotoResult>(camera_Completed);
        }

        public override void Activate()
```

```csharp
    {
        currentState = State.TakingPicture;
        camera.Show();
    }

    void camera_Completed(object sender, PhotoResult e)
    {
        if (e.ChosenPhoto == null)
        {
            currentState = State.PictureRejected;
        }
        else
        {
            selectedPhoto = Texture2D.FromStream(graphicsDevice,
                                                e.ChosenPhoto,
                                                480,
                                                800,
                                                true);
            currentState = State.ShowKeyboard;
        }
    }

    protected override void LoadScreenContent(ContentManager content)
    {
        backgroundSprite = new Background(content);
    }

    protected override void UpdateScreen(GameTime gameTime,
                            DisplayOrientation screenOrientation)
    {
        switch (currentState)
        {
            case (State.PictureRejected):
                {
                    changeScreenDelegate(ScreenState.Title);
                    break;
                }

            case (State.ShowKeyboard):
                {
                    currentState = State.NamingPicture;
                    Guide.BeginShowKeyboardInput(PlayerIndex.One,
                                                "Name your puzzle",
                                                "Puzzle Name",
                                                "",
                                                GetPuzzleName,
                                                null);
                    break;
                }

            case (State.PictureNamed):
                {
                    SaveNewPuzzle();
                    currentState = State.PuzzleSaved;
                    break;
```

continues

LISTING 15-3 *(continued)*

```
                    }
                case (State.PuzzleSaved):
                    {
                        changeScreenDelegate(ScreenState.SelectPuzzle);
                        break;
                    }
            }
        }

        protected void GetPuzzleName(IAsyncResult result)
        {
            puzzleName = Guide.EndShowKeyboardInput(result);
            currentState = State.PictureNamed;
        }

        private void SaveNewPuzzle()
        {
            using (MemoryStream stream = new MemoryStream())
            {
                selectedPhoto.SaveAsJpeg(stream, 480, 800);
                stream.Position = 0;
                MediaLibrary library = new MediaLibrary();
                library.SavePicture(puzzleName + "-PicturePuzzle", stream);
                stream.Close();
            }
            currentState = State.PuzzleSaved;
        }

        protected override void DrawScreen(SpriteBatch batch,
                                    DisplayOrientation screenOrientation)
        {
            backgroundSprite.Draw(batch);
            if (selectedPhoto != null)
            {
                batch.Draw(selectedPhoto, Vector2.Zero, Color.White);
            }
        }
    }
}
```

The `NewPuzzle` screen has its own state management. It starts by launching the Camera Task and having the state of `TakingPicture`.

Then, after the Camera Task closes, you check to see whether a picture was taken. (You can tell by checking to see if the chosen photo is being returned as `null`.) If a picture was taken, it shows the keyboard using the `Guide`. This allows the player to give the puzzle a name.

Once the player has finished naming the picture, the `GetPuzzleName()` method is called. The name is stored, and the state is changed. When the `UpdateScreen()` method detects that the picture has been named, it saves the picture to the user's media library. It adds the text

"-PicturePuzzle" so that those pictures can later be identified as being taken specifically to be puzzles.

When the picture has been saved, the screen switches and transfers the player to the `SelectPicture` screen.

> It's important to note that, when testing media-type things such as the Camera Task, you can't debug those items on the device while the Zune software is running. So, when you need to debug media tasks, you must launch the `WPConnect` tool that was installed on your system. Of course, you can use the Emulator but the pictures it takes aren't very interesting.

With the `NewPuzzle` screen added, you must do a little more work to get the screen hooked up and displaying. To start, you must change the `ScreenStateSwitchBoard` class to create the `NewPuzzle` screen (instead of returning `null`, as it does now).

In the `ScreenStateSwitchBoard` class file, modify the `CreateNewPuzzleScreen()` method to look like the following:

```
public Screen CreateNewPuzzleScreen()
{
    return new NewPuzzle(game,
                        game.GraphicsDevice,
                        game.Content,
                        batch,
                        new Screen.ChangeScreen(ChangeScreen));
}
```

Next, in the `TitleScreen` class, hook up the New Puzzle button so that it navigates to this screen. Modify the `UpdateScreen()` method in the `TitleScreen` class file to look like Listing 15-4.

LISTING 15-4: The UpdateScreen() Method of the TitleScreen Class

```
protected override void UpdateScreen(GameTime gameTime,
                                    DisplayOrientation displayOrientation)
{
    if (input.IsPressed(ActionCreateNewPuzzle))
    {
        soundEffects.PlaySound("SoundEffects/Select");
        changeScreenDelegate(ScreenState.NewPuzzle);
    }
    else if (input.IsPressed(ActionPlayExistingPuzzle))
    {
        soundEffects.PlaySound("SoundEffects/Select");
    }
    else if (input.IsPressed(ActionExit))
    {
        changeScreenDelegate(ScreenState.Exit);
    }
}
```

It's time to run `PicturePuzzle` again (by pressing F5) and test your new screen.

Click the New Puzzle button. This launches the Camera application, allowing you to take a picture of something nearby. Take a picture and click the `Accept` button. You are asked to name your new puzzle picture. Type a name for the puzzle, and click OK.

You are dumped out of the game, which is not really desirable behavior. In the `NewPuzzle` class, as soon as naming and saving are done, you navigate to the `SelectPuzzle` screen. As you may recall, the method to create that screen in the `ScreenStateSwitchboard` class currently returns `null`.

So, with the `NewPuzzle` screen working and waiting for the `SelectPuzzle` screen, now is a good time to start working toward creating that screen.

The `SelectPuzzle` screen is where users can select puzzles to play as part of the game, as well as ones they've created themselves. Before this screen gets created, however, you must create some other basic supporting classes.

The Pieces of the Puzzle

The main object that Picture Puzzle works with is the `Puzzle` object. But a `Puzzle` object is made up of many pieces, so those classes must be created first.

PuzzlePiece.cs

The `PuzzlePiece` class represents a single item that is part of a larger puzzle.

Right-click the `Sprites` folder and add a new class called `PuzzlePiece`. Modify the `PuzzlePiece` class file to look like Listing 15-5.

LISTING 15-5: The PuzzlePiece Class of Picture Puzzle

```
PuzzlePiece.cs
using Microsoft.Xna.Framework;
using Microsoft.Xna.Framework.Graphics;

namespace XNAPhoneGame.Sprites
{
    class PuzzlePiece
    {
        Texture2D pieceTexture;
        public Vector2 position;
        public Vector2 originalPosition;

        float rotation = 0.0f;
        int width;
        int height;

        public bool IsSelected = false;

        public PuzzlePiece(Texture2D theTexture,
                           Vector2 thePosition,
```

```
                          int theWidth,
                          int theHeight)
    {
        position = thePosition;
        originalPosition = thePosition;
        pieceTexture = theTexture;
        width = theWidth;
        height = theHeight;
    }

    public void Draw(SpriteBatch batch)
    {
        Color color = Color.White;
        float layerDepth = 1;
        if (IsSelected)
        {
            layerDepth = 0;
            color = Color.Yellow;
        }

        batch.Draw(pieceTexture,
                   position,
                   null,
                   color,
                   rotation,
                   Vector2.Zero,
                   1.0f,
                   SpriteEffects.None,
                   layerDepth);
    }

    public Rectangle OriginalCollisionRectangle
    {
        get { return new Rectangle((int)originalPosition.X,
                                   (int)originalPosition.Y,
                                   width,
                                   height); }
    }

    public Rectangle CollisionRectangle
    {
        get { return new Rectangle((int)position.X,
                                   (int)position.Y,
                                   width,
                                   height); }
    }
    }
}
```

Let's take a moment to examine how the game goes about "puzzleizing" the images. A lot of puzzle games just cut the image into squares, but you'll do something more interesting. You'll cut the original image into jigsaw-puzzle shapes. To do this, you use an image of a puzzle piece as a "cookie cutter" to cut the original image into jigsaw pieces.

StencilPiece.cs

Much like the `PuzzlePiece` class represents an individual puzzle piece, the `StencilPiece` class represents a single jigsaw cookie-cutter image.

Add a new class to the `Sprites` folder, and call it `StencilPiece`. Modify your new class file to look like Listing 15-6.

LISTING 15-6: The StencilPiece Class of Picture Puzzle

```
StencilPiece.cs
using Microsoft.Xna.Framework;
using Microsoft.Xna.Framework.Graphics;

namespace XNAPhoneGame.Sprites
{
    class StencilPiece
    {
        public Texture2D texture;
        public Vector2 position;
        public int width;
        public int height;

        public StencilPiece(Texture2D theTexture,
                            Vector2 thePosition,
                            int theWidth,
                            int theHeight)
        {
            position = thePosition;
            texture = theTexture;
            width = theWidth;
            height = theHeight;
        }

        public void Draw(SpriteBatch batch)
        {
            batch.Draw(texture, Vector2.Zero, Color.White);
        }
    }
}
```

Not much is going on in this class — just a simple wrapper to keep the size and position, and to draw it when necessary.

Next, you create the `Puzzle` class. But before you do that, you must add some new `Content` files that it depends on. To cut an image into jigsaw pieces, you must use a template for what those pieces will look like.

Copy the `Puzzle1` folder (and all the image files) from this book's files on the companion website (www.wrox.com) and paste it into the `Images` folder of the `PuzzlePieceContent` project.

A good future enhancement to Picture Puzzle would be to add more types of puzzle pieces to create variety and increase difficulty. For now, your puzzles will all look like the single template you just added.

Puzzle.cs

Now you must actually create the `Puzzle` class. Right-click the `Sprites` folder and add a new class called `Puzzle`. Modify the class file to look like Listing 15-7.

LISTING 15-7: The Puzzle Class of Picture Puzzle

```
using System;
using System.Collections.Generic;
using System.IO;

using Microsoft.Xna.Framework;
using Microsoft.Xna.Framework.Graphics;
using Microsoft.Xna.Framework.Content;

namespace XNAPhoneGame.Sprites
{
    class Puzzle
    {
        static List<StencilPiece> puzzleStencilPieces
            = new List<StencilPiece>();

        static List<PuzzlePiece> puzzlePieces = new List<PuzzlePiece>();

        Texture2D originalImage;
        ContentManager content;
        GraphicsDevice graphics;

        public string Name;
        PuzzlePiece selectedPiece;

        public Puzzle(string puzzleName,
                    Stream stream,
                    ContentManager theContent,
                    GraphicsDevice theGraphicsDevice)
        {
            Name = puzzleName;
            originalImage = Texture2D.FromStream(theGraphicsDevice, stream);
            content = theContent;
            graphics = theGraphicsDevice;
            stream.Dispose();
        }

        public Puzzle(string puzzleName,
```

continues

LISTING 15-7 *(continued)*

```
                string theOriginalAssetName,
                ContentManager theContent,
                GraphicsDevice theGraphicsDevice)
{
    Name = puzzleName;
    originalImage = theContent.Load<Texture2D>(theOriginalAssetName);
    content = theContent;
    graphics = theGraphicsDevice;
}

public void PuzzleizeImage()
{
    //Load the stencil pieces if they haven't been loaded before
    if (puzzleStencilPieces.Count == 0)
    {
        puzzleStencilPieces.Add(new
            StencilPiece(content.Load<Texture2D>
                ("Images/Puzzle1/Puzzle01"),
            new Vector2(0, 0),
            160,
            200));

        puzzleStencilPieces.Add(new
            StencilPiece(content.Load<Texture2D>
                ("Images/Puzzle1/Puzzle02"),
            new Vector2(160, 0),
            160,
            200));

        puzzleStencilPieces.Add(new
            StencilPiece(content.Load<Texture2D>
                ("Images/Puzzle1/Puzzle03"),
            new Vector2(320, 0),
            160,
            200));

        puzzleStencilPieces.Add(new
            StencilPiece(content.Load<Texture2D>
                ("Images/Puzzle1/Puzzle04"),
            new Vector2(0, 200),
            160,
            150));

        puzzleStencilPieces.Add(new
            StencilPiece(content.Load<Texture2D>
                ("Images/Puzzle1/Puzzle05"),
            new Vector2(160, 200),
            160,
            200));

        puzzleStencilPieces.Add(new
            StencilPiece(content.Load<Texture2D>
```

```
                    ("Images/Puzzle1/Puzzle06"),
                new Vector2(320, 200),
                160,
                150));

            puzzleStencilPieces.Add(new
                StencilPiece(content.Load<Texture2D>
                    ("Images/Puzzle1/Puzzle07"),
                new Vector2(0, 350),
                120,
                200));

            puzzleStencilPieces.Add(new
                StencilPiece(content.Load<Texture2D>
                    ("Images/Puzzle1/Puzzle08"),
                new Vector2(123, 398),
                200,
                200));

            puzzleStencilPieces.Add(new
                StencilPiece(content.Load<Texture2D>
                    ("Images/Puzzle1/Puzzle09"),
                new Vector2(320, 350),
                160,
                150));

            puzzleStencilPieces.Add(new
                StencilPiece(content.Load<Texture2D>
                    ("Images/Puzzle1/Puzzle10"),
                new Vector2(0, 550),
                120,
                250));

            puzzleStencilPieces.Add(new
                StencilPiece(content.Load<Texture2D>
                    ("Images/Puzzle1/Puzzle11"),
                new Vector2(123, 598),
                160,
                200));

            puzzleStencilPieces.Add(new
                StencilPiece(content.Load<Texture2D>
                    ("Images/Puzzle1/Puzzle12"),
                new Vector2(283, 598),
                200,
                200));
        }

        puzzlePieces.Clear();
        GC.Collect();

        SpriteBatch batch = new SpriteBatch(graphics);
        foreach (StencilPiece stencilPiece in puzzleStencilPieces)
        {
            RenderTarget2D puzzleImage
```

continues

LISTING 15-7 *(continued)*

```
            = new RenderTarget2D(graphics,
                                 480,
                                 800,
                                 false,
                                 SurfaceFormat.Color,
                                 DepthFormat.Depth24Stencil8);

    graphics.SetRenderTarget(puzzleImage);
    graphics.Clear(Color.Transparent);

    batch.Begin(SpriteSortMode.Immediate,
                null,
                null,
                StateObjects.StencilMaskBefore,
                null,
                StateObjects.AlphaEffect(graphics));

    batch.Draw(stencilPiece.texture,
               Vector2.Zero,
               null,
               Color.White,
               0.0f,
               Vector2.Zero,
               1.0f,
               SpriteEffects.None, 0.0f);

    batch.End();

    batch.Begin(SpriteSortMode.Immediate,
                null,
                null,
                StateObjects.StencilMaskAfter,
                null,
                StateObjects.AlphaEffect(graphics));

    batch.Draw(originalImage,
               Vector2.Zero - stencilPiece.position,
               null,
               Color.White,
               0.0f,
               Vector2.Zero,
               1.0f,
               SpriteEffects.None,
               0.0f);

    batch.End();

    graphics.SetRenderTarget(null);
    puzzlePieces.Add(new PuzzlePiece(puzzleImage,
                                    stencilPiece.position,
                                    stencilPiece.width,
                                    stencilPiece.height));
```

```csharp
        }
    }

    public void ScramblePuzzle()
    {
        Random random = new Random();
        foreach (PuzzlePiece piece in puzzlePieces)
        {
            piece.position = new Vector2(random.Next(100, 350),
                                        random.Next(100, 600));
        }
    }

    public void SelectPiece(Vector2 currentSelectPosition)
    {
        if (selectedPiece != null)
        {
            selectedPiece.IsSelected = false;
        }

        foreach (PuzzlePiece aPiece in puzzlePieces)
        {
            if (aPiece.CollisionRectangle.Contains(
                (int)currentSelectPosition.X,
                (int)currentSelectPosition.Y))
            {
                selectedPiece = aPiece;
            }
        }

        if (selectedPiece != null)
        {
            selectedPiece.IsSelected = true;
        }
    }

    public void MovePiece(Vector2 positionAdjustment)
    {
        if (selectedPiece == null)
        {
            return;
        }

        selectedPiece.position += positionAdjustment;

        float PositionX = MathHelper
            .Clamp(selectedPiece.position.X,
                0,
                480 - selectedPiece.CollisionRectangle.Width);

        float PositionY = MathHelper
            .Clamp(selectedPiece.position.Y,
                0,
                800 - selectedPiece.CollisionRectangle.Height);
```

continues

LISTING 15-7 *(continued)*

```
            selectedPiece.position = new Vector2(PositionX, PositionY);
        }

        public bool PlacePiece(Vector2 currentSelectPosition)
        {
            if (selectedPiece == null)
            {
                return false;
            }

            if (selectedPiece.OriginalCollisionRectangle
                .Contains((int)currentSelectPosition.X,
                          (int)currentSelectPosition.Y))
            {
                selectedPiece.position = selectedPiece.originalPosition;
                return true;
            }

            return false;
        }

        public bool IsSolved()
        {
            foreach (PuzzlePiece puzzle in puzzlePieces)
            {
                if (puzzle.position != puzzle.originalPosition)
                {
                    return false;
                }
            }

            return true;
        }

        public void Draw(SpriteBatch batch)
        {
            foreach (PuzzlePiece aPiece in puzzlePieces)
            {
                aPiece.Draw(batch);
            }

            if (selectedPiece != null)
            {
                selectedPiece.Draw(batch);
            }
        }
    }
}
```

After adding the `Puzzle` class code, you'll notice that a few compile errors remain. Those should all be within the `PuzzleizeImage()` method. This method takes your original image and cuts it into jigsaw pieces using the stencil pieces.

The most interesting method in this class is `PuzzleizeImage()`. This is where the original image is loaded from the `ContentManager` or via a stream from the user's media library, and turned into a puzzle.

The first thing to note in the `PuzzleizeImage()` method is that the `StencilPiece` objects are loaded only once for the `Puzzle` class. They're stored in a static `List` object, and after it's been loaded it's never loaded again. This was done to save memory and resources. You have to think about that a bit more when developing games for Windows Phone 7, because you're dealing with less.

With the Xbox 360 and PCs, it was unusual when you were dealing with a two-dimensional (2D) game to have to be overly concerned with memory conservation. But Windows Phone 7 will probably occasionally run out of memory if you aren't careful. Making sure to load into memory only the exact number of objects that you need is one way to save space.

Next, notice in the `PuzzleizeImage()` method that the *puzzlePieces* list is cleared and a `GC.Collect()` is called. This is another resource-clearing technique that is necessary to get this game working and to keep it from returning out-of-memory errors. (You could try removing the call to `GC.Collect` and changing both *puzzleStencilPieces* and *puzzlePieces* from static to private to see this happen.)

The *puzzlePieces* object is static so that only one list of puzzle pieces can exist at any point in time. When a new `Puzzle` object is "puzzleized," the list is cleared. `GC.Collect()` then allows the .NET framework to unload and clean up unused references and memory allocations.

Another technique that could have been used (but would have taken a bit more finagling to implement) would have been to use different `ContentManager` objects for each `Puzzle` class. These could have been loaded and unloaded to free up resources. The static route with the `GC.Collect()` call is just one possible approach. You can experiment with both techniques and see which one you think works better.

Now that the `Puzzle` class has freed up memory (and you should no longer be seeing memory errors), the puzzle pieces themselves are created using the following loop:

```
SpriteBatch batch = new SpriteBatch(graphics);

foreach (StencilPiece stencilPiece in puzzleStencilPieces)
{
    RenderTarget2D puzzleImage = new RenderTarget2D(graphics,
                                            480,
                                            800,
                                            false,
                                            SurfaceFormat.Color,
                                            DepthFormat.Depth24Stencil8);

    graphics.SetRenderTarget(puzzleImage);
    graphics.Clear(Color.Transparent);

    batch.Begin(SpriteSortMode.Immediate,
                null,
                null,
                StateObjects.StencilMaskBefore,
                null,
                StateObjects.AlphaEffect(graphics));
```

```
            batch.Draw(stencilPiece.texture,
                      Vector2.Zero,
                      null,
                      Color.White,
                      0.0f,
                      Vector2.Zero,
                      1.0f,
                      SpriteEffects.None,
                      0.0f);

        batch.End();

        batch.Begin(SpriteSortMode.Immediate,
                    null,
                    null,
                    StateObjects.StencilMaskAfter,
                    null,
                    StateObjects.AlphaEffect(graphics));

            batch.Draw(originalImage,
                      Vector2.Zero - stencilPiece.position,
                      null,
                      Color.White,
                      0.0f,
                      Vector2.Zero,
                      1.0f,
                      SpriteEffects.None,
                      0.0f);

        batch.End();

        graphics.SetRenderTarget(null);
        puzzlePieces.Add(new PuzzlePiece(puzzleImage,
                                        stencilPiece.position,
                                        stencilPiece.width,
                                        stencilPiece.height));
    }
```

Take a look at the puzzle images found in the `Puzzle1` folder (in your `Content` project). You see that they are black-and-white images of a puzzle piece. These puzzle pieces are used to cut out the shapes in black from whichever image this puzzle uses as its original image.

How It Works

First, a render target is created that's the size of the screen. This render target is then made the target of the graphics device. This means that anything drawn is now drawn onto this render target instead of the screen (which is normally the default render target). Once the render target has been set, the "screen" (your new render target) is cleared to a transparent color.

Next, the `SpriteBatch` object is signaled that you are ready to start drawing. Not only are you ready, but you also have some special state information for just how you want the `SpriteBatch` to draw. You pass that in using the various `StateObjects` (`StencilMaskBefore` and `AlphaEffect`).

These state objects just set and describe special instructions you want to give the `SpriteBatch` before it starts drawing. (You will create the `StateObjects` class and its members in the next step.)

Now that you've given the `SpriteBatch` the special instructions, draw the black-and-white puzzle-piece image, and then finish drawing with those particular instructions.

Next, you begin drawing to the same render target. But before you start, you give the `SpriteBatch` some new drawing instructions. The instructions tell the `SpriteBatch` that you want to draw the image only where the black exists from the drawing of the stencil shown in Figure 15-3.

This effectively "cuts out" the shape of the particular jigsaw piece from the original picture you're drawing to the render target.

FIGURE 15-3: The puzzle piece stencil

When you're finished drawing, end the batch and then add that puzzle piece to the dictionary object for storage. Repeat these steps for the next puzzle-piece shape. Those are the basics of how to "puzzleize" an image.

 You can use this technique to cut just about any shape out of an image. You'll definitely want to file away this process for future projects. A big thank-you goes to Michael McLaughlin for staying up late one night and helping to figure out this technique using XNA 4.0.

Managing State Objects

The code still has some compile errors; they are for the state objects you just read about. The capability to pass in various state objects to the `SpriteBatch` is new for XNA 4.0, and to use them effectively you must create static objects to represent them. With that in mind, it's time to create that class and its members.

StateObject.cs

Start by adding a new folder called `Misc` to your game. You'll use that to hold any miscellaneous class files that don't really fall into any of the other categories. Next, right-click the `Misc` folder and add a new class called `StateObject`. Modify the `StateObject` class file to look like Listing 15-8.

LISTING 15-8: The StateObject Class of Puzzle Piece

```
using Microsoft.Xna.Framework;
using Microsoft.Xna.Framework.Graphics;

namespace XNAPhoneGame
{
    static class StateObjects
    {
```

continues

LISTING 15-8 *(continued)*

```
        static AlphaTestEffect alphaEffect;

        public static AlphaTestEffect AlphaEffect(GraphicsDevice graphics)
        {
            if (alphaEffect == null)
            {
                alphaEffect = new AlphaTestEffect(graphics);
                alphaEffect.AlphaFunction = CompareFunction.Greater;
                alphaEffect.ReferenceAlpha = 0;
                Matrix projection
                    = Matrix.CreateOrthographicOffCenter(0,
                            graphics.PresentationParameters.BackBufferWidth,
                            graphics.PresentationParameters.BackBufferHeight,
                            0,
                            0,
                            1);
                alphaEffect.Projection = projection;
            }
            return alphaEffect;
        }

        public static DepthStencilState StencilMaskBefore
            = new DepthStencilState()
        {
            StencilEnable = true,
            ReferenceStencil = 1,
            StencilFunction = CompareFunction.Always,
            StencilPass = StencilOperation.Replace,
        };

        public static DepthStencilState StencilMaskAfter
            = new DepthStencilState()
        {
            StencilEnable = true,
            StencilFunction = CompareFunction.Equal,
            ReferenceStencil = 1,
            StencilPass = StencilOperation.Keep,
        };
    }
}
```

If you compile your project now, you should see no errors. With all the supporting classes created, you can now finally create the `SelectPuzzle` screen.

Creating the SelectPuzzle Screen

The `SelectPuzzle` screen loads a few standard puzzle images (just so that some preexist), so you need to add those to the `Images` folder of the `PicturePuzzleContent` project.

Add the `OceanSunset` and `Spring` images. You can download them from this book's companion website (www.wrox.com).

SelectPuzzleScreen.cs

Start by adding a new class to the Screens folder and naming it SelectPuzzleScreen. Modify the SelectPuzzleScreen class file to look like Listing 15-9.

LISTING 15-9: The SelectPuzzleScreen Class of Picture Puzzle

```
using System;
using System.Collections.Generic;

using Microsoft.Xna.Framework.Content;
using Microsoft.Xna.Framework.Graphics;
using Microsoft.Xna.Framework.Input.Touch;
using Microsoft.Xna.Framework;
using Microsoft.Xna.Framework.Media;

using XNAPhoneGame.Sprites;

namespace XNAPhoneGame.Screens
{
    class SelectPuzzleScreen : Screen
    {
        Background background;
        var puzzles = new Dictionary<string, Puzzle>();
        Puzzle selectedPuzzle;

        List<Button> buttons = new List<Button>();

        const string ActionSelectPuzzle = "Select";
        const string ActionPlayPuzzle = "Play";
        const string ActionScroll = "Scroll";

        public SelectPuzzleScreen(Game game,
                                  SpriteBatch batch,
                                  ChangeScreen changeScreen,
                                  GraphicsDevice graphics)
            : base(game,
                   batch,
                   changeScreen,
                   BackButtonScreenType.Other)
        {
            // Load the sample puzzles
            puzzles.Add("Spring",
                    new Puzzle("Spring",
                            "Images/Spring",
                            content,
                            graphics));

            puzzles.Add("Ocean Sunset",
                    new Puzzle("Ocean Sunset",
                            "Images/OceanSunset",
                            content,
                            graphics));
```

continues

LISTING 15-9 *(continued)*

```csharp
    // Load the puzzles that the user has saved
    MediaLibrary library = new MediaLibrary();

    foreach (Picture picture in library.Pictures)
    {
        if (picture.Name.Contains("-PicturePuzzle"))
        {
            string name
                = picture.Name.Replace("-PicturePuzzle.jpg", "");

            puzzles.Add(name,
                        new Puzzle(name,
                                   picture.GetImage(),
                                   content,
                                   graphics));
        }
    }

    background = new Background(content);

    int PositionY = 100;
    foreach (Puzzle puzzle in puzzles.Values)
    {
        buttons.Add(new Button(content,
                               puzzle.Name,
                               new Vector2(30, PositionY),
                               Color.SteelBlue));
        PositionY += 120;
    }
}

protected override void SetupInputs()
{
    input.AddTouchTapInput(ActionSelectPuzzle,
                           new Rectangle(0, 0, 480, 800),
                           false);
    input.AddTouchGestureInput(ActionPlayPuzzle,
                               GestureType.DoubleTap,
                               new Rectangle(0, 0, 480, 800));
    input.AddTouchGestureInput(ActionScroll,
                               GestureType.Flick,
                               new Rectangle(0, 0, 480, 800));
}

protected override void UpdateScreen(GameTime gameTime,
                                     DisplayOrientation screenOrientation)
{
    if (input.IsPressed(ActionScroll))
    {
        foreach (Button button in buttons)
        {
            Vector2 adjustment
```

```
                    = input.CurrentGestureDelta(ActionScroll);
                adjustment.X = 0;
                adjustment.Y = MathHelper.Clamp(adjustment.Y, -200, 200);
                button.ChangePosition(adjustment);
            }
        }
        else if (input.IsPressed(ActionPlayPuzzle))
        {
            foreach (Button button in buttons)
            {
                if (button.CollisionRectangle
                    .Contains(input
                        .CurrentTouchPoint("ActionSelectPuzzle")))
                {
                    selectedPuzzle = puzzles[button.DisplayText];
                    selectedPuzzle.PuzzleizeImage();
                    soundEffects.PlaySound("SoundEffects/Select");
                    GameInformation.CurrentPuzzle = selectedPuzzle;
                    changeScreenDelegate(ScreenState.MainGame);
                    break;
                }
            }
        }
        else if (input.IsPressed(ActionSelectPuzzle))
        {
            foreach (Button button in buttons)
            {
                if (button.CollisionRectangle.Contains
                    (input.CurrentTouchPoint("ActionSelectPuzzle")))
                {
                    selectedPuzzle = puzzles[button.DisplayText];
                    selectedPuzzle.PuzzleizeImage();
                    break;
                }
            }
        }
    }

    protected override void DrawScreen(SpriteBatch batch,
                                    DisplayOrientation
                                            screenOrientation)
    {
        background.Draw(batch);

        if (selectedPuzzle != null)
        {
            selectedPuzzle.Draw(batch);
        }

        foreach (Button button in buttons)
        {
            button.Draw(batch);
        }
    }
}
}
```

A compile error occurs in `GameInformation.CurrentPuzzle` because you haven't added that class yet. This is a common class that has information that many screens might need to access. It is time for you to add that class now.

Add a new class to the `Misc` folder, and name it `GameInformation`. Modify the `GameInformation` class file to look like Listing 15-10.

LISTING 15-10: The GameInformation Class

```
using XNAPhoneGame.Sprites;

namespace XNAPhoneGame
{
    class GameInformation
    {
        public static Puzzle CurrentPuzzle;
    }
}
```

There's not really a lot in this class, and that's a good sign that you're programming things fairly well. You don't want to create a ton of global variables.

With the `GameInformation` class created, the game again compiles, but you still must modify the `ScreenStateSwitchboard` class to create the file. You must also hook up the button on the `Title` screen to navigate to your new `SelectPuzzle` screen.

Modify the `CreateSelectPuzzleScreen()` method in the `ScreenStateSwitchboard` class file to look like Listing 15-11.

LISTING 15-11: The CreateSelectPuzzleScreen() Method of the ScreenStateSwitchboard Class

```
public Screen CreateSelectPuzzleScreen()
{
    return new SelectPuzzleScreen(game,
                                  batch,
                                  new Screen.ChangeScreen(ChangeScreen),
                                  game.GraphicsDevice);
}
```

Next, modify the `Update()` method in the `Title` class file to look like Listing 15-12.

LISTING 15-12: The Update() Method of the Title Class

```
protected override void UpdateScreen(GameTime gameTime,
                                     DisplayOrientation displayOrientation)
{
    if (input.IsPressed(ActionCreateNewPuzzle))
```

```
        {
            soundEffects.PlaySound("SoundEffects/Select");
            changeScreenDelegate(ScreenState.NewPuzzle);
        }
        else if (input.IsPressed(ActionPlayExistingPuzzle))
        {
            soundEffects.PlaySound("SoundEffects/Select");
            changeScreenDelegate(ScreenState.SelectPuzzle);
        }
        else if (input.IsPressed(ActionExit))
        {
            changeScreenDelegate(ScreenState.Exit);
        }
    }
}
```

That's it! Your new SelectPuzzle screen is now functional, as shown in Figure 15-4. You should now be able to navigate to it via the Title screen, and your phone should navigate there after you create a new puzzle image as well. Things are really starting to come along now!

If you select a puzzle to play, unfortunately your game will again crash. The CreateGameScreen() method in the ScreenStateSwitchboard class is currently returning a null value. You need to change that and make this game playable.

Creating the Playable Game Screen

The MainGame screen will use some new sound effects, so those need to be added first.

Download the Correct, Wrong, and Success.wav files from this book's companion website (www.wrox.com). Add them to the SoundEffects folder in the PicturePuzzleContent project.

MainGame.cs

Right-click the Screens folder and add the MainGame class to your project. Modify the MainGame class file to look like Listing 15-13.

FIGURE 15-4: The SelectPuzzle screen of Picture Puzzle

LISTING 15-13: The MainGame Class of Picture Puzzle

```
using Microsoft.Xna.Framework.Graphics;
using Microsoft.Xna.Framework.Input.Touch;
using Microsoft.Xna.Framework;
```

continues

LISTING 15-13 *(continued)*

```
using XNAPhoneGame.Sprites;

namespace XNAPhoneGame.Screens
{
    class MainGame : Screen
    {
        Puzzle puzzle;

        const string ActionDisplayMenu = "Menu";
        const string ActionSelectPuzzlePiece = "Select";
        const string ActionMovePuzzlePiece = "Move";
        const string ActionPlacePuzzlePiece = "Place";

        double scrambleCountdown;

        public MainGame(Game game,
                    SpriteBatch batch,
                    ChangeScreen changeScreen)
            : base(game,
                batch,
                changeScreen,
                BackButtonScreenType.Other)
        {
        }

        public override void Activate()
        {
            puzzle = GameInformation.CurrentPuzzle;
            scrambleCountdown = 2000;
        }

        protected override void SetupInputs()
        {
            input.AddTouchGestureInput(ActionDisplayMenu,
                                    GestureType.Hold,
                                    new Rectangle(0, 0, 480, 800));

            input.AddTouchGestureInput(ActionSelectPuzzlePiece,
                                    GestureType.Tap,
                                    new Rectangle(0, 0, 480, 800));

            input.AddTouchGestureInput(ActionMovePuzzlePiece,
                                    GestureType.FreeDrag,
                                    new Rectangle(0, 0, 480, 800));

            input.AddTouchGestureInput(ActionPlacePuzzlePiece,
                                    GestureType.DoubleTap,
                                    new Rectangle(0, 0, 480, 800));
        }

        protected override void UpdateScreen(GameTime gameTime,
```

```
                                    DisplayOrientation screenOrientation)
{
    if (scrambleCountdown > 0)
    {
        scrambleCountdown
            -= gameTime.ElapsedGameTime.TotalMilliseconds;
        if (scrambleCountdown <= 0)
        {
            puzzle.ScramblePuzzle();
        }
    }

    if (input.IsPressed(ActionDisplayMenu))
    {
        soundEffects.PlaySound("SoundEffects/Select");
        changeScreenDelegate(ScreenState.InGameMenu);
    }
    else if (input.IsPressed(ActionSelectPuzzlePiece)
        && scrambleCountdown <= 0)
    {
        puzzle.SelectPiece(input
            .CurrentGesturePosition(ActionSelectPuzzlePiece));
    }
    else if (input.IsPressed(ActionPlacePuzzlePiece)
        && scrambleCountdown <= 0)
    {
        if (puzzle.PlacePiece(input
            .CurrentGesturePosition(ActionPlacePuzzlePiece)))
        {
            if (puzzle.IsSolved())
            {
                soundEffects.PlaySound("SoundEffects/Success");
                changeScreenDelegate(ScreenState.PuzzleComplete);
            }
            else
            {
                soundEffects.PlaySound("SoundEffects/Correct");
            }
        }
        else
        {
            soundEffects.PlaySound("SoundEffects/Wrong");
        }
    }

    if (input.IsPressed(ActionMovePuzzlePiece)
        && scrambleCountdown <= 0)
    {
        Vector2 positionAdjustment
            = input.CurrentGestureDelta(ActionMovePuzzlePiece);
        positionAdjustment.X = MathHelper.Clamp(positionAdjustment.X,
                                                -100,
                                                100);
```

continues

LISTING 15-13 *(continued)*

```
                positionAdjustment.Y = MathHelper.Clamp(positionAdjustment.Y,
                                                        -100,
                                                        100);

                puzzle.MovePiece(positionAdjustment);
            }
        }

        protected override void DrawScreen(SpriteBatch batch,
                                            DisplayOrientation screenOrientation)
        {
            puzzle.Draw(batch);
        }
    }
}
```

Next, you need to go to the `ScreenStateSwitchboard` class and modify the `CreateMainGameScreen()` method to match Listing 15-14.

LISTING 15-14: The CreateMainGameScreen() Method of ScreenStateSwitchboard

```
public Screen CreateMainGameScreen()
{
    return new MainGame(game, batch, new Screen.ChangeScreen(ChangeScreen));
}
```

Run the game. You can now select and assemble a puzzle, as shown in Figure 15-5.

Making the InGameMenu Screen

The game still has two screens to go. If you press and hold on the game screen, you'll see that the in-game menu hasn't been styled and modified to match your Picture Puzzle game. And the completed message screen hasn't been created yet. So, if you finish a puzzle, your game again crashes.

InGameMenu.cs

Open the existing `InGameMenu` class file that you created when you created the base template, and modify it to look like Listing 15-15.

FIGURE 15-5: Picture Puzzle in action

LISTING 15-15: The InGameMenu Class of Picture Puzzle

```
using Microsoft.Xna.Framework;
using Microsoft.Xna.Framework.Content;
using Microsoft.Xna.Framework.Graphics;
using Microsoft.Xna.Framework.Input.Touch;

using XNAPhoneGame.Sprites;

namespace XNAPhoneGame.Screens
{
    class InGameMenu : Screen
    {
        Background backgroundSprite;

        Button resumeButton;
        Button restartButton;
        Button mainMenuButton;
        Button exitButton;
```

continues

LISTING 15-15 *(continued)*

```
        const string ActionResumePlaying = "Resume";
        const string ActionRestartPuzzle = "Restart";
        const string ActionMainMenu = "MainMenu";
        const string ActionExit = "Exit";

        public InGameMenu(Game game,
                         SpriteBatch batch,
                         ChangeScreen changeScreen)
            : base(game,
                   batch,
                   changeScreen,
                   BackButtonScreenType.InGameMenu)
        {
        }

        protected override void SetupInputs()
        {
            input.AddTouchGestureInput(ActionResumePlaying,
                                      GestureType.Tap,
                                      resumeButton.TouchArea);
            input.AddTouchGestureInput(ActionRestartPuzzle,
                                      GestureType.Tap,
                                      restartButton.TouchArea);

            input.AddTouchGestureInput(ActionMainMenu,
                                      GestureType.Tap,
                                      mainMenuButton.TouchArea);

            input.AddTouchGestureInput(ActionExit,
                                      GestureType.Tap,
                                      exitButton.TouchArea);
        }

        protected override void LoadScreenContent(ContentManager content)
        {
            backgroundSprite = new Background(content);

            resumeButton = new Button(content,
                                     "Resume",
                                     new Vector2(30, 200),
                                     Color.SteelBlue);

            restartButton = new Button(content,
                                      "Restart",
                                      new Vector2(30, 320),
                                      Color.SteelBlue);

            mainMenuButton = new Button(content,
                                       "Main Menu",
                                       new Vector2(30, 440),
```

```
                                          Color.SteelBlue);

            exitButton = new Button(content,
                                    "Exit",
                                    new Vector2(30, 560),
                                    Color.SteelBlue);
        }

        protected override void UpdateScreen(GameTime gameTime,
                                    DisplayOrientation displayOrientation)
        {
            if (input.IsPressed(ActionResumePlaying))
            {
                soundEffects.PlaySound("SoundEffects/Select");
                changeScreenDelegate(ScreenState.MainGame);
            }
            else if (input.IsPressed(ActionRestartPuzzle))
            {
                soundEffects.PlaySound("SoundEffects/Select");
                changeScreenDelegate(ScreenState.MainGame);
            }
            else if (input.IsPressed(ActionMainMenu))
            {
                soundEffects.PlaySound("SoundEffects/Select");
                changeScreenDelegate(ScreenState.Title);
            }
            else if (input.IsPressed(ActionExit))
            {
                changeScreenDelegate(ScreenState.Exit);
            }
        }

        protected override void DrawScreen(SpriteBatch batch,
                                    DisplayOrientation screenOrientation)
        {
            backgroundSprite.Draw(batch);

            resumeButton.Draw(batch);
            restartButton.Draw(batch);
            mainMenuButton.Draw(batch);
            exitButton.Draw(batch);
        }
    }
}
```

Now, run the game and check out your new in-game menu (see Figure 15-6). You access it by performing a `Hold` gesture on the main game screen.

Creating the PuzzleComplete Screen

The `PuzzleComplete` screen is just a generic `Message` screen letting the player know he or she completed the puzzle and offering congratulations.

FIGURE 15-6: The in-game menu of Picture Puzzle

Message.cs

Right-click the Screens folder and add a new Message class. Modify the Message class file to look like Listing 15-16.

LISTING 15-16: The Message Class of Picture Puzzle

```
using Microsoft.Xna.Framework;
using Microsoft.Xna.Framework.Graphics;
using Microsoft.Xna.Framework.Content;
using Microsoft.Xna.Framework.Input.Touch;

using XNAPhoneGame.Sprites;
using XNAPhoneGame.Texts;

namespace XNAPhoneGame.Screens
{
    class Message : Screen
    {
        string displayText;
        Text message;
        Button mainMenuButton;
        Button exitButton;

        const string ActionMainMenu = "Main";
```

```csharp
            const string ActionExit = "Exit";

        public Message(string message,
                       Game game,
                       SpriteBatch batch,
                       ChangeScreen changeScreen)
            : base(game,
                   batch,
                   changeScreen,
                   BackButtonScreenType.First)
        {
            this.displayText = message;
        }

        protected override void SetupInputs()
        {
            input.AddTouchGestureInput(ActionMainMenu,
                                      GestureType.Tap,
                                      mainMenuButton.CollisionRectangle);

            input.AddTouchGestureInput(ActionExit,
                                      GestureType.Tap,
                                      exitButton.CollisionRectangle);
        }

        protected override void LoadScreenContent(ContentManager content)
        {
            mainMenuButton = new Button(content,
                                        "Main Menu",
                                        new Vector2(30, 540),
                                        Color.SteelBlue);

            exitButton = new Button(content,
                                    "Exit",
                                    new Vector2(30, 650),
                                    Color.SteelBlue);

            message = new Text(font,
                               displayText,
                               new Vector2(0, 0),
                               Color.White,
                               Text.Alignment.None,
                               new Rectangle(0, 0, 480, 500));
        }

        protected override void UpdateScreen(GameTime gameTime,
                                             DisplayOrientation displayOrientation)
        {
            if (input.IsPressed(ActionMainMenu))
            {
                soundEffects.PlaySound("SoundEffects/Select");
                changeScreenDelegate(ScreenState.Title);
            }
```

continues

LISTING 15-16 *(continued)*

```
            else if (input.IsPressed(ActionExit))
            {
                changeScreenDelegate(ScreenState.Exit);
            }
        }

        protected override void DrawScreen(SpriteBatch batch,
                                DisplayOrientation displayOrientation)
        {
            message.Draw(batch);
            mainMenuButton.Draw(batch);
            exitButton.Draw(batch);
        }
    }
}
```

Next, you must modify the `ScreenStateSwitchboard` class file to navigate to that screen. Now, modify the `CreatePuzzleCompleteScreen()` method to look like Listing 15-17.

LISTING 15-17: The CreatePuzzleCompleteScreen() Method of the ScreenStateSwitchboard Class

```
public Screen CreatePuzzleCompleteScreen()
{
    return new Message("   Congratulations! \n You completed \n the puzzle!",
                    game,
                    batch,
                    new Screen.ChangeScreen(ChangeScreen));
}
```

This creates a new `Message` screen and gives it the message that should be displayed. Now when you complete a puzzle, you receive a congratulatory message for your efforts.

With that, you're done. Picture Puzzle is playable and complete, and you've created another Windows Phone 7 game! Congratulations!

ENHANCING YOUR GAME

So, what things can you think of that should be enhanced?

A few things you did when you created Drive & Dodge probably would be useful to add to Picture Puzzle as well. Some soothing background music might be nice.

Also, it's important to think about other key features that might be missing. You should get those thoughts percolating for when you make a game of your own.

What happens if the player is putting together a puzzle and the phone rings? Is there a way to save the state the puzzle is in? What about when the player resumes the game? Can you make it happen seamlessly?

Picture Puzzle was set up to have more types of puzzle stencils available. Try creating your own puzzle shapes, and see if you can figure out how to add them. Can you add the stencils so that the puzzle pieces can be rotated?

It's important to make sure when you're designing any game for any platform that you think through these types of things, and take the time to add polish.

Most game play can be written quickly, but it takes more than game play to make a successful game. The entire experience must be fun from start to finish. Always keep that in mind and, most of all, make games that you want to play, and have fun doing so!

SUMMARY

In this chapter you built a complete game from scratch. You learned a number of handy new techniques, including how to use the camera in your game. You also learned some interesting ways to enhance the sample game, and ideas for further development.

In Chapter 16, you will learn how to implement a trial mode and publish your games to the Marketplace.

16

Where Do You Go from Here?

WHAT'S IN THIS CHAPTER?

- Developing a trial mode for your game
- Letting your players invite their friends to buy your game
- Understanding the publishing process
- Submitting your game to the Windows Phone 7 Marketplace
- Where to find help if you need it

You're almost done. Congratulations on making it this far! You've made a few games, and now you're ready to learn about creating a compelling trial-mode experience and getting your game into the Windows Phone Marketplace.

TRIAL MODE

Imagine this scenario:

- You've made "The Greatest Game Ever Created" and have uploaded it to the Marketplace, complete with a few screenshots and a game-play video, but it's not selling like you thought it would.
- You've tried a word-of-mouth marketing campaign, purchased Facebook ads, and even got a good review in your favorite gaming magazine, but you aren't getting the sales you hoped for.
- Your buddy has published a game that's similar to yours. He hasn't done much advertising, but his sales are through the roof. Why? Your buddy's game has a trial mode.

Understanding Trial Mode

The preceding example may be a bit contrived, but it's not that far off the mark. Industry studies have shown that having a well-crafted trial mode can significantly increase sales.

Following are a few important things you need to know and understand about trial mode:

- Trial mode is not a separate download of your game, but rather the same executable file running with the isTrialMode flag set.
- Unlike Xbox Live Indie Games, trial mode is not time-limited. You can make trial mode last as long as you like, limiting it by functionality (such as the number of levels) rather than time.
- Having a trial mode is not required by the Windows Phone Marketplace. But if you have one, it must "reasonably represent" the game play and quality of your game.
- Do not rely solely on a time-limited trial mode to sell your game. If you don't tailor the trial experience to show off the best parts of your game, your players could waste precious time sitting through your opening cinematics and instruction screens without getting enough time to play the game.
- Networking and Xbox Live are disabled in trial mode, so don't make these options available to your players. Of course, this can be a very strong incentive for purchasing your game.
- Give your players a compelling reason to purchase the full version of your game, such as by limiting the number of levels available in the trial, or restricting other game play options (such as available character types, or game modes beyond single player).

Detecting Trial Mode

Since your customers will not be downloading a separate executable for the trial-mode version of your game, you must know how to detect which state the game is in.

The Microsoft.Xna.Framework.GamerServices.Guide class contains an interesting mix of methods and properties. They are useful for dealing with the social aspects of networked gaming (such as Friend Requests, Game Invites, and Party Sessions), along with the onscreen keyboard and trial-mode functionality.

The three items of interest right now are ShowMarketplace(), SimulateTrialMode(), and the read-only IsTrialMode().

ShowMarketplace()

This method offers to let the user purchase the full version of your game, but only if Guide .IsTrialMode() evaluates to true; otherwise, nothing happens. You are required to pass in a PlayerIndex value, which is always PlayerIndex.One in Windows Phone games.

A typical call to the ShowMarketplace() method looks like this:

```
if (Guide.IsTrialMode)
{
    Guide.ShowMarketplace(PlayerIndex.One);
}
```

Figure 16-1 shows what the call to ShowMarketplace() produces while your game is still in development.

FIGURE 16-1: The Test Purchase screen displayed by calling the ShowMarketplace() method

SimulateTrialMode()

To properly develop and test your game's trial mode, you need a way to force that status in your development environment. Use the SimulateTrialMode() property in your game while developing your trial mode. Leaving this turned on when submitting your game to the Windows Phone Marketplace can result in delays or rejection, because it can possibly render parts of your game untestable. So be sure you turn it off first!

 When developing for Xbox Live Indie Games, leaving SimulateTrialMode() *turned on when submitting your game for peer review is a valid fail reason. This can keep your game from being published (until it is corrected).*

To set your game to run in trial mode (for development purposes), add the following line to your Game1() constructor:

```
Guide.SimulateTrialMode = true;
```

Doing this, combined with IsTrialMode(), will let you develop a trial mode to entice your gaming audience to purchase the full version.

IsTrialMode()

Anywhere in your game that you draw a distinction between trial mode and full game play, you will want to check whether you are running in trial mode. Usually, this occurs in your Update() method (or in any code called by the Update() method).

To add a check for IsTrialMode(), use the following:

```
if (Guide.IsTrialMode)
{
```

```
        // Do Stuff Differently For Trial Mode
    }
    else
    {
        // Do Stuff Normally
    }
```

This is an extremely simple example and is fine in theory (and to show basic syntax). But in practice you would never do this in your game, because a call to `Guide.IsTrialMode()` can actually take 60 milliseconds (or more) to resolve. If you will be checking trial state frequently, you should cache the value and check against that, making calls to `Guide.IsTrialMode()` only occasionally.

It is a known issue that `IsTrialMode()` generates a false positive if checked while a game first starts. So, you should either check it again after the game has started, or introduce a delay before checking it for the first time. In addition to checking the trial state after your game has started, you should check it whenever your game resumes from being suspended or returns from having the Guide visible (such as when purchasing your game).

To see this in practice, look at Listing 16-1.

 If you want to work along with this sample, be sure to download the `PleaseBuyMe` *sample from this book's companion website (*www.wrox.com*).*

LISTING 16-1: The Game1 Class from the PleaseBuyMe Sample

```
using System;
using Microsoft.Xna.Framework;
using Microsoft.Xna.Framework.Content;
using Microsoft.Xna.Framework.GamerServices;
using Microsoft.Xna.Framework.Graphics;
using Microsoft.Xna.Framework.Input;
using Microsoft.Xna.Framework.Input.Touch;

namespace PleaseBuyMe
{
    public class Game1 : Microsoft.Xna.Framework.Game
    {
        GraphicsDeviceManager graphics;
        SpriteBatch spriteBatch;

        SpriteFont font;
        double checkTrialModeDelay = 1000.0;
        bool isTrialMode = true;

        public Game1()
        {
            graphics = new GraphicsDeviceManager(this);
            Content.RootDirectory = "Content";
```

```csharp
        // Frame rate is 30 fps by default for Windows Phone.
        TargetElapsedTime = TimeSpan.FromTicks(333333);

        Guide.SimulateTrialMode = true;
    }

    protected override void Initialize()
    {
        // TODO: Add your initialization logic here
        TouchPanel.EnabledGestures = GestureType.DoubleTap
                            | GestureType.Hold;

        base.Initialize();
    }

    protected override void LoadContent()
    {
        // Create a new SpriteBatch, which can be used to draw textures.
        spriteBatch = new SpriteBatch(GraphicsDevice);

        // TODO: use this.Content to load your game content here
        font = Content.Load<SpriteFont>("SpriteFont1");
    }

    protected override void UnloadContent()
    {
        // TODO: Unload any non ContentManager content here
    }

    protected override void Update(GameTime gameTime)
    {
        // Allows the game to exit
        if (GamePad.GetState(PlayerIndex.One).Buttons.Back
            == ButtonState.Pressed)
            this.Exit();

        // TODO: Add your update logic here

        // There's a chance that trial mode might be falsely
        // reported as the game first starts up so it's a good
        // idea to check it again shortly after the game has
        // started.
        if (isTrialMode && checkTrialModeDelay > 0)
        {
            checkTrialModeDelay -=
                gameTime.ElapsedGameTime.TotalMilliseconds;

            if (checkTrialModeDelay < 0)
            {
                isTrialMode = Guide.IsTrialMode;
            }
        }

        // Check to see if the user wants to buy the game
```

continues

LISTING 16-1 *(continued)*

```
            while (TouchPanel.IsGestureAvailable)
            {
                // read the next gesture from the queue
                GestureSample gesture = TouchPanel.ReadGesture();

                if (isTrialMode && gesture.GestureType
                    == GestureType.DoubleTap && !Guide.IsVisible)
                {
                    Guide.ShowMarketplace(PlayerIndex.One);
                    break;
                }
                else if (gesture.GestureType == GestureType.Hold)
                {
                    SendPurchaseMessage();
                }
            }

            base.Update(gameTime);
        }

        // Documentation on building the "buy this game" link
        // http://msdn.microsoft.com/en-us/library/ff967553%28VS.92%29.aspx
        private void SendPurchaseMessage()
        {
            Microsoft.Phone.Tasks.SmsComposeTask task
                = new Microsoft.Phone.Tasks.SmsComposeTask();

            task.To = "MyFriend";

            // There isn't any way to get the phoneAppID programmatically
            // so use this sample URL that doesn't actually point to a game
            task.Body = "Please buy this awesome game so we can play together!
                http://redirect.zune.net/redirect?type=phoneApp&id=cbd00900-
                0600-11db-89ca-0019b92a3933&source=MyGame";

            task.Show();
        }

        protected override void OnActivated(object sender, EventArgs args)
        {
            if (isTrialMode)
            {
                isTrialMode = Guide.IsTrialMode;
                checkTrialModeDelay = 1000.0f;
            }
        }

        protected override void Draw(GameTime gameTime)
        {
            GraphicsDevice.Clear(Color.CornflowerBlue);

            // TODO: Add your drawing code here
```

```
            spriteBatch.Begin();
            if (isTrialMode)
            {
                spriteBatch.DrawString(font,
                                "Please Buy Me!",
                                new Vector2(100, 200),
                                Color.White);
            }
            else
            {
                spriteBatch.DrawString(font,
                                "Thanks for buying me!",
                                new Vector2(100, 200),
                                Color.White);
            }
            spriteBatch.End();

            base.Draw(gameTime);
        }
    }
}
```

A fair amount of activity is going on in this listing, so let's go through the whole thing together, skipping the stuff that shows up in every project.

The first thing you should notice is the addition of some class-level variables. The first variable, *checkTrialModeDelay*, stores a value of 1,000 milliseconds (ms); the second variable, *isTrialMode*, stores the cached result of checking the Guide.IsTrialMode() property.

Next, in the Game1() class constructor, you turn on trial mode by setting Guide.SimulateTrialMode to true. You *will* comment out this line before submitting to the Windows Phone Marketplace, right? Right!

In the Initialize() method, you are setting the EnabledGestures property of the TouchPanel class to read the DoubleTap and Hold gestures.

For more on gestures, refer back to Chapter 4.

Skip over the LoadContent() and UnloadContent() methods, because they contain nothing new. You've seen how to load a SpriteFont a few dozen times by now, so there's no point boring you with it any further.

The Update() method contains two important blocks of code. The first one you will look at is responsible for setting the cache variable *isTrialMode* to contain the actual trial state, after the initial delay of 1,000 ms to prevent any false positives. The second important block of code responds to the gestures you added to the EnabledGestures collection.

If you perform a DoubleTap gesture while the game is running in trial mode, it calls the ShowMarketplace() method, which simulates purchasing the full version of your game (effectively turning off trial mode). You saw this screen in Figure 16-1. If you perform a `Hold` gesture, the game sends a "share with a friend" message. This topic hasn't been discussed yet, so let's finish looking at the rest of the code and then dig into that.

You should always check your trial state whenever your game returns from a suspended state. Your game may have been suspended because of an incoming phone call, or it could have been suspended because the player was actually buying your game. In the `OnActivated()` method, check the locally cached trial state first. Then, if you're in trial mode, do an actual call to `Guide.IsTrialMode()` to see if the trial state changed while the game was in a deactivated state.

In the `Draw()` method, you are checking the local *isTrialMode* again. You display a "nag" screen if the game is in a trial state or a "thank you" screen if you are no longer in trial mode.

Sharing with a Friend

The last remaining code to look at from Listing 16-1 is the `SendPurchaseMessage()` method.

Two things are going on here. The first is setting up the `SmsComposeTask`, which you've seen before, in Chapter 14. You will use this to send a direct link to the Windows Phone Marketplace page for your game, along with a brief message encouraging users to buy it.

The link to the game page is the more interesting piece of the puzzle. The link contains three parameters:

➤ The required `type` parameter must contain the string `"phoneApp"`, which indicates a phone application (and makes you wonder why it is parameterized at all).

➤ The optional `source` parameter is used only for reporting and can contain any value.

➤ The required `id` parameter contains the ID assigned to your game by the Windows Phone Marketplace once you submit it.

Read that last sentence again. Right now you should be wondering just how you are supposed to code the ID for your game if you don't receive it until you get through the submission service. Unfortunately, only two real options are possible:

➤ The first option is that you wait and add "tell a friend" capabilities to your first update as soon as you have the ID in hand. There's nothing inherently wrong with doing it this way, unless you really want that capability to be present from version 1 of your game.

➤ The second option is to have your game call an external service that you create and host (you learned about this in Chapter 11) to fetch your game ID value. Your game will use this value to build the URL pointing to your page. This way, the "tell a friend" feature is ready with your very first release. Just be sure to update the service as soon as you get the ID, or it won't work as expected.

Running the Sample

If you downloaded the code from this book's companion website (www.wrox.com), you're all set. Just open the `PleaseBuyMe` sample and press F5. If you typed the code from Listing 16-1, be sure to add a `SpriteFont`, and you should be ready to go.

After the sample starts, you see the "nag" screen, as shown in Figure 16-2.

FIGURE 16-2: The "nag" screen of the PleaseBuyMe sample

Double-tap the screen to get the simulated Marketplace screen (which you saw in Figure 16-1), and then tap the yes button to "purchase" the game.

At this point, the Marketplace screen goes away, and control returns to your game. This means that the `OnActivated()` method fires, checking your trial state. Once control returns to your game, you see the "thank you" screen shown in Figure 16-3, indicating that your purchase is complete.

FIGURE 16-3: The "thank you" screen of the PleaseBuyMe sample

You can also perform a `Hold` gesture to see the "tell a friend" text before it is sent.

PINNING YOUR GAME TILE TO THE START AREA

The Start area on Windows Phone 7 is what you see whenever you unlock your phone or press the Start button. There's not much there on the Emulator (typically, just an Internet Explorer icon). But on an actual device, it's a lot like your computer's desktop, in the sense that it gives you quick and easy access to any programs you have pinned there, along with the various hubs discussed in Chapter 1.

Pinning your game (or any application) to the Start screen is easy to do and definitely increases your game's visibility and accessibility.

If you use Tile notifications, having your game on the Start screen means those notifications will be seen (and possibly acted upon) sooner.

When you publish your game to a device or the Emulator, it is placed in the Games hub. Unfortunately, the Emulator doesn't display the Games hub, so you can't access the Start tile for your game unless you edit the `WMAppManifest.xml` file and change the `Genre` attribute of the `App` node from `Apps.Games` to `Apps.Apps`. (Hint: It's near the top of the file.)

After you do that, you can push your game to a device or the Emulator, and it shows up in the Programs list. Figure 16-4 shows the Programs list on the Windows Phone Emulator. If you have an actual device, the list is much longer.

 If you can't find the Programs screen, don't worry. Just tap the white arrow inside the circle in the top-left corner of the Start screen on your phone (or the Emulator).

To pin your game to the Start screen, find it in the Programs list and perform a `Hold` gesture. Remember that one from Chapter 4? Just tap the name of the game and keep your finger there. After about a second, a small menu pops up under your game, with options to "pin to start" and "uninstall," as shown in Figure 16-5.

FIGURE 16-4: The Programs list on the Windows Phone Emulator

FIGURE 16-5: The Programs list with the options menu displayed

Tap the "pin to start" option. Your game (or application) displays a 173-by-173-pixel tile on the Start screen, with plenty of room for tile notifications, as shown in Figure 16-6.

To remove a tile from the Start screen, do basically the same thing. Tap and hold your finger on the tile you want to remove; you see an icon resembling a pushpin with a circle and slash (see Figure 16-7). Tap that icon to remove the tile from the Start screen.

FIGURE 16-6: The Emulator Start screen with tiles added

FIGURE 16-7: Removing a tile from the Start screen

That's all there is to it. Now you can pin your games and applications to the Start menu, along with anything else listed in the Programs menu.

PUBLISHING

Several steps are involved with selling your game in the Windows Phone Marketplace. Much like with Apple's App Store, you must submit your game or application to Microsoft for certification before it can be sold in the Marketplace.

Requirements

Before submitting to the Marketplace, you should read through the Windows Phone 7 Application Certification Requirements document. You can download a copy of this in PDF form from the Microsoft App Hub site at http://create.msdn.com. This document contains the requirements you need to comply with for your game to pass certification and make it to the Marketplace.

The requirements document lists the four pillars of the certification program:

1. Applications are reliable.
2. Applications make efficient use of resources.
3. Applications do not interfere with the phone functionality.
4. Applications are free of malicious software.

Looking at each of these in order, Microsoft is basically asking that you write games that do not crash, do not waste battery life, do not ignore incoming calls, and do not have malware or viruses.

Submission

Before you can submit your game to the Marketplace, you need an account on the Microsoft App Hub site.

> *The previously mentioned requirements document occasionally refers to the Windows Phone Developer Portal. But these are just two names for the same thing.*

Currently, an account costs $99 per year and grants the following:

- Submitting unlimited paid games or applications (written in Silverlight or XNA) to the Windows Phone Marketplace.
- Submitting up to five free games or applications (written in Silverlight or XNA) to the Windows Phone Marketplace. You may submit another five for a small fee.
- Submitting up to five Xbox 360 games (written in XNA) to Xbox Live Indie Games.
- Access to premium content on the MSDN App Hub (formerly the XNA Creators Club).

Registering and paying for an account is as simple as filling in a form, so we won't go into details here. After you click Submit and pay your fee, the identity-verification process can take anywhere from a couple of days to a couple of weeks, so be patient. Eventually, you will get an e-mail from Microsoft letting you know that your account has been created and you're ready to roll.

> *The end result of the identity-verification process, aside from your being able to publish, is that you now have an Authenticode certificate that will be used to sign your game (or application) so that it can be installed and run on Windows Phones.*

Assuming that you were busy putting the finishing touches on your game while waiting on the background verification to complete, you are now ready to submit your game.

Unlike the Xbox Live Indie Games scene, which requires play test and peer review before being published, you submit your Windows Phone game directly to Microsoft for certification. The process works like this:

1. Sign in to the App Hub at http://create.msdn.com.
2. Create a new submission by clicking the Submit for Windows Phone button, as shown in Figure 16-8.

FIGURE 16-8: The App Hub main page

3. Fill in the requested information, as shown in Figure 16-9, and upload the game .xap file. If you have any special instructions for testers, be sure to include them on this screen as well. (The tester notes field shows up only after you add your .xap file.)

> *The .xap file can be found in the* bin\release *folder beneath your main game project folder. Be sure to do a release build before submitting your game to the Marketplace.*

4. Fill in the description information for your game, including selecting the correct subcategory of game from the following list:
   - Puzzle & Trivia
   - Action & Adventure

- Card & Casino
- Board & Classic
- Sports & Racing
- Strategy
- Family
- Music
- Shooter
- Xbox Companion

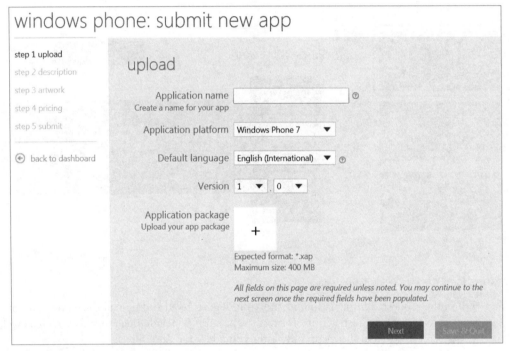

FIGURE 16-9: The App Hub upload page

5. If you have any rating certificates, you upload them at this point.
6. Upload the following graphics for your game:

- *Large mobile app icon* — This is the 173-by-173-pixel icon that shows up when your game is pinned to the Start screen.
- *Small mobile app icon* — This 99-by-99-pixel icon is displayed in the Programs list on the phone (or the Emulator).
- *Large PC app icon* — This 200-by-200-pixel icon is displayed in the Marketplace entry for your game.

- *Background art* — This 1422-by-800-pixel wallpaper is used as a background for your game's Marketplace entry.
- *Screenshots* — You can submit up to eight screenshots of your game, at a resolution of 480 by 800 pixels each.

7. Select what countries your game will be distributed to and how much you want to charge.
8. After your .xap upload has been validated (it takes a couple of minutes, but it happens behind the scenes while you are on Steps 5 through 7), you can choose to publish immediately after passing certification or to wait to publish.
9. The XAP file is deployed to a phone for manual and automated certification testing.
10. If your game passes certification testing, it is eligible for publication to the Windows Phone Marketplace. (If it fails, you get a failure report and your game is not published.)

Code Signing

Code signing happens automatically after your game passes the certification process. The game is signed with the Authenticode certificate that was created for you when you registered with the Marketplace (and waited for the identity verification).

> *All games or applications must be signed with the Authenticode certificate before they can be installed and run on any commercially available (that is, general public) Windows Phone.*

WHERE TO GET HELP

If you get stuck, you have options. Whether this happens during the development process or when you're trying to publish your game, don't worry: the XNA community is very active, and a number of resources are available.

Forums

This is one of the best places to turn when you have questions. Pretty much every part of the Windows Phone game development process is covered, from Design to Coding to Art and Sound to Publishing Your Game. The XNA Community forums are located at http://forums.create.msdn.com/forums/. They are staffed by Microsoft employees, XNA and Windows Phone MVPs, professional and amateur game developers, students and hobbyists, and the occasional artist.

A tremendous amount of knowledge is available in the forums, but for best results you should do a little legwork first. Before you post, search for keywords that match your question. There's a good chance that if you have run into a problem, others have as well — and your question may already have been answered.

If you search but can't find an answer, think about your problem, and try to provide as much information as possible in your post. If you are trying to troubleshoot a piece of code, include the code (or a link to it) in your post. The more information you can provide up front, the faster and more accurate your answer will be.

Blogs

A number of informative blogs focus on a variety of topics such as Windows Phone 7, XNA game development, C#, and more. Some blogs are worth bookmarking for repeat visits; the rest of the time, you may run into them while searching for information on a particular topic.

Here are a few blogs that the authors of this book consider especially reliable or interesting:

- *Shawn Hargreaves* (http://blogs.msdn.com/b/shawnhar/) is on the XNA team at Microsoft and frequently blogs technical information about the XNA Framework and Windows Phone 7.
- *Michael Klucher* (http://klucher.com) works with the XNA and Windows Phone teams. His blog contains much useful information.
- *Nick Gravelyn* (http://blogs.msdn.com/b/nicgrave/) is also on the XNA team at Microsoft and is an active participant in the XNA community.
- *Catalin's XNA Blog* (www.catalinzima.com) is an excellent resource full of examples and code from Microsoft MVP Catalin Zima.
- *Sgt. Conker* (www.sgtconker.com) is an interesting mix of community news, technical articles, and contests.

Search

When all else fails, try your favorite search engine.

For phone features, if you can't figure out how to do something in XNA, one helpful tip is to try searching for how to do it in Silverlight. In many cases, the code won't be all that different.

SUMMARY

Having a compelling trial mode is a critical part of any game if you want to convert downloads into sales. Be careful not to check trial state too often, or it can affect your game's performance.

Incorporate the ability for your users to "tell a friend," and send a link to the Marketplace page to increase word-of-mouth sales of your game.

Pinning your game to the Start area is quick and easy and makes your game much more visible.

To submit your game to the Windows Phone Marketplace, you need an App Hub account that lets you submit five free and unlimited paid games or applications. Be sure to read the Windows Phone 7 Application Certification Requirements document available from http://create.msdn.com. When your game passes certification, it is automatically signed with the Authenticode certificate that was generated for you as a result of the identity-verification process.

INDEX

3D models
    3DSampleContent project. *See*
        3DSampleContent project
    adding to Poker Dice project, 404–414
    creating, 247–251
    texturing in Blender, 254–257
3DSampleContent project
    3D animations, creating, 258–264
    adding models to, 251
    displaying models onscreen, 251–253
    Draw() method of Game1 class, 253
    LittleGuy.cs in 3DSample project, 251–252
    LoadContent() method of Game1 class, 253
    performing 3D transformations, 257–258
    rotating 3D objects, 257–258
    Update() method of Game1 class, 258
    Update() method of LittleGuy class, 257

A

accelerometer
    AccelerometerReadingChanged() method of the Game1 class (listing), 35
    AccelerometerSample project, 34–37
    class, 32–33
    defined, 4
AcceptGameRequest() method of MatchMakerService class (listing), 334
AcceptRequest() method of Gamer class (listing), 331
Action Editor (Blender), 262–263
Action object, passing, 78
Actions.cs class (listing), 85–86
Activate() method
    of GameOver class (listing), 234
    of MainGame class (listing), 232
    use of, 131, 151
AddGamepadInput() method, 65
AddInputs() method, 87–89
AddKeyboardInput() method, 65
addresses
    resolving asynchronously, 431–432
    resolving synchronously, 428–431
AddScore() method (listing), 314–315
AddTouchGesture() method, 66

AddTouchSlideInput() method, 66, 70
AddTouchTapInput() method, 65
aGPS, 4
Albums property, 131
All() property (Microphone class), 139
AlphaTestEffect class (XNA 4.0), 267
ambient light sensor, 5
animations
    in Blender, 262–263
    creating 3D, 258–264
Anonymous Live ID (ANID), 319
APIs, removal of, 266
App Hub, 509
Application Certification Requirements document, 512
Application Deployment tool, 445–446
ArgumentOutOfRangeException, 141
armatures (Blender), 259
Artists property, 131
asynchronous calls, 309
asynchronously resolving addresses, 431–432
audio
    Audio API (XNA Game Studio 4.0), 127
    Microphone class, 138–143
    playing music with MediaPlayer. *See* MediaPlayer, playing music with
    recording, 138
    saving/retrieving captured, 143–145
    SoundEffect class, 133–137
    XACT 3.0, 137–138
Authenticode certificates, 508, 511
Auto Link button (Blender), 256
automatic rotation, 26–29
AvailableGames() method of MatchMakerService class (listing), 333–334

B

Back button
    behavior (DriveAndDodge), 237
    defined, 6
    detecting, 115
    overriding, 115–116
backbuffer resolution, 26
background music, 129–131
BackgroundColor (screens), 110
Background.cs class (DriveAndDodge), 159–162

base game template – code listings

base game template, creating. *See* `XNAPhoneGame` template project
baseline pose, 263
`base.Update()` method, 27
`BasicEffect` class (XNA 4.0), 267
batch object, 209
battery power consumption, 426
bilinear filtering, 26
bin file (`WM70C1.bin`), 23
Bing Search screen, 7
Blender
    adding `FBX` export script to, 263–264
    animation in, 262–263
    downloading/installing, 248
    texturing 3D model in, 254–257
blogs, 512
Boolean flags, tracking game state with, 94–97
btn event handlers (listings), 328
`btn()` methods of `Game1` class (listing), 343
`BufferDuration` property (Microphone class), 141
`BufferIsReady()` method of `Game1` class (listing), 142
`Button.cs` class
    DriveAndDodge, 169–173
    listing, 170–172
    Poker Dice project, 385–386
`Buttons` enumeration (listing), 60–61
`ButtonState` enumeration, 115

C

callback delegates, 54
camera views, changing, 249
`camera_Completed()` method of `Game1` class (listing), 444
`CameraCaptureTask` class, 443–445
`CannotLoadException`, 129
capacitive-touch screens, 3–4
`Car.cs` class (listing), 210–212
`caResolver_ResolveAddressCompleted()` method, 432
`CenterText()` method, 167
`ChangeScreen()` method of `ScreenStateSwitchboard` class (listing), 205–206
`ChangeScreen` object, 151
`ChangeText()` method, 167
`channel_ChannelUriUpdated()` method (listing), 274, 281, 290, 322
`channel_HttpNotificationReceived()` method of `Game1` class (listing), 275
`channel_ShellToastNotificationReceived()` method (listing), 285, 322
chassis design, 2
`CivicAddress` class, 427
`CivicAddressResolver` class, 427–432
`client()` methods of `Game1` class (listing), 342
Clingerman, George, 323
code listings
    accelerometer class definition, 32–33

`AccelerometerReadingChanged()` method of `Game1` class, 35
`AccelerometerReadingEventArgs` class definition, 33
`AcceptGameRequest()` method of `MatchMakerService` class, 334
`AcceptRequest()` method of `Gamer` class, 331
`Actions` class, 86
`Activate()` method of `GameOver` class, 234
`Activate()` method of `MainGame` class, 232
`AddInputs()` method, 87–89
`AddScore()` method, 314–315
`AvailableGames()` method of `MatchMakerService` class, 333–334
`Background.cs` class, 159
btn event handlers, 328
`btn()` methods of `Game1` class, 343
`BufferIsReady()` method of `Game1` class, 142
`Button.cs` class, 170–172
`camera_Completed()` method of `Game1` class, 444
`Car.cs` class, 210–212
`caResolver_ResolveAddressCompleted()` method, 432
`ChangeScreen()` method of `ScreenStateSwitchboard` class, 205–206
`channel_ChannelUriUpdated()` method, 274, 281, 290, 322
`channel_HttpNotificationReceived()` method of `Game1` class, 275
`channel_ShellToastNotificationReceived()` method, 285, 322
`client()` methods of `Game1` class, 342
`CreateGameLobbyScreen()` method of `ScreenStateSwitchboard` class, 393
`CreateMainGameScreen()` method of `ScreenStateSwitchboard`, 488
`CreateNotificationChannel()` method, 273, 280, 289, 321
`CreatePuzzleCompleteScreen()` method, 494
`CreateRemoveGameScreen()` method of `ScreenStateSwitchboard` class, 397
`CreateRequestGameScreen()` method of `ScreenStateSwitchboard` class, 396
Create-Screen methods for `ScreenStateSwitchboard` class, 206–207
`CreateSelectPuzzleScreen()` method of `ScreenStateSwitchboard` class, 484
`CurrentHighScores()` method, 314
`DeclineGameRequest()` method of `MatchMakerService` class, 335
`DeclineRequest()` method of `Gamer` class, 331
`DiceGame` class of Poker Dice, 383–385
`DiceSelect` class of Poker Dice, 417–423
`Die` class of Poker Dice, 405–414
`DisplayOrientation` enumeration, 29
`Draw()` method of `Game1` class (3DSample), 253

Draw() method of Game1 class (AccelerometerSample), 36
Draw() method of Game1 class (DidYouOrderPizza), 430–431
Draw() method of Game1 class (FindMe), 437–438
Draw() method of Game1 class (MusicSample), 133
Draw() method of Game1 class (RotationSample), 30
Draw() method of Game1 class (WeatherWitch), 348
Draw() method (ScoreMe), 324
DrawScreen() method of GameOver class, 235–236
DrawScreen() method of MainGame class, 233–234
DrawScreen() method of Title class, 169, 173
eAddressChooser_Completed() method of Game1 class, 451
enum-based state management, 103–107
flag-based state management, 96–97
Form1() constructor, 341
Game class of PokerDiceService, 354–355
Game1 class constructor, 160
Game1.cs, 16–18
GameInfo class of Poker Dice, 398–404
GameInformation class of Poker Dice, 385
GameInformation class (Picture Puzzle), 484
GameInput.cs class, 174–179
GameLobby class of Poker Dice, 386–393
GameOver.cs class, 204–205, 222–223
Gamer class of PokerDiceService, 355–358
GeoCoordinateWatcher class, 434–435
GestureDefinition.cs class, 180
GestureSample properties, 46–47
GestureType enumerator, 45–46
GetWeather() methods of Game1 class, 346–347
HandleBackButtonInput() method of Screen class, 239–240
HandleCarCollision() method of MainGame class, 233
HandRank class of PokerDiceService, 359–363
Hazards.cs class, 212–214
highScores methods, 320, 327
HttpNotificationChannel class, 272–273
Identify() method of HighScore service, 313
IHighScore interface, 312–313
IMatchMaker interface file, 332
InGameMenu class (Picture Puzzle), 489–491
InGameMenu.cs class (DriveAndDodge), 204, 219–221
InGameMenu.cs class (Picture Puzzle), 488–489
Initialize() method of Game1 class, 36
Input.cs class, 181–193
IPokerDice Interface of PokerDiceService, 353–354
IService1.cs code file, 302–304
LittleGuy.cs (3DSample), 251–252
LoadContent() method (3DSample), 253
LoadContent() method (DriveAndDodge), 160–161, 168, 238
LoadContent() method (ScoreMe), 318–319
LoadContent() method (SkinningSample), 265
LoadScreenContent() method of GameOver class, 234–235
LoadScreenContent() method of MainGame class, 232
LoadScreenContent() method of Title class, 169, 172–173
locationWatcher_StatusChanged() method of Game1 class, 436–437
MainGame class of Poker Dice, 415
MainGame.cs class (DriveAndDodge), 203
MainGame.cs class (DriveAndDodge), 215–217
MainGame.cs class (Picture Puzzle), 485–488
MediaLocationType enumeration, 453
MediaPlaybackControls enumeration, 452
MediaPlayer class, 127–128
Message class of Poker Dice, 394–397
Message class (Picture Puzzle), 492–494
Microphone class, 138–139
Music.cs class, 198–199
NewPuzzle.cs class (Picture Puzzle), 463–466
NewReading() method of Game1 class, 35
photoChooser_Completed() method of Game1 class, 448
Player class, 311–312
PlayMusic() method of Game1 class, 130
PleaseBuyMe sample, Game1 class from, 500–503
PokerDice service, 363–365
PokerDiceTest form class, 367–371
Puzzle.cs class, 471–478
PuzzlePiece class, 468–469
ReadBuffer() method of Game1 class, 144–145
RequestGame() method of MatchMakerService class, 334
ResolveAddressSync() method of Game1 class, 428–429
Road.cs class, 207–209
Score class, 224, 226–227, 311
ScoreList.cs class, 225
Screen() class constructor (DriveAndDodge), 238
Screen class constructor (Poker Dice), 381–382
Screen() constructor of Screen class, 200–201
Screens.cs class, 149–151
ScreenState enumeration of ScreenStateSwitchboard class, 202
ScreenStateSwitchboard class of Poker Dice, 375–381
ScreenStateSwitchboard.cs (Picture Puzzle), 460–463
ScreenStateSwitchboard.cs class (DriveAndDodge), 153–155
SelectedPlayerID() method of Game1 class, 338, 344
SelectPuzzleScreen class, 481–483

SendRawNotification() method of Form1 class, 277
SendRequest() method of Gamer class, 331
SendTileNotification() method of Game1 class, 291–292
SendToastNotification() method, 283, 316–317
SerializableDictionary.cs class, 228–230
service1Client_CurrentTimeCompleted() method, 309
Service1.svc.cs code file, 301–302, 304
SetUpDelegates() method, 274, 281, 321
SetupInputs() method of Title class, 201
SoundEffectInstance class definition, 136–137
SoundEffects class, 134–135, 199–200
Sprite.cs class, 157–158
StartLocationWatcher() method of Game1 class, 435–436
StateObject class, 479–480
StencilPiece.cs class, 470
SubString() method of Game1 class, 347
Text.cs class, 163–167
Title class of Poker Dice, 373–374
Title.cs class (DriveAndDodge), 155–156
Title.cs class (Picture Puzzle), 457–459
TouchIndicatorCollection.cs class, 195–196
TouchIndicator.cs class, 193–195
Update() and Draw() methods (DriveAndDodge), 161
Update() method of Game1 class (3DSample), 258
Update() method of Game1 class (DidYouOrderPizza), 429–430
Update() method of Game1 class (MatchMe), 339
Update() method of LittleGuy class, 257
Update() method of Screen class (DriveAndDodge), 239
Update() method of Title class (Picture Puzzle), 484–485
Update() method (ScoreMe), 323
UpdateScreen() method of MainGame class (DriveAndDodge), 232
UpdateScreen() method of Title class (Poker Dice), 393
UpdateScreen() method of Title class (SoundEffects), 201
UpdateScreen() method of TitleScreen class (Picture Puzzle), 467
WriteBuffer() method of Game1 class, 144
code signing, 511
CollisionRectangle, 159
CollisionRectangle property, 168
colors, screen background, 109
command-line options (Emulator), 22–24
compass, 4
CompositeType class, 303
Concealed state, 120
configuring workspace in Blender, 254
consuming web services, 300
Content Processor property, 130

Content projects
    benefit of separate, 16
    DriveAndDodge, 159–160
Content.Load method, 136
Controls property (MediaPlayerLauncher class), 452
CreateGameLobbyScreen() method of ScreenStateSwitchboard class (listing), 393
CreateInstance() method (SoundEffect object), 136
CreateMainGameScreen() method of ScreenStateSwitchboard (listing), 488
CreateNotificationChannel() method (listing), 273, 280, 289, 321
CreatePuzzleCompleteScreen() method (listing), 494
CreateRemoveGameScreen() method of ScreenStateSwitchboard class (listing), 397
CreateRequestGameScreen() method of ScreenStateSwitchboard class (listing), 396
Create-Screen methods for ScreenStateSwitchboard class (listing), 206–207
CreateSelectPuzzleScreen() method of ScreenStateSwitchboard class (listing), 484
Cross-Platform Audio Creation Tool (XACT), 137–138
CurrentAccelerometerReading property, 74–75
CurrentHighScores() method (listing), 314
CurrentOrientation property, 29
CurrentTime() method, 305
CurrentTouchRectangle property, 74
custom gestures, 50–51

D

DeclineGameRequest() method of MatchMakerService class (listing), 335
DeclineRequest() method of Gamer class (listing), 331
Default() property (Microphone class), 139
Deployment namespace, 35
detecting
    back button, 115
    device orientation, 29–30
    touch input, 40–44
device orientation
    automatic rotation, 26–29
    detecting, 29–30
    full-screen mode, 30–32
    hardware scaling, 26
    setting, 25–29
DeviceType enumeration, 295
DiceGame.cs class, 383–385
DiceSelect screen, creating (Poker Dice), 417–423
Dictionary object, 130
DidYouOrderPizza project
    caResolver_ResolveAddressCompleted() method, 432
    CivicAddress class, 427–432
    creating, 427–428
    Draw() method of Game1 class, 430–431
    GeoCoordinate class, 432
    GeoCoordinateWatcher class, 433–435

ResolveAddressAsync() method, 431–432
ResolveAddressSync() method, 428–429
Update() method, 429–430
Die.cs class (Poker Dice), 405–414
digital camera, 5
Direction enumeration, 61
DirectX 9 acceleration, 6, 12
DisplayOrientation enumeration, 29
DisplayOrientation object, 152
DisplayText property, 386
DistanceScale property (sound effects), 135
DopplerScale property (sound effects), 135
DoubleTap action, 52
DoubleTap gesture, 47
downloading Blender, 248
Drag action (games), 53
DragComplete gesture, 49
Draw() method
    AccelerometerSample project (listing), 36
    DidYouOrderPizza project, 430–431
    DriveAndDodge project (listing), 161
    FindMe project, 437–438
    of Screen class (DriveAndDodge listing), 197
    RotationSample project (listing), 30
    ScoreMe project (listing), 324
    use of (DriveAndDodge), 152
    VisualizationSample project (listing), 133
    WeatherWitch project, 348
DrawScreen() method
    of GameOver class (DriveAndDodge listing), 235–236
    of MainGame class (DriveAndDodge listing), 233–234
    of Title class (DriveAndDodge listing), 169, 173
    use of (DriveAndDodge), 152
DrawSplashScreen() method, 101
DrawSprite() method, 209
Drive and Dodge project
    Activate() method of GameOver class, 234
    Activate() method of MainGame class, 232
    adding more screens to, 202
    Back button behavior, 237
    Background.cs class, 159–162
    Button.cs class, 169–173
    Car.cs class, 210–212
    Content project, 159–160
    DrawScreen() method of GameOver class, 235–236
    DrawScreen() method of MainGame class, 233–234
    DrawScreen() method of Title class, 169, 173
    Game1.cs class, 160–162
    GameOver.cs class, 204–207, 221–224, 234–236, 241
    HandleBackButtonInput() method of Screen class, 239–240
    HandleCarCollision() method of MainGame class, 233
    Hazards.cs class, 212–215
    InGameMenu.cs class, 204, 219–221, 241
    input wrapper classes. *See* input wrapper classes (DriveAndDodge)
    keeping score, 224
    LoadContent() method of Game1 class, 160–161
    LoadContent() method of Screen class, 168, 238
    LoadScreenContent() method of GameOver class, 234–235
    LoadScreenContent() method of MainGame class, 232
    LoadScreenContent() method of Title class, 169, 172–173
    main game screen, coding, 207
    MainGame.cs class, 203, 215–219, 231–234, 240–241
    mapping out screens for, 148–149
    Music.cs class, 198–199
    Road.cs class, 207–210
    Score.cs class, 224
    ScoreList.cs class, 225–226
    Scores.cs class, 226–228
    Screen() class constructor, 238
    Screen.cs class, 149–152, 231, 237–240
    screenFont.spritefont object, 168–170
    ScreenStateSwitchboard.cs class, 153–155
    SerializableDictionary.cs class, 228–230
    SoundEffects.cs class, 199–202
    sounds and music, adding to DriveAndDodge, 198
    Sprite.cs class, 157–159
    Text.cs class, 155–156, 162–168, 240
    Update() and Draw() methods of Game1 class, 161
    Update() Method of Screen class, 239
    UpdateScreen() method of MainGame class, 232
    XNAPhoneGame template project. *See* XNAPhoneGame template project
DualTextureEffect class (XNA 4.0), 267

E

eAddressChooser_Completed() method of Game1 class (listing), 451
effects, working with, 266–268
EmailAddressChooserTask class, 451–452
EmailComposeTask class, 450–451
Emulator, Windows Phone. *See* Windows Phone Emulator
EnabledGestures property, 140
enum-based state management (listing), 103–107
Environment class, 295
EnvironmentMapEffect class (XNA 4.0), 267
EventHandler object, 107
events
    Exiting, 120
    game-stopping, 120–121
    phone hardware, 115–116
Exiting events, 120
exporting shapes (Blender), 250–251

F

face buttons, 6–7
`FBX` export script, 263–264
features, phone, 3–7
filtering, bilinear, 26
`FindMe` project, 435–438
flag-based state management (listing), 96–97
`Flick` action (games), 53
`Flick` gesture, 49
`Form1.cs` class (`MatchMakerTester`), 340–344
forums, XNA Community, 511
`FreeDrag` gesture, 48–49
full-screen mode, 30–32

G

game state
    enum-based state management (listing), 103–107
    flag-based state management (listing), 96–97
    game interruptions, 116–121
    multiple layers of screens, 114–115
    object-oriented management of, 107–114
    overview, 93–94
    saving after interruptions, 121–125
    tracking with Boolean flags, 94–97
    tracking with enumerations, 98–107
game template, setting up (Poker Dice), 372
`Game1.cs` class
    `DriveAndDodge`, 160–162
    `InputHandlerDemo`, 86–91
    `ServeMe`, 308
`Game.cs` class (Poker Dice), 354–355
`GameHasControl` property, 128–129
`GameInfo` screen, creating (Poker Dice), 397–404
`GameInformation` class
    Picture Puzzle, 484
    Poker Dice project, 385
`GameInput.cs` class, 76–81, 174–179
`GameLobby.cs` class (Poker Dice), 386–394
`GameOver.cs` class (`DriveAndDodge`), 204–207, 222–223, 234–236, 241
`GamePadState` object, 61
`Gamer.cs` class
    `MatchMaker`, 330–332
    Poker Dice project, 355–358
GameRequest.cs class (`MatchMaker`), 330
games
    DirectX 9 acceleration, 6
    enhancement of (Picture Puzzle), 494–495
    enhancement of (Poker Dice), 423
    game hubs, 8–9, 506
    game interruptions, 116–121
    game-stopping events, 120–121
    landscape, 29
    pulling RSS feeds into, 348
    touch games, designing, 51–53
`GameScreen` class, 111–112

`GameState` class, 121
`GameWindow` class, 29
`GeoCoordinate` class, 433–438
`GeoCoordinateWatcher` class (listing), 434–435
`GeoPosition<T>` class, 439
`GeoPositionAccuracy.Default` method, 426
`GestureDefinition.cs` class, 75–76, 180
gestures
    custom gestures, 50–51
    `DoubleTap` gesture, 47
    `DragComplete` gesture, 49
    `Flick` gesture, 49
    `FreeDrag` gesture, 48–49
    `Gestures` project, 44–45
    `GestureSample` properties (listing), 46–47
    `GestureType` enumerator (listing), 45–46
    `Hold` gesture, 48
    `HorizontalDrag` gesture, 48
    `Pinch` gesture, 49–50
    `PinchComplete` gesture, 50
    `Tap` gesture, 47
    `VerticalDrag` gesture, 48
`GetData()` method
    example, 302
    `Microphone` class, 142
`GetDistanceTo()` method, 433
`GetSampleSizeInBytes()` method (microphone), 141
`GetWeather()` methods of `Game1` class (listing), 346–347
`GraphicsDeviceManager` class, 26
gravitational acceleration, 33
`Guide.IsVisible` property, 117–118
GUIDs (Guaranteed Unique Identifiers), 319

H

Half-size Video Graphics Array (HVGA), 26
`HandleBackButtonInput()` method of `Screen` class (listing), 239–240
`HandleCarCollision()` method, 218, 233
`HandRank.cs` class, 359–363
hardware scaling, 26
`Hazards.cs` class (listing), 212–214
`HighScoreClient` class, 319–320
`highScores` methods (listing), 320, 327
`HighScoreService` project, 310–317
`HighScoreTester` project, 325–329
Hodnick, Mike, 202
`Hold` action (games), 52–53
`Hold` gesture, 48
`HorizontalDrag` gesture, 48
HTTP requests, 345–349
`HttpNotificationChannel` class (listing), 272–273
`HttpWebRequest` class, 345
hubs, game, 8–10

I

`Identify()` method of `HighScore` service (listing), 313
`IHighScore` interface (listing), 312–313
`IMatchMaker` interface file (listing), 332
`IMatchMaker.cs` class, 332
InGameMenu screen, creating (Picture Puzzle), 488–491
`InGameMenu.cs` class
  `DriveAndDodge`, 204, 219–221, 241
  Picture Puzzle (listing), 488–491
`Initialize()` method (accelerometer project listing), 36
input management systems. *See* `InputHandlerDemo` project
input wrapper classes (`DriveAndDodge`)
  `GameInput.cs` class, 174–179
  `GestureDefinition.cs` class, 179–180
  `Input.cs` class, 181–193
  `TouchIndicatorCollection.cs` class, 195–197
  `TouchIndicator.cs` class, 193–195
`Input.cs` class, 59, 181–193
`InputHandlerDemo` project
  Action objects, passing in, 78
  `Actions.cs` class, 85–86
  `AddGamepadInput()` method, 65
  `AddInputs()` method, 87–89
  `AddKeyboardInput()` method, 65
  `AddTouchGesture()` method, 66
  `AddTouchSlideInput()` method, 66, 70
  `AddTouchTapInput()` method, 65
  `Buttons` enumeration (listing), 60–61
  creating, 60
  `CurrentAccelerometerReading` property, 74–75
  `CurrentTouchRectangle` property, 74
  `Game1.cs` class, 86–91
  `GameInput.cs` class, 76–81
  `GestureDefinition.cs` class, 75–76
  `Input.cs` class, 59
  `InputHandlerDemo.Inputs` namespace, 86
  `IsAccelerometerInputPressed()` method, 72–73
  `IsConnected()` method, 67, 77
  `IsGestureInputPressed` method, 71–72
  `IsKeyboardInputPressed()` method, 68–69
  `IsPressed()` method, 67–68, 77
  `IsTouchSlideInputPressed()` method, 70
  `IsTouchTapInputPressed()` method, 69
  mapping multiple inputs to perform same action, 64–65
  methods to map game actions/behavior to input, 79
  `PlayerIndex`, 78–79
  `PlayerIndex.One`, 69
  properties for returning current accelerator reading, 81
  properties for returnning current touch point data, 80
  properties to grab `Position` and `Delta` information, 79–80
  properties to loop through touch locations, 73–74
  properties to provide `Position` and `Delta` info, 73
  property used with `Pinch` gesture type, 80–81

rectangle definitions for touch regions, 87
testing, 90–91
`TouchIndicatorCollection.cs` class, 84–85
`TouchIndicator.cs` class, 81–84
`Update()` method, 63
installing XNA Game Studio 4.0, 13
interfaces, touch, 40
interruptions, game, 116–125
`InterruptionSample` project, 116
`InvalidOperation` exception, 46
`IPokerDice.cs` class, 353–354
`IsAccelerometerInputPressed()` method, 72–73
`IsCollidingWith()` method, 159
`IsConnected()` method, 67, 77
`IService1.cs` code file (listing), 302–304
`IsGestureInputPressed` method, 71–72
`IsKeyboardInputPressed()` method, 68–69
`IsKeyUp()` method, 56
`IsolatedStorageFileStream` object, 123
`IsPressed()` method, 67–68, 77
`IsTouchSlideInputPressed()` method, 70
`IsTouchTapInputPressed()` method, 69
`IsTrialMode()`, 499–500
`IsUnknown` property (`GeoCoordinate` class), 433

J

JavaScript Notation (JSON), 345
JibJab website, 447

K

`keyboardCallback()` method, 55
`Keys` enumeration, 56

L

Landscape orientation, 25, 29
Launchers and Choosers, 441–442
layers of screens, handling, 114–115
light sensor, ambient, 5
`LinearWrap`, 210
listings, code. *See* code listings
`LittleGuy.cs` (3DSample listing), 251–252
`LiveToServeYou` project, 300–305
`LoadContent()` method
  3DSampleContent, 253
  DrivebdDodge, 152
  DrivebdDodge (listing), 160–161
  ScoreMe (listing), 318–319
  of `Screen` class (`DriveAndDodge` listing), 168, 238
  `SkinningSampleContent` (listing), 265
`LoadScreenContent()` method (`DriveAndDodge`)
  of `GameOver` class (listing), 234–235
  of `MainGame` class (listing), 232
  of `Title` class (listing), 169, 172–173
Location API, 425

`Location` property (`MediaPlayerLauncher` class), 453
Location Services
    best practices for using, 425–426
    `CivicAddress` class, 427–432
    `CivicAddressResolver` class, 427–432
    `FindMe` project, 435–438
    `GeoCoordinate` class, 433–438
    `GeoCoordinateWatcher` class, 433–435
    `GeoPosition<T>` class, 439
    using in games, 426
`locationWatcher_StatusChanged()` method (listing), 436–437
Lock screen, 8
`LocRotScale` key, 263

M

`MainGame` screen
    coding (`DriveAndDodge`), 207
    creating (Poker Dice), 414–417
`MainGame.cs` class (`DriveAndDodge`), 203, 215–217, 231–234, 240–241
`MainGame.cs` class (Picture Puzzle), 485–488
Map Input tab (Blender), 256
mapping multiple inputs to perform same action, 64–65
Marketplace Certification, 426
Marketplace hub, 9
`MatchMaker` project, 329–335
`MatchMakerService.svc.cs` class, 333–335
`MatchMakerTester` project, 340–345
`MatchMe` project, 335–339
Material Button (Blender), 256
McLaughlin, Michael, 479
`Media` property (`MediaPlayerLauncher` class), 453
`MediaLibrary` properties, 131
`MediaLocationType` enumeration (listing), 453
`MediaPlayer`, playing music with
    background music, 129–131
    `GameHasControl` property, 128–129
    `MediaPlaybackControls` enumeration (listing), 452
    `MediaPlayer` class (listing), 127–128
    `MediaPlayerLauncher` class, 452–454
    song collections, 131
    visualizations, 132–133
megapixels, calculating, 5
memory size, simulating (Emulator), 22
`memoryStream` variable, 144
Message class (Picture Puzzle listing), 492–494
`Message.cs` class (Poker Dice), 394–397
`messagePos` variable, 50
messaging tasks, classes for, 449–452
metric craploud, defined, 202
`micButtons` variable, 140
Microphone class, 138–143
`MicrophoneSample` project, 139
Microsoft Cross-Platform Audio Creation Tool (XACT), 137–138

`Microsoft.Devices.Sensors` namespace, 174
Microsoft Push Notification Service, 269
Microsoft Skinning Sample, 264–266
`Microsoft.Devices.Sensors` namespace, 32
`Microsoft.Phone` dynamic link library, 443
`Microsoft.Phone.Info` namespace, 319
`Microsoft.Phone.Tasks` namespace, 441
`Microsoft.XNA.Framework.Audio` namespace, 127, 138
`Microsoft.XNA.Framework.Content` namespace, 127
`Microsoft.XNA.Framework.GamerServices.Guide` class, 498
`Microsoft.XNA.Framework.Input` namespace, 40
`Microsoft.XNA.Framework.Media` namespace, 127
milliGal units, 33
Model workspace (Blender), 259
`MovementThreshold` property, 426, 438
.mp3 files, 130
multiple layers of screens, 114–115
`MultiTouchMe` game project, 43–44
music
    Music + Video hub, 8
    `Music.cs` class (listing), 198–199
    `MusicSample` project, 129
    playing with MediaPlayer, see `MediaPlayer`, playing music with

N

nag screens, 102–103, 108
`NewPuzzle` screen, 463–468
`NewReading()` method (`Accelerometer` listing), 35
notifications
    temporary interruptions and, 117–120
    toast, 279
`NowPictureThis` project, 443–449

O

object-oriented management of game state, 107–114
Office hub, 9–10
`onDeactivated()`/`onActivated()` methods, 118
`OnExiting()` method, 120–121
`OOStateManagement` project, 107
`[OperationContract]` attribute, 303
orientation, device. See device orientation
overriding Back button, 115–116

P

parameters, command-line (Emulator), 23
`PassTheToastSample` project
    `channel_ChannelUriUpdated()` method, 281
    consuming toasts as raw notifications, 284–286
    `CreateNotificationChannel()` method, 280
    overview, 279–280
    `SetupDelegates()` method, 281
`PassTheToastWindows` project, 281–284

People hub, 8
phone hardware events, 115–116
`PhoneTitleSafe` area project, 31–32
`photoChooser_Completed()` method class (listing), 448
`PhotoChooserTask` class, 447–449
Picture Puzzle project
    base game setup, 456–457
    game enhancement, 494–495
    how to "puzzleize" images, 478–479
    `InGameMenu` screen, creating, 488–491
    `NewPuzzle` screen, 463–468
    overview, 455
    playable game screen, creating (`MainGame.cs`), 485–488
    `PuzzleComplete` screen, creating, 491–494
    `Puzzle.cs` class, 471–478
    `PuzzlePiece.cs` class, 468–469
    screen flow, designing, 456
    `ScreenStateSwitchboard.cs` class, enhancing, 460–463
    `SelectPuzzle` screen, creating, 480–485
    state objects, managing, 479–480
    `StencilPiece.cs` class, 470–471
    title screen, creating, 457–460
Pictures hub, 8
Pinch action, 53
Pinch gesture, 49–50
`PinchComplete` gesture, 50
pinning game tiles to Start area, 505–507
playable game screen, creating (`MainGame.cs`), 485–488
Player class (listing), 311–312
`PlayerIndex`, 78–79
`PlayerIndex.One`, 69
`PlayMusic()` method (listing), 130
Play/Record buttons (microphone), 142–143
`PleaseBuyMe` sample, `Game1` class from (listing), 500–505
Poker Dice project
    3D dice models, adding, 404–414
    `Button.cs` class, 385–386
    `DiceGame.cs` class, 383–385
    `DiceSelect` screen, creating, 417–423
    `Die.cs` class, 405–414
    game enhancement, 423
    game template, setting up, 372
    `Game.cs` class, 354–355
    `GameInfo` screen, creating, 397–405
    `GameInformation.cs` class, 385
    `GameLobby.cs` class, 386–394
    `Gamer.cs` class, 355–358
    `HandRank.cs` class, 359–363
    `IPokerDice.cs` class, 353–354
    `MainGame` screen, creating, 414–417
    `Message.cs` class, 394–397
    overview, 351–352
    `PokerDiceService`, 353, 382–383
    `PokerDice.svc`, 363–365
    `PokerDiceTester` application, 365–372

    `ScreenStateSwitchboard` class, enhancing, 374–383
    service flow vs. screen flow, 352–353
    `Title.cs` class, modifying, 373–374
    web service, creating, 353–365
Portrait orientation, 25, 29
Pose mode (Blender), 263
projects (examples)
    `3DSampleContent` project. *See* `3DSampleContent` project
    `AccelerometerSample`, 34–37
    `DidYouOrderPizza` project. *See* `DidYouOrderPizza` project
    Drive and Dodge project. *See* Drive and Dodge project
    `FindMe` project, 435–438
    Game project, 94
    `HighScoreService` project, 310–317
    `HighScoreTester` project, 325–328
    `InputHandlerDemo` project. *See* `InputHandlerDemo` project
    `InterruptionSample` project, 116
    `LiveToServeYou` project, 300–305
    `MatchMaker` project, 329–335
    `MatchMakerTester` project, 340–345
    `MatchMe` project, 335–339
    `MicrophoneSample` project, 139
    `MultiTouchMe` game project, 43–44
    `MusicSample` project, 129
    `NowPictureThis` project, 443–449
    `OOStateManagement` project, 107
    `PassTheToastSample` project. *See* `PassTheToastSample` project
    `PassTheToastWindows` project, 281–284
    `PhoneTitleSafe` area, 31–32
    Picture Puzzle project. *See* Picture Puzzle project
    Poker Dice project. *See* Poker Dice project
    `PushingTileSample` project, 287–290
    `PushingTileWindows` project, 290–294
    `PushItRawSample` project, 271–276
    `PushItRawWindows` project, 276–279
    `ScoreMe` project, 317–319
    `ServeMe` project, 305–310
    `SIPSample` project, 53–54
    `SoundEffectSample` project, 134
    `StateManagementWithEnum` project, 98
    `VibrationSample` project, 294–297
    `VisualizationSampleContent` project, 132
    `WeatherWitch` project, 345–348
proximity sensor, 5
publishing games
    accounts for submitting games, 508–511
    code signing, 511
    requirements for, 507–508
push notifications
    basics, 269–270
    raw notifications. *See* raw notifications
    `ScoreMe` project, 321–325
`PushingTileSample` project, 287–290

PushingTileWindows project, 290–294
PushItRawSample project, 271–276
PushItRawWindows project, 276–279
PuzzleComplete screen, creating, 491–494
Puzzle.cs class, 471–478
PuzzlePiece.cs class, 468–469

Q

QWERTY keyboard, 7

R

raw notifications
    overview, 270–271
        PushItRawSample project, 271–276
Reach Graphics Demo (effects), 267–268
ReadBuffer() method (listing), 144–145
ReadingChanged() event, 33
recorderbuttons.png file, 140
recording, audio, 138
Record/Play buttons (microphone), 142–143
rectangle definitions for touch regions, 87
Representational State Transfer (REST) Services, 349
RequestGame() method of MatchMakerService class (listing), 334
Reset() method, 208
ResolveAddressAsync() method (listing), 431–432
ResolveAddressSync() method (listing), 428–429
RetrieveGameState() method, 122, 123
Road.cs class (listing), 207–209
rotating 3D objects, 257–258
rotation, automatic, 26–29
RSS feeds, consumimg, 348

S

Safe Area Sample, 30–31
SaveGameState() method, 122–123
SaveState() / SaveScreenState() methods, 152
saving
    game state after interruptions, 121–125
    and retrieving captured audio, 143–145
scaling, hardware, 26
Score class (listing), 224, 311
ScoreList.cs class (listing), 225
ScoreMe project, 317–319
Scores.cs class (listing), 226–227
Screen class, 107
Screen() class constructor
    DriveAndDodge (listing), 200–201, 238
    Poker Dice (listing), 381–382
screen flow
    designing (Picture Puzzle), 456
    vs. service flow (Poker Dice), 352–353
screen resolution, 3, 51–52
Screen.cs class (DriveAndDodge), 149–152, 231, 237–240

ScreenEvent.Invoke() statement, 109–110
screenFont.spritefont object (DriveAndDodge), 168–170
screens. *See also* game state
    backgropund colors, 109
    multiple layers of, 114–115
    splash, 101–103, 108–110
ScreenState enumeration of
    ScreenStateSwitchboard class (listing), 202
ScreenStateSwitchboard class
    DriveAndDodge, 153–155
    Picture Puzzle project, 460–463
    Poker Dice project, 374–383
Search button, 7
SelectedPlayerID() method (listing), 338, 344
SelectPuzzle screen, creating, 480–485
SendPurchaseMessage() method, 504
SendRawNotification() method of Form1 class (listing), 277
SendRequest() method (listing), 331
SendTileNotification() method (listing), 291–292
SendToastNotification() method (listing), 283, 316–317
sensors, 4–5
serializing
    defined, 303
    SerializableDictionary object, 227–228
    SerializableDictionary.cs class (listing), 228–230
ServeMe project, 305–310
service flow vs. screen flow (Poker Dice), 352–353
service1Client variable, 308
service1Client_CurrentTimeCompleted() method (listing), 309
Service1.svc.cs code file (listing), 301–302, 304
SetUpDelegates() method (listing), 274, 281, 321
SetupInputs() method
    defined, 152
    of Title class (listing), 201
shader APIs, removal of, 266
Shading mode (Blender), 255
shapes
    combining, 249–250
    creating primitive, 248–249
    exporting, 250–251
ShowCamera Boolean property, 448
ShowMarketplace() method, 498–499
SimulateTrialMode() property, 499
SIPSample project, 53–54
skin files, loading (Emulator), 22
SkinnedEffect class (XNA 4.0), 267
SkinningSampleContent project, 264–266
SmsComposeTask class, 449–450
SOAP (Simple Object Access Protocol) web services, 300
Soft Input Panel (SIP), 21, 53–56
software features, 7–10
song collections, 131
soundCrash.Play() method, 136
SoundEffectInstance objects, 136–137

`SoundEffects` class (listing), 134–135
`SoundEffectSample` project, 134
`SoundEffects.cs` class (listing), 199–200
sounds and music, adding to `DriveAndDodge`, 198
`SpeedOfSound` property (sound effects), 135–136
splash screens, 101–103, 108–110
`SpriteBatch.Draw()` method, 210
`Sprite.cs` class (`DriveAndDodge`), 157–159
`SpriteFont`, 34, 99
Start button, 6–7
Start screen, 7, 20
`StartLocationWatcher()` method (listing), 435–436
state management
    game interruptions, 116–121
    game state. *See* game state
    phone hardware events, 115–116
    `StateManagementWithEnum` project, 98
state objects (Picture Puzzle)
    managing, 479–480
    `StateObject` class (listing), 479–480
`StencilPiece.cs` class (Picture Puzzle), 470–471
stock effects, 267
`Stop()` method (`Microphone` object), 143
storage cards, simulating (Emulator), 22
`StreamReader` object, 275
`SubString()` method (listing), 347
`SupportedOrientations` property, 26, 29
Swipe action, 53
Swipe gesture, 51
synchronously resolving addresses, 428–431
system tray (Emulator), 19
`System.Device` dynamic link library, 427
system/software requirements for development, 12–13

T

Tap action, 52
Tap gesture, 47
`TargetElapsedTime` property, 18
testing
    `HighScoreService` project, 328–329
    `InputHandlerDemo` project, 90–91
    `MatchMaker` service, 344–345
    `NowPictureThis` project, 447
`Text.cs` class (`DriveAndDodge`), 162–168
texture, defined, 158
`Texture2D` variable, 140
texturing 3D models in Blender, 254–257
tile notifications
    overview, 286
    `PushingTileSample` project, 287–290
    `PushingTileWindows` project, 290–294
tilt sensor, 4
`TimeState` variable, 122
title screens, 99, 103, 108–110, 457–460
`Title.cs` class
    `DriveAndDodge`, 155–156, 240
    Poker Dice project, 373–374

title-safe area, 30–31
toast notifications, 279
touch input
    detecting, 40–44
    gestures, detecting. *See* gestures
    overview, 39–40
    Soft Input Panel (SIP), 53–56
    touch games, designing for, 51–53
    touch interfaces, 40
`TouchIndicatorCollection.cs` class, 84–85, 195–196
`TouchIndicator.cs` class, 81–84, 193–195
`TouchPanel` class, 140
`TouchSlide` gesture, 62
tracking
    game state with Boolean flags, 94–97
    game state with enumerations, 98–107
transformations, 3D, 257–258
trial mode
    basics of, 497–498
    detecting, 498–505
try/catch blocks, 37

U

`UnloadContent()` method, 36
Unwrap menu (Blender), 254
`Update()` method, 18
    3DSampleContent (listing), 258
    `DidYouOrderPizza`, 429–430
    `DriveAndDodge`, 152, 161
    of `LittleGuy` class (3DSampleContent listing), 257
    MatchMe (listing), 339
    ScoreMe, 323
    of `Screen` class (Back button), 239
    of `Screen` class (`DriveAndDodge` listing), 195–196
    of `Title` class (Picture Puzzle listing), 484–485
`UpdateMainGameScreen()` method, 99
`UpdateNagScreen()` method, 100
`UpdateScreen()` method
    of `MainGame` class (`DriveAndDodge`), 232–233
    of `Title` class (Poker Dice), 393
    of `Title` class (SoundEffects), 201
    of `TitleScreen` Class (Picture Puzzle), 467
`UpdateSplashScreen()` method, 95, 99
`UpdateSprite()` method, 209
`UpdateTitleScreen()` method, 95, 99
`UserExtendedProperties` class, 319
using statements, 123, 143
UV Texture Editor workspace (Blender), 259
UV/Image Editor (Blender), 254

V

velocity variable, 202
`VerticalDrag` gesture, 48

`VibrateController` class, 295–297
`VibrationSample` project, 294–297
Visual C# 2010 Express, 276
Visual Studio 2010 Express for Windows Phone, 13, 14
visualizations (`MediaPlayer`), 132–133
`VisualizationSampleContent` project, 132

W

.wav files, 130
WCF service applications
    `HighScoreService` project, 310–317
    `LiveToServeYou` project, 300–305
    `MatchMaker` project, 329–335
    `PokerDiceService`, 353
WCF Test Client, 305–306, 383
`WeatherWitch` project, 345–348
web services
    consuming, 300
    `PokerDiceService`, 353–365, 382–383
websites, for downloading
    Blender, 248
    code for projects, 15
    development unlock code, 19
    Microsoft Skinning Sample, 264
    Reach Graphics Demo (effects), 267
    tools for creating games with XNA, 24
    Visual C# 2010 Express, 276, 282
    Windows Phone 7 development tools, 11
websites, for further information
    3D models, 248
    App Hub, 509
    Application Certification Requirements document, 512
    blogs, 512
    Hodnick, Mike, 202
    Launchers and Choosers, 442
    `using` statements, 123
    Windows Phone 7 Application Certification Requirements document, 9
    XNA Community forums, 511
weight painting, 260–262
Wide Video Graphics Array (WVGA), 3, 26
Windows Forms applications
    `HighScoreTester`, 325
    `PokerDiceTest`, 366–372
Windows Phone 7
    Application Certification Requirements document, 9, 129
    applications shipping with, 10
    blogs, 512
    capacitive-touch screens, 3–4
    chassis design, 2
    Developer Tools, 13
    development tools for, 11–13
    digital camera, 5
    DirectX 9 acceleration, 6
    face buttons, 6–7
    hubs, 8–10
    Lock screen, 8
    minimum specifications, 1–3
    phone features, 3–7
    QWERTY keyboard, 7
    screen resolution, 3
    SDK, 13
    sensors, 4–5
    software features, 7–10
    Start screen, 7
Windows Phone device, setting up, 18–19
Windows Phone Emulator
    command-line options, 22–24
    using, 19–22
Windows Phone Game (4.0) project. *See* accelerometer
`WMAppManifest.xml` file, 282, 382
workspace, configuring in Blender, 254
`WriteBuffer()` method (listing), 144

X

XACT (Microsoft Cross-Platform Audio Creation Tool), 137–138
.XAP files, 445–446
Xbox Live Indie Games (XBLIG), 30, 118, 499
Xbox Live integration, 9
`XDE.exe` folder, 23
XML web services, 282
XNA
    framework, 13
    help, 511–512
    Start button in, 116
XNA Game Studio 4.0
    Deployment Device drop-down, 18–19
    installing, 13
    project, creating, 14–18
`XNAPhoneGame` template project
    creating/using templates, 244–245
    overview, 241–242
    `ScreenStateSwitchboard.cs` class, 243–244
    stripping down `DriveAndDodge` game, 242
    `Title.cs` class, modifying, 242–243
X-Ray button (Blender), 259

Z

Zune developers, 32
Zune HD, 8